THE THIRD REICH FROM ORIGINAL SOURCES

# ALBERT SPEER ON TRIAL
## Evidence from Nuremberg

The Illustrated Edition

EDITED AND INTRODUCED BY
BOB CARRUTHERS

This book is published in Great Britain in 2013 by
Coda Books Ltd,
Office Suite 2, Shrieves Walk, Sheep Street,
Stratford upon Avon, Warwickshire CV37 6GJ.

www.codabooks.com

Copyright © 2013 Coda Books Ltd

ISBN 978-1-78158-336-4

A CIP catalogue record for this book is available from the British Library.

All rights reserved. No part of this publication may be reproduced or transmitted in any form or by any means (electronic or mechanical, including photocopy, recording, or any information storage and retrieval system, without the prior permission in writing from the publisher.

This book includes excerpts from "The Trial of German Major War Criminals Proceedings of the International Military Tribunal Sitting at Nuremberg, Germany" published under the authority of H.M. Attorney-General by His Majesty's Stationery Office, London 1946/1947.

# CONTENTS

**FOREWORD** ............................................................................................ 4

**STATEMENT OF INDIVIDUAL RESPONSIBILITY FOR CRIMES SET OUT IN COUNTS ONE, TWO, THREE AND FOUR** ............... 7

**THE CASE ON FORCED LABOUR**

    Tuesday, 11th December, 1945 ........................................................ 8

    Wednesday, 12th December, 1945 .................................................. 19

    Thursday, 13th December, 1945 ...................................................... 74

**THE BRIEF RELATING TO FORCED LABOUR**

    Saturday, January 19th, 1946 ........................................................ 150

**INDIVIDUAL RESPONSIBILITY OF THE DEFENDANT**

    Wednesday, 6th February, 1946 .................................................... 172

    Thursday, 7th February, 1946 ........................................................ 175

**THE CASE FOR ALBERT SPEER**

    Wednesday, 19th June, 1946 ......................................................... 179

    Thursday, 20th June, 1946 ............................................................ 193

    Friday, 21st June, 1946 ................................................................. 252

**CONCLUDING SPEECH FROM THE DEFENSE**

    Tuesday, 23rd July, 1946 ............................................................... 317

**CONCLUDING SPEECHES FROM THE PROSECUTION**

    Friday, 26 July 1946 ...................................................................... 354

    Tuesday, 30 July 1946 .................................................................. 362

**THE FINAL STATEMENT BY THE DEFENDANT**

    Saturday, 31st August, 1946 ......................................................... 365

**THE JUDGMENT**

    1st October, 1946 ......................................................................... 368

    The Sentence ................................................................................. 371

# Foreword

The Nuremberg Trials were held by the four victorious Allied forces in the Palace of Justice, Nuremberg from November 1945 to October 1946. Famous for prosecuting the major German war criminals, they also tried the various groups and organisations that were at the heart of Nazi Germany.

There were four counts against the accused:
Count One: The Common Plan or Conspiracy
Count Two: Crimes against Peace
Count Three: War Crimes
Count Four: Crimes against Humanity

The Rt. Hon. Sir Geoffrey Lawrence of Great Britain was the President of the court, and the United States of America, France, the United Kingdom, and the Union of Soviet Socialist Republics each provided one judge and an alternate, as well as a prosecutor and their assistants. Each defendant was given counsel, the majority of whom were German, along with a team of assistants, clerks and lawyers.

This volume is concerned with the trial of Albert Speer, Hitler's architect and the Minister of Armaments and War Production. It includes all the testimony regarding his trial, including his cross-examination by the Court, the concluding speeches from the defence and prosecution, and the final judgment on his case. Because of his close links with the Nazi system of forced labour, the book also includes evidence regarding this policy. Speer's defense counsel was Dr. Hans Flaechsner.

Albert Speer was born in 1905 in Mannheim and had a typical wealthy, middle-class upbringing. Following in the family tradition, he trained as an architect, initially at the University of Karlsruhe, then the Technical University of Munich and finally to the Technical University of Berlin, where he qualified in 1927. In December 1930, he attended a Nazi rally in Berlin, where Hitler and his ideas made a huge impression on him, and on 1st March, 1931, he became a member of the Nazi Party.

Karl Hanke, the Party leader for the West End of Berlin, commissioned Speer to redecorate his villa, and enthusiastic about the results, recommended him to Josef Goebbels to renovate the Party's headquarters in Berlin. When Hitler took office in 1933, Goebbels again instructed Speer to redevelop the building of the Reich Ministry of Public Enlightenment and Propaganda. The organisers of the Nuremberg Nazi Party rally then asked Speer to submit designs, which Hitler approved. Speer's career within the Nazi Party was starting to take off, and he became the "Commissioner for the Artistic and Technical Presentation of Party Rallies and Demonstrations". He finally met Hitler in person during the renovation of the Chancellery, and was invited to lunch. They found they had much in common, and Speer became part of

*A portrait of Albert Speer from 1933.*
Bundesarchiv, Bild 146II-277 / Binder / CC-BY-SA

Hitler's inner circle. In 1934, he was appointed head of the Chief Office for Construction, which placed him nominally on Hess's staff.

Further promotions and awards followed; in 1937 Speer was appointed General Building Inspector for the Reich Capital with the rank of undersecretary of state in the Reich government. Hitler ordered him to make plans to rebuild Berlin but the outbreak of war led to the abandonment of these proposals. He did, however, succeed in rebuilding the Reich Chancellery in 1938. The structure included the "Marble Gallery", at 146 metres long it was almost twice as long as the Hall of Mirrors in the Palace of Versailles.

Speer witnessed much of the early brutality of Hitler's regime. After the Night of the Long Knives in 1934, Speer began the conversion of the offices of Vice-Chancellor Franz von Papen and was confronted with a pool of blood, apparently from the body of Herbert von Bose, von Papen's secretary. Speer related in his book 'Inside the Third Reich' that the sight had no effect on him, other than to cause him to avoid that room. He also did not feel it necessary to mention the events of Kristallnacht in November 1938 in his book until urged to do so by his publisher, and then it was just a cursory mention of seeing the ruins of the Central Synagogue in Berlin. He supported the invasion of Poland and the military ambitions of Hitler in full; "all I wanted was for this great man to dominate the globe."[1]

In February 1942, Fritz Todt, the Minister of Armaments died in a plane crash, and Speer was appointed as his successor. Even at this stage in the war, Germany was not fully equipped for war production; most factories still had just one shift, few women employees and many were still engaged in manufacturing purely consumer goods. Speer's genius for organisation overcame these problems and gave the factories autonomy or "self-responsibility" and made each plant concentrate on a single product, and put experts, not civil servants in charge. Speer advocated using female labour, but was overruled by Fritz Sauckel, the General Plenipotentiary for Labour Deployment who favoured importing workers from the occupied nations. In December 1943 he visited the underground Mittelwek V2 rocket factory and was shocked by the state of the workforce. He ordered improvements, but over half of them died by the end of the war.

In March 1945, with the end of the war in sight, Hitler ordered a scorched earth policy in Germany and the occupied territories (the Nero Decree). Speer demanded the right to implement the order and Hitler finally agreed, but instead, Speer persuaded many generals and Gauleiters to defy the order to avoid needless death and destruction. Speer visited Hitler in the bunker the week before his suicide, and confessed that he had flouted the order, and as a result, Hitler's final testament omitted Speer from the successive Government to be formed upon his death. However, Karl Doenitz used Speer's administrative skills as Minister of Industry and Production in the short-lived 'Flensburg Government'. In May 1945, he was arrested by the Allies.

Speer, almost uniquely in this trial, accepted responsibility for his actions. However, he denied any knowledge of the Holocaust, or of the appalling conditions of the enslaved workers at the Krupp factories. He was told by Karl Hanke, by then Gauleiter of Lower Silesia, never to accept an invitation to inspect a concentration camp as "he had seen something there which he was not permitted to describe and moreover could not describe,"[2] referring to Auschwitz. He certainly did not favour the Jews during the war, and was fully aware of the displacement of 75,000 Jewish occupants to make way for non-Jewish tenants made homeless by redevelopment or bombing. What he did or did not know about the Jewish Problem and its Solution is still a matter of speculation today.

At the end of the Nuremberg Trials, Albert Speer was sentenced to 20 years imprisonment in Spandau Prison, and was released in October 1966. He wrote his biography and these books became best-sellers, and he donated a considerable amount to Jewish charities. He died of a stroke in London in September 1981.

**Bob Carruthers**

---

1 'Albert Speer: His Battle With Truth', by Sereny Gitta, 1995
2 'Inside the Third Reich', Albert Speer 1970

# Statement of Individual Responsibility for Crimes set out in Counts One, Two, Three and Four

**ALBERT SPEER:**

The defendant Speer between 1932-1945 was a member of the Nazi Party, Reichsleiter, member of the Reichstag, Reich Minister for Armament and Munitions, Chief of the Organisation Todt, General Plenipotentiary for Armaments in the Office of the Four Year Plan, and Chairman of the Armaments Council. The defendant Speer used the foregoing positions and his personal influence in such a manner that: he participated in the military and economic planning and preparation of the Nazi conspirators for Wars of Aggression and Wars in Violation of International Treaties, Agreements and Assurances set forth in Counts One and Two of the Indictment; and he authorised, directed and participated in the War Crimes set forth in Count Three of the Indictment and the Crimes against Humanity set forth in Count Four of the Indictment, including more particularly the abuse and exploitation of human beings for forced labour in the conduct of aggressive war.

# The Case on Forced Labour

## TUESDAY, 11TH DECEMBER, 1945

MR. DODD: We propose to submit during the next several days evidence concerning the conspirators' criminal deportation and enslavement of foreign labour, their illegal use of prisoners of war, their infamous concentration camps and their relentless persecution of the Jews. We will present evidence regarding the general aspects of these programmes, and our French and Soviet colleagues will present evidence of the specific application of these programmes in the West and the East, respectively.

These crimes were committed both before and after Nazi Germany had launched its series of aggressions. They were committed within Germany and in foreign countries as well. Although separated in time and space, these crimes had, of course, an inter-relationship which resulted from their having a common source in Nazi ideology; for within Germany the conspirators had made hatred and destruction of the Jew an official philosophy and a public duty; they had preached the concept of the master race with its corollary of slavery for others, they had denied and destroyed the dignity and the rights of the individual human being. They had organised force, brutality and terror into instruments of political power and had made them commonplaces of daily existence. We propose to prove that they had placed the concentration camp and a vast apparatus of force behind their racial and political myths, their laws and their policies. As every German Cabinet Minister or high official knew, behind the laws and decrees in the Reichsgesetzblatt was not the agreement of the people or their representatives, but the terror of the concentration camps and the Police State. The conspirators had preached that war was a noble activity and that force was the appropriate means of resolving international differences and, having mobilised all aspects of German life for war, they plunged Germany and the world into war.

We say that this system of hatred, savagery, and denial of individual rights, which the conspirators erected into a philosophy of government within Germany, into what we may call the Nazi Constitution, followed the Nazi armies as they swept over Europe. For the Jews of the occupied countries suffered the same fate as the Jews of Germany, and foreign labourers became the serfs of the master race—they were deported and enslaved by the millions. Many deported and enslaved labourers joined the victims of the concentration camps where they were literally worked to death in the course of the Nazi programme of extermination through work. We propose to show that this Nazi combination of the assembly line, the torture chamber and the executioner's rack in a single institution has a horrible repugnance to the twentieth century mind.

We say that it is plain that the programme of the concentration camp, the anti-Jewish programme, the forced labour programme, are all parts of a larger pattern, and this will become even more plain as we examine the evidence regarding these programmes and then test their legality by applying the relevant principles of International Law.

The evidence relating to the Nazi Slave Labour Programme has been assembled in a document book bearing the letter "R", and, in addition, there is an appendix to the document book consisting of certain photographs contained in a manila folder. Your Honours will observe that on some of the books we have placed some tabs, so that it will be easier for the Tribunal to locate the documents. Unfortunately, we did not have a sufficient number of tabs to do the work completely, and that will account for tabs missing on some of the document books.

It may illuminate the specific items of evidence which will be offered later if we first describe in rather general terms the elements of the Nazi foreign labour policy. It was a policy of mass deportation and mass enslavement, as I said a moment ago, and it was also carried out by force, by fraud, by terror, by arson, by means unrestrained by the laws of war, and laws of humanity, or the considerations of mercy. This labour policy was a policy as well of underfeeding and overworking foreign labourers, of subjecting them to every form of degradation, brutality and inhumanity. It was a policy which compelled foreign workers and prisoners of war to manufacture armaments and to engage in other operations of war directed against their own countries. It was a policy, as we propose to establish, which constituted a flagrant violation of the laws of war and the laws of humanity.

We shall show that defendants Sauckel and Speer are principally responsible for the formulation of the policy and for its execution, that defendant Sauckel, the Nazi Plenipotentiary General for Manpower, directed the recruitment, deportation and allocation of foreign civilian labour, that he sanctioned and directed the use of force as the instrument of recruitment, and that he was responsible for the care and treatment of the enslaved millions; that the defendant Speer, as Reich Minister for Armament and Munitions, Director of the Organisation Todt and member of the Central Planning Board, bears responsibility for the determination of the numbers of foreign slaves required by the German war machine responsible for the decision to recruit by force, and for the use under brutal, inhuman and degrading conditions, of foreign civilians and prisoners of war in the manufacture of armaments and munitions, the construction of fortifications, and in active military operations.

We shall also show in this presentation that the defendant Goering, as Plenipotentiary General for the Four Year Plan, is responsible for all of the crimes involved in the Nazi Slave Labour Programme. Finally, we propose to show that the defendant Rosenberg, as Reich Minister for the Eastern Occupied Territories, and the defendant Frank, as Governor of the Government General of Poland, and the defendant Seyss-Inquart, as Reich

Commissar for the Occupied Netherlands, and the defendant Keitel, as Chief of the O.K.W., share responsibility for the recruitment by force and terror and for the deportation to Germany of the citizens of the areas overrun or subjugated by the Wehrmacht.

The use of vast numbers of foreign workers was planned before Germany went to war and was an integral part of the conspiracy for waging aggressive war. On 23rd May, 1939, a meeting was held in Hitler's study at the Reich Chancellery. Present were the defendants Goering, Raeder and Keitel.

I now refer to Document L-79 which has already been introduced in evidence as Exhibit USA 27. The document presents the minutes of this meeting, at which Hitler stated, as your Honours will recall, that he intended to attack Poland at the first suitable opportunity; but I wish to quote from Page 2 of the English text starting with Paragraph 13. In the German text the passage, by the way, appears at Page 4, Paragraphs 6 and 7. Quoting directly from the English text:

"If fate brings us into conflict with the West, the possession of extensive areas in the East will be advantageous. We shall be able to rely upon record harvests even less in time of war than in peace.

The population of non-German areas will perform no military service, and will be available as a source of labour."

We say the Slave Labour Programme of the Nazi conspirators was designed to achieve two purposes, both of which were criminal. The primary purpose, of course, was to satisfy the labour requirements of the Nazi war machine by compelling these foreign workers, in effect, to make war against their own countries and their allies. The secondary purpose was to destroy or weaken peoples deemed inferior by the Nazi racialists, or deemed potentially hostile by the Nazi planners of world supremacy.

These purposes were expressed by the conspirators themselves.

I wish to refer at this point and to offer in evidence Document 016-PS, which is Exhibit USA 168. This document was sent by the defendant Sauckel to the defendant Rosenberg on 20th April, 1942, and it describes Sauckel's Labour Mobilisation Programme. I wish to quote now from Page 2 of the English text, starting with the sixth paragraph, and in the German text, again, it appears at Page 2 of the second paragraph. Quoting from the text directly:

"The aim of this new, gigantic labour mobilisation is to use all the rich and tremendous sources, conquered and secured for us by our fighting Armed Forces under the Leadership of Adolf Hitler, for the armament of the Armed Forces and also for the nutrition of the Homeland. The raw materials as well as the fertility of the conquered territories and their human labour power are to be used completely and conscientiously to the profit of Germany and her allies."

The theory of the master race underlay the conspirators' labour policy in the East.

I now refer to Document 1130-PS, which is marked Exhibit USA 16q. This document consists of a statement made by one Erich Koch, Reich Commissar for the Ukraine, on 5th March, 1943, at a meeting of the National Socialist Party in Kiev. I quote from the first page of the English text, starting with the first paragraph, and in the German text it appears at Page 2, Paragraph 1. Quoting directly again from the English text, Koch said:—

"We are the master race and must govern hardly but justly..I will draw the very last out of this country. I did not come to spread bliss. I have come to help the Fuehrer. The population must work, work, and work again. for some people are getting excited, that the population may not get enough to eat. The population cannot demand that, one has only to remember what our heroes were deprived of in Stalingrad .. We definitely did not come here to give out manna. We have come here to create the basis for victory. We are a master race, which must remember that the lowliest German worker is racially and biologically a thousand times more valuable than the population here."

At this point I should like to offer in evidence Document 1919-PS, which is Exhibit USA 170. This is a document which contains a speech delivered by Himmler, the Reichsfuehrer S.S., to a group of S.S. Generals on 4th October, 1943, at Posen, and I am referring to the first page of the English text, starting with the third paragraph. For the benefit of the interpreters, in the German text it appears at Page 23 in the first paragraph. Quoting direct from this document, starting with the third paragraph:—

"What happens to a Russian, or to a Czech, does not interest me in the slightest. What the nations can offer in the way of good blood of our type, we will take, if necessary by kidnapping their children and raising them here with us. Whether nations live in prosperity or starve to death interests me only in so far as we need them as slaves for our Kultur: otherwise, it is of no interest to me. Whether 10,000 Russian females fall down from exhaustion while digging an anti-tank ditch interests me only in so far as the anti-tank ditch for Germany is finished—"

**THE PRESIDENT:** Who is the author of that document?

**MR. DODD:** The author of that quotation was the Reichsfuehrer S.S., Heinrich Himmler.

The next document to which I make reference is 031-PS, which is Exhibit USA 171. This document is a top secret memorandum prepared for the Ministry for the Eastern Occupied Territories on 12th June, 1944, and approved by the defendant Rosenberg; and from it I wish to quote from the English text, starting with the first paragraph, and in the German text the passage appears at Page 2 in the first paragraph. Quoting directly:—

"The Army Group Centre has the intention to apprehend 40,000— 50,000 youths of the ages of 10 to 14 who are in the Army area, and to transport them to the Reich..."

I wish to pass now to line 21 of Paragraph 1, and quoting directly I read as follows:—

"It is intended to allot these juveniles primarily to the German trades as apprentices, to be used as skilled workers after 2 years' training. This is to be arranged through the Organisation Todt, which is especially equipped for such a task through its technical and other set-ups. This action is being greatly welcomed by the German trade since it represents a decisive measure for the alleviation of the shortage of apprentices."

Passing a little further on in that document, I wish to call to the attention of the Tribunal Paragraph 1 on Page 2, and to quote it directly:—

"This action is aimed not only at preventing a direct reinforcement of the enemy's military strength, but also at a reduction of his biological potentialities as viewed from the perspective of the future. These ideas have been voiced not only by the Reichsfuehrer of the S.S. but also by the Fuehrer. Corresponding orders were given during last year's withdrawals in the Southern Sector."

I call to your Honour's attention particularly, that the approval of the defendant Rosenberg is noted on Page 3 of the document. It is a note in ink in the original, and I quote it-:

"Regarding the above Obergruppenfuehrer Berger received the memorandum on 14th June. Consequently the Reich Minister has approved the action."

THE PRESIDENT: Mr. Dodd, did you mean to leave out the sentence at the bottom of Page 1?

MR. DODD: No, your Honour, I did not, but I did not want to refer to it at this time. I will refer to it a little later on.

THE PRESIDENT: Is not it really a part of what follows at the top of Page 2, the words "Following are the arguments—"

MR. DODD: I did omit that. I thought you were referring to the sentence above. I am sorry. "Following are the arguments against this decision of the minister"; and then, quoting:—

"This action is not only aimed at preventing direct reinforcement of any military—"

THE PRESIDENT: Yes, and you were telling us how the defendant Rosenberg was implicated.

MR. DODD: Yes. On the last page of that document, the original bears a note in ink, and in the mimeographed copy it is typewritten:

"Regarding the above Obergruppenfuehrer Berger received the memorandum on 14th June. Consequently the Reich Minister has approved the action."

One page back on that same document, from the first paragraph, four sentences down, the sentence begins:

"The Minister has approved the execution of the high action in the Army Territories, under the conditions and provisions arrived at in talks with Army Group Centre."

The purposes of the Slave Labour Programme which we have just been describing, namely the strengthening of the Nazi war machine and the destruction or weakening of peoples deemed inferior by the Nazi conspirators, were achieved, we repeat, by the impressment and deportation of millions of persons into Germany for forced labour. It involved the separation of husbands from their wives and children from their parents, and the imposition of conditions unfit for human existence, with the result that countless numbers were killed.

Poland was the first victim. The defendant Frank, as Governor of the Government General of Poland, announced that under his programme 1,000,000 workers were to be sent to Germany, and he recommended that police surround Polish villages and seize the inhabitants for deportation.

I wish to refer to Document 1375-PS, which is Exhibit USA 172. This document is a letter from the defendant Frank to the defendant Goering and it is dated the 25th January, 1940. I wish to quote from the first page of the English text, starting with the first paragraph, and in the German text, again, it appears at Page 1 of the first paragraph, and, quoting directly:—

> "In view of the present requirements of the Reich for the defence industry, it is at present fundamentally impossible to carry on long term economic policy in the Government General. Rather, it is necessary so to steer the economy of the Government General that it will, in the shortest possible time, accomplish results representing the maximum that can be obtained from the economic strength of the Government General for the immediate strengthening of our capacity for defence.
>
> In particular the following performances are expected of the total economy of the Government General."

I wish to pass on a little bit in this text to the second page and particularly to Paragraph (g) of the English text. In the German text, the same passage appears on Page 3 in Paragraph (g). I am quoting directly again:—

> "Supply and transportation of at least one million male and female agricultural and industrial workers to the Reich—among them at least 750,000 agricultural workers of whom at least 50 per cent. must be women—in order to guarantee agricultural production in the Reich and as a replacement for industrial workers lacking in the Reich."

The methods by which these workers were to be supplied were considered by the defendant Frank, as revealed in the document to which we now refer.

It is an entry in the defendant Frank's own diary, to which we have assigned our Document 2233-PS-A, and which we offer as Exhibit USA 173. The portion which I shall read is the entry for Friday, 10th May, 1940. It appears in the document book as 2233-PS-A, on the third page, in the centre of the page. Just above are the words "Page 23", Paragraph 1, to the left, just above it:—

> "Then the Governor General deals with the problem of the Compulsory Labour Service of the Poles. Upon the demands from the Reich it has now been decreed that compulsion may be exercised, in view of the fact that sufficient manpower was not voluntarily available for service inside the German Reich. This compulsion means the possibility of arrest of male and female Poles. Because of these measures a certain disquietude had developed which, according to individual reports,

was spreading very much, and which might produce difficulties everywhere. General Field Marshal Goering some time ago pointed out in a long speech the necessity to deport into the Reich a million workers. The supply so far was 160,000. However, great difficulties had to be overcome. Therefore it would be advisable to consult the district and town chiefs in the execution of the compulsion, so that one could be sure from the start that this action would be reasonably successful. The arrest of young Poles when leaving church service or the cinema would bring about an increasing nervousness among them. Generally speaking, he had no objections at all if the rubbish, capable of work yet often loitering about, were snatched from the streets. The best method for this, however, would be the organisation of a raid, and it would be absolutely justifiable to stop a Pole in the street and to question him what he was doing, where he was working, etc."

I should like to refer to another entry in the diary of the defendant Frank, and I offer in evidence an extract from the entry made on 16th March, 1940, which appears in the document book as 2233-PS-B, and it is Exhibit USA 174. I wish particularly to quote from the third page of the English text:—

"The Governor General remarks that he had long negotiations in Berlin with the representatives of the Reich Ministry for Finance and the Reich Ministry for Food. An urgent demand was made there that Polish farm workers should be sent to the Reich in greater numbers. He has made the statement in Berlin that he, if it is demanded from him, could naturally exercise force in such a manner as to order the police to surround a village, and get the men and women in question out by force, and then send them to Germany. One can however also work in another way, besides these police measures, by retaining the unemployment compensation of those workers in question."

**THE PRESIDENT:** Why is it that this document is dated the 16th March, 1943

**MR. DODD:** That is clearly an error in the translation—I am sorry, your Honour. It is the 16th March, 1940. It is a mistake in the mimeographing.

The instruments of force and terror used to carry out this programme reached into many phases of Polish life. German labour authorities raided churches and theatres, seized those present and shipped them back to Germany. This appears in a memorandum to Himmler, which we offer in evidence as Document 2220-PS, and it becomes Exhibit USA 175. This memorandum is dated the 17th April, 1943, and it was written by Dr. Lammers, the Chief of the Reich Chancellery, and deals with the situation in the Government General of Poland.

**DR. SERVATIUS (Counsel for defendant Sauckel):** I should like to call the attention of the Court to the fact that the last three documents which have just been read were not made available to me beforehand. They did not appear in the original list of documents, and when checking the later list I could not find them either.

*Speer's Cathedral of Light above the Zeppelintribune at the Nuremberg parade ground was featured in Leni Riefenstahl's famous propaganda film 'Triumph of the Will'.*
*Bundesarchiv, Bild 183-1982-1130-502 / CC-BY-SA*

I therefore request that the reading of these documents be held in abeyance until I have had an opportunity to peruse them, and to discuss the matter with my client.

Perhaps I may, at the same time, lodge an additional complaint. I received some interrogation material in German the day before yesterday. My client, when asked, told me that they are not transcripts of the interrogation in the real sense of the word; that he was interrogated in German; that an interpreter translated his deposition into English, and that this was taken down.

**THE PRESIDENT:** I did not hear what you said last. I heard what you said about the three last documents not being available to you, and you went on to say something about interrogations.

**DR. SERVATIUS:** With regard to the interrogation document—as I shall call it—which was submitted to me I should like to make the following complaint. These documents cannot have the value of evidence as they were not presented to the defendant for approval; he did not sign them, nor were they read to him. They are transcripts in English, a language which the defendant understands but little or not at all.

I have also ascertained that another interrogation document, concerning the defendant Speer, contains statements detrimental to my client's interests, statements which are evidently incorrect too, as I established after talking to him.

I should like to have an opportunity of discussing the matter with the representatives of the prosecution, in order to clear up these differences and to decide whether I can agree to the use of these documents. For the time being I must object to use being made of these documents, which are to be presented by the prosecution today, or tomorrow at the latest.

**THE PRESIDENT:** As I understand it, you said to us that the last three documents were not available to you and that they were not in the original list. Is that right?

**DR. SERVATIUS:** Not available so far. I should like to have an opportunity to peruse these documents beforehand. They are being read here prior to my even having seen them.

**THE PRESIDENT:** And then you went on to deal with the interrogations which have not been put into evidence.

**DR. SERVATIUS:** It is, however, probable that the material will be put into evidence today, and I wish to take the opportunity of calling the Court's attention to the fact that I wish to discuss the matter with the prosecution beforehand, in case the material should be used during tomorrow's proceedings. Meanwhile I must object to this material being used as evidence.

**THE PRESIDENT:** Mr. Dodd, do you know what the circumstances are about these three documents which have not been supplied.

**MR. DODD:** I do not, your Honour. They have been placed in the defendants' Information Centre and they partly have been in the information list. It may be that through some oversight these entries of this diary were neglected.

**DR. SERVATIUS:** I have these documents in my hand; they are not numbered. The first document concerning Sauckel begins on Page 10, question and answer on Pages 11, 12. It is, therefore, not a coherent document, but consists of fragments of a transcript, the origin of which I should like to investigate.

**THE PRESIDENT:** Counsel for the prosecution will supply you with these documents at the adjournment this afternoon. With reference to the interrogation, if they propose to use any interrogation in the trial tomorrow, they can also supply you with any documents which are material to that interrogation.

**DR. SERVATIUS:** I agree to that.

**MR. DODD:** I believe I was referring to Document 2220-PS.

**THE PRESIDENT:** That is right. You have not begun to read it yet.

**MR. DODD:** I propose to read from the fourth page of the English text, Paragraph 2 at the top of the page, particularly the last two sentences of the paragraph; and in the German text the passage is found in Page 10, Paragraph 1. Quoting directly, it is as follows:—

> "As things were, the utilisation of manpower had to be enforced by means of more or less forceful methods, such as the instances when certain groups appointed by the Labour Offices caught churchgoers and cinema audiences here and there, and transported them into the Reich. That such methods undermine the people's willingness to work and the people's confidence to such a degree that it cannot be checked

even with terror, is just as clear as the consequences brought about by a strengthening of the political resistance movement."

That is the end of the quotation. We say that Polish farmland was confiscated with the aid of the S.S. and was distributed to German inhabitants or held in trust for the German community, and the farm owners were employed as labourers, or transported to Germany against their will. We refer to Document 1352-PS, which becomes Exhibit USA 176. This document is a report of the S.S., and it bears the title "Achievement of Confiscations of Polish Agricultural Enterprises with the Purpose to Transfer the Poles to the Old Reich and to Employ Them as Agricultural Workers."

I wish to read from the first page of the English text beginning with the fifth paragraph; and in the German text it appears on Page 9, Paragraph 1. Quoting:—

"It is possible without difficulty to accomplish the confiscation of small agricultural enterprises in the villages in which larger agricultural enterprises have been already confiscated, and are under the management of the East German Corporation for Agricultural Development."

And then passing down three sentences, there is this statement which I quote:—

"The former owners of Polish farms, together with their families, will be transferred to the old Reich by the employment agencies, for employment as farm workers. In this way many hundreds of Polish agricultural workers can be placed at the disposal of agriculture in the old Reich in the shortest and simplest manner. In this way the most pressing shortage, that which is now felt especially in the root-crop districts, would be overcome."

Pursuant to the directions of the defendant Sauckel, his agents and the S.S. men deported Polish men to Germany without their families, thereby accomplishing one of the basic purposes of the programme, the supplying of labour for the German war effort, and at the same time, weakening the reproductive potential of the Polish people.

I wish to refer directly to Document L-61, which becomes Exhibit USA 177. This document is a letter from the defendant Sauckel to the Presidents of the "Landes" Employment Offices. It is dated 26th November, 1942, and I want to read from the first paragraph of that letter, which states as follows:—

"In agreement with the Chief of the Security Police and the S.D., Jews who are still in employment are, from now on, to be evacuated from the territory of the Reich and are to be replaced by Poles, who are being deported from the Government General."

Passing to the third paragraph of that same letter, we find this statement.

"The Poles who are to be evacuated as a result of this measure will be put into concentration camps and put to work whether they are criminal or asocial elements. The remaining Poles where they are suitable for labour will be transported without family into the Reich, particularly to Berlin, where they will be put at the disposal of the labour allocation offices, to work in armament factories instead of the Jews who are to be replaced."

**THE PRESIDENT:** Who is the Chief of the Security Police, mentioned in the second paragraph?

**MR. DODD:** The Chief of the Security Police was Heinrich Himmler. He was also the Reichsfuehrer of the S.S.

**DR. SERVATIUS:** I would like to add something with regard to this document. The defendant Sauckel denies knowledge of it, and the place of issue, not mentioned during the reading of this document, is relevant. This document, according to its letterhead, was written at 36 Saarland Strasse, a place which has never been the office of defendant Sauckel.

The second point is; this document was not signed by the defendant Sauckel, and contrary to the statement in the document list classifying it as an original letter, it is merely a copy marked "Signed Sauckel". The usual certification of the signature customary for all documents is missing. I should like the prosecution to take note of this, so that I can refer to this document in the defence later.

**THE PRESIDENT:** If the procedure which the Tribunal has laid down has been carried out, either the original document or a photostat copy will be in your Information Centre, and you can then compare or show to your client either the photostat or the original.

**DR. SERVATIUS:** I have done this, and only object to the fact that this document is being read with the exclusion of some parts which I consider important. If this letter is being read here it will have to be read in its entirety, and with parts considered essential by me, and, of course, we also attach importance to the kind of signature.

**THE PRESIDENT:** Will you repeat that.

**DR. SERVATIUS:** I beg that the letter be read in its entirety if it is to be used here; namely, with its complete heading and the signature of the defendant, such as it is. The certification of the signature is missing, a fact from which my client draws certain conclusions in his favour.

**THE PRESIDENT:** You will have an opportunity, after adjournment, of seeing this document, and you have been told already that you can refer, when your turn comes to present your defence, to the whole of any document. It is inconvenient to the Tribunal to have many interruptions of this sort, and if you wish to refer to the whole document, you will be able to do so at a later stage.

**DR. SERVATIUS:** I draw the conclusion therefrom that it is admissible to present parts of a document instead of a complete document. Do I understand the Court correctly?

**THE PRESIDENT:** Yes, certainly. You can put in a part or the whole of the document when your turn comes. We will adjourn now; but, Mr. Dodd, you will satisfy this counsel for the defence as to the reason why he had not got these documents.

**MR. DODD:** Yes, I will.

**THE PRESIDENT:** And you will make them available to him and ensure that he has an opportunity of seeing the original of this document so that he can check the signature.

**MR. DODD:** We will have and furnish a photostat of the document, and I will see that the original is available to him.

**THE PRESIDENT:** All right, we will adjourn now.

*(The Tribunal adjourned until 1000 hours, on 12th December, 1945.)*

## WEDNESDAY, 12TH DECEMBER, 1945

**THE PRESIDENT:** The Tribunal will adjourn this morning at 12.30 for a closed session and sit again at 2 o'clock.

**MR. DODD:** May it please the Tribunal, I should like to report to the Tribunal this morning with reference to the questions which arose yesterday afternoon concerning three documents.

After adjournment we found that Document 2220-PS was in the defendants' Information Centre in photostatic form, and that the two other documents, being respectively two entries from the Frank diary, were also there but in a different form. The Frank diary consists of some 40 odd volumes which we, of course, were not able to photostat, so we had placed instead in the defendants' room the excerpts. As a matter of fact, we had placed the entire document book there.

**DR. ALFRED SEIDL (Counsel for defendant Frank):** Yesterday the prosecution showed documents concerning the defendant Frank. The documents concerned were 2233-PS-A and 2233-PS-B, Exhibits USA 173 and 174. These are not ordinary documents, but excerpts from the diary of Frank. Six weeks ago I applied in writing to have this diary, which consists of 42 heavy, thick volumes, submitted to me. I first made this request on 2nd September, the second time on 16th November, the third time on 18th November and the fourth time on 3rd December.

In spite of this I have not received this diary, and I should like to ask the Tribunal that this diary be submitted to me as soon as possible, if for no other reason, because evidence is involved which the defendant Frank before his arrest handed over to the officer who was to arrest him so that it could be used as evidence for his defence.

I am not in a position to work through all this material in a few days, and I should like to ask the Tribunal that this diary be put at my disposal without delay.

In this connection I should like to call the attention of the Tribunal to another point. The Tribunal has already granted that the four long speeches delivered by defendant Frank in Germany in 1942, which led to his dismissal from his offices by Hitler, should be put at my disposal. The General Secretary of the Tribunal gave me notice of this as early as the 4th

December. Unfortunately I have not received copies of these speeches up to this day. I should be very grateful therefore if the Tribunal will make certain that decisions of the Tribunal are being carried out and that the documents be submitted to me.

**THE PRESIDENT:** The Tribunal will look into these matters with the General Secretary of the Tribunal, and doubtless it will be able to arrange that you should have these documents submitted to you in the defendants' counsel Information Centre.

**DR. SEIDL:** Thank you.

**THE PRESIDENT:** Yes, Mr. Dodd.

**MR. DODD:** May I refer briefly to the discussion that we were engaged in yesterday in order to pick up the train of thought.

I wish to remind the Tribunal that we were discussing or had just completed a discussion of Document L-61, which had to do with a letter written by the defendant Sauckel to the residents of the "Landes" Employment Offices. I had read two excerpts from that letter.

Referring to the letter, we say that the Nazi campaign of force and terror and abduction was described in another letter to the defendant Frank, which we wish to refer to as Document 1526-PS.

**THE PRESIDENT:** Before you pass from that, Mr. Dodd, has either the original or the photostatic copy been shown to Sauckel's counsel?

**MR. DODD:** Oh, yes, sir. A photostatic copy was in the defendants' Information Centre, and after adjournment yesterday we got the original and handed it to him here in this room.

**THE PRESIDENT:** And he saw it?

**MR. DODD:** Yes, sir.

**THE PRESIDENT:** Very well.

**MR. DODD:** This Document, 1526-PS, Exhibit USA 178, is a letter written by the Chairman of the Ukrainian Main Committee, at Cracow, in February, 1943. I wish to read from the third page of the English text, beginning with the second paragraph. The same passage in the German text at Page 2, Paragraph 5. I quote:—

"The general nervousness is still more enhanced by the wrong methods of finding labour which have been used more and more frequently in recent months.

The wild and ruthless man-hunt as exercised everywhere in towns and country, in streets, squares, stations, even in churches, at night in houses, has badly shaken the feeling of security of the inhabitants. Everybody is exposed to the danger, to be seized anywhere and at any time by members of the police, suddenly and unexpectedly, and to be brought into an assembly camp. None of his relatives knows what has happened to him, and only months later one or the other gets news of his fate by a postcard."

I wish to turn to enclosure 5 on Page 8 of this document, which I quote:—

"In November of last year an inspection of all males of the age groups

1910 to 1920 was ordered in the area of Zaleschozyki (district of Czortkow). After the men had appeared for inspection, all those who were chosen were arrested at once, loaded into trains and sent to the Reich. Such recruiting of labourers for the Reich also took place in other areas of this district. Following some interventions the action was then stopped."

The resistance of the Polish people to this enslavement programme and the necessity for increased force were described by the defendant Sauckel's deputy, one Timm, at a meeting of the Central Planning Board, which was, by the way, Hitler's war-time planning agency. It was made up of the defendant Speer, Field Marshal Milch and State Secretary Korner. The Central Planning Board was the highest level economic planning agency, exercising production controls by allocating raw materials and labour to industrial users.

Now, Document R-124, Exhibit USA 179. This document consists of excerpts from minutes of the meetings of this Central Planning Board, and minutes of conferences between the defendant Speer and Hitler. Only the excerpts, of course, from these minutes upon which we rely are being offered in evidence. I would say to the Tribunal, however, that the balance of the minutes are available, or can or be made available if the Tribunal so desires.

This deputy of Sauckel, his name being Timm, made a statement at the 36th conference of the Central Planning Board, and it appears on Page 14, Paragraph 2, of the English text of Document R-124, and on Page 10, Paragraph 2, of the German text:—

"Especially in Poland the situation at the moment is extraordinarily serious. It is well known that violent battles occurred just because of these actions. The resistance against the administration established by us is very strong. Quite a number of our men have been exposed to increased dangers, and it was only in the last two or three weeks that some of them were shot dead, e.g., the head of the Labour Office of Warsaw who was shot in his office, and yesterday again, another man. This is how matters stand at present, and the recruiting itself, even if done with the best will, remains extremely difficult unless police reinforcements are at hand."

Deportation and enslavement of civilians reached unprecedented levels in the so-called Eastern Occupied Territories. These wholesale deportations resulted directly from labour demands made by the defendant Sauckel on the defendant Rosenberg, who was the Reich Minister for the Eastern Occupied Territories, and his subordinates, and also on the Armed Forces—a demand made directly on the Armed Forces by the defendant Sauckel.

On the 5th October, 1942, for example, the defendant Sauckel wrote to the defendant Rosenberg, stating that two million foreign labourers were required, and that the majority of these would have to be drafted from the recently Occupied Eastern Territories and especially from the Ukraine.

I wish to refer at this point to Document 017-PS, which will be Exhibit USA 180. This letter from the defendant Sauckel to the defendant Rosenberg

I wish to quote in full. It begins by saying:—

"The Fuehrer has worked out new and most urgent plans for the armament industry which require the quick mobilisation of two million more foreign labour forces. The Fuehrer therefore has granted me, for the execution of my decree of 21st March, 1942, new powers for my new duties, and has especially authorised me to take whatever measures I think are necessary in the Reich, the Protectorate, the General Government, as well as in the occupied territories, in order to assure at all costs an orderly mobilisation of labour for the German armament industry. The additional labour forces required will have to be drafted for the majority from the recently Occupied Eastern Territories, especially from the Reichskommissariat Ukraine. Therefore, the Reichskommissariat Ukraine must furnish:—

225,000 labour forces by 31st December, 1942, and 225,000 more by 1st May, 1943.

I ask you to inform Reichskommissar, Gauleiter, Party Member Koch about the new situation and requirements and especially to see to it that he will support personally in any way possible the execution of this new requirement.

I have the intention to visit Party Member Koch shortly and I would be grateful to you if you could inform me as to where and when I could meet him for a personal discussion. But I ask that the procurement be taken up at once with every possible pressure and the commitment of all powers, especially those of the experts of the labour offices. All the directives which had limited temporarily the procurement of Eastern labourers are annulled. The Reich procurement for the next months must be given priority over all other measures.

I do not ignore the difficulties which exist for the execution of this new requirement, but I am convinced that with the ruthless commitment of all resources, and with the full co-operation of all those interested, the execution of the new demands can be accomplished by the fixed date. I have already communicated the new demands to the Reichskommissar Ukraine by mail. In reference to our long-distance phone call of today I will send you the text of the Fuehrer's decree at the beginning of next week."

I should like to remind the Tribunal that we referred previously, yesterday afternoon, to this Reichskommissar, Gauleiter, Party Member Koch, and we quoted him as stating, the Tribunal will recall: "We are the master race. We must be hard," and so forth.

On the 17th March, 1943, the defendant Sauckel wrote again to the defendant Rosenberg, and on this occasion he demanded the importation of another 1,000,000 men and women from the Eastern territories within the following four months. I wish to refer at this point to Document 019-PS, which will be Exhibit USA 181. Quoting that letter in full:—

"After a protracted illness my Deputy for Labour Supply in the occupied

Eastern territories, State Councillor Peuckert, is going there to regulate the supply both for Germany and the territories themselves.

I ask you sincerely, dear Party Member Rosenberg, to assist him to your utmost on account of the pressing urgency of his mission. I thank you for the hitherto good reception accorded to Peuckert. He himself has been charged by me with the absolute and completely unreserved co-operation with all bureaux of the Eastern territories. In particular the labour supply for German agriculture, and likewise for the most urgent armament production programmes ordered by the Fuehrer make the rapid importation of approximately one million men and women from the Eastern territories within the next four months imperative. Starting 15th March, the daily shipment must have reached 5,000 female and male workers respectively, while by the beginning of April this number has to be stepped up to 10,000. This is a requisite of the most urgent programmes, and the spring tillage and other agricultural tasks are not to suffer to the detriment of the nutrition and of the Armed Forces. I have foreseen the allotment of the draft quotas for the individual territories in agreement with your experts for the labour supply as follows:-

Daily quota starting 15th March, 1943
- General Commissariat White Ruthenia—500 people
- Economic Inspection Centre—500 people
- Reichs Commissariat Ukraine—3,000 people
- Economic Inspection South—1,000 people
- Total—5,000 people

Starting 1st April, 1943, the daily quota is to be doubled, corresponding to the doubling of the entire quota. I hope to visit personally the Eastern territories towards the end of the month, and ask you once more for your kind support."

The defendant Sauckel did travel to the East. He travelled to Kauen in Lithuania to press his demands. We offer in evidence Document 204-PS, which will be Exhibit USA 182. This document is a synopsis of a report of the City Commissioner of Kauen and minutes of a meeting in which the defendant Sauckel participated. I read from the second page of the English text, beginning with the first paragraph. The same passage appears in the German text at Page 5, Paragraph 2. Quoting directly as follows:—

"In a lecture in which the Plenipotentiary for the Arbeitseinsatz, Gauleiter Sauckel, made on 18th July, 1943, in Kauen, and in an official conference following it, between Gauleiter Sauckel and the General Commissar, the pool of labour in the Reich was again brought up urgently; Gauleiter Sauckel again demanded that Lithuanian labour be furnished in greater volume for the purpose of the Reich."

**THE PRESIDENT:** Who was the General Commissar, Rosenberg?

**MR. DODD:** The Plenipotentiary for the Arbeitseinsatz?

**THE PRESIDENT:** No, the General Commissar.

*Speer, Hitler and the architect Franz Ruff looking at building plans and models of the Nuremberg Party Congress Hall in 1934.*
*Bundesarchiv, Bild 146-1971-016-31 / CC-BY-SA*

**MR. DODD:** His name is not known to us. He was apparently a local functionary in the Party.

**THE PRESIDENT:** Very well.

**MR. DODD:** The defendant Sauckel also visited Riga, in Latvia, to assert his demands, and the purpose of this visit is described in Document 2280-PS, which will be Exhibit USA 183. This document is a letter from the Reich Commissar for the Ostland to the Commissioner General in Riga and it is dated 3rd May, 1943. I wish to read from Page 1 of the English text, beginning with the first paragraph:—

> "Following the basic statements of the Plenipotentiary General for manpower, Gauleiter Sauckel, on the occasion of his visit to Riga, on 21st April, 1943, it was decided in view of the critical situation and in disregard of all adverse considerations, that a total of 183,000 workers have to be supplied from the Eastern territories to the Reich territory. This task must definitely be accomplished within the next four months and at the latest must be completed by the end of August."

Here again we are not informed as to the name and identity of the Reich Commissar for the Ostland.

Sauckel asked the German Army for assistance in the recruitment and deportation of civilian labour from the Eastern territories. We refer now to Document 3010-PS, which will be Exhibit USA 184.

**THE PRESIDENT:** Mr. Dodd, were you saying that it was not known from whom that document emanated?

**MR. DODD:** No, sir. We say it is a letter from the Reichskommissar for the Ostland to the Commissioner General in Riga, but we do not know their names specifically at the time of the writing of the letter.

**THE PRESIDENT:** You do not know who the Reichskommissar of the Eastern territories was?

**MR. DODD:** We only know him by that title, "The Reichskommissar for the Ostland."

**THE PRESIDENT:** Very well.

**MR. DODD:** Lohse, I am now informed, was his name. I understood that we did not know it.

**THE PRESIDENT:** All right.

**MR. DODD:** Referring to this Document 3010-PS, it is a secret organisation order of the Army Group South, dated 17th August, 1943. I wish to read from the first page of the English text, the first two paragraphs, as follows:—

> "The Plenipotentiary General for Labour Employment ordered the recruitment and employment of all born during the two years 1926 and 1927 for the whole of the newly occupied Eastern territory in Decree AZ. VI A 5780.28 (Enclosure I), copy of which is enclosed.
>
> The Reich Minister for Armament and Munitions approved this order.
>
> According to this order by the Plenipotentiary General for Labour Employment (B.G.A.) you have to recruit and to transport to the Reich immediately all labour force in your territory born during 1926 and 1927. The decree relative to labour duty and labour employment in the theatre of operations of the newly occupied Eastern territory of 6th February, 1943, and the executive orders therefore are the authority for the execution of this measure. Enlistment must be completed by 30th September, 1943, at the latest."

We say it is clear that the demands made by the defendant Sauckel resulted in the deportation of civilians from the occupied Eastern territories. The defendant Speer has recorded conferences with Hitler on 10th, 11th and 12th August, 1942, and this record is contained in Document R-124, which is already in as Exhibit USA 179. I now wish to quote from Page 34, of that same document in Paragraph 1 of the English text. In the German text it appears at Page 23, Paragraph 2. Quoting directly:—

> "Gauleiter Sauckel promises to make Russian labour available for the fulfilment of the iron and coal programme and reports that—if required—he can supply a further million Russian labourers for the German armament industry up to and including October, 1942. He has already supplied 1,000,000 for the industry and 700,000 for agriculture. In this connection the Fuehrer states that the problem of providing labour can be solved in all cases and to any extent; he authorises Gauleiter Sauckel to take all measures required. He would agree to any necessary compulsion in the East as well as in the West if this question could not be solved on a voluntary basis."

In order to meet these demands of 1,700,000, 100,000 here and there, the Nazi conspirators made terror, violence and arson, as we said yesterday, fundamental instruments of their labour enslavement policy. Twenty days after the defendant Sauckel's demands of 5th October, 1942, a top official in the defendant Rosenberg's Ministry described the measures taken to meet these demands. I wish to refer now to Document 294-PS, which is Exhibit USA 185. This document is a top secret memorandum dated 25th October, 1942, signed by one Brautigam. I wish to quote from Page 4 of the English text starting with the last paragraph, as follows. In the German text it appears at Page 8, Paragraph 2. Quoting directly:—

"We now experienced the grotesque picture of having to recruit millions of labourers from the Occupied Eastern Territories, after prisoners of war have died of hunger like flies, in order to fill the gaps that have formed within Germany. Now the food question no longer existed, In the prevailing limitless abuse of the Slavic humanity, 'recruiting' methods were used which probably have their origin in the blackest periods of the slave trade. A regular man-hunt was inaugurated. Without consideration of health or age the people were shipped to Germany where it turned out immediately that more than 100,000 had to be sent back because of serious illnesses and other incapabilities for work."

The defendant Rosenberg wrote concerning these brutalities to the instigator of them, the defendant Sauckel, and we refer now to Document 018-PS, which is Exhibit USA 186.

**THE PRESIDENT:** Mr. Dodd, from where did that top secret document come?

**MR. DODD:** It came from the files of the defendant Rosenberg.

This Document, 018-PS, is a letter from the defendant Rosenberg to the defendant Sauckel, and it is dated the 21st December, 1942, with attachments. I wish to quote from Page 1 of the English text starting at the middle of the second paragraph which reads as follows:—

"The report I have received shows that the increase of the guerrilla bands in the occupied Eastern Regions is largely due to the fact that the methods used for procuring labourers in these regions are felt to be forced measures of mass deportations, so that the endangered persons prefer to escape their fate by withdrawing into the woods or going to the guerrilla bands."

Passing now to Page 4 of the same English text, there is an attachment to Rosenberg's letter consisting of parts excerpted from letters of residents of the occupied Eastern territories, excerpted by Nazi censors apparently. In the German text it appears at Page 6, Paragraphs 1 and 2. Starting the quotation:—

"At our place, new things have happened. People are being taken to Germany. On 5th December, some people from the Kowkuski district were scheduled to go, but they did not want to and the village was set afire. They threatened to do the same thing in Borowytschi, as not all who were scheduled to depart wanted to go. Thereupon three truck loads of Germans arrived and set fire to their houses. In Wrasnytschi, twelve houses and in Borowytschi, three houses were burned.

On 1st October a new conscription of labour forces took place. I will describe the most important events to you. You cannot imagine the bestiality. You probably remember what we were told about the Soviets during their rule of the Poles. We did not believe it then, and now it seems just as incredible. The order came to supply 25 workers, but no one reported. All had fled. Then the German militia came and began to ignite the houses of those who had fled. The fire became very violent, since it had not rained for two months. In addition the grain stacks were in the farm yards. You can imagine what took place. The people who had hurried to the scene were forbidden to extinguish the flames and were beaten and arrested, so that seven homesteads burned down. The policemen meanwhile ignited other houses. The people fell on their knees and kissed the policemen's hands, but they beat them with rubber truncheons and threatened to burn down the whole village. I do not know how this would have ended if Sapurkany had not intervened. He promised that there would be labourers by morning. During the fire the militia went through the adjoining villages, seized the labourers, and put them under arrest. Wherever they did not find any labourers, they detained the parents, until the children appeared. That is how they raged throughout the night in Bieloserka. The workers who had not yet appeared by then were to be shot. All schools were closed and the married teachers were sent to work here, while the unmarried ones go to work in Germany. They are now catching humans like the dog-catchers used to catch dogs. They have already been hunting for one week and have not yet got enough. The imprisoned workers are locked in the schoolhouse. They cannot even go to perform their natural functions, but have to do it like pigs in the same room. People from many villages went on a certain day to a pilgrimage to the Monastery Potschaew. They were all arrested, locked in, and will be sent to work. Among them there are lame, blind and aged people."

Despite the fact that the defendant Rosenberg wrote this letter with this attachment, we say he nevertheless countenanced the use of force in order to furnish slave labour to Germany and admitted his responsibility for the "unusual and hard measures" that were employed. I refer to excerpts from the transcript of an interrogation under oath of the defendant Rosenberg on 6th October, 1945, which is Exhibit USA 187, and I wish to quote from Page 1 of the English text starting with the ninth paragraph.

**THE PRESIDENT:** You have not given us the PS number.

**MR. DODD:** It has no PS number.

**THE PRESIDENT:** I beg your pardon. Has a copy of it been given to Rosenberg's counsel?

**MR. DODD:** Yes, it has been. It is at the end of the document book, if your Honour pleases, the document book the Tribunal has.

THE PRESIDENT: I see.

DR. ALFRED THOMA (Counsel for defendant Rosenberg): In the name of my client, I object to the reading of this document for the following reasons. My client has been asked in the preliminary hearings several times about these questions concerning employment of labour. He declared that the defendant Sauckel, by virtue of plenary authority received from the Fuehrer and by order of the Plenipotentiary for the Four Year Plan, had the right to give him orders and that he (the defendant Rosenberg), despite this, demanded a recruitment of labour on a voluntary basis; that this was carried through, and that Sauckel agreed, providing the quota and the time limit could be met. Rosenberg further stated that his Ministry demanded in joint meetings that the quota be reduced and had in part been granted such a reduction.

This document which is going to be presented does not say anything about all these statements. The document which is to be presented contains only fragments of this declaration.

In order to give the Court a complete picture and in order to give the defence the possibility of a complete survey, I ask the Court to request the prosecution to present the record of the entire declaration and then, before this document is presented officially, to discuss the translation with the defence in order to prevent misunderstandings.

THE PRESIDENT: I am not sure that I understand your objection. You say, as I understood it, that Sauckel had authority from Hitler; is that right?

DR. THOMA: Yes.

THE PRESIDENT: And that Rosenberg was carrying out that authority.

DR. THOMA: Yes.

THE PRESIDENT: But all that counsel for the prosecution is attempting to do at the moment is to put in evidence an interrogation of Rosenberg. With reference to that, you ask that he should put in the whole interrogation?

DR. THOMA: Yes.

THE PRESIDENT: Well, we do not know yet whether he intends to put in the whole interrogation or a part of it.

DR. THOMA: I know only one thing. I have the document which the prosecution wishes to submit already in my hands, and I can see that it contains only fragments of the whole interrogation. What it particularly does not contain is the fact that Rosenberg always insisted that only voluntary recruitment be taken into consideration and that Rosenberg desired a reduction of the quotas, This is not contained in the document that is to be submitted.

THE PRESIDENT: If counsel for the prosecution reads a part of the interrogation, and you wish to refer to another part of the interrogation, in order that the part he has read should not be misleading, you will be at liberty to do so, when he has read his part of the interrogation; is that clear?

DR. THOMA: Yes. Then I will request the Tribunal to ask counsel for the prosecution if the document, which he intends to submit, contains the whole of Rosenberg's declaration.

**THE PRESIDENT:** Mr. Dodd, were you going to put in the whole of Rosenberg's interrogation?

**MR. DODD:** No, your Honour, I was not prepared to put in the whole of Rosenberg's interrogation, but only certain parts of it. These parts are available, and have been for some time, to counsel. The whole of the Rosenberg interrogation, in English, was given to Sauckel's counsel, however, and he has the entire text of it, the only available copy that we have.

**THE PRESIDENT:** Has counsel for Rosenberg not got the entire document?

**MR. DODD:** He has only the excerpt that we propose to read into the record here at this time.

**DR. THOMA:** May I please speak?

**THE PRESIDENT:** Mr. Dodd, the Tribunal considers that if you propose to put in a part of the interrogation, the whole interrogation ought to be submitted to the defendant's counsel, that then you may read what part you like of the interrogation, and then defendant's counsel may refer to any other part of the interrogation directly, if it is necessary for the purpose of explaining the part which has been read by counsel for the prosecution. So before you use this interrogation, Rosenberg's counsel must have a copy of the whole interrogation.

**MR. DODD:** I might say, your Honour, that we turned over the whole interrogation to counsel for the defendant Sauckel, and we understood that he would make it available to all other defence counsel. Apparently, that did not happen.

**DR. THOMA:** Thank you, my Lord.

**DR. SERVATIUS (Counsel for defendant Sauckel):** Last night I received from the prosecution these documents in English. That, of course, is sufficient for me, but counsel for the other defendants are not all in a position to follow the English text, so that certain difficulties have arisen, and I must have sufficient time to interpret these matters for my colleagues. Or perhaps the prosecution could give us the German text—for the interrogation took place in German and was translated into English—so that the original German text should be on hand.

Those are the difficulties, and I would like to have the German translation as soon as possible.

**MR. DODD:** With reference to the so-called German text, the original is an English text. These interrogations were made through an interpreter and they were transcribed in English, so that the original text is an English text, and that is what was turned over to the attorney for the defendant Sauckel with the understanding that it would be made available to all other counsel.

**THE PRESIDENT:** But of course that does not quite meet their difficulties because they do not all of them speak English, or are not all able to read English, so I am afraid you must wait until Rosenberg's counsel has got a copy of the entire interrogation in his own language.

**MR. DODD:** Very well.

Passing on beyond the document which we have just referred to, and which we now withdraw in view of the ruling, but which we will offer at a later date after we have complied with the ruling of the Court, we have a letter dated 21st December, 1942, which is Document 018-PS, and which will be Exhibit USA 186—which, by the way, is a letter from the defendant Rosenberg to the defendant Sauckel—and I wish to quote from Page 1, Paragraph 3 of the English text. In the German text it appears at Page 4, Paragraph 1. Quoting directly:—

> "Even if I do not close my eyes to the necessity that the numbers demanded by the Reich Minister for Armament and Munitions, as well as by the agricultural economy, justify unusual and hard measures, I have to ask, due to the responsibility for the occupied Eastern territories which lies upon me, that in the accomplishment of the ordered tasks such measures be excluded, the toleration and prosecution of which will some day be held against me, and my collaborators."

In the Ukraine area, arson was indeed used as a terror instrument to enforce these conscription measures, and we refer now to Document 254-PS, which is Exhibit USA 188. This document is from an official of the Rosenberg Ministry and was also found in the Rosenberg file. It is dated 29th June, 1943, and encloses a copy of a letter from one Paul Kaab, a district commissioner in the territory of Wassilkow, to the defendant Rosenberg. I wish to quote from Kaab's letter, Page 1, starting with Paragraph 1 of the English text which reads as follows:—

> "According to a charge by the Supreme Command of the Armed Forces—"

**THE PRESIDENT:** Mr. Dodd, I thought you said the date of it was 29th June, 1943.

**MR. DODD:** Yes, I did, your Honour. That was the date on the document.

**THE PRESIDENT:** The mimeographed copy of the document I have appears to have as date of the original document the 29th June, 1945, and the date below is 7th June, 1944.

**MR. DODD:** We will get the original document.

I am sorry, your Honour. There are two errors here. The document is dated the 29th June, 1944.

**THE PRESIDENT:** I see. And the enclosure is 7th June, 1944?

**MR. DODD:** Yes.

> "Answering to a charge by the Supreme Command of the Armed Forces that I burned down a few houses in the territory of Wassilkow, Ukraine, belonging to insubordinate people ordered for work-duty, this accusation is true."

Passing now to the third paragraph:—

> "During the year of 1942, the conscription of workers was accomplished by way of propaganda. Only very rarely was force necessary. Only in August, 1942, did measures have to be taken against two families in the

villages Glewenka and Salisny/Chutter, each of which were to supply one person for labour. Both were requested in June for the first time, but did not obey, although requested repeatedly. They had to be brought up by force, but succeeded twice in escaping from the collecting camp, or when on transport. Before the second arrest, the fathers of both of the men were taken into custody, to be kept as hostages and to be released only when their sons should show up. When, after the second escape, rearrest of both the fathers and boys was ordered, the police patrols ordered to do so, found the houses to be empty."

Passing to Paragraph 4, it is stated, and I quote directly:—

"That time I decided to take measures—"

**THE PRESIDENT:** Should not you read on at the top of that Page 2? You had read, had not you, "I ordered the burning down of the houses of the fugitives"?

**MR. DODD:** Yes, I have.

**THE PRESIDENT:** I thought you ought to go on after that "The result was ..." Do you see?

**MR. DODD:** "The result was that in the future the people obeyed willingly."

**THE PRESIDENT:** Wait a minute. My colleague doubts whether you have read the passage at the bottom of Page 1. I thought you had read it, beginning, "That time I decided to take measures—"

**MR. DODD:** No, I was just beginning to read it.

**THE PRESIDENT:** I beg your pardon.

**MR. DODD:** That is the fourth paragraph:

"That time I decided to take measures to show the increasingly rebellious Ukrainian youth that our orders had to be followed. I ordered the burning down of the houses of the fugitives."

Would your Honour like to have the rest of that paragraph?

**THE PRESIDENT:** I think you should read the next few lines.

**MR. DODD:**

"The result was that in the future people willingly obeyed orders concerning labour obligations. However, the measure of burning houses has not become known for the first time by my actions, but was suggested in a secret letter from the commissioner for the commitment of labour as a forced measure in case other measures should fail. This harsh punishment was accepted by the population with satisfaction."

**THE TRIBUNAL (Mr. Biddle):** The Commissioner for Labour, Mr. Dodd—you just said, "an order from the Commissioner of Labour." Who was that?

**MR. DODD:** Well, we have discussed this matter previous to our appearance here today. The document does not identify him by name. We are not sure. The defendant Sauckel was called Plenipotentiary General for Labour, and we think we cannot go much further, and must say we do not know. It just does not appear.

**THE TRIBUNAL (Mr. Biddle):** Thank you.

**MR. DODD:** Reading that last sentence,

"This harsh punishment was accepted by the population with satisfaction previous to the measures, because both families ridiculed all the other duty-anxious families which sent their children partly voluntarily to the labour commitment."

Turning to Paragraph 2 on Page 2, beginning about two-thirds of the way through the paragraph, I wish to read as follows. In the German text it appears at Page 3, Paragraph 1:—

"After the initial successes, a passive resistance of the population started, which finally forced me to start again making arrests, confiscations, and transfers to labour camps. After a while a transport of people, obliged to work, overran the police in the railroad station in Wassilkow and escaped. I saw again the necessity for strict measures.

A few ring-leaders of course escaped before they were found in Plisseskoje and in Mitmitza. After repeated attempts to get hold of them, their houses were burned down."

Finally, I wish to pass to the last paragraph on Page 3 of that same document. In the German text it appears at Page 5, Paragraph 7. Quoting from that last paragraph on the third page:—

"My actions against fugitive people obliged to work were always reported to District Commissioner Dohrer, in office in Wassilkow; and to the general-commissioner (Generalkommissar) in Kiev. Both of them knew the circumstances and agreed with my measures because of their success."

That is the end of that part of the quotation.

That Generalkommissar in Kiev, as we indicated yesterday and again this morning, was the man Koch, concerning whom we quoted his statement about the master race.

Another document confirms the arson as an instrument of enforcing this labour programme in the village of Bieloserka in the Ukraine in cases of resistance to forced labour recruitment. Atrocities committed in this village are related in Document 118-PS, which is already in evidence as Exhibit USA 186. But in addition there is Document 290-PS which is Exhibit USA 189. This document consists of correspondence originating within the Rosenberg Ministry, which was, of course, the office headquarters of the defendant Rosenberg, and it is dated 12th November, 1943. I wish to quote from Page 1 of the English text, starting with the last line, as follows:—

"But even if Muller had been present at the burning of houses in connection with the national conscription in Bieloserka, this should by no means lead to his relief from office. It is mentioned specifically in a directive of the Commissioner General in Luck of 21st September, 1942, referring to the extreme urgency of the national conscription.

Estates of those who refuse to work are to be burned, and their relatives are to be arrested as hostages and to be brought to forced labour camps."

The S.S. troops were directed to participate in the abduction of these forced labourers and also in the raids on villages, burning of villages, and were directed to turn the entire population over for slave labour in Germany.

We refer to Document 3012-PS, which is Exhibit USA 190. This document is a secret S.S. order and it is dated the 19th March, 1943. I wish to quote from Page 3 of the English text starting with the third paragraph. In the German text it appears at Page 2, Paragraph 3. It says and I quote it:—

"The activity of the labour offices, that is, of recruiting commissions, is to be supported to the greatest extent possible. It will not be possible always to refrain from using force. During a conference with the Chief of the Labour Commitment Staffs, an agreement was reached stating that whatever prisoners can be released, should be put at the disposal of the Commissioner of the Labour Office. When searching villages, when it has become necessary to burn down these villages, the whole population will be put at the disposal of the Commissioner by force."

**THE PRESIDENT:** Should not you read No. 4 which follows it?

**MR. DODD:** No. 4 says:

"As a rule, no more children will be shot."

I might say to your Honour that parts of these documents are going to be relied on for other purposes later and it sometimes may appear to the Tribunal that we are overlooking some of these excerpts, but nevertheless I am grateful to have them called to our attention because they are most pertinent to these allegations as well.

From the community of Zhitomir, where the defendant Sauckel appealed for more workers for the Reich, the Commissioner General reported on the brutality of the conspirators' programme, which he described as a programme of coercion and slavery. And I now refer to Document 266-PS, which is Exhibit USA 191. This document is a secret report of a conference between the Commissioner General of Zhitomir and the defendant Rosenberg in the community of Winniza on 17th June, 1943. The report itself is dated 30th June, 1943, and is signed by Leyser. I wish to quote from Page 1 of the English text, beginning with the last paragraph, and in the German text it appears at Page 2, Paragraph 3. Quoting it directly:—

"The symptoms created by the recruiting of workers are, no doubt, well known to the Reich Minister through reports and his own observations. Therefore I shall not report them. It is certain that a recruitment of labour, in this sense of the word, can hardly be spoken of. In most cases it is nowadays a matter of actual conscription by force."

Passing now to Page 2 of that same document, and to Paragraph 1, Line 11 in the German text it appears at Page 3, Paragraph 2—it says, and I quote it directly:—

"But as the Chief Plenipotentiary for the mobilisation of labour explained to us the gravity of the situation we had no other device. I consequently have authorised the commissioners of the areas to apply the severest measures in order to achieve the imposed quota.

The deterioration of morale, in conjunction with this, does not need any further proof. It is nevertheless essential to win the war on this front too. The problem of labour mobilisation cannot be handled with gloves."

The recruitment measures which we have been discussing enslaved so many citizens of occupied countries that whole areas were depopulated.

I now wish to refer to our Document 3000-PS, which is Exhibit USA 192. This document is a partial translation of a report from the Chief of Main Office III with the High Command in Minsk, and it is dated 28th June, 1943. It was sent to Ministerialdirektor Riecke, who was a top official in the Rosenberg Ministry. I wish to read from Page 1 of the English text, starting with the second paragraph, as follows:—

"The recruitment of labour for the Reich, however necessary, had disastrous effects. The recruitment measures in the last months and weeks were absolute man- hunts, which have an irreparable political and economic effect. From White Ruthenia approximately 50,000 people have been obtained for the Reich so far. Another 130,000 are to be obtained. Considering the 2.4 million total population, these figures are impossible.

Due to the sweeping drives of the S.S. and police in November, 1942, about 115,000 hectares of farmland is not used, as the population is not there and the villages have been razed."

We have already referred to the conspirators' objective of permanently weakening the enemy through the enslavement of labour and the breaking up of families, and we invite the Tribunal's attention to Document 031-PS, which is in evidence as Exhibit USA 171, for we desire to emphasise that the policy was applied in the Eastern Occupied Territories, with the defendant Rosenberg's approval, of a plan for the apprehension and deportation of 40,000 to 50,000 youths of the ages of 10 to 14. Now, the stated purpose of this plan was to prevent a reinforcement of the enemy's military strength and to reduce the enemy's biological potentialities. We have already quoted from Page 3 of the English text of that document to establish that the defendant Rosenberg approved that plan, the so-called high action plan. We referred to it yesterday afternoon.

Further evidence of the conspirators' plan to weaken their enemies, in utter disregard of the rules of International Law, is contained in Document 1702-PS, which is Exhibit USA 193. This document is a secret order, issued by a Rear Area Military Commandant to the District Commissar at Kasatin, dated 25th December, 1943. I quote from Page 3 of the English text at Paragraph 1. In the German text it appears at Page 12, Paragraph 1.

"1. The able-bodied male population between 15 and 65 years of age and the cattle are to be shipped back from the district East of the line Belilowka-Berditschen- Zhitomir."

This programme, which we have been describing, and the brutal measures that it employed, were not limited to Poland and the Occupied Eastern

*The Marble Gallery from the New reich Chancellery. This was damaged during the Battle of Berlin and the Soviet Union used the stone for a war memorial.*
Bundesarchiv, Bild 183-K1216-501 / Hoffmann / CC-BY-SA

Territories but covered and cursed Western Europe as well. Frenchmen, Dutchmen, Belgians, Italians, all came to know the yoke of slavery and the brutality of their slave-masters.

In France these slave-masters intensified their programme in the early part of 1943, pursuant to instructions which the defendant Speer telephoned to the defendant Sauckel at 8 o'clock in the evening on the 4th January, 1943, from Hitler's headquarters. I now refer to Document 556-PS 13, which is Exhibit USA 194. This document, incidentally, is a note from his own files, signed by the defendant Sauckel, dated 5th January, 1943. I wish to quote from Page 1 of the English text, Paragraph 1 as follows:—

"1. On 4th January, 1943, at 8 p.m. Minister Speer telephones from the Fuehrer's headquarters and communicates that on the basis of the Fuehrer's decision, it is no longer necessary to give special consideration to Frenchmen in the further recruiting of specialists and helpers in France. The recruiting can proceed with emphasis and sharpened measures."

To overcome resistance to his slave labour programme, the defendant Sauckel improvised new impressment measures which were applied to both France and Italy by his own agents and which he himself labelled as grotesque. I now refer to Document R-124, which is Exhibit USA 179, and particularly Page 2 and Paragraph 2 of the English text; in the German text it appears at Page 2, Paragraph 1. Quoting directly from that page and that paragraph a statement made by Sauckel on 1st March, 1944, at a meeting of the Central Planning Board:—

"The most abominable point made by my adversaries is their claim that no executive had been provided within these areas in order to recruit in a sensible manner the Frenchmen, Belgians, and Italians and to dispatch them to work. Thereupon, I even proceeded to employ and train a whole batch of French male and female agents who for good pay, just as was done in olden times for "shanghai-ing", went hunting for men and made them drunk by using liquor as well as words, in order to dispatch them to Germany.

Moreover, I charged some able men with founding a special labour supply executive of our own, and this they did by training, and arming, with the help of the higher S.S. and Police Fuehrer a number of natives, but I still have to ask the Munitions Ministry for arms for the use of these men, for during the last year alone several dozens of very able labour executive officers have been shot dead. All these means I have to apply, grotesque as it sounds, to refute the allegation there was no executive to bring labour to Germany from these countries."

This same slave labour hunt proceeded in Holland as it did in France, with terror and abduction. I now refer to Document 1726-PS, which is Exhibit USA 195. This document is entitled "Statement of the Netherlands Government in view of the Prosecution and Punishment of the German Major War Criminals." I wish to quote from enclosure "h", entitled "Central Bureau for Statistics—The Deportation of Netherlands Workmen to Germany." It is Page 1 of the English text, starting with the first paragraph, and in the German text it appears at Page 1, also Paragraph 1. Quoting directly, it reads as follows:—

"Many large or reasonably large business concerns, especially in the metal industry, were visited by German commissions who appointed workmen for deportation. This combing out of the concerns was called the "Sauckel-action", so named after its leader, who was charged with the appointment of foreign workmen in Germany.

The employers had to cancel the contract with the appointed workmen temporarily, and the latter were forced to register at the labour offices, which then took care of the deportation under supervision of German 'Fachberater'.

Workmen who refused—relatively few—were prosecuted by the 'Sicherheitsdienst' (S.D.). If captured by this service, they were mostly lodged for some time in one of the infamous prisoners' camps in the Netherlands and eventually put to work in Germany.

In this prosecution the Sicherheitsdienst (S.D.) was supported by the German Police Service, which was connected with the labour offices, and was composed of members of the N.S.D.A.P. and the like.

At the end of April, 1942, the deportation of working labourers started on a grand scale. Consequently, in the months of May and June, the number of deportees amounted to not less than 22,000 and 24,000 respectively of which number many were metal workers.

After that the action slackened somewhat, but in October, 1942, another top figure was reached (26,000). After the big concerns, the smaller ones had, in their turn, to give up their personnel.

This changed in November, 1944. The Germans then started a ruthless campaign for manpower, by-passing the labour offices. Without warning, they lined off whole quarters of the towns, seized people in the streets or in the houses and deported them.

Rotterdam and Schiedam, where these raids took place on 10th and 11th November, the number of people thus deported was estimated at 50,000 and 5,000 respectively.

In other places where the raids were held later, the numbers were much lower, because one was forewarned by what had happened. The exact figures are not known, as they have never been published by the occupants.

The people thus seized were put to work partly in the Netherlands, partly in Germany ..."

A document found in the O.K.H. files furnishes evidence of the seizure of workers in Holland and I refer to Document 3003-PS, which is Exhibit USA 196. This document is a partial translation of the text of a lecture delivered by one Lieutenant Haupt, of the German Wehrmacht, concerning the situation of the war economy in the Netherlands. I wish to quote from Page 1 of the English text, starting with the fourth line of Paragraph 1, quoting that directly, which reads as follows:—

"There had been some difficulties with the Arbeitseinsatz, that is, during the man-catching action, which became very noticeable because it was unorganised and unprepared. People were arrested in the streets and taken out of their homes. It had been impossible to carry out a unified release procedure in advance, because for security reasons, the time for the action had not been previously announced. Certificates of release, furthermore, were to some extent not recognised by the officials who carried out the action. Not only workers who had become available through the stoppage of industry but also those who were employed in our installations producing things for our immediate need, were apprehended or did not dare to go into the streets. In any case it proved to be a great loss to us ..."

I might say to the Tribunal, that the hordes of people displaced in Germany today indicate, to a very considerable extent, the length to which the conspirators' labour programme proceeded. The best available Allied and German data reveal that by January, 1945, approximately 4,795,000 foreign civilian workers had been put to work for the German war effort in the Old Reich, and among them were forced labourers of more than 14 different nationalities. I now refer to Document 2520-PS, Exhibit USA 197, which is an affidavit executed by Edward L. Duess, an economic analyst.

At the top of the first page there are tables setting forth the nationality and then the numbers of the various nations, and other groupings of prisoners of war and politicals, so-called. The workers alone total, according to Mr.

Duess, who is an expert in this field, the 4,795,000 figure to which I have just referred. In the second paragraph of this statement of Duess, I should like to read for the record and quote directly:—

"I, Edward, L. Duess, for three years employed by the Foreign Economic Administration, Washington, as an economic analyst in London, Paris and Germany, specialising in labour and population problems of Germany during the war, do hereby certify that the figures of foreign labour employed in the Old Reich have been compiled on the basis of the best available material from German and Allied sources. The accompanying table represents a combination of German official estimates of foreigners working in Germany in January, 1945, and of American, British and French figures of the number of foreigners, actually discovered in the Old Reich since 10th May, 1945."

Only a very small proportion of these imported labourers came to Germany on a voluntary basis. At the 1st March, 1944, meeting of this same Central Planning Board, to which we have made reference before, the defendant Sauckel made clear himself the vast scale on which free men had been forced into this labour slavery. He made the statement, and I quote from Document R-124, which is in evidence as Exhibit USA 179, and from which I have quoted earlier this morning. I wish to refer to Page 11 of that document, the middle paragraph, Paragraph 3. In the German text it appears at Page 4, Paragraph 2 (the defendant Sauckel speaking), and I quote directly from that document:—

"Out of five million foreign workers who arrived in Germany, not even two hundred thousand came voluntarily."

The Nazi conspirators were not satisfied just to tear five million odd persons from their children, from their homes, from their native lands, but in addition, these defendants, who sit today in this Court room, insisted that this vast number of wretched human beings, who were in the so-called Old Reich as forced labourers, must be starved, given less than sufficient to eat, often beaten and mistreated, and permitted to die wholesale for want of food, for want of even the fundamental requirements of decent clothing, for the want of adequate shelter or indeed sometimes just because they produced too little.

Now, these conditions of deportation are vividly described in Document 054-PS, which is a report made to the defendant Rosenberg, concerning the treatment of Ukrainian labour. I wish to refer to Document 054-PS, which is Exhibit USA 198. Before quoting from it directly, according to this report the plight of these hapless victims was aggravated because many were dragged off without opportunity to collect their possessions. Indeed, men and women were snatched from bed and lodged in cellars, pending deportation. Some arrived in night clothing. Brutal guards beat them. They were locked in railroad cars for long periods without any toilet facilities at all, without food, without water, without heat. The women were subjected to physical and moral indignities and indecencies during medical examinations.

I refer now specifically to this Document 054-PS, which consists of a covering letter to the defendant Rosenberg, first of all, and is signed by one Theurer—a Lieutenant in the Wehrmacht-to which is attached a copy of a report by the Commandant of the Collecting Centre for Ukrainian Specialists at Charkow, and it also consists of a letter written by one of the specialists, in the Rosenberg office—no, by one of the workers, not in the Rosenberg office, but one of the specialists they were recruiting, by the name of Grigori. I wish to quote from the report at Page 2, starting at Paragraph 4 of the English text, and in the German text it appears at Page 3, Paragraph 4. Quoting directly from that page of the English text:—

"The starosts, that is the village elders, are frequently corruptible, they continue to have the skilled workers, whom they drafted, dragged from their beds at night to be locked up in cellars until they are shipped. Since the male and female workers often are not given any time to pick up their luggage, and so forth, many arrive at the Collecting Centre for Skilled Workers with entirely insufficient equipment (without shoes, only two dresses, no eating and drinking utensils, no blankets, etc.). In particularly extreme cases, new arrivals therefore have to be sent back again immediately to get the things most necessary for them. If people do not come along at once, threatening and beating of skilled workers by the above-mentioned militia is a daily occurrence and is reported from most of the communities. In some cases women were beaten until they could no longer march. One bad case in particular was reported by me to the commander of the civil police here (Colonel Samek) for severe punishment (place Sozokinkow, district Dergatschni). The encroachments of the starosts; and the militia are of a particularly grave nature because they usually justify themselves by claiming that all this is done in the name of the German Armed Forces. In reality, the latter have conducted themselves throughout in a highly understanding manner toward the skilled workers and the Ukrainian population. The same, however, cannot be said of some of the administrative agencies. To illustrate this, be it mentioned that a woman once arrived dressed in little more than a shirt."

Passing now to Page 4 of this same document, starting with the tenth line of the third paragraph and in the German text it appears at Page 5, Paragraph 2. Quoting directly again:—

"On the basis of reported incidents, attention must be called to the fact that it is irresponsible to keep workers locked in the cars for many hours so that they cannot even take care of the calls of nature. It is evident that the people of a transport must be given an opportunity from time to time, to get drinking water, to wash, and to relieve themselves. Cars have been shown in which people had made holes so that they could take care of the calls of nature. Persons should, if possible, relieve themselves well before reaching the larger stations."

Turning to Page 5 of the same document, Paragraph 12, in the German text it appears at Page 6, Paragraph 1:—

"The following abuses were reported from the delousing stations: In the women's and girls' shower rooms, services were partly performed by men, or men would join in or even help with the soaping and, on the other hand, there were female personnel in the men's shower rooms; men also for some time were taking photographs in the women's shower rooms. Since mainly Ukrainian peasants were transported in the last months, as far as the female portion of these are concerned, they were mostly of a high moral standard and used to strict decency, and they must have considered such a treatment as a national degradation. The above-mentioned abuses have been, according to our knowledge, settled by the intervention of the transport commanders. The reports of the photographing were made from Halle; the reports about the other incidents were made from Kiewerce. Such incidents, in complete disregard of honour and respect of the Greater German Reich, may still occur again here or there."

Sick and infirm people of the occupied countries were taken indiscriminately with the rest. Those who managed to survive the trip into Germany, but who arrived too sick to work, were returned like cattle together with those who fell ill at work, because they were of no further use to the Germans. The return trip took place under the same terrible conditions as the initial journey, and without any kind of medical supervision. Death came to many and their corpses were unceremoniously dumped out of the cars, with no provision for burial.

I quote from Page 3, Paragraph 3 of Document 054-PS. In the German text it appears at Page 2, Paragraph 3. Quoting directly:—

"Very depressing for the morale of the skilled workers and the population is the effect of those persons shipped back from Germany for having become disabled or not having been fit for labour commitment from the very beginning. Several times already transports of skilled workers on their way to Germany have crossed returning transports of such disabled persons, and have stood on the tracks alongside of each other for a long time. These returning transports are insufficiently cared for. Sick, injured or weak people, mostly 56 to 60 in a car, are usually escorted by only three to four men. There is neither sufficient care nor enough food. Those returning frequently made unfavourable—but surely exaggerated—statements about their treatment in Germany and on the way. As a result of all this and of what the people could see with their own eyes, a psychosis of fear was evoked among the specialist workers, that is, about the whole transport to Germany. Several transport leaders of the 62nd and 63rd in particular reported thereto in detail. In one case the leader of the transport of skilled workers observed with his own eyes how a person who died of hunger was unloaded from a returning transport on the side track. (First Lt. Hofman of the 63rd Transport Station, Darniza.) Another time it was reported that three dead had to be deposited by the side of the tracks on the way and had to be left behind unburied by the escort. It is also regrettable that these disabled persons arrive here without any identification. According to the reports of the transport commanders, one gets the impression that these persons unable to work, are assembled, penned into the wagons and sent off, provided with only a few male escorts, and without special care for food and medical or other attendance. The Labour Office at the place of arrival as well as the transport commanders confirm this impression."

Incredible as it may seem, mothers in the throes of childbirth shared cars with those infected with tuberculosis or venereal diseases. Babies, when born, were hurled out of these car windows and dying persons lay on the bare floors of freight cars without even the small comfort of straw.

I refer to Document 984-PS, which is Exhibit USA 199. This document is an inter-departmental report, prepared by Dr. Gutkelch, in the defendant Rosenberg's Ministry and it is dated 30th September, 1942. I wish to quote from Page 10 of the English text, starting with the fourth line from the top of the page. In the German text it appears at Page 22, Paragraph 1. Quoting directly from that paragraph:—

"How necessary this interference was is shown by the fact that this train with returning labourers had stopped at the same place where a train with newly recruited Eastern labourers had stopped. Because of the corpses in the trainload of returning labourers, a catastrophe might have been precipitated had it not been for the mediation of Mrs. Miller. In this train women gave birth to babies who were thrown out of the windows during the journey, people having tuberculosis and venereal diseases rode in the same car, dying people lay in freight cars without straw, and one of the dead was thrown on the railway embankment. The same must have occurred in other returning transports."

Some aspects of the Nazi transport were described by the defendant Sauckel himself in a decree which he issued on 20th July, 1942; and I refer specifically to Document 2241-PS 3, which is Exhibit USA 200. I ask that the Tribunal take judicial notice of the original decree, which is published in Section B 1 a, at Page 48 e, of a book entitled Die Beschaeftigung von Auslaendischen Arbeitskraeften in Deutschland. I quote from Page 1, Paragraph 2, of the English text, and I am quoting directly:—

"According to reports of transportation commanders (Transportleiter) presented to me, the special trains provided for this purpose have frequently been in a really deficient condition. Numerous window panes have been missing in the coaches. Old French coaches without lavatories have been partly employed so that the workers had to fit up an emptied compartment as a lavatory. In other cases, the coaches were not heated in winter so that the lavatories quickly became unusable because the water system was frozen and the flushing apparatus was therefore without water."

The Tribunal will unquestionably have noticed, or observed, that a number of the documents which we have referred to—and which we have offered—consist of complaints by functionaries of the defendant Rosenberg's Ministry, or by others, concerning the conditions under which foreign workers were recruited and lived. I think it is appropriate to say that these documents have been presented by the prosecution really for two purposes, or for a dual purpose, to establish, first, the facts recited therein, of course, but also to show that these conspirators had knowledge of these conditions, and that notwithstanding their knowledge of these conditions, these conspirators continued to countenance and assist in this enslavement programme of a vast number of citizens of occupied countries.

Once within Germany, slave labourers were subjected to almost unbelievable brutality and degradation by their captors; and the character of this treatment was in part made plain by the conspirators' own statements, as in Document 016-PS, which is in evidence as Exhibit USA 168, and I refer to Page 12, Paragraph 2 of the English text; in the German text it appears at Page 17, Paragraph 4. Quoting directly:—

> "All the men must be fed, sheltered, and treated in such a way as to exploit them to the highest possible extent at the lowest conceivable degree of expenditure."

Force and brutality as instruments of production found a ready adherent in the defendant Speer who, in the presence of the defendant Sauckel, said at a meeting of the Central Planning Board—and I refer to Document R-124, which is already in evidence and which has been referred to previously. It is Exhibit USA 179. I refer particularly to Page 42 of that Document R-124, and Paragraph 2 of that Page 42. The defendant Speer, speaking at that meeting, stated:—

> "We must also discuss the slackers. Ley has ascertained that the sick-list decreased to one-fourth or one-fifth in factories where there are doctors on the staff to examine the sick men. There is nothing to be said against S.S. and police taking drastic steps and putting those known as slackers into concentration camps. There is no alternative. Let it happen several times and the news will soon go around."

At a later meeting of the Central Planning Board, Field Marshal Milch agreed that so far as workers were concerned—and again I refer to Document R-124, and to Page 26, Paragraph 2 in the English text; and in the German text at Page 17, Paragraph 1. Field Marshal Milch, speaking at a meeting of the Central Planning Board when the defendant Speer was present, stated—and I am quoting directly:—

> "The list of the shirkers should be entrusted to Himmler's trustworthy hands."

**THE PRESIDENT:** Page 17?

**MR. DODD:** No, your Honour; Page 26, Paragraph 2. The Page 17 was of the German text; in the English text it is at Page 26.

**THE PRESIDENT:** Thank you.

**MR. DODD:** Milch made particular reference to foreign workers—again in this Document R-124, at Page 26, Paragraph 3; in the German text it appears at Page 18, Paragraph 3—when he said, and I am quoting him directly:—

"It is therefore not possible to exploit fully all the foreigners unless we put them on piece-work rates, or are authorised to take measures against those who are not doing their utmost."

The policy as actually executed was even more fearful than the policy as expressed by the conspirators. Indeed, these impressed workers were underfed and overworked, and they were forced to live in grossly overcrowded camps where they were held as virtual prisoners, and were otherwise denied adequate shelter, adequate clothing, adequate medical care and treatment. As a consequence, they suffered from many diseases and ailments. They were generally forced to work long hours, up to and beyond the point of exhaustion. They were beaten and subjected to all manner of inhuman indignities.

An example of this mistreatment is found in the conditions which prevailed in the Krupp factories. Foreign labourers at the Krupp works were given insufficient food to enable them to perform the work required of them.

I refer to Document D-316, which is Exhibit USA 201. This document was found in the Krupp files. It is a memorandum upon the Krupp stationery to a Hert Hupe, a director of the Krupp Locomotive Factory in Essen, Germany, dated 14th March, 1942. I wish to refer to Page 1 of the English text, starting with Paragraph 1, as follows, and I am quoting directly:—

"During the last few days we established that the food for the Russians employed here is so miserable, that the people are getting weaker from day to day.

Investigations showed that single Russians are not able to place a piece of metal for turning into position, for instance, because of lack of physical strength. The same conditions exist in all places of work where Russians are employed."

The condition of foreign workers in Krupp workers' camps is described in detail in an affidavit executed in Essen, Germany, by Dr. Wilhelm Jaeger, who was the senior camp doctor. It is Document D-288, which is Exhibit USA 202.

"I, Dr. Wilhelm Jaeger, am a general practitioner in Essen, Germany, and its surroundings. I was born in Germany on 2nd December, 1888, and now live at Kettwig, Sengenholz, Germany. I make the following statement of my own free will. I have not been threatened in any way and I have not been promised any sort of reward.

On 1st October, 1942, I became senior camp doctor in Krupp's workers' camp, and was generally charged with the medical supervision of all Krupp's workers' camps in Essen. In the course of my duties it was my responsibility to report to my superiors in the Krupp works upon the sanitary and health conditions of the workers' camps. It was a part of my task to visit every Krupp camp which housed foreign civilian workers, and I am therefore able to make this statement on the basis of my personal knowledge.

My first official act as senior camp doctor was to make a thorough inspection of the various camps. At that time, in October, 1942, I found the following conditions:

The Eastern workers and Poles who worked in the Krupp works at Essen were kept at camps at Seumannstrasse, Spenlestrasse, Grieperstrasse, Heecstrasse, Germaniastrasse, Kapitan-Lehmannstrasse, Dechenschule, and Kramerplatz." (When the term "Eastern workers" is hereinafter used, it is to be taken as including Poles.) "All of the camps were surrounded by barbed wire and were closely guarded.

Conditions in all of these camps were extremely bad. The camps were greatly overcrowded. In some camps there were twice as many people in a barrack as health conditions permitted. At Kramerplatz, the inhabitants slept in treble-tiered bunks, and in the other camps they slept in double-tiered bunks. The health authorities prescribed a minimum space between beds of 50 cm., but the bunks in these camps were separated by a maximum of 20 to 30 cm.

The diet prescribed for the Eastern workers was altogether insufficient. They were given 1,000 calories a day less than the minimum prescribed for any German. Moreover, while German workers engaged in the heaviest work received 5,000 calories a day, the Eastern workers with comparable jobs received only 2,000 calories. These workers were given only two meals a day and their bread ration. One of these two meals consisted of a thin, watery soup. I had no assurance that they did in fact, receive the minimum which was prescribed. Subsequently, in 1943, when I undertook to inspect the food prepared by the cooks, I discovered a number of instances in which food was withheld from the workers.

The plan for food distribution called for a small quantity of meat per week. Only inferior meats, rejected by the veterinary, such as horse meat or tuberculin-infested, was permitted for this purpose. This meat was usually cooked into a soup.

The percentage of Eastern workers who were ill was twice as great as among the Germans. Tuberculosis was particularly widespread among these workers. The tuberculosis rate among them was four times the normal rate (2 per cent. Eastern workers, German,—5 per cent.). At Dechenschule approximately 2.5 per cent. of the workers suffered from open tuberculosis. These were all active tuberculosis cases. The Tartars and Kirghises suffered most; as soon as they were overcome by this disease they collapsed like flies, The cause was bad housing, the poor quality and insufficient quantity of food, overwork, and insufficient rest.

These workers were likewise afflicted with spotted fever. Lice, the carrier of this disease, together with countless fleas, bugs and other vermin tortured the inhabitants of these camps. As a result of the filthy conditions, nearly all Eastern workers were afflicted with skin disease. The shortage of food also caused many cases of hunger-oedema, nephritis and shiga-kruse.

It was the general rule that workers were compelled to go to work unless a camp doctor had prescribed that they were unfit for work. At Seumannstrasse, Grieperstrasse, Germaniastrasse, Kapitan-Lehmannstrasse, and Dechenschule, there was no daily sick call. At these camps the doctors did not appear for two or three days. As a consequence, workers were forced to go to work despite illness.

I undertook to improve conditions as well as I could. I insisted upon the erection of some new barracks in order to relieve the overcrowded conditions of the camps. Despite this, the camps were still greatly overcrowded, but not as much as before. I tried to alleviate the poor sanitary conditions in Kramerplatz and Dechenschule by causing the installation of some emergency toilets, but the number was insufficient, and the situation was not materially altered.

With the onset of heavy air raids in March, 1943, conditions in the camps greatly deteriorated. The problem of housing, feeding, and medical attention became more acute than ever. The workers lived in the ruins of their former barracks. Medical supplies which were used up, lost or destroyed, were difficult to replace. At times the water supply at the camps was completely shut off for periods of eight to fourteen days. We installed a few emergency toilets in the camps, but there were far too few of them to cope with the situation.

During the period immediately following the March, 1943, raids, many foreign workers were made to sleep at the Krupp factories in the same rooms in which they worked. The day workers slept there at night, and the night workers slept there during the day, despite the noise which constantly prevailed. I believe that this condition continued until the entrance of American troops into Essen.

As the pace of air raids was stepped up, conditions became progressively worse. On 28th July, 1944, I reported to my superiors that:

> The sick barrack in camp Rabenhorst is in such a bad condition that one cannot speak of a sick barrack any more. The rain leaks through in every corner. The housing of the sick is therefore impossible. The necessary labour for production is in danger because those persons who are ill cannot recover.

At the end of 1943, or the beginning of 1944—I am not completely sure of the exact date—I obtained permission for the first time to visit the prisoner of war camps. My inspection revealed that conditions at these camps were worse than those I had found at the camps of the Eastern workers in 1942. Medical supplies at such camps were virtually nonexistent. In an effort to cure this intolerable situation, I contacted the Wehrmacht authorities whose duty it was to provide medical care for the prisoners of war. My persistent efforts came to nothing. After visiting and pressing them over a period of two weeks, I was given a total of 100 aspirin tablets for over 3,000 prisoners of war.

The French prisoner of war camp in Nogerratstrasse had been destroyed in an air raid attack and its inhabitants were kept for nearly half a year in dog kennels, urinals, and old baking houses. The dog kennels were 3 ft. high, 9 ft. long, and 6 ft. wide. Five men slept in each of them. The prisoners had to crawl into these kennels on all fours. The camp contained no tables, chairs, or cupboards. The supply of blankets was inadequate. There was no water in the camp. That treatment which was extended was given in the open. Many of these conditions were mentioned to me in a report by Dr. Stinnesbeck dated 12th June, 1944, in which he said:—

Three hundred and fifteen prisoners are still accommodated in the camp. One hundred and seventy of these are no longer in barracks but in the tunnel in Grunertstrasse under the Essen-Muelheum railway line. This tunnel is damp and is not suitable for continued accommodation of human beings. The rest of the prisoners are accommodated in ten different factories in the Krupp works. The first medical attention is given by a French Military Doctor who takes great pains with his fellow countrymen. Sick people from Krupp factories must be brought to the sick parade. This parade is held in the lavatory of a burned-out public house outside the camp. The sleeping accommodation of the four French orderlies is in what was the men's room. In the sick bay there is a double tier wooden bed. In general, the treatment takes place in the open. In rainy weather it is held in the above-mentioned small room. These are insufferable conditions. There are no chairs, tables, cupboards, or water. The keeping of a register of sick people is impossible. Bandages and medical supplies are very scarce, all those badly hurt in the works are very often brought here for first aid and have to be bandaged here before being transported to hospital. There are many loud and lively complaints about food, which the guard personnel confirm as being correct.

Illness and loss of manpower must be reckoned with under these conditions.

In my report to my superiors at Krupps dated 2nd September, 1944, I stated:—

Camp Humboldtstrasse has been inhabited by Italian prisoners of war. After it had been destroyed by an air raid, the Italians were removed and 600 Jewish females from Buchenwald concentration camp were brought to work at the Krupp factories. Upon my first visit at Camp Humboldtstrasse, I found these females suffering from open festering wounds and other diseases.

I was the first doctor they had seen for at least a fortnight. There was no doctor in attendance at the camp. There were no medical supplies in the camp. They had no shoes and went about in their bare feet. The sole clothing of each consisted of a sack with holes for their arms and head. Their hair was shorn. The camp was surrounded by barbed wire and closely guarded by S.S. guards.

The amount of food in the camp was extremely meagre and of very poor quality. The houses in which they lived consisted of the ruins of former barracks and they afforded no shelter against rain and other weather conditions. I reported to my superiors that the guards lived and slept outside their barracks as one could not enter them without being attacked by 10, 20 and up to 50 fleas. One camp doctor employed by me refused to enter the camp again after he had been bitten very badly. I visited this camp with Dr. Grosne on two occasions and both times we left the camp badly bitten. We had great difficulty in getting rid of the fleas and insects which had attacked us. As a result of this attack by insects of this camp, I got large boils on my arms and the rest of my body. I asked my superiors at the Krupp works to undertake the necessary steps to delouse the camp so as to put an end to this unbearable vermin-infested condition. Despite this report, I did not find any improvement in sanitary conditions at the camp on my second visit a fortnight later.

When foreign workers finally became too sick to work or were completely disabled, they were returned to the Labour Exchange in Essen and from there they were sent to a camp at Friedrichsfeld. Among persons who were returned to the Labour Exchange were aggravated cases of tuberculosis, malaria, neurosis, cancer which could not be treated by operation, old age, and general feebleness. I know nothing about conditions at this camp because I have never visited it. I only know that it was a place to which workers who were no longer of any use to Krupp were sent.

My colleagues and I reported all of the foregoing matters to Herr Inn, Director of Friedrich Krupp A.G., Dr. Wiels, personal physician of Gustav Krupp von Bohlen and Halbach, Senior Camp Leader Kupke, and at all times to the health department. Moreover, I know that these gentlemen personally visited the camps.

Signed Dr. Wilhelm Jaeger."

**THE PRESIDENT:** We will adjourn now until 2 o'clock.

*(A recess was taken until 1400 hours)*

**MR. DODD:** May it please the Tribunal: We had just completed the reading of the affidavit executed by Dr. Wilhelm Jaeger at the noon recess. The conditions which were described in this affidavit were not confined to the Krupp factories alone but existed throughout Germany, and we turn to a report of the Polish Main Committee made to the Administration of the General Government of Poland, Document R-103, which is Exhibit USA 204. This document is dated 17th May, 1944, and describes the situation of the Polish workers in Germany, and I wish to refer particularly to Page 2 of the English translation, starting with Paragraph 2; in the German text it appears

*Hitler and Speer discussing plans at the Berghof, 1938.*
*Bundesarchiv, Bild 183-2004-0312-506 / CC-BY-SA*

at Page 2, Paragraph 2, also. In quoting from the document, it reads:—
 "The provision for cleanliness at many overcrowded camp rooms is contrary to the most elementary requirements. Often there is no opportunity to obtain warm water for washing; therefore, the cleanest parents are unable to maintain even the most primitive standard of

hygiene for their children or, often, even to wash their only set of linen. A consequence of this is the spreading of scabies which cannot be eradicated.

We receive imploring letters from the camps of Eastern workers and their prolific families, beseeching us for food. The quantity and quality of camp rations mentioned therein—the so-called fourth grade of rations—is absolutely insufficient to maintain the energies spent in heavy work. 3.5 kg. of bread weekly and a thin soup at lunch time, cooked with swedes or other vegetables without any meat or fat, with a meagre addition of potatoes now and then is a hunger ration for a heavy worker.

Sometimes punishment consists of starvation which is inflicted, e.g. for refusal to wear the badge 'East'. Such punishment has the result that workers faint at work (Klosterteich Camp, Grunheim, Saxony). The consequence is complete exhaustion, an ailing state of health, and tuberculosis. The spreading of tuberculosis among the Polish factory workers is a result of the deficient food rations meted out in the community camps, because energy spent in heavy work cannot be replaced.

The call for help which reaches us brings to light starvation and hunger, severe stomach intestinal trouble, especially in the case of children, resulting from the insufficiency of food which does not take into consideration the needs of children. Proper medical treatment or care for the sick is not available in the mass camps."

We now refer to Page 3 of this same document, and particularly to the first paragraph. In the German text it appears at Page 5, Paragraph 1:—

"In addition to these bad conditions, there is lack of systematic occupation for and supervision of these hosts of children, which affects the life of prolific families in the camps. The children, left to themselves, without schooling or religious care, must run wild and grow up illiterate. Idleness in rough surroundings may and will create unwanted results in these children. An indication of the awful conditions this may lead to, is given by the fact that in the camps for Eastern workers (camp for Eastern workers, 'Waldlust', Post Office Lauf, Pegnitz) there are cases of 8-year-old delicate and undernourished children put to forced labour and perishing from such treatment.

The fact that these bad conditions dangerously affect the state of health and the vitality of the workers is proved by the many cases of tuberculosis found in very young people returning from the Reich to the General Government as unfit for work. Their state of health is usually so bad that recovery is out of the question. The reason is that a state of exhaustion resulting from overwork and a starvation diet is not recognised as an ailment until the illness betrays itself by high fever and fainting spells.

Although some hostels for unfit workers have been provided as a precautionary measure, one can only go there when recovery may no longer be expected (Neumarkt in Bavaria). Even there the incurables waste away slowly, and nothing is done even to alleviate the state of the sick by suitable food and medicines. There are children there with tuberculosis whose cure would not be hopeless and men in their prime who, if sent home in time to their families in rural districts, might still be able to recover. No less suffering is caused by the separation of families when wives and mothers of small children are away from their families and sent to the Reich for forced labour."

And finally, from Page 4 of the same document, starting with the first paragraph. In the German text it appears at Page 7, Paragraph 4:—

"If, under these conditions, there is no moral support such as is normally based on regular family life, then at least such moral support which the religious feelings of the Polish population require should be maintained and increased. The elimination of religious services, religious practice and religious care from the life of the Polish workers, the prohibition of church attendance, at a time when there is a religious service for other people, and other measures, show a certain contempt for the influence of religion on the feelings and opinions of the workers."

**THE PRESIDENT:** Can you tell us who the Polish Central Committee were; or, I mean, how they were founded?

**MR. DODD:** Well, so far as we are aware, it was a committee apparently set up by the Nazi State when it occupied Poland, to work in some sort of co-operation with it during the days of the occupation. We do not know the names of the members, and we have not any more specific information.

**THE PRESIDENT:** Is it a captured document?

**MR. DODD:** It is a captured document, yes, sir. All of the documents that I am presenting in connection with this case are, excepting the Netherlands Government's report and one or two other official reports, the Dois affidavit and such other matters. That particular document, it has just been called to my attention, was captured by the United States Third Army.

Particularly harsh and brutal treatment was reserved for workers imported from the conquered Eastern territories. As we have illustrated, they did indeed live in bondage, and they were subjected to almost every form of degradation, quartered in stables with animals, denied the right of free worship, and the ordinary pleasures of human society.

Illustrative of this treatment is Document EC-68, Exhibit USA 205. This Document, EC-68, bears the title "Directives on the Treatment of Foreign Farmworkers of Polish Nationality", issued by the Minister for Finance and Economy of Baden, Germany, on 6th March, 1941. We do not know his name, nor have we been able to ascertain it.

Quoting from the English text of this document from the beginning:—

"The agencies of the Reich Food Administration, State Peasant Association of Baden, have received the result of the negotiations with the Higher S.S. and Police Officers in Stuttgart on 14th February, 1941, with great satisfaction. Appropriate memoranda have already been turned over to the District Peasants Associations. Below, I promulgate the individual regulations, as they have been laid down during the conference, and how they are now to be applied accordingly:

1. Fundamentally, farmworkers of Polish nationality no longer have the right to complain, and thus no complaints may be accepted any more by any official agency.

2. The farmworkers of Polish nationality may not leave the localities in which they are employed, and have a curfew from 1st October to 31st March from 2000 hours to 0600 hours, and from 1st April to 30th September from 2100 hours to 0500 hours.

3. The use of bicycles is strictly prohibited. Exceptions are possible for riding to the place of work in the field if a relative of the employer or the employer himself is present.

4. The visit to churches, regardless of faith, is strictly prohibited, even when there is no service in progress. Individual spiritual care by clergymen outside of the church is permitted.

5. Visits to theatres, motion pictures, or other cultural entertainment are strictly prohibited for farmworkers of Polish nationality.

6. The visit to restaurants is strictly prohibited to farmworkers of Polish nationality, except for one restaurant in the village, which will be selected by the Rural Councillor's office (Landratsamt), and then only one day per week. The day to visit the restaurant will also be determined by the Landratsamt. This regulation does not change the curfew regulation mentioned above under No. 2.

7. Sexual intercourse with women and girls is strictly prohibited, and wherever it is established, it must be reported.

8. Gatherings of farmworkers of Polish nationality after work is prohibited, whether it is on other farms, in the stables, or in the living quarters of the Poles.

9. The use of railroads, buses or other public conveyances by farmworkers of Polish nationality is prohibited.

10. Permits to leave the village may only be granted in very exceptional cases, by the local police authority (Mayor's office). However, in no case may it be granted if the applicant wants to visit a public agency on his own, whether it is a labour office or the District Peasants Association or whether he wants to change his place of employment.

11. Arbitrary change of employment is strictly prohibited. The farmworkers of Polish nationality have to work daily so long as the interests of the enterprise demand it, and as it is demanded by the employer. There are no time limits to the working time.

12. Every employer has the right to give corporal punishment to farmworkers of Polish nationality, if instructions and good words fail: The employer may not be held accountable in any such case by an official agency.

13. Farmworkers of Polish nationality should, if possible, be removed from the community of the home, and they can be quartered in stables, etc. No remorse whatever should restrict such action.

14. Report to the authorities is compulsory in all cases, when crimes have been committed by farmworkers of Polish nationality, such as sabotage of the enterprise or slowing down work, for instance, unwillingness to work, or impertinent behaviour; it is compulsory even in minor cases. An employer who loses his Pole through the latter having to serve a long prison sentence because of such a compulsory report, will receive another Pole from the competent labour office on preferential request.

15. In all other cases, only the State Police are still competent.

For the employer himself, severe punishment is contemplated if it is established that the necessary distance from farmworkers of Polish nationality has not been kept. The same applies to women and girls. Extra rations are strictly prohibited. Non-compliance with the Reich tariffs for farmworkers of Polish nationality will be punished by the competent labour office by the removal of the workers."

The women of the conquered territories were led away against their will to serve as domestics, and the defendant Sauckel described this programme in his own words, which appear in Document 016-PS, already offered in evidence as Exhibit USA 168, and particularly Page 7, fourth paragraph of the English text; in the German text it appears on Page 10, Paragraph 1, and I quote directly:—

"In order to relieve considerably the German housewife, especially the mother with many children, and the extremely busy farmwoman, and in order to avoid any further danger to their health, the Fuehrer also charges me with the procurement of 400,000-500,000 selected, healthy and strong girls from the territories of the East, for Germany."

Once captured, once forced to become labourers in Germany, or workers in Germany, these Eastern women, by order of the slavemaster, defendant Sauckel, were bound to the household to which they were assigned, permitted at the most three hours of freedom a week, and denied the right to return to their homes. I now refer to Document 3044 (b)-PS. That is Exhibit USA 206. The document is a decree issued by the defendant Sauckel containing instructions for housewives concerning Eastern household workers, and I ask that the Court take judicial notice of the original decree which appears on Pages 592 and 593 of the second volume of a publication of the Zentralverlag of the N.S.D.A.P., entitled "Verfuegungen, Anordnungen und Bekanntgaben", and I quote from the first paragraph of the English translation of a portion of the decree as follows:

"There is no claim for free time. Female domestic workers from the East may, on principle, leave the household only to take care of domestic tasks.

As a reward for good work, however, they may be given the opportunity to stay outside the home without work for three hours once a week. This leave must end with the onset of darkness, at the latest at 2000 hours.

It is prohibited to enter restaurants, movies, or other theatres, and similar establishments provided for German, or foreign workers. Attending church is also prohibited. Special events may be arranged for Eastern domestics in urban homes by the German Workers' Front, for Eastern domestics in rural homes by the Reich Food Administration with the German Women's League. Outside the home, the Eastern domestic must always carry her work card as a personal pass. Vacations, return to homes, are not granted as yet. The recruiting of Eastern domestics is for an indefinite period."

Always over these enslaved workers was the shadow of the Gestapo, and the torture of the concentration camps. Like other major programmes of the Nazi conspirators, the black-shirted guards of the S.S., and Himmler's methods of dealing with people were the instruments employed for enforcement.

On the subject of the slave labourers, a secret order dated 20th February,1942, issued by Reichsfuehrer S.S. Himmler to S.D. and Security Police Officers concerning Eastern workers, spells out the violence which was applied against them. I offer this order in evidence. It is our Document 3040-PS, which is Exhibit USA 207, and I ask this Court to take judicial notice of the original order, which is published in the "Allgemeine Erlassammlung," Part II, Section 2-A, III, small letter "f", Pages 15 to 24. I wish to quote from Page 3 of the English text starting with Paragraph III, in the German text it appears in Section 2-A, III, "f", at Page 19 of the publication as follows:—

"III. Combating violations against discipline.—(1) According to the equal status of labourers from the original Soviet Russian territory with prisoners of war, a strict discipline must be exercised in the quarters and at the working place. Violations against discipline, including work refusal and loafing at work, will be fought exclusively by the Secret State Police. The smaller cases will be settled by the leader of the guard according to instruction of the State Police administration offices, with measures as provided for in the enclosure. To break acute resistance, the guards shall be permitted to use also physical compulsion against the labourers. But this may be done only for a cogent cause. The manpower should always be informed about the fact that they will be treated decently when conducting themselves with discipline and accomplishing good work. In severe cases, that is in such cases where the measures at the disposal of the leader of the guard do not suffice, the State police office has to act with its means. Accordingly, they will be treated, as a rule, only with strict measures, that is, with transfer to a concentration camp, or with special treatment. The transfer to a concentration camp is to be done in the usual manner. In especially severe cases special treatment is to be requested at the Reich Security Main Office, stating personal data, and the exact facts.

Special treatment is hanging. It should not take place in the immediate vicinity of the camp. A certain number of labourers from the original Soviet Russian territory should attend the special treatment; they are then warned of the circumstances which lead to this treatment. Should special treatment be required within the camp for exceptional reasons of camp discipline, this is also to be requested."

And I turn now to Page 4 of the original text, Paragraph VI; in the German text it appears at Section 2-A, VI, "f", on Page 20.

"VI. Sexual intercourse.—Sexual intercourse is forbidden to labourers of the original Soviet Russian territory. By means of their closely confined quarters they have no opportunity for it. For every case of sexual intercourse with men or women of the German race, special treatment is to be requested for male labour from the original Soviet Russian territory, and, for female labour, transfer to a concentration camp."

And finally from Page 5 of the same document, Paragraph VIII, and in the German text it appears at Section 2-A, VIII, "f", at Page 21:—

"VIII. Search.—Fugitive workers from the original Soviet Russian territory are to be announced primarily in the German search book. Furthermore, search measures are to be decreed locally. When caught the fugitive must receive special treatment."

We have said to this Tribunal more than once that the primary purpose of the entire slave labour programme was, of course, to compel the people of the occupied country to work for German war economy. The decree by which defendant Sauckel was appointed Plenipotentiary General for manpower reveals that the purpose of the appointment was to facilitate acquisition of the manpower required for German war industries, and in particular the armaments industry, by centralising under Sauckel responsibility for the recruitment and allocation of foreign labour and prisoners of war in these industries. I refer to the document bearing our Number 1666-PS, Exhibit USA 208. This document is a decree signed by Hitler, Lammers, and the defendant Keitel, and it is dated 21st March, 1942, appointing the defendant Sauckel the Plenipotentiary General for the utilisation of labour. I ask that the Court take judicial notice of the original decree, which is published at Page 179, Part I, of the 194z Reichsgesetzblatt; referring to the English text starting at Paragraph 1, as follows, and quoting directly:—

"In order to secure the manpower requisite for war industries as a whole, and particularly for armaments, it is necessary that the utilisation of all available manpower, including that of workers recruited abroad, and of prisoners of war, should be subject to a uniform control, directed in a manner appropriate to the requirements of war industry, and further that all still incompletely utilised manpower in the Greater German Reich, including the Protectorate, and in the Government General, and in the occupied territories should be mobilised. Reichsstatthalter and Gauleiter Fritz Sauckel will carry out this task within the framework of the Four Year Plan, as Plenipotentiary General, for the utilisation of labour. In that capacity he will be directly responsible to the Commissioner for the Four Year Plan. Section III (Wages) and Section V (Utilisation of Labour) of the Reich Labour Ministry, together with their subordinate authorities, will be placed at the disposal of the Plenipotentiary General for the accomplishment of his task."

Sauckel's success can be measured from a letter which he himself wrote to Hitler on 15th April, 1943, and which contained his report on the one year of his activities. We refer to the Document 407-PS, VI, which will be Exhibit USA 209. I wish to quote from Paragraphs 6 and 9 on Page 1 of the English text; in the German text it appears at Page 2, Paragraphs 1 and 2:—

"After one year's activity as Plenipotentiary for the Direction of Labour, I can report that 3,638,056 new foreign workers were given to the German war economy from 1st April of last year to 31st March of this year. The 3,638,056 are distributed amongst the following branches of the German war economy. Armament- 1,568,801."

Still further evidence of this steady use of this enslaved foreign labour is found again in a report of the Central Planning Board, to which we have referred so many times this morning and yesterday. Another meeting of this Central Planning Board was held on 16th February, 1944, and I refer to our Document R-124, which contains the minutes of this meeting of the Central Planning Board, and which has been already offered in evidence as Exhibit USA 179, and I want to refer particularly to Page 26, Paragraph 1 of the English text of Document R-124. It is at Page 16, in Paragraph 2, of the German text:—

"The armament industry employs foreign workmen to a large extent; according to the latest figures—40 per cent."

Moreover, our Document 2520-PS, which is in evidence as Exhibit USA 197, records that, according to Speer Ministry tabulations, as of 31st December, 1944, approximately two million civilian foreign workers were employed directly in the manufacture of armaments and munitions (end products or components). That the bulk of these workers had been forced to come to Germany against their will is made clear by Sauckel's statement which I previously quoted from Paragraph 3 of Page 11 of Document R-124. We quoted it this morning, the statement being that of five million foreign workers only two hundred thousand or less came voluntarily.

The defendants Sauckel, Speer and Keitel succeeded in the enforcement of foreign labour to construct military fortifications. Thus, citizens of France, Holland and Belgium were compelled against their will to engage in the construction of the "Atlantic Wall", and we refer to our Document 556-PS-2, which is Exhibit USA 194. This is a Hitler order dated 8th September, 1942, and it is initialled by the defendant Keitel.

Quoting the order directly:—

"The extensive coastal fortifications which I have ordered to be erected in the area of Army Group West make it necessary that in the occupied territory all available workers should be committed and should give the fullest extent of their productive capacities. The previous allotment of domestic workers is insufficient. In order to increase it I order the introduction of compulsory labour and the prohibition of changing the place of employment without permission of the authorities in the occupied territories. Furthermore, the distribution of food and clothing ration cards to those subject to labour draft should in the future depend on the possession of a certificate of employment. Refusal to accept an assigned job, as well as abandoning the place of work without the consent of the authorities in charge, will result in the withdrawal of the food and clothing ration cards. The G.B.A. (Deputy General for Arbeitseinsatz) in agreement with the military commander, as well as the Reich Commissar, will issue the corresponding decrees for execution."

Indeed, the defendant Sauckel boasted to Hitler concerning the contribution of the forced labour programme to the construction of the Atlantic Wall by the defendant Speer's "Organisation Todt". And we refer to Document 407-PS VIII, which is Exhibit USA 210. This document is a letter from the defendant Sauckel to Hitler dated the 17th May, 1943. I refer to the second and last paragraphs:—

"In addition to the labour allotted to the total German economy by the Arbeitseinsatz since I took office, the Organisation Todt was supplied with new labour continually". Thus: "The Arbeitseinsatz has done everything to help make possible the completion of the Atlantic Wall."

Similarly, Russian civilians were forced into labour battalions and compelled to build fortifications to be used against their own countrymen. In Document 031-PS, in evidence as Exhibit USA 171, which is a memorandum of the Rosenberg Ministry, it is stated in Paragraph 1 at Page 1 of that document:—

"The men and women in the theatres of operations have been—and will be conscripted into labour battalions to be used in the construction of fortifications."

In addition, the conspirators compelled prisoners of war to engage in operations of war against their own country and its allies. At a meeting of the Central Planning Board, again held on 19th February, 1943, attended by the defendant Speer and the defendant Sauckel and Field Marshal Milch, the following conversation occurred and is recorded in out Document R-124, at Page 32, Paragraph 5, of the English text. It is Page 20, the last paragraph, of the German text, and I quote it, the defendant Sauckel speaking:—

"Sauckel: If any prisoners are taken there, they will be needed.

Milch: We have made a request for an order that a certain percentage of men in the anti-aircraft artillery must be Russians. 50,000 will be taken altogether, 30,000 are already employed as gunners. This is an amusing thing that Russians must work the guns."

We refer now to Documents 3027 and 3028. They are respectively Exhibits USA 211 and 212. They will be found at the very back, I believe, of the document book, in a separate manila folder. They are official German Army photographs, and if your Honours will examine Document 3027- PS the caption states that Russian prisoners of war are acting as ammunition bearers during the attack upon Tschedowe. Document 3028-PS consists of a series of official German Army photographs taken in July and August, 1941, showing Russian prisoners of war in Latvia and the Ukraine being compelled to load and unload ammunition trains and trucks, and being required to stack ammunition, all, we say, in flagrant disregard of the rules of International Law, particularly Article 6 of the regulations annexed to The Hague Convention, No. IV of 1907, which provides that the tasks of prisoners of war shall have no connection with the operations of war. The use of prisoners of war in the German armament industry was as widespread and as extensive almost as in the use of the forced foreign civilian labour. We refer to Document 3005-PS, which is Exhibit USA 213. This document is a secret letter from the Reich Minister of Labour to the presidents of the Regional Labour Exchange Offices, which refers to an order of the defendant Goering to the effect that—I quote now from Paragraph 1 of that document—I am quoting it directly:—

"Upon personal order of the Reich Marshal 100,000 men are to be taken from among the French prisoners of war not yet employed in armament industry and are to be assigned to the armament industry (aeroplane industry). Gaps in manpower supply resulting therefrom will be filled by Soviet prisoners of war. The transfer of the above-named French prisoners of war is to be accomplished by 1st October."

The Reich Marshal referred to in that quotation is, of course, the defendant Goering.

A similar policy was followed with respect to Russian, prisoners of war. The defendant Keitel directed the execution of Hitler's order to use prisoners of war in the German war economy, and I now make reference to our Document EC-194, which is Exhibit USA 24. This document is also a secret memorandum, according to its label, issued from Hitler's Headquarters on the 31st October, 1941, and I read from Page 1, Paragraphs 1 and 2, quoting it directly as follows:—

"The lack of workers is becoming an increasingly dangerous hindrance for the future German war and armament industry. The expected relief through discharges from the Armed Forces is uncertain as to the extent and date; however, even its greatest possible extent will by no means correspond to expectations and requirements in view of the great demand.

The Fuehrer has now ordered that even the working power of the Russian prisoners of war should be utilised to a large extent by large scale assignments for the requirements of the war industry. The prerequisite for production is adequate nourishment. Also very small wages are to be planned for the most modest supply, with a few consumers' goods for everyday life as eventual rewards for production."

And quoting now from the same document, Paragraph 2, II and III—I am quoting directly:—

"II. Construction and Armament Industry.

(a) Work units for construction of all kinds, particularly for the fortification of coastal defences (concrete workers unloading units for essential war plants.)

(b) Suitable armament factories which have to be selected in such a way that their personnel should consist in the majority of prisoners of war under guidance and supervision (eventually after withdrawal and other employment of the German workers).

III. Other War Industries.

(a) Mining as under 11 (b).

(b) Railroad construction units for building tracks, etc.

(c) Agriculture and forestry in closed units. The utilisation of Russian prisoners of war is to be regulated on the basis of the above examples by:

To I. The Armed Forces.

To II. The Reich Minister for Armament and Munitions and the Inspector General for the German Road System in agreement with the Reich Minister for Labour and Supreme Commander of the Armed Forces. Deputies of the Reich Minister for Armament and Munitions are to be admitted to the prisoner of war camps to assist in the selection of skilled workers."

The defendant Goering, at a conference at the Air Ministry on the 7th November, 1941, also discussed the use of prisoners of war in the armament industry. We refer now to our Document 1206-PS, which becomes Exhibit USA 215. This document consists of top secret notes on Goering's instructions as to the employment and treatment of prisoners of war in many phases of the German war industry. And I wish to quote from Paragraph 1 of Page 1 and Paragraph 4 of Page 2 of the English text, and from Paragraph 1, Page 1, and Paragraph 1, Page 3 of the German text as follows:—

"The Fuehrer's point of view as to employment of prisoners of war in war industries has changed basically. So far a total of 5,000,000 prisoners of war- employed so far 2,000,000."

And on Page 2:—

"In the Interior and the Protectorate it would be ideal if entire factories could be manned by Russian prisoners of war except the employees necessary for direction. For employment in the Interior and the Protectorate the following are to have priority:—

(a) At the top, coal mining industry. Order by the Fuehrer to investigate all mines as to suitability for employment of Russians, at times manning the entire plant with Russian labourers.

(b) Transportation (construction of locomotives and cars, repair shops). Railroad repair and industry workers are to be sought out from the prisoners of war. Railroad is most important means of transportation in the East.

(c) Armament Industries. Preferably factories of armour and guns.

Possibly also construction of parts for aeroplane engines. Suitable complete sections of factories to be manned exclusively by Russians. For the remainder, employment in columns. Use in factories of tool machinery, production of farm tractors, generators, etc. In emergency, erect in individual places barracks for occasional workers who are used as unloading details and for similar purposes. (Reich Minister of the Interior through communal authorities.)

O.K.W./A.W.A. is competent for transporting Russian prisoners of war employment through 'Planning Board for Employment of all prisoners of war.' If necessary, offices of Reich Commissariats.

No employment where danger to men or their supply exists, that is, factories exposed to explosives, waterworks, powerworks, etc. No contact with German population, especially no 'solidarity'. German worker as a rule is foreman of Russians.

Food is a matter of the Four Year Plan. Supply their own food (cats, horses, etc.)

Clothes, billeting, messing somewhat better than at home where part of the people live in caverns.

Supply of shoes for Russians as a rule wooden shoes; if necessary install Russian shoe repair shops.

Examination of physical fitness in order to avoid importation of diseases.

Clearing of mines as a rule by Russians; if possible by selected Russian engineers."

The defendant Goering was not the only one of these defendants who sponsored and applied the policy for using prisoners of war in the armament industry. The defendant Speer also sponsored and applied this same policy of using prisoners of war in the armament industry. And we refer to Document 1435-PS, which is Exhibit USA 20. This document is a speech to the Nazi, Gauleiters delivered by the defendant Speer on 24th February, 1942, and I read from Paragraph 2 of that document:—

"I therefore proposed to the Fuehrer at the end of December, that all my labour force, including specialists, be released for mass employment in the East. Subsequently the remaining prisoners of war, about 10,000, were put at the disposal of the armament industry by me."

He also reported at the 36th meeting of the Central Planning Board, held on 22nd April, 1943, that only 30 per cent. of the Russian prisoners of war were engaged in the armament industry. This the defendant Speer found unsatisfactory. Referring again to Document R-124, the minutes of the Central Planning Board, and particularly to Page 17 of that document, and to Paragraph 10 of the English text, and Page 14, Paragraph 7 of the German text, we find this statement by the defendant Speer: quoting directly:—

"There is a specified statement showing in what sectors the Russian prisoners of war have been distributed, and this statement is quite interesting. It shows that the armaments industry only received 30 per cent. I always complained about this."

At Page 20 of the same Document, R-124, Paragraph 11 on Page 20 of the English text, and Page 14, the last paragraph of the German text, the defendant Speer stated, and I quote from that paragraph directly:—

> "The 90,000 Russian prisoners of war employed in the whole of the armament industry are for the greatest part skilled men."

The defendant Sauckel, who was appointed Plenipotentiary General for the utilisation of labour for the express purpose, among others, of integrating prisoners of war into the German war industry, made it plain that prisoners of war were to be compelled to serve the German armament industry. His labour mobilisation programme, which is Document 016-PS, already marked Exhibit USA 168, contains this statement on Page 6, Paragraph 10 of the English text, and Page 9, Paragraph 1 of the German text:—

> "All prisoners of war, from the territories of the West as well as of the East, actually in Germany, must be completely incorporated into the German armament and nutrition industries. Their production must be brought to the highest possible level."

I wish to turn now from the exploitation of foreign labour in general to a rather special Nazi programme which appears to us to have combined the brutality and the purposes of the slave labour programme with those of the concentration camp. The Nazis placed all Allied nationals in concentration camps and forced them, along with the other inmates of the concentration camps, to work under conditions which were set actually to exterminate them. This was what we call the Nazi programme of "extermination through work".

In the spring of 1942 these conspirators turned to the concentration camps as a further source of slave labour for the armament industry. I refer to a new Document R-129, being Exhibit USA 217. This document is a letter to Himmler, the Reichsfuehrer S. S., dated the 30th April, 1942, from one of his subordinates, an individual named Pohl, S.S. Obergruppenfuehrer and General of the Waffen S.S.; and I wish to quote directly from the first page of that document.

> "Today I report about the present situation of the concentration camps and about measures I have taken to carry out your order of 3rd March, 1942."

Then moving on from Paragraphs 1, 2 and 3 on Page 2 of the English text, and at Page 1 of the German text, I quote as follows:—

> "1. The war has brought about a marked change in the structure of the concentration camps and has changed their duties with regard to the employment of the prisoners. The custody of prisoners for the sole reasons of security, education, or prevention is no longer the main consideration. The mobilisation of all prisoners who are fit for work for purposes of the war now, and for purposes of construction in the forthcoming peace, comes to the foreground more and more.
> 
> 2. From this knowledge some necessary measures result with the

aim of transforming the concentration camps into organisations more suitable for the economic tasks, whilst they were formerly merely politically interested.

3. For this reason I gathered together all the leaders of the former inspectorate of concentration camps, all camp commanders, and all managers and supervisors of work on 23rd and 24th April, 1942; I explained personally to them this new development. I compiled in the order attached the main essentials, which have to be brought into effect with the utmost urgency if the commencement of work for the purposes of the armament industry is not to be delayed."

Now, the order referred to in that third paragraph set the framework for a programme of relentless exploitation, providing in part as follows; and I now refer to the enclosure appended to the quoted letter which is also a part of Document R-129, found at Page 3, Paragraphs 4, 5 and 6 of the English text, and Page 3 of the German text:—

"4. The camp commander alone is responsible for the employment of the labour available. This employment must be, in the true meaning of the word, exhaustive, in order to obtain the greatest measure of performance. Work is allotted by the Chief of the Department D centrally and alone. The camp commanders themselves may not accept, on their own initiative, work offered by third parties, and may not negotiate about it.

5. There is no limit to working hours. Their duration depends on the kind of working establishments in the camps and the kind of work to be done. They are fixed by the camp commanders alone.

6 .Any circumstances which may result in a shortening of working hours (e.g. meals, roll-calls) have therefore to be restricted to the minimum which cannot be condensed any more. It is forbidden to allow long walks to work, and noon intervals are only for eating purposes."

The armament production programme we have just described was not merely a scheme for mobilising the manpower potential of the camps. It actually was integrated directly into the larger Nazi programme of extermination; and I wish to refer at this point to our Document 654-PS, being Exhibit USA 218.

**THE PRESIDENT:** Do you think it will be convenient to break off now for a few minutes?

**MR. DODD:** Very well.

*(A recess was taken.)*

**MR. DODD:** At the recess time I had made reference to Document 654-PS which is Exhibit USA 218. This document is a memorandum of an agreement between Himmler, Reichsfuehrer S.S., and the Minister of Justice, Thierack. It is dated 18th September, 1942. The concept of extermination to which I referred shortly before the recess, was embodied in this document and I wish to quote from Page 1, Paragraph 2.

"2. The transfer of anti-social elements from prison to the Reichsfuehrer for extermination through work. Persons under protective arrest, Jews,

Gypsies, Russians and Ukrainians, Poles with more than three-year sentences, Czechs and Germans with more than eight-year sentences, according to the decision of the Reich Minister for justice. First of all the worst anti-social elements amongst those just mentioned are to be handed over. I shall inform the Fuehrer of this through Reichsleiter Bormann."

Now, this agreement further provided in Paragraph 12 on Page 2 of the English text, and Page 3, Paragraph 14 of the German text, as follows:—

"14. It is agreed that, in consideration of the intended aims of the Government for the clearing up of the Eastern problems, in future Jews, Poles, Gypsies, Russians and Ukrainians are no longer to be tried by the ordinary courts, so far as punishable offences are concerned, but are to be dealt with by the Reichsfuehrer S.S. This does not apply to civil lawsuits, nor to Poles whose names are announced or entered in the German Racial Lists."

Now, in September, 1942, the defendant Speer made arrangements to bring this new source of labour within his jurisdiction. Speer convinced Hitler that significant production could be obtained only if the concentration camp prisoners were employed in factories under the technical control of the Speer Ministry instead of the control in the camps. In fact, without defendant Speer's co-operation, we say it would have been most difficult to utilise the prisoners on any large scale for war production, since he would not allocate to Himmler the machine tools and other necessary equipment. Accordingly, it was agreed that the prisoners were to be exploited in factories under the defendant Speer's control. To compensate Himmler for surrendering this jurisdiction to Speer, the defendant Speer proposed, and Hitler agreed, that Himmler would receive a share of the armaments' output, fixed in relation to the man hours contributed by his prisoners. In the minutes of the defendant Speer's conference with Hitler on 20th, 21st, and the 22nd September, 1942, Document R-124, which is Exhibit USA 179, I wish to refer particularly to Page 34 of the English text. These are the defendant Speer's minutes on this conference. I am quoting from Page 34, Paragraph 36, beginning at the middle of the page, and it is at the top of Page 26 in the German text:—

"I pointed out to the Fuehrer that, apart from an insignificant amount of work, no possibility exists of organising armament production in the concentration camps, because: (1) the machine tools required are missing; (2) there are no suitable premises. Both these assets would be available in the armament industry, if use could be made of them by a second shift.

The Fuehrer agrees to my proposal that the numerous factories set up outside towns for A.R.P. reasons should release their workers for supplementing the second shift in town factories, and should in return be supplied with labour from the concentration camps—also two shifts.

I pointed out to the Fuehrer the difficulties which I expected to encounter if Reichsfuehrer S.S. Himmler should be able, as he requests, to exercise authoritative influence over these factories. The Fuehrer, too, does not consider such an influence necessary.

The Fuehrer, however, agrees that Reichsfuehrer S.S. Himmler should draw advantages from making his prisoners available; he should get equipment for his division.

I suggest giving him a share in kind (war equipment) in ratio to the working hours done by his prisoners. A 3 to 5 per cent. share is suggested, the equipment also being calculated according to working hours. The Fuehrer would agree to such a solution.

The Fuehrer is prepared to order the additional delivery of this equipment and weapons to the S. S., according to a list submitted to him."

After a demand for concentration camp labour had been created, and after a mechanism had been set up by the defendant Speer for exploiting this labour in armament factories, measures were evolved for increasing the supply of victims for extermination through work. A steady flow was assured by an agreement between Himmler and the Minister of Justice mentioned above, which was implemented by such programmes as the following, and I refer to Document L-61, Exhibit USA 177, and I wish to quote from Paragraph 3. That document, the Tribunal will recall, is the defendant Sauckel's letter dated 26th November, 1942, to the Presidents of the Landes Employment Offices, and I wish to quote from Paragraph 3 of that letter.

"The Poles who are to be evacuated as a result of this measure will be put into concentration camps and put to work whether they are criminal or asocial elements."

General measures were supplemented by special drives for persons who would not otherwise have been sent to concentration camps.

**THE PRESIDENT:** Did you not read that this morning?

**MR. DODD:** Yes, I did, your Honour. I was reading it again with particular reference to this feature of the proof.

For example, for "reasons of war necessity" Himmler ordered that at least 35,000 prisoners qualified for work should be transferred to concentration camps. I now offer in evidence Document 1063-PS D, which is Exhibit USA 219. This document is a Himmler order dated the 17th December, 1942. The order provides, and I quote in part, beginning with the first paragraph of that document:—

"For reasons of war necessity not to be discussed further here, the Reichsfuehrer S.S. and Chief of the German Police on 14th December, 1942, has ordered that until the end of January, 1943, at least 35,000 prisoners qualified for work, are to be sent to the concentration camps. In order to reach this number, the following measures are required:

(1) Up to this date (so far until 1st February, 1943) all Eastern workers or such foreign workers who have been fugitives, or who have broken contracts, and who do not belong to allied, friendly or neutral States are to be brought by the quickest means to the nearest concentration

camps.

(2) The commanders and the commandants of the Security Police and the Security Service, and the chiefs of the State Police Headquarters will check immediately on the basis of a close and strict ruling:

(a) the prisons,

(b) the labour reformatory camps.

All prisoners qualified for work, if it is essentially and humanly possible, will be committed at once to the nearest concentration camp, according to the following instructions, for instance if penal procedures were to be established in the near future. Only such prisoners who in the interest of investigation procedures are to remain absolutely in solitary confinement can be left there.

Every single labourer counts!"

Measures were also adopted to ensure that this extermination through work was practised with maximum efficiency. Subsidiary concentration camps were established near important war plants. The defendant Speer has admitted that he personally toured Upper Austria and selected sites for concentration camps near various munitions factories in the area. I am about to refer to the transcript of an interrogation under oath of the defendant Albert Speer.

**THE PRESIDENT:** Mr. Dodd, do you understand the last document you read, 1063-PS to refer to prisoners of war or prisoners in ordinary prisons or what?

**MR. DODD:** We understood it to refer to prisoners in ordinary prisons. In view of the Tribunal's ruling this morning, I think I should state that, with respect to this interrogation of defendant Speer, we had provided the defendants' counsel with the entire text in German. It happens to be a brief interrogation, and so we were able to complete that translation, and it has been placed in their Information Centre.

**DR. FLAECHSNER (Counsel for defendant Speer):** In reference to the transcript of the interrogation the reading of which the prosecutor has just announced, I should like to say the following:—

"It is true that we have received the German transcript of the English protocol, if one may call it a protocol. A comparison of the English text with the German transcript shows that there are, both in the English text and in the German transcript, mistakes which change the meaning and which I believe are to be attributed to misunderstandings on the part of the certifying interpreter. I believe, therefore, that the so-called protocol, as well as the English text, does not actually give the contents of what defendant Speer tried to express during the interrogation. It would, therefore, not further the establishment of the truth should this protocol ever be used."

**THE PRESIDENT:** Mr. Dodd, when was the German translation given to counsel for the defendant?

**MR. DODD:** About four days ago, your Honour.

**THE PRESIDENT:** Mr. Dodd, is there any certification by the interrogator as to the English translation?

MR. DODD: There is, your Honour. There is a certification at the end of the interrogation by the interrogator and by the interpreter, and by the reporter as well. There are three certifications.

THE PRESIDENT: I think the best course will be in these circumstances to receive the interrogation now. You will have an opportunity, by calling the defendant, to show in what way he alleges, or you allege, that the interrogation is inaccurately translated.

DR. FLAECHSNER: Thank you, sir.

MR. DODD: May I respectfully refer your Honour to the last document in the document book, four pages from the end?

THE PRESIDENT: Which page do you refer to?

MR. DODD: I refer to the page bearing the number 16 of the English text of the transcript of the interrogation and Page 21 of the German text. The answer quoted is:—

"The fact that we were anxious to use workers from concentration camps in factories and to establish small concentration camps near factories in order to use the manpower that was then available there was a general one, but it did not come up only in connection with this trip."—Exhibit USA 270, i.e. Speer's trip to Austria.

THE PRESIDENT: I think I ought to say to defendant's counsel that if he had waited until he heard that piece of evidence read, he would have seen that it was quite unnecessary to make any objection.

MR. DODD: Defendant Goering endorsed this use of concentration camp labour and asked for more. We refer to our Document 1584-PS, Part I, which is Exhibit USA 221. This document is a teletype message from Goering to Himmler dated 14th February, 1944. I quote from the document beginning with the second sentence:—

"At the same time I ask you to put at my disposal as great a number of concentration-camp (K.Z.) convicts as possible for air armament, as this kind of manpower proved to be very useful according to previous experience. The situation of the air war makes subterranean transfer of industry necessary. For work of this kind concentration-camp (K.Z.) convicts can be especially well concentrated at work and in the camp."

Defendant Speer subsequently assumed responsibility for this programme and Hitler promised Speer that if the necessary labour for the programme could not be obtained, 100,000 Hungarian Jews would be brought in by the S.S.

Speer recorded his conferences with Hitler on 6th April and 7th April, 1944, in Document R-124, which is Exhibit USA 179, already in evidence. I quote from Page 36 of the English text, Page 29 of the German text as follows:—

"Suggested to the Fuehrer that, due to lack of builders and equipment, the second big building project should not be set up in German territory, but in close vicinity to the border on suitable soil (preferably on gravel base and with transport facilities) on French, Belgian or

Dutch territory. The Fuehrer agrees to this suggestion if the works could be set up behind a fortified zone. For the suggestion of setting up works in French territory speaks mainly the fact that it would be much easier to procure the necessary workers. Nevertheless, the Fuehrer asks that an attempt be made to set up the second works in a safer area, namely, in the Protectorate. If it should prove impossible there, too, to get hold of the necessary workers, the Fuehrer himself will contact the Reichsfuehrer S.S. and will give an order that the required 100,000 men are to be made available by bringing in Jews from Hungary. Stressing the fact that the building organisation was a failure, the Fuehrer demands that these works must be built by the O.T. exclusively and that the workers should be made available by the Reichsfuehrer S.S. He wants to hold a meeting shortly in order to discuss details with all the men concerned."

The unspeakably brutal, inhuman, and degrading treatment inflicted on Allied nationals and other victims of concentration camps while they were indeed being literally worked to death is described in Document L-159, which is not in the document book. It is an official report prepared by a U.S. Congressional Committee, U.S. Senate Document 47. This Congressional Committee had inspected the liberated camps at the request of General Eisenhower. It will be Exhibit USA 222. 1 would like to quote from the document briefly, first. from Page 14, the last paragraph, and from the first two paragraphs of the English text.

"The treatment accorded to these prisoners in the concentration camps was generally as follows: They were herded together in some wooden barracks not large enough for one-tenth of their number. They were forced to sleep on wooden frames covered with wooden boards in tiers of two, three and even four, sometimes with no covering, sometimes with a bundle of dirty rags serving both as pallet and coverlet.

Their food consisted generally of about one-half of a pound of black bread per day and a bowl of watery soup at noon and night, and not always that. Owing to the great numbers crowded into a small space and to the lack of adequate sustenance, lice and vermin multiplied, disease became rampant, and those who did not soon die of disease or torture began the long, slow process of starvation. Notwithstanding the deliberate starvation programme inflicted upon these prisoners by lack of adequate food, we found no evidence that the people of Germany, as a whole, were suffering from any lack of sufficient food or clothing. The contrast was so striking that the only conclusion which we could reach was that the starvation of the inmates of these camps was deliberate.

Upon entrance into these camps, newcomers were forced to work either at an adjoining war factory or were placed 'in commando' on various jobs in the vicinity, being returned each night to their stall in the barracks. Generally a German criminal was placed in charge of each 'block' or shed in which the prisoners slept. Periodically he would choose the one prisoner of his block who seemed the most alert or intelligent or showed most leadership qualities. These would report to the guards' room and would never be heard of again. The generally accepted belief of the prisoners was that these were shot or gassed or hanged and then cremated. A refusal to work or an infraction of the rules usually meant flogging and other types of torture, such as having the fingernails pulled out, and in each case usually ended in death after extensive suffering. The policies described constituted a calculated programme of planned torture and extermination on the part of those who were in control of the German Government ..."

I quote next from Page 11 of the English text beginning with the second sentence of Paragraph 2, a description of Camp Dora at Nordhausen; Page 12, Paragraph 1 of the German text, quoting as follows:—

"On the whole, we found this camp to have been operated and administered much in the same manner as Buchenwald had been operated and managed. When the efficiency of the workers decreased as a result of the conditions under which they were required to live, their rations were decreased as punishment. This brought about a vicious circle in which the weak became weaker and were ultimately exterminated."

Such was the cycle of work, torture, starvation and death for concentration camp labour—labour which the defendant Goering, while requesting that more of it be placed at his disposal, said had proved very useful; labour which the defendant Speer was "anxious" to use in the factories under his control.

The policy underlying this programme, the manner in which it was executed, and the responsibility of the conspirators in connection with it has been dwelt upon at length. Therefore, we should like, at this point, to discuss the special responsibility of the defendant Sauckel.

The defendant Sauckel's appointment as Plenipotentiary General for Manpower is explained probably first of all by his having been an old and trusted Nazi. He certified in Document 2974-PS, dated 17th November, 1945, which is already in evidence before this Tribunal as Exhibit USA 15, that he held the following positions:

Starting with his membership in the N.S.D.A.P., he was thereafter a member of the Reichstag; he was Gauleiter of Thuringia; he was a member of the Thuringian Legislature; he was Minister of Interior and head of the Thuringian State Ministry; he was Reichsstatthalter for Thuringia; he was an S.A. Obergruppenfuehrer, S. S. Obergruppenfuehrer; he was Administrator for the Berlin-Suhler Waffen and Fahrzeugwerke in 1935. He was head of the Gustloff Werke Nationalsozialistische Industrie-Stiftung, 1936, and the Honorary Head of the Foundation. And from 21st March, 1942, until 1945, he was the General Plenipotentiary for Labour Allocation.

Sauckel's official responsibilities are borne out by evidence. His appointment as Plenipotentiary General for Manpower was effected by a decree of 21st March, 1942, which we have read and which was signed by Hitler, Lammers, and the defendant Keitel. By that decree Sauckel was given authority as well as responsibility subordinate only to that of Hitler, and Goering, who was the head of the Four Year Plan, subordinate only to those two for all matters relating to recruitment, allocation, and handling of foreign and domestic manpower.

The defendant Goering, to whom Sauckel was directly responsible, abolished the recruitment and allocation agencies of his Four Year Plan and delegated their powers to the defendant Sauckel, and placed his far-reaching authority as deputy for the Four Year Plan at Sauckel's disposal.

In Document 1666-PS, a second 1666-PS, but of another date, the 27th March, 1942, I ask the Tribunal to take judicial notice of this original decree which is published in the 1942 Reichsgesetzblatt, Part 1, at Page 180:—

"In pursuance of the Fuehrer's Decree of 21st March, 1942, I decree as follows:—

1. My manpower sections are hereby abolished (circular letter of 22nd October, 1936). Their duties (recruitment and allocation of manpower, regulations for labour conditions) are taken over by the Plenipotentiary General for Arbeitseinsatz, who is directly under me.

2. The Plenipotentiary General for Arbeitseinsatz will be responsible for regulating the conditions of labour (wage policy) employed in the Reich territory, having regard to the requirements of Arbeitseinsatz.

3. The Plenipotentiary General for Arbeitseinsatz is part of the Four Year Plan. In cases where new legislation is required, or existing laws required to be modified, he will submit appropriate proposals to me.

4. The Plenipotentiary General for Arbeitseinsatz will have at his disposal for the performance of his task the right delegated to me by the Fuehrer for issuing instructions to the higher Reich authorities, their branches and the Party Offices, and their associated organisms and also the Reich Protector, the Governor General, the Commander-in-Chief, and heads of the civil administrations. In the case of ordinances and instructions of fundamental importance a report is to be submitted to me in advance."

Document 1903-PS is a Hitler Decree of 30th September, 1942, giving the defendant Sauckel extraordinary powers over the civil and military authority of the territories occupied by Germany. We ask that judicial notice be taken by this Tribunal of the original decree, which is published in Volume II, Page 510, of the "Verfuegungen/Anordnungen/Bekanntgaben", published by the Party Chancellery. This decree states as follows:—

"I herewith authorise the Deputy General for the Arbeitseinsatz, Reich Governor and District Leader (Gauleiter) Fritz Sauckel to take all necessary measures for the enforcement of my decree referring to a Deputy General for the Arbeitseinsatz of 21st March, 1942 (Reichsgesetzblatt I, Page 179) according to his own judgement in the Greater German Reich, in the Protectorate, and in the Government General as well as in the occupied territories, measures which

*The opening ceremony of the Nazi Party Rally at Nuremberg, September 1938.*
Bundesarchiv, Bild 121-0042 / CC-BY-SA

will safeguard under all circumstances the regulated deployment of labour for the German war economy. For this purpose he may appoint commissioners to the bureaux of the military and civilian administration. These are subordinated directly to Deputy General for the Arbeitseinsatz. In order to carry out their tasks, they are entitled to issue directives to the competent military and civilian authorities in charge of the Arbeitseinsatz; and of wage policy.

More detailed directives will be issued by the Deputy General for the Arbeitseinsatz.

Fuehrer Headquarters, 30th September, 1942. The Fuehrer, signed Adolf Hitler."

Within one month after his appointment, the defendant Sauckel sent defendant Rosenberg his "Labour Mobilisation Programme". This programme—Document 016-PS, already in evidence as Exhibit USA 168—envisaged a recruitment by force, and the maximum exploitation of the entire labour resources of the conquered areas and of prisoners of war, in the interests of the Nazi war machine at the lowest conceivable degree of expenditure to the German State.

The defendant Sauckel states—and I refer now to the bottom of Page 6 of the English text of that document. It is Page 9, Paragraph 2, of the German text, and I quote as follows:—

"It must be emphasised, however, that an additional tremendous number of foreign labourers has to be found for the Reich. The greatest pools for that purpose are the occupied territories of the East. Consequently, it is an immediate necessity to use the human reserves of the conquered Soviet territory to the fullest extent. Should we not succeed in obtaining the necessary amount of labour on a voluntary basis, we must immediately institute conscription of forced labour.

Apart from the prisoners of war still in the occupied territories, we must, therefore, requisition skilled or unskilled male and female labour from the Soviet territory, from the age of 15 up, for the labour mobilisation."

Passing to Page 11 of the English text, first paragraph, and Page 17, Paragraph 4 of the German text, I quote directly; as follows:

"The complete employment of all prisoners of war as well as the use of a gigantic number of new foreign civilian workers, men and women, has become an indisputable necessity for the solution of the mobilisation of labour programme in this war."

The defendant Sauckel proceeded to implement this plan, which he submitted with certain basic directives. He provided that if voluntary recruitment of foreign workers was unsuccessful, compulsory service should be instituted.

Document 3044-PS is the defendant Sauckel's Regulation No. 4, dated 7th May, 1942. We ask that the Tribunal take judicial notice of the original regulation published in Volume II, Pages 516 to 527 of the "Verfuegungen/Anordnungen/Bekanntgaben", to which I have previously referred. Reading from Page 1, Paragraph 3, of the English text:—

"The recruitment of foreign labour will be carried out on the fundamental basis of volunteering. Where, however, in the occupied territories the appeal for volunteers does not suffice, obligatory service and drafting must, under all circumstances, be resorted to. This is an indisputable requirement of our labour situation."

Sauckel provided also for the allocation of foreign labour in the order of its importance to the Nazi war machine. We refer to Document 3044-(A)-PS, which is the defendant Sauckel's Regulation No. 10, and ask that the Court take judicial notice of the original regulation, published in Volume II, "Verfuegungen/Anordnungen/Bekanntgaben", at Pages 531 to 533—Paragraph 3 of this regulation I quote as follows:

"The resources of manpower that are available in the occupied territories are to be employed primarily to satisfy the requirements of importance for the war in Germany itself. In allocating the said labour resources in the Occupied territories, the following order of priority will be observed:

(a) Labour required for the troops, the occupation authorities, and the civil authorities.

(b) Labour required for German armaments.

(c) Labour required for food and agriculture.

(d) Labour required for industrial work other than armaments.

(e) Labour required for industrial work in the interests of the population of the territory in question."

The defendant Sauckel, and agencies subordinate to him, exercised exclusive authority over the recruitment of workers from every area in Europe occupied by, controlled by, or friendly to the German nation. He affirmed—the defendant Sauckel himself did—this authority in a decree, Document 3044-PS, already in evidence as Exhibit USA 206. I refer to Paragraph 5 on Page 1 of the English text of that document, and I am quoting it directly:—

"The recruitment of foreign labour in the areas occupied by Germany, in allied, friendly or neutral States will be carried out exclusively by my Commissioners, or by the competent German military or civil agencies for the tasks of labour mobilisation."

**THE PRESIDENT:** Have not you read that already?

**MR. DODD:** No, I have not, if your Honour pleases. We have referred to that decree before, but we have not referred to this portion of it.

I am passing to Paragraph 2, 1-a on Page 2, and quoting, again, directly:—

"For the carrying out of recruitment in allied, friendly, or neutral foreign countries, my Commissioners are solely responsible."

In addition, the following defendant, who was informed by Sauckel of the quotas of foreign labourers which he required, collaborated with Sauckel and his agents in filling these quotas:—

The defendant Keitel, Chief of the O.K.W.-which was the Supreme Command.

We refer to Document 3012-PS-1, which is Exhibit USA 190. This document is the record of a telephone conversation of the Chief of the Economic Staff East of the German Army, and it is dated 11th March, 1943. I wish to quote from the first two paragraphs of the document as follows:—

"The Plenipotentiary for the Arbeitseinsatz, Gauleiter Sauckel, points out to me, in an urgent teletype, that the Arbeitseinsatz in German agriculture, as well as all the most urgent armament programmes, ordered by the Fuehrer, make the most rapid procurement of approximately 1,000,000 women and men from the newly occupied territories an imperative necessity. For this purpose, Gauleiter Sauckel demands the daily shipment of 5,000 workers beginning on 15th March; 10,000 workers, male and female, beginning 1st April, from the newly occupied territories."

I am passing down to the next paragraph:—

"In consideration of the extraordinary losses of workers, which occurred in German war industry because of the developments of the past months, it is now necessary that the recruiting of workers be taken up again everywhere with all emphasis. The tendency momentarily noticeable in that territory, to limit and/or entirely stop the Reich recruiting programme, is absolutely intolerable in view of this state of affairs. Gauleiter Sauckel, who is informed about these events, has, because of this, turned immediately to General Field Marshal Keitel on 10th March, 1943, in a teletype, and has emphasised on this occasion, that, as in all other occupied territories, where all other methods fail, a certain pressure must be used by order of the Fuehrer."

At this point we were prepared to offer a transcript of an interrogation under oath of the defendant Sauckel. The English only, of the transcript of the interrogation has been seen by the counsel for the defendant Sauckel. He has had it, however, for some time, and the excerpts on which we intended to rely were furnished to him as well in German.

If I understood the ruling of the Tribunal correctly, it would be necessary for us to have furnished the entire record in German.

**THE PRESIDENT:** I think you might use this interrogation, as the excerpts have been submitted in German.

**MR. DODD:** Yes, they have, your Honour, and the entire English text as well.

**THE PRESIDENT:** Very well.

**MR. DODD:** I refer to a transcript of an interrogation, under oath of the defendant Sauckel, held on the morning of 5th October, 1945, Exhibit USA 224. That is the very last document in the document book. I wish to quote from the bottom of Page 1 of the English text, and Page 1, Paragraph 11 of the German text, as follows:—

Q. Was it necessary, in order to accomplish the completion of the quotas given, to have liaison with O.K.W.

A. I remember that the Fuehrer had given directives to Marshal Keitel, telling him that my task was a very important one, and I, too, have often conferred with Keitel after such discussions with the Fuehrer, when I asked him for his support.

Q. It was his task to supervise the proper performance of the military commanders in the occupied countries in carrying out their missions, was it not?

A. Yes, the Fuehrer had told me that he would inform the Chief of the O.K.W., and the Chief of the Reich Chancellery, as to these missions. The same applies to the Foreign Minister."

We are also prepared to offer the transcript of an interrogation of the defendant Alfred Rosenberg. There is this distinction in so far as this record is concerned. While we have supplied the counsel with the German translation of those parts of it which we propose to use, we have not had an opportunity to supply the whole text to counsel. However, they have been supplied with the German of the parts which we propose to use and to offer to this Tribunal.

**THE PRESIDENT:** Well, you are prepared to do it hereafter, I suppose?

**MR. DODD:** Yes, we will, your Honour, as soon as we can get these papers down to their Information Centre.

**THE PRESIDENT:** Yes.

**MR. DODD:** The next document is rather lengthy, and I wonder what the Tribunal's pleasure is. Do I understand that I may proceed with the interrogation?

**THE PRESIDENT:** Yes.

**MR. DODD:** I wish to refer to the defendant Alfred Rosenberg, the Reich Minister for Eastern Occupied Territories, as one who also collaborated with the defendant Sauckel, and specifically, to refer to a transcript of an interrogation under oath of the defendant Rosenberg, on the afternoon of 6th October, 1945, Exhibit USA 187. That record may be found about the third from the last of the interrogation records in the document book, and I wish to read from Page 1 of the transcript:—

Q. Is not it a fact that Sauckel would allocate to the various areas under your jurisdiction the number of persons to be obtained for labour purposes?

A. Yes.

Q. And that, thereafter, your agents would obtain that labour in order to meet the quota which had been given; is that right?

A. Sauckel, normally, had very far-reaching desires, which one could not fulfil unless one looked very closely into the matter.

Q. Never mind about Sauckel's desires being far-reaching or not being far-reaching. That has nothing to do with it. You were given quotas for the areas over which you had jurisdiction, and it was up to you to meet that quota?

A. Yes; it was the responsibility of the administrative officials to receive this quota and to distribute the allotments over the districts in such a way, according to number and according to the age groups, that they would be most reasonably met.

Q. These administrative officials were part of your organisation, is not that right?

A. They were functionaries or officials of the Reichskommissar for the Ukraine, but, as such, they were placed in their office by the Ministry for the Eastern Occupied Territories.

Q. You recognised, did you not, that the quotas set by Sauckel could not be filled by voluntary labour, and you did not disapprove of the impressment of forced labour; is not that right?

A. I regretted that the demands of Sauckel were so urgent that they could not be met by a continuation of voluntary recruitments, and thus I submitted to the necessity of forced impressment."

Then, passing a little further down on that page:—

"Q. The letters that we have already seen between you and Sauckel do not indicate, do they, any disagreements on your part with the principle of recruiting labour against their will? They indicate, as I remember, that you were opposed to the treatment that was later accorded these workers, but that you did not oppose their initial impressment."

THE PRESIDENT: Mr. Dodd, I think you ought to read the next two answers, in fairness to the defendant Rosenberg, after the one where he said he submitted to the necessity of forced impressment.

MR. DODD: Very well, I will read those, your Honour.

THE PRESIDENT: Did you ever argue with Sauckel.

MR. DODD: Yes.

"Q. Did you ever argue with Sauckel that perhaps in view of the fact that quotas could not be met by voluntary labour, the labour recruiting programme be abandoned, except for such recruits as could be voluntarily enrolled?

A. I could not do that because the numbers or allotments that Sauckel had received from the Fuehrer to meet were absolutely binding for him, and I could not do anything about that."

And then, referring again to the question which I had just read, the answer is as follows:—

"That is right. In those matters I mostly discussed the possibility of finding the least harsh methods of handling the matter, though in no way placing myself in opposition to the orders that he was carrying out for the Fuehrer."

**THE PRESIDENT:** I think the Tribunal might adjourn now.

**MR. DODD:** Very well, your Honour.

*(The Tribunal adjourned until 13th December, 1945, at 1000 hours.)*

## THURSDAY, 13TH DECEMBER, 1945

**MR. DODD:** May it please the Tribunal, at the close of yesterday's session, we were discussing and had just completed reading the excerpts from the interrogation of 6th October, 1945, wherein the defendant Alfred Rosenberg was questioned.

There have been introduced Documents 017-PS and 019-PS and I have read excerpts from them. The Tribunal will recall that they are letters written by the defendant Sauckel to the defendant Rosenberg, requesting the assistance of the defendant Rosenberg in the recruitment of additional foreign labourers. I refer to them in passing, by way of recapitulation, with respect to the defendant Sauckel's participation in this slave labour programme and also the assistance of the defendant Rosenberg. Also the defendant Sauckel received help from the defendant Seyss-Inquart, who was the Reichskommissar for the Occupied Netherlands.

I refer again to the transcript of the interrogation under oath of the defendant Sauckel, which was read from yesterday, and I now refer to another part of it. The transcript of this interrogation will be found at the back of the document book. It is the very last document and I wish to quote particularly from it.

"Q. For a moment, I want to turn our attention to Holland. It is my understanding that the quotas for the workers from Holland were agreed upon, and then the numbers given to the Reichskommissar Seyss-Inquart to fulfil, is that correct?

A. Yes, that is correct.

Q. After the quota was given to Seyss-Inquart, it was his mission to fulfil it—with the aid of your representatives; was it not?

A. Yes. This was the only possible thing for me to do and the same applied to other countries."

And the defendant Hans Frank, who was the Governor General of the Government General of Poland, participated in the filling of defendant Sauckel's quota requirements.

I refer again to the interrogation of the defendant Sauckel and to Page 1 of the excerpts from the transcript of this interrogation, as it appears in the document book:

"Q. Was the same procedure substantially followed of allocating quotas in the Government General of Poland?

A. Yes. I have to basically state again that the only possibility I had of carrying through these missions was to get in touch with the highest German military authorities in the respective country and to transfer to them the orders of the Fuehrer and ask them very urgently, as I have always done, to fulfil these orders.

Q. Such discussions in Poland, of course, were with the Governor General Frank?

A. Yes. I spent a morning and afternoon in Cracow two or three times and I personally spoke to Governor General Frank. Naturally, there was also present Secretary Dr. Goebbels."

The S.S., as in most matters involving the use of force and brutality, also extended its assistance. We refer to Document 1292-PS, which is Exhibit USA 225. This Document, 1292-PS, is the report of the Reichschancellor Lammers of a conference with Hitler, which was attended by, among others, the defendant Sauckel, the defendant Speer, and Himmler, the Reichsfuehrer S.S. I turn to Page 2 of the document, beginning with the third line from the top of the page of the English text; and it is Page 4, Paragraph 2 of the German text. The quotation reads as follows:

"The Plenipotentiary for Employment and Labour, Sauckel, declares that he will attempt with fanatical determination to obtain these workers. Until now, he has always kept his promises as to the number of workers to be furnished. With the best of intentions, however, he is unable to make a definite promise for 1944. He will do everything in his power to furnish the requested manpower in 1944. Whether it will succeed depends primarily on what German enforcement agents will be made available. His project cannot be carried out with domestic enforcement agents."

There are additional quotations, as the Tribunal may observe, in this very part from which I have been reading, but I intend to refer to them again a little further on.

The defendant Sauckel participated in the formulation of the overall labour requirements for Germany, and passed out quotas to be filled by and with the assistance of the individuals and agencies referred to, in the certain knowledge that force and brutality were the only means whereby his demands could be met. Turning to Document 1292- PS again, and quoting from Page 1:—

"A conference took place with the Fuehrer today which was attended by: the Plenipotentiary for the Employment of Labour, Gauleiter Sauckel; the Secretary for Armament and War Production, Speer; the Chief of the Supreme Command of the Army, General Field Marshal Keitel; General Field Marshal Milch; the Minister of the Interior, Reichsfuehrer of the S.S. Himmler; and myself. (The Minister for Foreign Affairs and the Minister of National Economy had repeatedly asked to be permitted to participate prior to the Conference, but the Fuehrer did not wish their attendance.)

The Fuehrer declared in his introductory remarks:

I want a clear picture:

1. How many workers are required for the maintenance of German War Economy?

   (a) For the maintenance of present output?

   (b) To increase its output?

2. How many workers can be obtained from occupied countries, or how many can still be gained in the Reich by suitable means (increased output)? For one thing, it is this matter of making up for losses by death, infirmity, the constant fluctuation of workers, and so forth, and for another it is a matter of procuring additional workers.

The Plenipotentiary for the Employment of Labour, Sauckel, declared that, in order to maintain the present pool of workers, he would have to add at least 2.5 but probably 3 million new workers in 1944. Otherwise production would fall off. Reichsminister Speer declared that he needed an additional 1.3 million labourers. However, this would depend on whether it would be possible to increase production of iron ore. Should this not be possible, he would need no additional workers. Procurement of additional workers from occupied territory would, however, be subject to the condition that these workers would not be withdrawn from armament and auxiliary industries already working there, for this would mean a decrease of production of these industries which he could not tolerate. Those, for instance, who were already working in France in industries mentioned above must be protected against being sent to work in Germany by the Plenipotentiary for the Employment of Labour. The Fuehrer agreed with the opinions of Reichsminister Speer and emphasised that the measures taken by the Plenipotentiary for the Employment of Labour should under no circumstances lead to the withdrawal of workers from armament and auxiliary industries working in occupied territories, because such a shift of workers would only cause disturbances of production in occupied countries.

The Fuehrer further called attention to the fact that at least 250,000 labourers would be required for preparations against air attacks in the field of civilian air raid protection. For Vienna alone 2,000- 2,500 were required immediately. The Plenipotentiary for the Employment of Labour must add at least 4 million workers to the manpower pool, considering that he required 21 million workers for maintenance of the present level, that Reich Minister Speer needed 1.3 million additional workers, and that the above-mentioned preparations for security measures against air attacks called for 0.25 million labourers."

Referring again to Page 2, the first full paragraph of the English text of this document, and Page 5, Paragraph 1 of the German text:

"The Reichsfuehrer S.S. explained that the enforcement agents put at his disposal were extremely few, but that he would try to help the Sauckel project to succeed by increasing them and working them harder. The Reichsfuehrer S.S. made immediately available 2,000 to 2,500 men from concentration camps for air raid preparations in Vienna."

Passing the next paragraph of this document and continuing with the paragraph entitled "Results of the Conference", and quoting it directly after the small figure II:

"The Plenipotentiary for Employment of Labour shall procure at least 4,000,000 new workers from occupied territories."

Moreover, as Document 3012-PS, which has already been offered as Exhibit USA 190, revealed, the defendant Sauckel in requesting the assistance of the Army for the recruitment of 1,000,000 men and women from the occupied Eastern territories informed the defendant Keitel that prompt action was required and that, as in all other occupied countries, pressure had to be used if other measures were not successful. Again, as revealed by Document 018-PS, which has been offered and from which excerpts have been read, the defendant Sauckel was informed by the defendant Rosenberg, that the enslavement of foreign labour was achieved by force and brutality.

Notwithstanding his knowledge of conditions, the defendant Sauckel continued to request greater supplies of manpower from the areas in which the most ruthless methods had been applied. Indeed, when German Field Commanders on the Eastern Front attempted to resist or restrain the defendant Sauckel's demands, because forced recruitment was swelling the ranks of the partisans and making the Army's task more difficult, Sauckel sent a telegram to Hitler, in which he implored him, Hitler, to intervene.

I make reference to Document 407-II-PS, which is Exhibit USA 226. This document is a telegram from the defendant Sauckel to Hitler, dated 10th March, 1943, It is a rather long message, but I wish to call particularly to the attention of the Tribunal the last paragraph on Page 1 of the English text. It is Page 2, Paragraph 5 of the German text. Quoting the last paragraph of the English text:—

"Therefore, my Fuehrer I ask you to abolish all orders which oppose the compulsion of foreign workers for labour, and to report to me kindly whether the concept of the mission presented here is still right."

Turning to Paragraph 5 on the first page of this English text, we find these words, quoting them directly:

"If the compulsion for labour and the forced recruiting of workers in the East is not possible any more, then the German war industries and agriculture cannot fulfil their tasks to the full extent."

The next paragraph:—

"I myself have the opinion that our Army leaders should not give credence under any circumstances to the atrocity and propaganda campaign of the partisans. The Generals themselves are greatly interested that the support for the troops is made possible in time. I should like to point out that hundreds of thousands of excellent workers going into the field as soldiers now cannot possibly be substituted by German women not used to work, even if they are trying to do their best. Therefore, I have to use the people of the Eastern territories."

**THE PRESIDENT:** I think you should read the next paragraph.

**MR. DODD:**

"I myself report to you that the workers belonging to all foreign nations are treated humanely and correctly and cleanly, are fed and housed well and are even clothed. On the basis of my own services with foreign nations I go as far as to state that never before in the world were foreign workers treated as correctly as is now happening, in the hardest of all wars, by the German people."

In addition to being responsible for the recruitment of foreign civilian labour by force defendant Sauckel was responsible for the conditions under which foreign workers were deported to Germany and for the treatment to which they were subjected within Germany.

We have already referred to the conditions under which these imported persons were transported to Germany and we have read from Document 2241-PS-3 to show that Sauckel knew of these conditions. Yesterday we referred at length to the brutal, degrading, and inhuman conditions under which these labourers worked and lived within Germany. We invite the attention again of the Tribunal to Document 3044-PS, already offered as Exhibit USA 206. It is Regulation No. 4 of 7th May, 1942, issued by Sauckel, as the Plenipotentiary General for the Mobilisation of Labour, concerning recruitment, care, lodging, feeding and treatment of foreign workers of both sexes. By this decree defendant Sauckel expressly directed that the assembly and operation of rail transports and the supplying of food therefor was the responsibility of his agents until the transports arrived in Germany. By the same regulation defendant Sauckel directed that within Germany the care of foreign industrial workers was to be carried out by the German Labour Front, and that the care of foreign agricultural workers was to be carried out by the Reich Food Administration. By the terms of the regulation, Sauckel reserved for himself ultimate responsibility for all aspects of care, treatment, lodging and feeding of foreign workers while in transit to and within Germany.

I refer particularly to the English text of this Document 3044-PS, Exhibit USA 206, and the part of it that I make reference to is at the bottom of Page 1 in the English text, and it appears at Page 518 of the volume in the German text. Quoting directly from the English text:—

"The care of foreign labour will be carried out.

(a) Up to the Reich border by my commissioners or-in the occupied areas-by competent military or civil labour mobilisation agencies. Care of the labour will be carried out in co-operation with the respective competent foreign organisation.

(b) Within the area of the Reich

(1) By the German Labour Front in the cases of non-agricultural workers.

(2) By the Reich Food Administration in the case of agricultural workers.

The German Labour Front and the German Food Administration are bound by my directives in the carrying out of their tasks of caring for the workers.

The agencies of the labour mobilisation administration are to give far-reaching support to the German Labour Front and the German Food Administration in the fulfilment of their assigned tasks.

My competence for the execution of the care for foreign labour is not prejudiced by the assignment of these tasks to the German Labour Front and the Reich Food Administration."

**THE PRESIDENT:** Mr. Dodd, do not you think that that is the sort of passage which might be summarised and not read, because all that it is really stating is that Sauckel, his department and commissioners were responsible, and that is what he is saying.

**MR. DODD:** Yes, indeed, your Honour, we spelled it out, thinking that perhaps under the rule of getting it into the record it must be read fully. I quite agree.

**THE PRESIDENT:** A summary will be quite sufficient, I think.

**MR. DODD:** In the same document, I should like to make reference to the data on Page 3, Paragraph 3 of the English text, which indicates, under the title of "Composition and Operation of the Transports", that this function is the obligation of the representatives of the defendant Sauckel; and in Paragraph "c", on Page 5 of the English text, under the title of "Supply for the Transport", after setting out some responsibility for the office of the German Workers Front, the defendant Sauckel states that for the rest his offices effect the supply for the transport.

The defendant Sauckel had an agreement with the head of the German Labour Front, Dr. Robert Ley, and in this agreement, the defendant Sauckel emphasised his ultimate responsibility by creating a Central Inspectorate, charged with examining the working and living conditions of foreign workers. We refer to Document 1913-PS, Exhibit USA 227. This agreement between the defendant Sauckel and the then Chief of the German Labour Front is published in the 1943 edition of the Reichsarbeitsblatt, Part 1, at Page 588. It is a rather lengthy agreement, and I shall not read it all or any great part of it, except such part as will indicate the basic agreements between the defendant Sauckel and Ley, with respect to the foreign workers and their living conditions and working conditions.

On the first page of the English text:—

"The Reichsleiter of the German Labour Front, Dr. Ley, in collaboration with the Plenipotentiary General for the Arbeitseinsatz, Gauleiter Sauckel, will establish a 'Zentral Inspektion' for the continuous supervision of all measures concerning the care of the foreign workers mentioned under 1. This will have the designation:

'Central Inspection for Care of Foreign Workers.'"

Paragraph 4, marked with the Roman numeral IV, in the same text, states:—

"The offices of the administration of the Arbeitseinsatz will be constantly informed by the 'Central Inspection for the Care of Foreign Workers' of its observations, in particular, immediately in each case in which action of State organisations seems to be necessary."

I should also like to call the attention of the Tribunal to this paragraph, which is quoted on the same page. It is the fourth paragraph down, after the small number 2, and it begins with the words:—

"The authority of the Plenipotentiary General for the Arbeitseinsatz to empower the members of his staff and the presidents of the State employment offices to get direct information on the conditions regarding the employment of foreigners in the factories and camps, will remain untouched."

We have already offered to the Court, proof that the defendant Sauckel was responsible for compelling citizens of the occupied countries, against their will, to manufacture arms and munitions and to construct military fortifications for use in war operations against their own country and its allies. He was, moreover, responsible for compelling prisoners of war to produce arms and munitions for use against their own countries and their actively resisting allies.

The decree appointing Sauckel indicated that he was appointed Plenipotentiary General for Manpower for the express purpose, among others, of integrating prisoners of war into the German war industry; and in a series of reports to Hitler, Sauckel described how successful he had been in carrying out that programme. One such report states that in a single year, the defendant Sauckel had incorporated 1,622,829 prisoners of war into the German economy.

I refer to Document 407-V-PS, which is Exhibit USA 228. It is a letter from the defendant Sauckel to Hitler, on 14th April, 1943. Although the figures in the document have been contained in another one, this is the first introduction of this particular one. Quoting from Paragraphs 1 and 2 of the English text, it begins:—

"My Fuehrer,

After having been active as Plenipotentiary for Arbeitseinsatz for one year, I have the honour to report to you that 3,638,056 new foreign workers have been added to the German war economy between 1st April of the last year and 31st March of this year."

**THE PRESIDENT:** Are you reading Paragraph I?

**MR. DODD:** Yes, your Honour.

**THE PRESIDENT:** It says 5,000,000, not three.

**MR. DODD:** I think it is 3,000,000, if your Honour pleases.

**THE PRESIDENT:** It should be three?

**MR. DODD:** I think so. The original looks to us like three.

Passing on a little bit, with particular reference to the prisoners of war, we find this statement:—

"Besides the foreign civilian workers another 1,622,829 prisoners of war are employed in the German economy."

A later report states that 846,511 additional foreign labourers and prisoners of war were incorporated into the German war industry, and quoting from Document 407-IX-PS, Exhibit USA 229, which is also a letter from the defendant Sauckel to Hitler, I read in part from Page I, Paragraphs 1 and 2:—

"My Fuehrer,

I beg to be permitted to report to you on the situation of the Arbeitseinsatz for the first five months of 1943. For the first time the following number of new foreign labourers and prisoners of war were employed in the German war industry: Total, 846,511."

This use of prisoners of war in the manufacture of armaments allocated by the defendant Sauckel was confirmed by the defendant Speer, who stated that 40 per cent. of all prisoners of war were employed in the production of weapons and munitions and in subsidiary industries. I wish to refer briefly to Paragraphs 6, 7 and 8, on Page 15 of the English text of an interrogation of the defendant Speer on 18th October, 1945, which was offered and referred to yesterday Exhibit USA 220.

Quoting from Paragraphs 6, 7 and 8, on Page 15, Paragraph 1, on Page 2 of the German text. There are three questions which will establish the background for this answer:—

"Q. Let me understand, when you wanted labour from prisoners of war did you requisition prisoners of war separately, or did you ask for a total number of workers?

A. Only Schmelter can answer that directly. As far as the commitment of prisoners of war for labour goes, it was effected through employment offices of the Stalags. I tried several times to increase the total number of prisoners of war that were occupied in the production at the expense of the other demand factors.

Q. Will you explain that a little more?

A. In the last phase of production, that is, in the year 1944, when everything collapsed, I had 40 per cent. of all prisoners of war employed in the production. I wanted to have this percentage increased.

Q. And when you say 'employed in the production', you mean in these subsidiary industries that you have discussed, and also in the production of weapons and munitions, is that right?

A. Yes. That was the total extent of my task."

**THE TRIBUNAL (Mr. Biddle):** What do you mean by "subsidiary industries", Mr. Dodd? Is that war industries?

MR. DODD: Yes, sir; war industries, as we understand it. It was referred to many times by these defendants as the component parts of the plans.

I also would like to call the attention of the Tribunal again to the "Minutes of the 36th Meeting of the Central Planning Board", Document R-124, from which we read a number of excerpts yesterday, and remind the Tribunal that in the report of the minutes of that meeting the defendant Speer stated that:—

"90,000 Russian prisoners of war employed in the whole of the armament industry are for the greatest part skilled men."

We should like, at this point, to turn to the special responsibility of the defendant Speer, and to discuss the evidence of the various crimes committed by, the defendant Speer in planning and participating in the vast programme of forcible deportation of the citizens of occupied countries. He was the Reich Minister of Armaments and Munitions and Chief of the Organisation Todt, both of which positions he acquired on 15th February, 1942, and by virtue of his later acquisition of control over the armament offices of the Army, Navy and Air Force and the production offices of the Ministry of Economics, the defendant Speer was responsible for the entire war production of the Reich, as well as for the construction of fortifications and installations for the Wehrmacht. Proof of the positions held by him is supplied in his own statement, as contained in Document 2980-PS, which has already been offered to the Tribunal and which is Exhibit USA 18.

The industries under the defendant Speer's control were really the most important users of manpower in Germany; and thus, according to the defendant Sauckel, Speer's labour requirements received unconditional priority over all other demands for labour. We refer to the transcript of the interrogation of the defendant Sauckel on 22nd September, 1945, It is Exhibit USA 230. It is next to the last document in the document book. I wish to refer to Page 1 of that document, Paragraph 4. It is a brief reference, the last answer on the page. The question was asked of the defendant Sauckel:—

"Q. Except for Speer, they would give the requirements in general for the broad field, but in Speer's work he would get them allocated to industry, and so on; is that right?

A. The others only got whatever was left. Because Speer told me once in the presence of the Fuehrer that I was there to work for Speer and that mainly I was his man."

The defendant Speer has admitted under oath that he participated in the discussions, during which the decision to use foreign forced labour was made. He has also said that he concurred in the decision and that it was the basis for the programme of bringing foreign workers into Germany by compulsion. I make reference to the interrogation of this defendant of 18th October, 1945. It is Exhibit USA 220. We have already read from it; and I particularly refer to the bottom of Page 12 and the top of Page 13 of the English text:—

"Q. But is it clear to you, Herr Speer, that in 1942 when the decisions were being made concerning the use of forced foreign labour you participated in the discussions yourself?

A. Yes.

Q. So that I take it that the execution of the programme of bringing foreign workers into Germany by compulsion under Sauckel was based on earlier decisions that had been made with your agreement?

A. Yes, but I must point out that only a very small part of the manpower that Sauckel brought into Germany was made available to me; a far larger part of it was allocated to other departments that demanded it."

This admission is confirmed by the minutes of Speer's conference with Hitler on 10th, 11th and 12th August, 1942, in Document R-124, which has been offered here and from which excerpts have been read. Page 34 of that document, Paragraph 1 of the English text, has already been quoted, and those excerpts were read before the Tribunal yesterday. The Tribunal will recall that the defendant Speer related the outcome of his negotiations concerning the forcible recruitment of 1,000,000 Russian labourers for the German armaments industry, and this use of force was again discussed by Hitler and Speer on 4th January, 1943, as shown by the excerpts read from the Document 556-PS-13, where it was decided that stronger measures were to be used to accelerate the conscription of French civilian workers.

We say the defendant Speer demanded foreign workers for the industries under his control and used those workers with the knowledge that they had been deported by force and were being compelled to work. Speer has stated under oath in his interrogation of 18th October, 1945, Page 5, Paragraph 9 of the English text, quoting it directly:—

"I do not wish to give the impression that I want to deny the fact that I demanded manpower and foreign manpower from Sauckel very energetically."

He has admitted that he knew he was obtaining foreign labour, a large part of which was forced labour; and referring again to that same interrogation of 18th October, 1945, and to Pages 8 and 9 of the English text and Page 10 of the German text:—

"Q. So that during the period when you were asking for labour, it seems clear, does it not, that you knew you were obtaining foreign labour as well as domestic labour in response to your requests, and that a large part of the foreign labour was forced labour.

A. Yes.

Q. So that, simply by way of illustration, suppose that on 1st January, 1944, you require 50,000 workers for a given purpose, would you put in a requisition for 50,000 workers, knowing that in that 50,000 there would be forced foreign workers?

A. Yes."

The defendant Speer has also stated under oath that he knew at least as early as September, 1942, that workers from the Ukraine were being forcibly deported for labour into Germany. Likewise he knew that the great majority of the workers of the Western occupied countries were slave labourers, forced against their will to come to Germany; and again referring to his interrogation of this 18th day of October, 1945, and beginning with the fourth paragraph from the bottom of Page 5 of the English text, Paragraph 10 on Page 6 of the German text, we find this series of questions and answers:

"Q. When did you first find out then that some of the manpower from the Ukraine was not coming voluntarily?

A. It is rather difficult to answer this here, that is, to name a certain date to you. However, it is certain that I knew that at some particular point of time that the manpower from the Ukraine did not come voluntarily.

Q. And does that apply also to the manpower from other occupied countries; that is, did there come a time when you knew that they were not coming voluntarily?

A. Yes.

Q. When in general, would you say that time was, without naming a particular month of the year?

A. As far as the Ukraine situation goes, I believe that they did not come voluntarily any more after a few months, because immense mistakes were made in their treatment by us. I should say off-hand that this time was either in July, August or September, 1942."

Turning to Paragraph 11 on Page 6 of the English text of this same interrogation and Page 7 and Paragraph 8 of the German text, we find this series of questions and answers—and I am quoting:—

"Q. But many workers did come from the West, did they not, to Germany?

A. Yes.

Q. That means, then, that the great majority of the workers that came from the Western countries, the Western occupied countries, came against their will to Germany?

A. Yes."

These admissions are borne out, of course, by other evidence, for, as Document R-124 shows, and as we have shown by the readings from it, in all countries conscription for work in Germany could be carried out only with the active assistance of the police, and the prevailing methods of recruitment had provoked such violence that many German recruiting agents had been killed.

And again, at a meeting with Hitler to discuss the manpower requirements for 1944, which is reported in Document 1292-PS, Speer was informed by the defendant Sauckel that the requirements—including Speer's requirement for 1,300,000 additional labourers—could be met only if German enforcement agents were furnished to carry out the enslavement programme in the occupied countries.

Now we say that, notwithstanding his knowledge that these workers were conscripted and deported to Germany against their will, Speer nevertheless continued to formulate requirements for the foreign workers and requested their allocation to those industries which were subject to his control. This is borne out by the minutes of the Central Planning Board, as contained in

Document R-124, and particularly Page 13, Paragraph 4 of the English text; and that is Page 6 and Paragraph 4 of the German text.

Speer speaking:—

"Now, to the labour problem in Germany. I believe it is still possible to transfer some workers from the Western territories. The Fuehrer stated only recently that he wished to dissolve these foreign volunteers as he had the impression that the army groups were carting around with them a lot of ballast. Therefore, if we cannot settle this matter ourselves, we shall have to call a meeting with the Fuehrer to clear up the coal situation. Keitel and Keitzler will be invited to attend in order to determine the number of Russians from the rear army territories that can be sent to us. However, I see another possibility: We might organise another drive to screen out workers for the mines from the Russian Prisoners of War in the Reich. But this possibility is none too promising."

At another meeting of the Central Planning Board the defendant Speer rejected a suggestion that labour for industries under his control be furnished from German sources instead of from foreign sources. And again, in this Document R-124, on Page 16, Paragraphs 3, 4 and 5 of the English text, and Page 12, Paragraphs 6 and 7 of the German text—I quote Speer:—

"We do it this way: Kehrl collects the demands for labour necessary to complete the coal-and-iron plan and communicates the numbers to Sauckel. Probably there will be a conference at the Reich Marshal's next week, and an answer from Sauckel should have arrived by then. The question of recruitment for the armaments industry will be solved together with Weger."

Then Kehrl speaking:—

"I wish to urge that the allotments to the mines should not be made dependent on the recruitment of men abroad. We were completely frustrated these last three months because this principle had been applied. We ended December with a deficit of 25,000 and we never get replacements.

The number must be made up by men from Germany.

Speer: No, nothing doing."

We say also that the defendant Speer is guilty of advocating terror and brutality as a means of maximising production by slave labourers. And again I refer to this Document R-124. At Page 42 there is a discussion concerning the supply and exploitation of labour. That excerpt has been read to the Tribunal before, and I simply refer to it in passing. It is the excerpt wherein Speer said it would be a good thing; the effect of it was that nothing could be said against the S.S. and the police taking a hand and making these men work and produce more.

We say he is also guilty of compelling allied nationals and prisoners of war to engage in the production of armaments and munitions and in direct military operations against their own country.

*A German soldier guarding part of the Atlantic Wall at Cap Gris Nez, France, 1942.*
*Bundesarchiv, Bild 146-1973-036-05 / Maier / CC-BY-SA*

We say that, as Chief of the "Organisation Todt," he is accountable for its policies, which were in direct conflict with the laws of war, for the "Organisation Todt," in violation of the laws of war, impressed allied nationals into its service.

Document L-191, Exhibit USA 231, is an International Labour Office study of the exploitation of foreign labour by Germany. We have only one copy of this document, being this International Labour Office study, printed at Montreal, Canada, in 1945. We ask that the Tribunal take judicial notice of it as an official publication of the International Labour Office.

I might say to the Tribunal, with some apology, that this arrived at a time when we were not able even to have the excerpt mimeographed and printed, to place in your document book, so this is the one document which is missing from the document book which is in your hands. However, I should like to quote from Page 73, Paragraph 2, of this study by the International Labour Office. It is not long; it is very brief. I am quoting directly. It says:—

"The methods used for the recruitment of foreign workers who were destined for employment in the Organisation did not greatly differ from the methods used for the recruitment of foreigners for deportation to Germany."

The Organisation, by the way, is the "Organisation Todt."

"The main difference was that, since the principal activities of the Organisation lay outside the frontiers of Germany, foreigners were not transported to Germany but had either to work in their own country or in some other occupied territory.

In the recruitment drives for foreign workers for the Organisation methods of compulsion as well as methods of persuasion were used, the latter usually with very little result."

Moreover, conscripted allied nationals were compelled by this same Organisation to actually engage in operations of war against their country.

Document 407-PS, VIII, discloses that the foreign workers who were impressed into the "Organisation Todt," through the efforts of the defendant Sauckel, did participate in the building of the Atlantic Wall fortifications.

As Chief of German War Production this defendant Speer sponsored and approved the use of these prisoners of war in the production of armaments and munitions. This has been made plain by the evidence already discussed.

To sum it up briefly, we say that it shows first that, after Speer assumed the responsibility for the armament production, his concern, in his discussions with his co-conspirators, was to secure a larger allocation of prisoners of war for his armament factories. That has been shown by the quotations from the excerpts of Document R-124, the minutes of the meeting of the Central Planning Board; and in this same meeting the Tribunal will recall that Speer complained because only 30 per cent. of the Russian prisoners of war were engaged in the armaments industry.

We have referred to a speech of Speer, Document 1435-PS—we quoted from it—in which he said that 10,000 prisoners of war were put at the disposal of the armaments industry upon his orders.

And, finally, Speer advocated the returning of escaped prisoners of war to factories as convicts. That is shown again by Document R-124, Page 13, Paragraph 5 of the English text, where Speer says that he has come to an arrangement—

**THE PRESIDENT:** Mr. Dodd, do not you think that we really have got this sufficiently now?

**MR. DODD:** Yes, sir.

**THE PRESIDENT:** We have Speer's own admission and any number of documents which prove the way in which these prisoners of war and other labourers were brought into Germany.

**MR. DODD:** Well I just wanted to refer briefly to that passage in that Document R-124 as showing that this defendant advocated having escaped prisoners of war returned to the munitions factories. I do not want to enlarge on this responsibility of the defendant Speer. I was anxious—or perhaps I should say we are all over-anxious—to have the documents in the record and before the Tribunal.

**THE PRESIDENT:** Which is the passage you want to refer to on Page 13?

**MR. DODD:** I just referred in passing to the statement which begins with the words "We have come to an arrangement with the Reichsfuehrer S.S." And in the next to the last sentence says: "The men should be put into the factories as convicts."

Finally, with reference to this defendant, I should like to say to the Tribunal that he visited the concentration camp at Mauthausen and he also visited factories such as those conducted by the Krupp industries, where concentration camp labour was exploited under degrading conditions. Despite this first-hand knowledge of these conditions in Mauthausen and places where these forced labourers were at work in factories, he continued to direct the use of this type of labour in factories under his own jurisdiction.

**THE PRESIDENT:** How do you intend to prove it as to these concentration camps?

**MR. DODD:** I was going to refer the Tribunal to Page 9 of the interrogation of 18th October, 1945, and I refer to Page 11, Paragraph 5 of the German text and Page 9, beginning with Paragraph 9, of the English text:—

"Q. But, in general, the use of concentration camp labour was known to you and approved by you as a source of labour?

A. Yes.

Q. And you knew also, I take it, that among the inmates of the concentration camps there were both Germans and foreigners?

A. I did not think about it at that time.

Q. As a matter of fact, you visited the Austrian concentration camp personally, did you not?

A. I did not—well, I was in Mauthausen once, but at that time I was not told just to what categories the inmates of the concentration camps belonged.

Q. But in general everybody knew, did they not, that foreigners who were taken away by the Gestapo or arrested by the Gestapo, as well as Germans, found their way into the concentration camps?

A. Of course, yes. I did not mean to imply anything like that."

And on Page 15 of this same interrogation, beginning with the 13th paragraph of the English text, and Page 20 in the German text, we find these questions:

"Q. Did you ever discuss, by the way, the requirements of Krupp for foreign labour?

A. It is certain that it was reported to me what shortage Krupp had in foreign workers.

Q. Did you ever discuss it with any of the members of the Krupp firm?

A. I cannot say that exactly, but during the time of my activities I visited the Krupp factory more than once and it is certain that this was discussed, that is, the lack of manpower."

Before closing, I should like to take two minutes of the time of the Tribunal to refer to what we consider to be some of the applicable laws of the case for the assistance of the Tribunal in considering these documents which we have offered.

We refer, of course, first of all, to Sections 6 (b) and 6 (c) of the Charter of this Tribunal. We also say that the acts of the conspirators constituted a flagrant violation of Articles 46 and 52 of the Regulations annexed to the Hague Convention No. IV of 1907.

Article 46 seeks to safeguard the family honour, the rights and the lives of persons in areas under belligerent occupation.

Article 52 provides in part that: "Requisitions in kind and services shall not be demanded from municipalities or inhabitants except for the needs of the army of occupation. They shall be in proportion to the resources of the country".

We say that these conspirators violated this Article because the labour which they conscripted was not used to satisfy the needs of the army of occupation, but, on the contrary, was forcibly removed from the occupied areas and exploited in the interest of the German war effort.

Finally, we say that these conspirators, and particularly the defendants Sauckel and Speer, by virtue of their planning, of their execution, and of their approval of this programme which we have been describing yesterday and today, the enslavement and the misuse of the forced labour of prisoners of war—that for this they bear a special responsibility for their Crimes Against Humanity and their War Crimes.

**THE PRESIDENT:** Are you finishing, Mr. Dodd?

**MR. DODD:** Yes, I have finished.

**THE PRESIDENT:** I should like to ask you why you have not read Document 3057-PS, which is Sauckel's statement.

**MR. DODD:** Yes. We had intended to offer that document. Counsel for the defendant Sauckel informed me a day or two ago that his client maintained that he had been coerced into making the statement. Because we had not ample time to ascertain the facts of the matter, we preferred to withhold it, rather than to offer it to the Tribunal under any question of doubt.

**THE PRESIDENT:** He objects to it, and therefore you have not put it in?

**MR. DODD:** No, we did not offer it while there was any question about it.

**THE PRESIDENT:** Very well.

**MR. DODD:** Might I suggest to the Tribunal that a recess be taken at this time? I am sorry to have to say that I am due to be before the Tribunal for some little time—that is, I am sorry for the Tribunal—with the matters on the concentration camps.

**THE PRESIDENT:** You mean a recess now?

**MR. DODD:** If your Honour pleases.

**THE PRESIDENT:** Certainly, yes; ten minutes.

*(A recess was taken.)*

**MR. DODD:** May it please the Tribunal, we propose to offer additional evidence at this time concerning the use of Nazi concentration camps against the people of Germany and allied nationals. We propose to examine the purposes and the role of the concentration camp in the larger Nazi scheme of things. We propose to show that the concentration camp was one of the fundamental institutions of the Nazi regime, that it was a pillar of the system of terror by which the Nazis consolidated their power over Germany and imposed their ideology upon the German people, that it was really a primary weapon in the battle against the Jews, against the Christian Church, against Labour, against those who wanted peace, against opposition or nonconformity of any kind. We say it involved the systematic use of terror to achieve the cohesion within Germany which was necessary for the execution of the conspirators' plans for aggression.

We propose to show that a concentration camp was one of the principal instruments used by the conspirators for the commission on an enormous scale of Crimes Against Humanity and War Crimes; that it was the final link in a chain of terror and repression which involved the S.S. and the Gestapo, and which resulted in the apprehension of victims and their confinement, without trial, often without charges, generally with no indication of the length of their detention.

My colleagues will present full evidence concerning the criminal role of the S.S. and Gestapo in this phase of Nazi terrorism, the concentration camp, but at this point, I wish simply to point out that the S.S., through its espionage system, tracked down the victims, that the criminal police and the Gestapo seized them and brought them to the camps, and that the concentration camps were administered by the S.S.

This Tribunal, we feel, is already aware of the sickening evidence of the brutality of the concentration camp from the showing of the moving picture. More than that, individual prosecutions are going on, going forward before other courts, which will record these outrages in detail. Therefore, we do not propose to present a catalogue of individual brutalities, but, rather, to submit evidence showing the fundamental purposes for which the camps were used, the techniques of terror which were employed, the large number of victims and the death and the anguish which they caused.

The evidence relating to concentration camps has been assembled in a document book bearing the letter "S". I might say that the documents in this book have been arranged in the order of presentation, rather than, as we have been doing, numerically. In this book we have put them in as they occur in the presentation. One document in this book, 2309- PS, is cited several times, so we have marked it with a tab with a view to facilitating reference back to it. It will be referred to more than once.

The Nazis realised early that, without the most drastic repression of actual and potential opposition, they could not consolidate their power over the German people. We have seen that, immediately after Hitler became Chancellor, the conspirators promptly destroyed civil liberty by issuing the Presidential Emergency Decree of 28th February, 1933. It is Document 1390-PS, and it sets forth that decree, which has already been introduced in evidence before the Tribunal and is included in Exhibit USA B. It was this decree which was the basis for the so-called "Schutshaft", that is, protective custody—the terrible power to imprison people without judicial proceedings. This is made clear by Document 2499-PS, which is a typical order for protective custody. We offer it for that purpose, as a typical order for protective custody which has come into the possession of the prosecution. It is Exhibit USA 232. I should like to quote from the body of that order:—

"Order of Protective Custody.

Based on Article 1 of the Decree of the Reich President for the Protection of People and State of 28th February, 1933 (Reichsgesetzblatt, Page 83), you are taken into protective custody in the interest of public security and order.

Reason: Suspicion of activities inimical toward the State."

Defendant Goering in a book entitled 'Aufbau einer Nation', published in 1934, sought to give the impression, it appears, that the camps were originally directed at those whom the Nazis considered Communists and Social Democrats. We refer to Document 2324-PS, Exhibit USA 233. This document is an excerpt from Page 89 of the German book. We refer to the third and fourth paragraphs of the document, which I read as follows:

"We had to deal ruthlessly with these enemies of the State. It must not be forgotten that at the moment of our seizure of power over 6,000,000 people officially voted for Communism and about 8,000,000 for Marxism in the Reichstag elections in March.

Thus the Concentration Camps were created, to which we had to send first, thousands of functionaries of the Communist and Social Democratic parties."

In practical operations, the power to order confinement in these camps was almost without limit. The defendant Frick, in an order which he issued on 25th January, 1938, as Minister of the Interior, made this quite clear. An extract from this order is set forth in Document 1723-PS, to which we make reference. It is Exhibit USA 206. I wish to read Article 1, beginning at the bottom of Page 5 of the English translation of this order:—

"Protective custody can be decreed as a coercive measure of the Secret State Police against persons who endanger the security of the people and the State through their attitude, in order to counter all aspirations of enemies of the people and State."

I wish also to read into the record the first two paragraphs of that order, which are found at the top of Page 1 of the English translation:—

"In a summary of all the previously issued decrees on the co-operation between the Party and the Gestapo I refer to the following and ordain:—

1. To the Gestapo has been entrusted the mission by the Fuehrer to watch over and to eliminate all enemies of the Party and the National Socialist State, as well as all disintegrating forces of all kinds directed against both. The successful solution of this mission forms one of the most essential prerequisites for the unhampered and frictionless work of the Party. The Gestapo, in their extremely difficult task, are to be granted support and assistance in every possible way by the N.S.D.A.P."

The conspirators then were directing their apparatus of terror against the "enemies of the State", against "disintegrating forces", against those people who endangered the State "with their attitude". Whom did they consider as belonging to those broad categories? Well, first, there were the men in Germany who wanted peace. We refer to Document L-83, Exhibit USA 231.

**THE PRESIDENT:** What was the date of that document that you have been referring to, 1723-PS?

**MR. DODD:** 25th January, 1938. This document consists of an affidavit of Gerhart H. Segar, and I wish to read only from Page 1, Paragraph 2 of that affidavit:

"2. During the period after World War One, up to my commitment to the Leipzig Gaol and Oranienburg Concentration Camp in the spring of 1933, following the Nazi accession to power in January of that year, my business and political affiliations exposed me to the full impact of the Nazi theories and practice of violent regimentation and terroristic tactics. My conflict with the Nazis by virtue of my identification with the peace movement and as a duly elected member of the Reichstag representing a political faith (Social Democratic Party) hostile to National Socialism, clearly demonstrated that, even in the period prior to 1933, the Nazis considered crimes and terrorism a necessary and desirable weapon in overcoming democratic opposition."

Passing to Page 5 of the same document, and the paragraph marked (e):—

"'That the Nazis had already conceived the device of the Concentration Camp as a means of suppressing and regimenting opposition elements, was forcefully brought to my attention during the course of a conversation which I had with Dr. Wilhelm Frick in December, 1932. Frick at that time was Chairman of the Foreign Affairs Committee of the Reichstag, of which I was a member. When I gave an emphatic answer to Frick concerning the particular matter discussed, he replied, 'Do not worry, when we are in power we shall put all of you into Concentration Camps.' When the Nazis came into power, Frick was appointed Reichsminister of the Interior and promptly carried out his threat in collaboration with Goering, as Chief of the Prussian State Police, and Himmler."

This paragraph shows that, even before the Nazis had seized power in Germany, they had conceived the plan to repress any potential opposition by terror, and Frick's statement to Segar is completely consistent with an earlier statement which he made on the 18th October, 1929. We refer to Document 2513-PS, Exhibit USA 235, which has also been received in evidence and has been included in Exhibit USA B. We refer to the first page of the English translation, Page 48 of the German text. On Page 1 the quotation begins:—

> "This fateful struggle will first be taken up with the ballot, but this cannot continue indefinitely, for history has taught us that in a battle blood must be shed and iron broken. The ballot is the beginning of the fateful struggle. We are determined to promulgate by force that which we preach. Just as Mussolini exterminated the Marxists in Italy, so must we also succeed in accomplishing the same through dictatorship and terror."

**THE PRESIDENT:** This is the defendant, is it?

**MR. DODD:** Yes, the defendant Frick.

There are many additional cases of the use of the concentration camp against the men who wanted peace. There was, for example, a group called the Bibelforschers, that is, Bible Research Workers, most of whom were known as Jehovah's Witnesses. They were pacifists, and so the conspirators provided not only for their prosecution in the regular courts but also for their confinement in the concentration camps after they had served the judicial sentences, and we refer to Document D-84, Exhibit USA 236.

This document is dated 5th August, 1937, and it is an order by the Secret State Police at Berlin, and I refer particularly to the first and last paragraphs of this order, as follows:—

> "The Reichsminister of Justice had informed me that he does not share the opinion voiced by subordinate departments on various occasions, according to which the arrest of the Bibelforschers, after they have served a sentence, is supposed to jeopardise the authority of the Law Courts. He is fully aware of the necessity for measures by the State Police after the sentence has been served. He asks, however, not to bring the Bibelforschers into protective custody under circumstances detrimental to the respect of the Law Courts."

And then, the paragraph (2):—

> "If information regarding the impending release of a Bibelforscher from arrest is received from the authorities carrying out the sentence, my decision regarding the ordering of measures by the State Police will be asked for in accordance with my circular decree dated 22nd April, 1937, so that transfer to a Concentration Camp can take place immediately after the sentence has been served. Should a transfer into concentration camp immediately after the serving of the sentence not be possible, Bibelforschers will be detained in police prisons."

The Labour Unions, of which I think it is safe to say the majority are traditionally opposed to wars of aggression, also felt the full force of Nazi terror. A member of the American staff, Major Wallis, has already submitted evidence before this Tribunal concerning the conspirators' campaign against the trade unions. But the concentration camp was an important weapon in this campaign, and the Tribunal will recall that in Document 2324-PS, to which I made reference this morning, the defendant Goering made it plain that members of the Social Democratic Party were to be confined in concentration camps. Now labour leaders were very largely members of that Party, and they soon learned the horrors of protective custody. We refer to Document 2330-PS, Exhibit USA 237, which has already been received as part of Exhibit USA G, which consists of an order that one Joseph Simon should be placed in protective custody. We refer to the middle of the first page of the English translation of that order, beginning with the material under the word "Reasons".

**THE PRESIDENT:** I think you should read the sentence before that the two lines before it. The words are: "The arrestee has no right to appeal against the decree of protective custody."

**MR. DODD:** "The arrestee has no right to appeal against the decree of protective custody." Then comes a title "Reasons":—

"Simon was for many years a member of the Socialist Party and temporarily a member of the Union Socialists Populaire. From 1907 to 1918 he was Lantag deputy of the Socialist Party; from 1908 to 1930 Social Democratic City Counsellor (Stadtrat) in Nuremberg. In view of the decisive role which Simon played in international socialism, and in regard to his connection with international Marxist leaders and central agencies, which he continued after the national recovery, he was placed under protective custody on the 3rd May, 1933, and was kept, until 25th January, 1934, in the Dachau Concentration Camp. Simon was strongly suspected, even after this date, of playing an active part in the illegal continuation of the Socialist Party. He took part in meetings which aimed at the illegal continuation of the Socialist Party and propagation of illegal Marxist printed matter in Germany. Through this radical attitude, which is hostile to the State, Simon directly endangered public security and order."

We do not wish to burden these proceedings with a multiplication of such instances, but I refer the Tribunal to documents which have already been offered in connection with the presentation of the evidence concerning the destruction of the trade unions. In particular, we wish to refer to Document 2334-PS and Document 2928-PS, Exhibits USA 238 and 239, both of which are included within Exhibit USA G.

Thousands of Jews, as the world so well knows, were, of course, confined in these concentration camps. The evidence on this point will be developed in a later presentation by another member of the prosecuting staff of the United States. But among the wealth of evidence available on this point showing the confinement of Germans only because they were Jews, we wish to offer a Document 3051-PS, Exhibit USA 240. This is a copy of a teletype from S.S.

Gruppenfuehrer Heydrich, and it is dated 16th November, 1938. It was sent to all Headquarters of the State Police and all Districts and Sub-districts of the S.D. We refer to Paragraph 5 of this teletype. Paragraph 5 is found on Page 3 of the English translation. It begins at the bottom of Page 2 and runs over to Page 3. Quoting from Paragraph 5:

"As soon as the course of events of this night allows the use of the officials employed for this purpose, as many Jews, especially rich ones, as can be accommodated in the existing prisons are to be arrested in all districts. For the time being only healthy men, not too old, are to be arrested. Upon their arrest, the appropriate concentration camps should be contacted immediately, in order to confine them in these camps as soon as possible.

Special care should be taken that the Jews arrested in accordance with these instructions are not mistreated."

Himmler in 1943 indicated that use of the concentration camp against the Jews had been motivated not simply by Nazi racialism. He indicated that this policy had been motivated by a fear that the Jews might have been an obstacle to aggression. There is no necessity to consider whether this fear was justified. The important consideration is that the fear existed, and with reference to it we refer to Document 1919-PS, Exhibit USA 170. The document is a speech delivered by Himmler at the meeting of the S.S. Major Generals at Posen on 4th October, 1943, in the course of which he sought to justify the Nazi anti-Jewish policy. We refer to a portion of this document of this speech which is found on Page 4, Paragraph 3, of the English translation, starting with the words "I mean the clearing out of the Jews".

"I mean the clearing out of the Jews, the extermination of the Jewish race. It is one of those things it is easy to talk about. 'The Jewish race is being exterminated', says one party member, 'that is quite clear, it is in our programme, elimination of the Jews, and we are doing it, exterminating them'. And then there come 80,000,000 worthy Germans, and each one has his 'decent Jew'. Of course, the others are vermin, but this one is 'an A-1 Jew'. Not one of all those who talk this way has witnessed it, not one of them has been through it. Most of you must know what it means when 100 corpses are lying side by side, or 500 or 1,000. To have stuck it out and at the same time—apart from exceptions caused by human weakness—to have remained decent fellows, that is what has made us hard. This is a page of glory in our history which has never been written and is never to be written, for we know how difficult we should have made it for ourselves, if—with bombing raids, the burden and privations of war—we still had Jews today in every town as secret saboteurs, agitators and trouble- mongers."

It is clear, we say, from the foregoing that prior to the launching of the Nazi aggression, the concentration camp had been one of the principal weapons by which the conspirators achieved the social cohesion which was needed for the execution of their plans for aggression. After they launched this aggression and their armies swept over Europe, they brought the concentration camp to occupied countries, and they also brought the citizens of the occupied countries to Germany and subjected them to the whole apparatus of Nazi brutality.

Document R-91 is Exhibit USA 241. This document consists of a communication dated 16th December, 1942, sent by Muller to Himmler, for the Chief of the Security Police and S.D., and deals with the seizure of Polish Jews for deportation to concentration camps in Germany. I am beginning with the first paragraph. It says, quoting directly:—

"In connection with the increase of the transfer of labour to the concentration camps, ordered to be completed by 30th January, 1943, the following procedure may be applied in the Jewish section:

1. Total number: 45,000 Jews.

2. Start of transportation: 11th January, 1943. End of transportation: 31st January, 1943. The Reich railroads are unable to provide special trains for the evacuation during the period from 15th December, 1942, to 10th January, 1943, because of the increased traffic of Armed Forces leave trains.

3. Composition: The 45,000 Jews are to consist of 30,000 Jews from the district of Byalystock. 20,000 Jews from the Ghetto Theresienstadt, 5,000 of whom are Jews fit for work who heretofore had been used for smaller jobs required for the ghetto, and 5,000 Jews who are generally incapable of working, also Jews over 60 years old."

And passing the next sentence:—

"As heretofore only such Jews would be taken for the evacuation who have no particular connections and who are not in possession of any high, decorations. 3,000 Jews from the occupied Dutch territories, 2,000 Jews from Berlin—45,000. The figure of 45,000 includes the invalid (old Jews and children). By use of a practical standard the screening of the arriving Jews in Auschwitz should yield at least 10,000 to 15,000 people fit for work."

The Jews of Hungary suffered the same tragic fate. Between 19th March, 1944, and the 1st August, 1944, more than 400,000 Hungarian Jews were rounded up. Many of these were put in wagons and sent to extermination camps, and we refer to Document 2605-PS, Exhibit USA 242. This document is an affidavit made in London by Dr. Rudolph Kastner, a former official of the Hungarian Zionist Organisation. We refer to Page 3 of the document, the third full paragraph:—

"In March, 1944,"—quoting—"together with the German Military Occupation arrived in Budapest a 'Special Section Commando' of the German Secret Police, with the sole object of liquidating the Hungarian Jews. It was headed by Adolf Aichmann, S.S. Obersturmbannfuehrer, Chief of Section IV. B of the Reich Security Head Office. His immediate collaborators were: S.S. Obersturmbannfuehrer Hermann Krumcy, Hauptsturmfuehrer Wisliczeny, Hunsche, Novak, Dr. Seidl, and later

Danegger, Wrtok. They arrested and later deported to Mauthausen all the leaders of Jewish political and business life, and journalists, together with the Hungarian democratic and anti-Fascist politicians. Taking advantage of the 'interregnum' following upon the German occupation and lasting four days, they placed their Quislings in the Ministry of the Interior."

On Page 7 of that same document, the eighth paragraph, beginning with the words "Commanders of the death camps", and quoting:—

"Commanders of the death camps gassed only on direct or indirect instructions of Aichmann [sic]. The particular officer of IV. B who directed the deportations from some particular country had the authority to indicate whether the train should go to a death camp or not, and what should happen to the passengers. The instructions were usually carried by the S.S.—N.C.O. escorting the train. The letter 'A' or "M"—capital letters "A" or "M"—"on the escorting instruction documents indicated Auschwitz or Majdanck; it means that the passengers were to be gassed."

And passing over the next sentence, we come to these words:—

"Regarding Hungarian Jews the following general ruling was laid down in Auschwitz: children up to the age of 12 or 14, older people over 50, as well as the sick, or people with criminal records, who were transported in specially marked wagons, were taken immediately on their arrival to the gas chambers.

The others passed before an S.S. doctor who, on sight, indicated who was fit for work and who was not. Those unfit were sent to the gas chambers, while the others were distributed in various labour camps."

In the so-called "Eastern territories" these victims were apprehended for extermination—

**THE PRESIDENT:** Mr. Dodd, do not you want Page 5 for the numbers which you have stated-up to 27th June, 1944? You have not yet given us any authority for the numbers that you have stated.

**MR. DODD:** Oh, yes. On Page 5 of that same Document, 2605-PS, quoting: "Up to 27th June, 1944, 475,000 Jews were deported."

In the so-called "Eastern territories" these victims were apprehended for extermination in concentration camps without any charges having been made against them. In the Eastern occupied territories charges seemed to have been made against some of the victims. Some of the charges which the Nazi conspirators considered sufficient basis for confinement in the concentration camps are shown by reference to Document L-215, which becomes Exhibit USA 243. This document is the summary of the file, the dossier, of 25 persons arrested in Luxembourg for commitment to various concentration camps and sets forth the charges made against each person. Beginning with the paragraph after the name "Henricy", at the bottom of the first page, and quoting:—

"The name: Henricy. Charge: For associating with members of illegal resistance movements and making money for them, violating legal foreign exchange rates, for harming the interests of the Reich and being expected in the future to disobey official administrative regulations and act as an enemy of the Reich. Place of confinement: Natzweiler."

Next comes the name of "Krier" and the charge:—

"For being responsible for advanced sabotage of labour and causing fear because of his political and criminal past. Freedom would only further his anti-social urge. Place of confinement: Buchenwald."

Passing to the middle of Page 2, after the name "Monti":—

"Charge: For being strongly suspected of aiding desertion. Place of confinement: Sachsenhausen."

Next, after the name "Junker":—

"Charge: Because as a relative of a deserter he is expected to endanger the interests of the German Reich if allowed to go free. Place of confinement: Sachsenhausen."

"Jaeger" is the next name and the charge against Jaeger, quoting:—

"Because as a relative of a deserter he is expected to take advantage of every occasion to harm the German Reich. Place of confinement: Sachsenhausen."

And down to the name "Ludwig" and the charge against Ludwig:—

"For being strongly suspected of aiding desertion. Place of confinement: Dachau."

Not only civilians of the occupied countries but also prisoners of war were subjected to the horrors and the brutality of the concentration camps; and we refer to Document 1165-PS, Exhibit USA 244. This document is a memorandum to all officers of the State Police signed by Muller, the Chief of the Gestapo, dated 9th November, 1941. The memorandum has the revealing title of, and I quote, "Transportation of Russian Prisoners of War, Destined for Execution, into the Concentration Camps."

I wish to quote also from the body of this memorandum which is found on Page 2 of the English translation and I quote directly:—

"The commandants of the concentration camps are complaining that 5 to 10 per cent. of the Soviet Russians destined for execution are arriving in the camps dead or half dead. Therefore the impression has arisen that the Stalags are getting rid of such prisoners in this way.

It was particularly noted that, when marching, for example, from the railroad station to the camp, a rather large number of prisoners of war collapsed on the way from exhaustion, either dead or half dead, and had to be picked up by a truck following the convoy.

It cannot be prevented that the German people take notice of these occurrences.

Even if the transportation to the camps is generally taken care of by the Wehrmacht, the population will attribute this situation to the S.S.

In order to prevent, if possible, similar occurrences in the future, I therefore order that, effective from today on, Soviet Russians, declared definitely suspect and obviously marked for death (for example with typhus) and therefore not able to withstand the exertions of even a short march on foot, shall in the future, as a matter of basic principle, be excluded from the transport into the concentration camps for execution."

More evidence of the confinement of Russian prisoners of war in concentration camps is found in an official report of the investigation of the Flossenburg concentration camp by the Headquarters of the United States Third Army, the Judge Advocate Section, and particularly the War Crimes Branch, under the date of 21st June, 1945. It is our Document 2309- PS, and is Exhibit USA 245. At the bottom of Page 2 of the English text the last two sentences of that last paragraph say, and I quote:—

"In 1941 an additional stockade was added at the Flossenburg Camp to hold 2,000 Russian prisoners. Of these 2,000 prisoners only 102 survived."

Soviet prisoners of war found their allies in the concentration camps too and at Page 4 of this same Document 2309-PS it will show, particularly Paragraph 5, on Page 4, and I quote it:—

"The victims of Flossenburg included among them Russian civilians and prisoners of war, German nationals, Italians, Belgians, Poles, Czechs, Hungarians, British and American prisoners of war. No practical means was available to complete a list of victims of this camp; however, since the foundation of the Camp in 1938 until the day of liberation it is estimated that more than 29,000 inmates died."

Escaped prisoners of war were sent to concentration camps by the conspirators, and these camps were specially set up as extermination centres; and we refer to Document 1650-PS, being Exhibit USA 246. This document is a communication from the Secret State Police of Cologne and it is dated the 4th March, 1944. At the very top of the English text it says "To be transmitted in secret—to be handled as a secret Government matter." In the third paragraph, quoting:—

"Concerns: Measures to be taken against captured escaped prisoners of war who are officers or non-working non-commissioned officers, except British and American prisoners of war. The Supreme Command of the Army has ordered as follows:

1. Every captured escaped prisoner of war who is an officer or a non-working non-commissioned officer, except British and American prisoners of war, is to be turned over to the Chief of the Security Police and of the Security Service under the classification 'Step III', regardless of whether the escape occurred during a transport, whether it was a mass escape or an individual one.

2. Since the transfer of the prisoners of war to the Security Police and Security Service must not become officially known to the outside under any circumstances, other prisoners of war must by no means be informed of the capture. The captured prisoners are to be reported

to the Army Information Bureau as 'escaped and not captured'. Their mail is to be handled accordingly. Inquiries of representatives of the Protective Power of the International Red Cross and of other aid societies will be given the same answer."

The same communication carried a copy of an order of S.S. General Muller, acting for the Chief of the Security Police and S.D., directing the Gestapo to transport escaped prisoners directly to Mauthausen; and I quote the first two paragraphs of Muller's order, which begins on the bottom of Page 1 and runs over to Page 2 of the English text. Quoting:—

"The State Police Directorates will accept the captured escaped officer prisoners of war from the prisoner of war camp commandants and will transport them to the concentration camp Mauthausen following the procedure previously used, unless the circumstances render a special transport imperative. The prisoners of war are to be put in irons on the transport—not on the station if it is subject to view by the public. The camp commandant at Mauthausen is to be notified that the transfer occurs within the scope of the action 'Kugel'. The State Police Directorates will submit semi-yearly reports on these transfers giving merely the figures, the first report being due on 5th July, 1944."

Passing the next three sentences, we come to this line:—

"For the sake of secrecy the Supreme Command of the Armed Forces has been requested to inform the prisoner of war camps to turn the captured prisoners over to the local State Police Office and not to send them directly to Mauthausen."

It is no coincidence that the literal translation for the German word 'Kugel' is the English word 'bullet', since Mauthausen, where the escaped prisoners were sent, was an extermination centre.

Nazi conquest was marked by the establishment of concentration camps over all Europe. In this connection we refer to Document R-129. It is a report on the location of concentration camps, signed by Pohl, who was an S.S. General in charge of concentration camp labour policies. Document R- 129 is Exhibit USA 217.

I wish to refer particularly to Section 1, Paragraphs 1 and 2 of this document, which are found on Page 1 of the English translation. It is addressed to the Reichsfuehrer S.S. and bears the stamp "Secret":—

"Reichsfuehrer: Today I report about the present situation of the concentration camps and about measures I have taken in order to carry out your order of the 3rd March, 1942:

1. At the outbreak of war there existed the following concentration camps:

(a) Dachau—1939, 4,000 prisoners; today, 8,000.

(b) Sachsenhausen—1939, 6,500 prisoners; today, 10,000.

(c) Buchenwald—1939, 5,300 prisoners; today, 9,000.

(d) Mauthausen—1939, 1,500 prisoners; today, 5,500.

(e) Flossenburg—1939, 1,600 prisoners; today, 4,700.

(f) Ravensbruek—1939, 2,500 prisoners; today, 7,500."

And then it goes on to say in Paragraph 2, quoting:

"In the years 1940 to 1942 nine further camps were erected:

(a) Auschwitz.

(b) Neuengamme.

(c) Guson.

(d) Natzweiter.

(e) Gross-Rosen.

(f) Lublin.

(g) Niederhagen.

(h) Stutthof.

(i) Arbeitsdorf."

In addition to the camps in the occupied territory mentioned in this Document R-129, from which I have just read these names and figures, there were many, many others. I refer to the official report by the United States Third Army Headquarters, to which we have already made reference, Document 2309-PS, on Page 2 in the English text, Section IV, Paragraph 4, quoting:_

"Concentration Camp Flossenburg was founded in 1938 as a camp for political prisoners. Construction was commenced on the camp in 1938 and it was not until April, 1940, that the first transport of prisoners was received. From this time on prisoners began to flow steadily into the camp. (Exhibit B-1.) Flossenburg was the mother camp and under its direct control and jurisdiction were 47 satellite camps or outer-commandos for male prisoners and 27 camps for female workers. To these outer- commandos were supplied the necessary prisoners for the various work projects undertaken.

Of all these outer-commandos Hersbruck and Leitmeritz (in Czechoslovakia), Oberstaubling, Mulsen and Sall, located on the Danube, were considered to be the worst."

I do not wish to take the time of the Tribunal to discuss each of the Nazi concentration camps which dotted the map of Europe. We feel that the widespread use of these camps is commonly known and notorious. We do, however, wish to invite the Tribunal's attention to a chart which we have had prepared. The solid black line marks the boundary of Germany after the "Anschluss", and we invite the Tribunal's attention to the fact that the majority of the camps shown on the chart are located within the territorial limits of Germany itself. They are the red spots, of course, on the map. In the centre of Germany there is the Buchenwald camp located near the city of Weimar, and at the extreme bottom of the chart there is Dachau, several miles outside Munich. At the top of the chart are Neuengamme and Bergen-Belsen, located near Hamburg. To the left is the Niederhagen camp in the Ruhr Valley. In the upper right there are a number of camps near Berlin, one named Sachsenhausen (formerly Oranienburg, which was one of the first camps established after the Nazis came into power). Near to that is the camp

*The famous photograph of Hitler and his cohorts walking by the Eiffel Tower in June 1940. Speer is third on the left in the front next to Hitler.*

of Ravensbruck, which was used exclusively for women. Some of the most notorious camps were indeed located outside Germany. Mauthausen was in Austria. In Poland was the infamous Auschwitz; and to the left of the chart is a camp called Hertogenbosch which was located in Holland, as the chart shows; and below it is Natzweiler, located in France.

The camps were established in networks, and it may be observed that surrounding each of the major camps-the larger red dots—is a group of satellite camps, and the names of the principal camps, the most notorious camps, at least, are above the map and below it on the chart; and those names, for most people, symbolise the Nazi system of concentration camps as they have become known to the world since May or a little later in 1945.

I should like to direct your attention briefly to the treatment which was meted out in these camps. The motion picture to which I have made reference a short time ago and which was shown to the members of this High Tribunal, has disclosed the terrible and savage treatment which was inflicted upon these Allied nationals, prisoners of war and other victims of Nazi terror. Because the moving picture has so well shown the situation, as of the time of its taking at least, I shall confine myself to a very brief discussion of the subject.

The conditions which existed inside these camps were, of course, we say, directly related to the objectives which these Nazi conspirators sought to achieve outside the camps through their employment of terror.

It is truly remarkable, it seems to us, how easily the words "concentration camps" rolled off the lips of these men. How simple all problems became when they could turn to the terror institution of these camps. I refer to Document R- 124, which is already before the Tribunal as Exhibit USA

179. It is again that document covering the minutes of the Central Planning Committee on which the defendant Speer sat, and where the high strategy of the high Nazi armament production was formulated. I do not intend to read from the document again, because I read from it this morning, to illustrate another point, but the Tribunal will recall that it was at this meeting that the defendant Speer and others were discussing the so-called slackers, and the conversation had to do with having drastic steps taken against these workers, who were not putting out sufficient work to please their masters. Speer suggested that "there is nothing to be said against the S.S. and Police taking steps and putting those known as slackers into concentration camps," and he used the words "concentration camps ". And he said "Let it happen several times and the news will soon get around."

Words spoken in this fashion, we say, sealed the fate of many victims. As for getting the news around, as suggested by the defendant Speer, this was not left to chance, as we shall presently show.

The deterrent effect of the concentration camps upon the public was a carefully planned thing. To heighten the atmosphere of terror, these camps were shrouded in secrecy. What went on in the barbed wire enclosures was a matter of fearful conjecture in Germany and countries under Nazi control; and this was the policy from the very beginning, when the Nazis first came into power and set up this system of concentration camps. We refer now to Document 778-PS, Exhibit USA 247. This document is an order issued on the 1st October, 1933, by the camp commander of Dachau. The document prescribed a programme of floggings, solitary confinement and executions for the inmates for infractions of the rules.

Among the rules were those prescribing a rigid censorship concerning conditions within the camp; and I refer to the first page of the English text, paragraph numbered Article 11, and quoting:—

"By virtue of the law on revolutionaries, the following offenders, considered as agitators, will be hanged: anyone who, for the purpose of agitating, does the following in the camp, at work, in the quarters, in the kitchens and workshops, toilets and places of rest: talks politics, holds inciting speeches and meetings, forms cliques, loiters around with others; who, for the purpose of supplying the propaganda of the opposition with atrocity stories, collects true or false information about the concentration camp and its institution, receives such information, buries it, talks about it to others, smuggles it out of the camp into the hands of foreign visitors or others by means of clandestine or other methods, passes it on in writing or orally to released prisoners or prisoners who are placed above them, conceals it in clothing or other articles, throws stones and other objects over the camp wall containing such information, or produces secret documents; who, for the purpose of agitating, climbs on barracks roofs and trees, seeks contact with the outside by giving light or other signals, or induces others to escape or commit a crime, gives them advice to that effect or supports such undertakings in any way whatsoever."

The censorship in the camps themselves was complemented by an officially inspired rumour campaign outside the camps. Concentration camps were spoken of in whispers, and the whispers were spread by agents of the Secret Police. When the defendant Speer said that if the threat of the concentration camp were used, the news would get around soon enough, he knew whereof he spoke.

We refer to Document 1531-PS. With reference to this document, I wish to submit a word of explanation. The original German text, the original German document, the captured document was here in the document room and was translated into English as our translation shows. Yesterday we were advised that it had either been lost or misplaced, the original German text, and unfortunately no photostatic copy was available here in Nuremberg. A certified copy is, however, being sent to the office here from Frankfurt and it is on its way today, and I ask the Tribunal's permission to offer the English translation of the German original, which is certified to be accurate by the translator, into evidence, subject to a motion to strike it from the record if the certified copy of the original German document does not arrive.

**M. HERZOG:** Mr. President and your Honours.

The National Socialist doctrine, by the high place which it gives to the idea of the State, by the contempt in which it holds individuals and personal rights, contains a conception of work which agrees with the principles of its general philosophy.

Work is not, in this philosophy, one of the forms of the manifestation of individual personalities, it is a duty imposed by the community on its members.

"The relationship of labour, according to National Socialist ideas," a German writer has said, "is not merely a judicial relationship between the worker and his employer; it is a living phenomenon in which the worker becomes a cog in the National Socialist machine for collective production." The conception of compulsory labour is thus, for National Socialism, necessarily complementary to the conception of work itself.

Compulsory Labour Service was first of all imposed on the German people. German Labour Service was instituted by a law of 26th June, 1935, which bears Hitler's signature and that of the defendant Frick, Minister of the Interior. This law was published in the "Reichsgesetzblatt," Part I, Page 769. I submit it to the Tribunal as Document RF-6.

From 1939 the mobilisation of workers was added to the compulsory labour service. Decrees were promulgated to that effect by the defendant Goering in his capacity as Plenipotentiary for the Four Year Plan. I do not stress this point; it arises from the conspiracy entered into by the accused to commit their Crime against Peace, and of which my American colleagues have already informed the Tribunal. I merely point out that the mobilisation of workers was applicable to foreigners resident in German territory, because I find in this fact the proof that the principle of compulsory recruitment of foreign workers existed prior to the war. Far from being the spontaneous result of the needs of German war industry, the compulsory recruitment of foreign workers is the putting into practice of a concerted policy. I lay before the Tribunal a document which proves this. It is Document 382 of the French classification, which I offer as Exhibit RF 7. This is a memorandum of the High Command of the German Armies of 1st October, 1938; the memorandum, drawn up in anticipation of the invasion of Czechoslovakia, contains a classification of possible violations of International Law; the explanation which the High Command of the Armed Forces thinks it possible to give appears in connection with each violation. The document appears in the form of a list in four columns; in the first is a statement of the violations of International Law; the second gives a concrete example; the third contains the points of view of International Law on the one hand and, on the other hand, the conclusions which can be drawn from them; the fourth column is reserved for the explanation of the Propaganda Ministry.

I read the passage which deals with the forced labour of civilians and prisoners of war, which is found on Page 6 of the German original, Page 7 of the French translation, the document which is referred to in my document book as Exhibit RF-7.

I read at the bottom of Page 7 of the French translation:

"Compulsory use of prisoners of war and civilians for war work, construction of roads, digging trenches, munition work, transport."

Second column:

"Captured Czech soldiers and civilians are detailed to construct roads and to load munitions."

Third column:

"Article 31 of an agreement signed 27th July, 1929, concerning the treatment of prisoners of war engaged on work which is directly connected with the War to force them to do such work is in any case contrary to International Law; prisoners of war and civilians can be used on highway construction but not on munition work."

Last column:

"The use of such measures can be justified by the necessity of war or by the assertion that the enemy acted in the same way first."

The compulsory recruitment of foreign workers is thus in accordance with National Socialist doctrine, one of the elements of the policy of German domination. Hitler himself recognised this on several occasions. I quote in this connection his speech of 9th November, 1941, which was printed in the "Volkischer Beobachter" of 10th November, 1941, No. 314, Page 4, which I submit to the Tribunal as Exhibit RF 8. I read the extract of this speech, columns 1 and 2 and the first paragraph below, in the German original.

THE PRESIDENT: Exhibit RF 8, is it not?

M. HERZOG: Yes, your Honour.

"The territory which now works for us contains more than 250,000,000 men, but the territory in Europe which works indirectly for this struggle now includes more than 350,000,000. In so far as German territory is concerned, occupied territory, the domain which we have taken under our administration, it is certain that we shall succeed in harnessing the very last man to this work."

The recruitment of foreign workers thus proceeds in a systematic manner. It constitutes the putting into practice of the political principles applied to all the territories occupied by Germany. These principles, the concrete development of which in other departments of German criminal activity will be pointed out to you by my colleagues, are materially of two kinds: employment of all active forces of the occupied or dominated territories; extermination of all their non-productive forces.

These are the two justifications which the defendants have given for the establishment of the recruitment of foreign workers. There are many documents to this effect; I confine myself to the most explicit.

The justification for the recruitment of foreign workers, because of the necessity of associating the enslaved peoples with the German war effort, is primarily a result of the exposition of the motives of the decree of 21st March, 1942.

**DR. STAHMER (Counsel for defendant Goering):** Mr. President, I should like to point out that the translation into German is faulty. Whole sentences are omitted. This is apparently the result of the fact that the prosecutor is speaking too rapidly.

**THE PRESIDENT:** Will you go a little more slowly?

**M. HERZOG:** Yes.

The justification for the recruitment of foreign workers, on account of the necessity for associating the enslaved peoples with the German war effort, is primarily a result of the exposition of the motives of the decree of 21st March, 1942, appointing the defendant Sauckel as plenipotentiary for the employment of labour. The decree was published in the "Reichsgesetzblatt," 1942, Part 1, Page 179. I submit it and will read its complete text to the Tribunal as Exhibit RF 9.

"The decree of the Fuehrer concerning the creation of a plenipotentiary for the employment of labour, dated 21st March, 1942.

To assure to the whole of the war economy, and, in particular, the armament industry, necessary labour, it is important to establish a unified direction, which answers the needs of the war economy for the use of available labour, including hired foreigners and war prisoners, as well as the mobilisation of all labour still unemployed in the Greater German Reich, including the Protectorate as well as the Government General and the other occupied regions. This mission will be accomplished by Reichsstatthalter and Gauleiter Fritz Sauckel, in the capacity of general plenipotentiary for the employment of labour in the framework of the Four Year Plan. In this capacity he is directly responsible for the Four Year Plan."

I would like to point out here that the defendant Sauckel developed the same theme at the Congress of Gauleiter and Reichsleiter, held on 5th and 6th February, 1943, at Posen. He expressed himself in plain terms: he justified compulsory recruitment on the basis of National Socialist philosophy, and on the basis of the necessity of associating all the European peoples in the struggle carried on by Germany. His speech constitutes Document 1739-PS. I submit it as Exhibit RF 10, and I request the Court to accept the following passages in evidence against the defendant Sauckel. At first, Page 5 of the German text, fourth paragraph—this is found in the first page of the French translation:

"The unprecedented violence of the war has forced me to mobilise in the name of the Fuehrer a great number of foreigners for labour in the domain of the German war economy, and to force them to large-scale production.

The purpose of this is to insure in the labour domain the material means required by war in the struggle for the preservation of the life and liberty, in the first place, of our people, and also for the preservation of our Western culture for those peoples who, in contrast to the parasitical Jews and plutocrats, lead a life of work and endeavour and are honest and strong.

Such is the enormous difference between, on the one hand, the work which was demanded at one period by the power and authority of the Jews in the Treaty of Versailles and the Dawes and Young Plans, work which took the form of slavery and tributary efforts, and, on the other' hand, the utilisation of labour which, in my capacity as a National Socialist, I have the honour to prefer and to carry out, and which represents a participation in the struggle by Germany for the liberty of Germany and for the liberty of friendly nations."

The compulsory recruitment of foreign workers did not have as its only object the maintenance of the level of German industrial production. There was also the conscious desire to weaken the human potential of the occupied countries.

The idea of extermination by work was familiar to the theorists of National Socialism and to the leaders of Germany; it constituted one of the bases of the policy of domination of the invaded territories. I lay before the Court the proof that the National Socialist conspirators envisaged the destruction by work of whole ethnical groups. A discussion which took place on 14th September, 1942, between Goebbels and Thierack is significant. It constitutes Document 682-PS, which I file with the Tribunal as Exhibit RF 11, from which I take the following passage:

"Concerning the extermination of the social elements, Doctor Goebbels is of the opinion that the following groups must be exterminated: Jews and Gypsies, without discrimination; Poles who have still to serve three or four years' sentence; Czechoslovakians and Germans who have been condemned to death or to penal servitude for life or have been placed in protective custody for life. The idea to exterminate them by work is best."

The idea of extermination by work was not applied to ethnical groups alone, the disappearance of which was desired by the defendants; it also led to the employment of foreign manual labour in the German war industry to the extreme limit of the individual's strength. I will revert to this aspect of the policy of forced labour when I lay before the Tribunal the treatment of foreign workers in Germany: the cruelties to which they were subjected sprang from this main conception of National Socialism, that the human forces of the occupied countries must be utilised to the limit of extermination, which is the final goal.

The defendants have not only admitted the principle of compulsory recruitment of foreign workers; they have followed a consistent policy of putting their principle into practice, applying it in the same concrete manner in the various occupied territories. To do this they resorted to identical methods of recruitment; they set up everywhere the same recruitment administration and promulgated the same orders.

In the first place, it was a question of urging the foreign workers to work in their own countries for the Army of Occupation and the services connected with it. The German military and civil authorities organised workyards in order to carry out on the spot work useful to their war policy. The workyards or shops of the Todt organisation, which, after the death of their founder, were under the direction of the defendant Speer, and those of the Wehrmacht, Luftwaffe, Kriegsmarine and the N.S.K.K. organisation, employed numerous foreign workers in all areas of Western Europe.

But the essential undertaking of the German labour services was the deportation of foreign workers to the munition factories of the Reich. The most varied means were used to this end. They were built up into a recruiting policy which can be analysed as follows:

In the beginning, this policy took on the cloak of legality. The use of labour took the form of requisition under the terms of Article 52 of the Appendix to the Fourth Hague Convention; it was also effected by means of voluntary recruitment of workers, to whom the German recruiting offices offered labour contracts.

I shall provide the Tribunal with proof that the labour requisitions effected by the National Socialist authorities were a deliberate misinterpretation of the letter and spirit of the international convention by virtue of which they were carried out. I shall show that the voluntary character of the recruitment of certain foreign workers was entirely fictitious; in reality their work contracts were made under the pressure which the occupation authorities brought to bear on their will.

The defendants lost no time in flinging aside their mask of legality. They compelled the prisoners of war to do work forbidden by international conventions. I shall show how the work of prisoners of war was incorporated in the general plan for the employment of labour from the occupied areas.

It was finally by force that the defendants brought to fruition their recruitment plans. They did not hesitate to resort to violent methods. Thus they established the compulsory labour service in the areas which they occupied. Sometimes they directly promulgated orders bearing the signature of military commanders or Reich Commissars; this is the case with Belgium and Holland. Sometimes they forced the de facto authorities themselves, whom they had set up in the occupied areas, to take legislative measures; this is particularly the case with France and Norway; sometimes they simply took direct action, that is, they transferred foreign workers to factories in Germany without providing a written order for this; this happened in Denmark. Finally in certain occupied areas where they began to carry out Germanisation, the defendants made the inhabitants of these territories a part of the labour service of the Reich. This was the case in the French provinces of Haut-Rhin, Bas-Rhin and Moselle, and in Luxembourg.

The policy of compulsory labour was asserted and systematised from the day when the defendant Sauckel was appointed General Plenipotentiary for the Employment of Labour.

Member of the National Socialist Party since its formation, member of the Diet of Thuringia and member of the Reichstag, Obergruppenfuehrer of the criminal organisations S.S. and S.A., the defendant Sauckel was Gauleiter and Reichsstatthalter of Thuringia. On 21st March, 1942, he was appointed General Plenipotentiary for the Employment of Labour by a decree of the Fuehrer. This decree was countersigned by Lammers, in his capacity as Reich Minister and Chief of the Chancellery and by the defendant Keitel; the responsibility of these latter is confirmed by this countersignature. The defendant Keitel has associated himself, by appointing Sauckel, with the policy of compulsory labour, the principle and the method of which he has approved.

I have already read this decree nominating Sauckel to the Tribunal. I would remind you that it placed Sauckel, in his capacity as General Plenipotentiary for the Employment of Labour, under the immediate orders of the Trustee for the Four Year Plan, the defendant Goering. The latter bears a direct responsibility in pursuing the plan for recruitment of compulsory labour. I shall produce numerous proofs of this. I ask the Tribunal to authorise me to produce, as first proof, the decree signed by the defendant Goering the day after the appointment of the defendant Sauckel. This decree, dated 27th March, 1942, was published in the "Reichsgesetzblatt," 1942, Part 1, Page 180. I file it with the Tribunal as Exhibit RF 12. Goering by this decree did away with all the administrative offices of the Four Year Plan which had been charged with the recruitment of labour, he transmitted their powers to Sauckel's department, thus confirming his appointment.

The powers of Sauckel between 1942 and 1944 were considerably reinforced by decrees of Hitler and Goering. These decrees gave full significance to the defendant Sauckel's title of Plenipotentiary. They gave him administrative autonomy and even legislative competency such as he could not aspire to, had he confined himself to executive tasks. The importance of the political part which he played during the last two years of the war increases in this measure the weight of the responsibility devolving upon him.

I would particularly draw the attention of the Tribunal to the decrees of the Fuehrer of 30th September, 1942, and of 14th March, 1943, and to the decree of the defendant Goering, of 25th May, 1942.

I will not read these decrees, which have been commented on by my American colleague, Mr. Dodd. I submit them in support of my contention.

I will first refer to the decree of the defendant Goering of 25th May, 1942. It was published in the "Reichsgesetzblatt," 1942, Part 1, Page 347. He delegates to Sauckel part of the powers relating to labour held by the Minister of Labour. I submit it to the Tribunal as Exhibit RF 13.

Hitler's decree of 30th September, 1942, gave Sauckel considerable power over the civil and military authorities of the territories occupied by the German Armed Forces. It made it possible for the defendant to introduce into the staffs of the occupying authorities personal representatives, to whom he gave his orders directly. The decree is countersigned by Lammers and by the defendant Keitel, and this appears in the collection of the directive decrees of 1942, second volume, Page 510, and I submit it as Exhibit RF 14.

In the carrying out of this decree representatives of Sauckel's department were in fact introduced into the Headquarters Staffs of the military commands. The interrogation of General von Falkenhausen, Military Governor of Belgium and Northern France, gives, in this connection, a proof which I would ask the Tribunal to be good enough to remember. General von Falkenhausen was interrogated on 27th November, 1945, by the head of the Investigation Section of the French delegation. I submit his evidence to the Tribunal as Exhibit RF 15. I read the following extract (Page 2, the seventh paragraph, of the French translation, and Page 2, the fifth paragraph, of the German translation):

"Q. Can the witness tell us what was the line of demarcation between his own powers and the powers of the Arbeitseinsatz?

A. Up to a certain time there existed in my department a labour service which dealt with the hiring of voluntary workers.

I no longer remember the exact date—perhaps autumn 1942-when this labour service was placed under the order of Sauckel, and the only thing I had to do was to carry out the orders which came through this way.

I do not remember, but Raeder, who is also in prison"—Raeder was a civilian official in the staff of General von Falkenhausen—"is very well informed about the dates and can undoubtedly give them better than I can.

Q. Before the question of labour was entirely entrusted to Sauckel's organisation, did there exist in the General Staff or in its services an officer who was in charge of this question? Afterwards, was there a delegate from Sauckel's service in this department?

A. Until Sauckel came into power there was, in my service, Raeder, who directed the Bureau of Labour in my office. This labour office functioned as an employment office in Germany, that is to say, it concerned itself with the requests for labour which would naturally be voluntary.

Q. What took place when this change happened?

A. After this change the office continued to exist, but the orders were given directly by Sauckel to the Arbeitseinsatz and passed through my office."

**THE PRESIDENT:** Would this be a convenient time to break off for 10 minutes?

Before the Tribunal adjourns I want to announce that the Tribunal will sit tomorrow, Saturday, until 1 o'clock.

*(A recess was taken.)*

**M. HERZOG:** I have just reminded the Tribunal of the legislative framework through which the activity of the defendant Sauckel was exercised. This framework was reinforced by the defendant's own decree. The first document attests that Sauckel deliberately assumed the responsibility of the general policy for the recruiting of foreign workers—the decree of the 22nd August, 1942, which appeared in the "Reichsgesetzblatt," 1942, Part I, Page 382. This decree lays down the principle of forced recruiting, and makes the necessary provisions for all the human potential of the occupied territories to be put in the service of the German war economy.

Sauckel forces the inhabitants of the conquered countries to participate in the war of Germany against their Fatherland. It is not only a violation of International Law, it is a crime against the rights of nations. I submit the decree to the Tribunal as Exhibit RF 17, and I shall read it:

"Ordinance No. 10 of the General Plenipotentiary for the Employment of Labour regarding the Arbeitseinsatz in the occupied territories under date of 22nd August, 1942.

In order to mobilise the labour of the occupied territories in the new organisation of the Arbeitseinsatz within the European framework, one must submit these forces to one central authority; it is necessary to assure a maximum return as well as a useful and rational distribution of this force, in order to satisfy the labour needs of the Reich and of the occupied territories. By virtue of the full powers which are conferred upon me, I order:

(1) By virtue of the decree of the Fuehrer, under date of 21st March, 1942, relative to the General Plenipotentiary for the Employment of Labour and by virtue of the ordinance of the Trustee for the Four Year Plan, under date of 27th March, 1942, relative to the application of this decree, I likewise have powers to employ, when necessary, the labour of occupied territories, as well as to take all the measures necessary to increase its production. Those German offices which dealt with Arbeitseinsatz and for the policy of wages or my commissioners will, according to my directives, carry out this employment of labour and

take all measures necessary to increase production.

(2) This ordinance extends to all the territories occupied during the war by the Wehrmacht, if they are under a German administration.

(3) The labour available in the occupied territories must be utilised in the first place to fulfil the primary war needs of Germany. This labour must be utilised in the occupied territories in the following order:

(a) For the needs of the army, of the services of occupation and of the civilian services.

(b) For the German armament needs.

(c) For the food and agriculture.

(d) For industrial needs other than those of armament, in which Germany is interested.

(e) For industrial needs of the population of the territory in question."

A second document shows the willingness of the defendant Sauckel to take the responsibility for the treatment of foreign workers. It is an agreement concluded on 2nd June, 1943, with the Chief of the German Labour Front. I shall not read this document to the Tribunal. The document has been discussed by Mr. Dodd. I recall that it was published in the "Reichsarbeitsblatt" in 1943, Part 1, Page 588. I submit it in support of my brief as Exhibit RF 18.

Designated by Hitler and by the defendants Keitel and Goering, in order to pursue, under the control of the latter, the policy of recruitment of compulsory labour, the defendant Sauckel has consequently carried out his task in virtue of the responsibilities which he had assumed. I request that the Tribunal bear this in mind.

I request the Tribunal, likewise, to note that the policy of recruitment of foreign workers involves the responsibility of all German Ministers responsible for the economic and social life of the Reich. An interministerial office, or at any rate, an interadministrative office, the Central Planning Board for the Four Year Plan, has proceeded to formulate the programme for the recruitment of foreign workers.

All departments interested in the labour problem were represented at the meetings of the Central Office. General Milch presided at the meetings, in the name of the defendant Goering.

The defendant Sauckel and the defendant Speer took part, in person, and I shall submit to the Tribunal certain statements made by them. The defendant Funk also took part; he therefore knew of, and approved, the programme for the deportation of workers. He even collaborated in its formulation. As proof thereof I produce three documents inculpating him.

The first is a letter of 9th February, 1944, in which Funk is summoned to a meeting of the Central Planning Board. It is Document 674, which I submit to the Tribunal as Exhibit RF 19. I read:

"Sir: In the name of the Central Planning Board, I invite you to a meeting concerning the question of the utilisation of labour. It will take place on Wednesday, the 16th February, 1944, at 10 o'clock, in a boardroom of the Secretaries of State at the Air Ministry, Leipziger Strasse, in Berlin.

In the Appendix I transmit to you some statistics on the subject of the development of the utilisation of labour. These statistics will serve as a basis for the discussion at the meeting."

Funk was unable personally to attend the meeting, but he arranged to be represented by Undersecretary of State Hayler. He received the minutes of the meeting and, on 7th March, 1944, he wrote to General Milch, in order to excuse his frequent absences from the meetings of the Board. I submit this document to the Tribunal. It is Document 675, which I submit as Exhibit RF 20. It is the report of the fifty-third meeting of the Planning Board. The Tribunal will note on Page 2 of the French translation that Minister Funk received a report of this meeting. He is mentioned on the second line of the distribution list: Reich Minister Speer first and on the second line Reich Minister Funk.

I now produce as Exhibit RF 21 the letter in which Funk excuses himself to Marshal Milch because of his inability to be present at the meeting.

"Very honoured and very dear Field Marshal:

Unfortunately the meetings of the Central Planning Board have always been set for dates on which I am already engaged by other important meetings. So it is to my great regret that I shall be unable to be present on Saturday at the meeting of the Central Planning Board, inasmuch as I have to speak on that day in Vienna in the course of a great demonstration in honour of the Anniversary of the day of the Anschluss.

Secretary Hayler will likewise be in Vienna on Friday and Saturday, where there will be an important South- European Conference, in which foreign delegates will participate and at which I must also speak.

Under these conditions I beg you to allow Ministerial Director and General of Police, Brigadefuehrer of S.S. Ohlendorf, who is the permanent deputy of State Secretary Hayler, to attend as my representative."

**THE PRESIDENT:** Does this document tell us anything more than that the defendant Funk was unable to be present?

**M. HERZOG:** This document, Mr. President, was given to me by my American colleagues, who asked me to use it in the case on compulsory labour, because they have not had time to use it in their charge against Funk. It is presented to the Tribunal to prove that Funk was following the meetings of the Central Planning Board and that he had permanent representatives there to represent him on all occasions who, by their report, kept him in touch with the work of the Central Planning Board. That is why we present to the Tribunal this document on defendant Funk.

I shall continue to quote:

"Under these circumstances, I beg you to allow the Major- General of Police, Brigadefuehrer of the S.S., Ohlendorf, who is the permanent deputy of State Secretary Hayler, to attend as my representative. Herr

Ohlendorf will have Ministerial Director Koelsen as a consultant for questions of consumer goods, and Counsellor of State Janke for questions concerning foreign trade."

The policy of the Central Planning Board for the Four Year Plan pursued by the defendant Sauckel is shown by the mass deportation of workers. The principle of this deportation is a criminal one, but the manner of its execution was even more criminal. I shall give the proof of this to the Tribunal by submitting, in succession, the methods of compulsory recruitment, its results and the conditions of deportation.

I wish here to thank the members of the French delegation and of the foreign delegations who have come to my aid in the preparation of my work, in particular, my colleague M. Pierre Portal, a Lyons barrister.

The brief which I have the honour of presenting to the Tribunal will be limited to the account of the recruiting of foreign labour in occupied territories of Western Europe, since the deportation of workers coming from Eastern Europe will be dealt with by my Soviet colleagues.

Throughout the occupation the local field commanders imposed requisitions of labour on the populations of the occupied territories. Fortification works considered necessary for the furtherance of military operations, and guard duties for the security of the occupation troops were carried out by the inhabitants of the occupied areas. The labour requisitions affected not only isolated individuals but entire groups.

In France, for instance, they affected, in turn, groups of Indo-Chinese workers, workers from North Africa, foreign workers, and Chantiers de Jeunesse (Youth workyards). I produce in evidence an extract from the report on forced labour and the deportation of workers drawn up by the Institute of Statistics of the French Government. This report bears the number 515 and I submit this to the Tribunal as Exhibit RF 22. This document, because of its size, has been taken out of the document book. I quote first of all Page 17 of the French text and 17, likewise, of the German translation.

I read the second paragraph before the end—

**THE PRESIDENT:** Is this it? *(indicating).*

**M. HERZOG:** No, it is the document in the blue cover, on Page 17.

"Paragraph 6: The Forced Labour Recruitment of Constituted Groups: Finally, a last procedure adopted by the Germans on a number of occasions during the whole course of the occupations for direct forced labour, as well as for indirect forced labour: the 'requisition' of constituted groups already trained and disciplined and consequently an excellent contribution.

(a) Indo-Chinese Labour (M.O.I.): This formation of colonial workers had been intended from the beginning of the hostilities to satisfy the needs of French industry in non-specialised labour. Under the control of officers and non-commissioned officers of the French Army, transformed into civilian functionaries after the month of July, 1940, Indo-Chinese labour was, from 1945 on, obliged to do part-time forced labour, directly as well as indirectly."

I leave out the table on Page 16 and I read:

"(b) The North African work: Between 17th August and 6th November, 1942, the home country received two contingents of workers from North Africa; one was composed of 5,560 Algerians, the other of 1,825 Moroccans. These workers were immediately obliged to do direct forced labour which brought the number of North African workers enrolled in the Todt organisation to 17,582.

(c) Foreign labour: The law of 11th July, 1938, concerning the organisation of the nation in time of war provided for the cases of foreigners living in France, and obliged them to render services; under-officers and non-commissioned officers transformed into civilian functionaries by the law of the 9th October, 1940, the foreign labour was progressively subjected by the Germans to direct forced labour."

I leave out the table and I read:

"(d) Youth workyards (Chantiers de Jeunesse): On 29th January, 1943, the labour staff of the German Armistice Commission in Paris announced that the Commander-in- Chief 'West' was examining whether and in which way the formations of French workers might be called upon to perform tasks important for both countries. This resulted in partial recruiting and was followed by demands for young people from the workyards to supply direct labour."

Similar requisitions took place in all the other territories of Western Europe. These requisitions were illegal: they were carried out by virtue of Article 52 of the Appendix to the Fourth Hague Convention. In reality they systematically violated the letter and the spirit of this text of International Law.

What does Article 52 of the Appendix to the Fourth Hague Convention say? It is worded as follows:

"Requisitions in kind and services shall not be demanded from municipalities or inhabitants except for the needs of the Army of Occupation. They shall be in proportion to the resources of the country and be of such a nature that the populations will not be obliged to take part in operations against their own country. These requisitions and services shall only be demanded on the authority of the commander of the locality occupied."

Thus the terms in which Article 52 authorises the requisition of services by an Army of Occupation are expressly formulated. These terms are four in number:

1. The rendering of services can be demanded only for the needs of the Army of Occupation. All requisitions made for the general economic needs of the occupying power are thus forbidden.

2. Services demanded by way of requisition must not entail an obligation to take part in military operations against the country of those rendering them. The rendering of any service exacted in the interests of the war economy of the occupying power, all guard duties

or exercise of military control are forbidden.

3. Services rendered in a given area must be in proportion to its economic resources, the development of which must not be hampered. It follows that any requisitioning of labour is contrary to International Law if it results in the impeding or prevention of the normal utilisation of the riches of the occupied country.

4. Finally, labour requisitions must, under the provisions of the second paragraph of Article 52, be carried out in the area of the locality under the administration of the occupation authority who has signed the requisition order. The transfer of conscripted workers from one part of the occupied area to another and, especially, their deportation to the country of the occupied power are prohibited.

Labour requisitions exacted by German civilian and military authorities in the occupied areas did not conform to the spirit of Article 52. They were carried out to satisfy either the needs of German economy or even the needs of military strategy of the enemy forces. They deliberately refused to acknowledge the need of ensuring facilities for a reasonable utilisation of local resources; they finally took the form of migrations of workers. The case of those workers who were conscripted from all countries of Western Europe, and formed an integral part of the Todt organisation to help in building the system of fortifications known under the name of the "Atlantic Wall," may be taken as a typical example.

This violation of international agreements is a flagrant one; it called forth repeated protests from General Doyen, delegate of the French authorities with the German Armistice Commission. I ask the Tribunal to accept as evidence the letter of General Doyen, 25th May, 1941. This letter constitutes Document 283, and it is placed before the Tribunal as Exhibit RF 23. I read:

"Wiesbaden, 25th May, 1941. From the General de Corps d'Armée Doyen, President of the French delegation at the German Armistice Commission to Monsieur le General der Artillerie Vogl, President of the German Armistice Commission.

On several occasions, and notably in my letters No. 14,263/A.E. and 14,887/A.E. of 26th February and 8th March, I respectfully protested to you against the use for which French labour has been employed within the framework of the Todt organisation in the execution of military work on the coast of Bretagne.

I have today the duty of calling your attention to other cases in which the occupation authorities have had recourse to the recruiting of French civilians to carry out services of a strictly military character, cases which are even more serious than those which I have already called to your attention.

If, indeed, in the case of the workers engaged by the Todt organisation, it could be argued that certain workers among them accepted voluntarily an employment for which they are being remunerated (although in practice most often they were not given the possibility of refusing this employment), this argument can by no means be invoked when the prefects themselves are obliged, at the expense of the departments and the communities, to set up guard services at important points, such as bridges, tunnels, works of art, telephone lines, munitions depots, and areas surrounding aviation fields.

The accompanying note furnishes some examples of the guard services which have been imposed upon Frenchmen in this way, services which before this were assumed by the German Army and which normally fall to the latter, since it is a question of participating in watches or of safe-guarding the German Army against risks arising from the state of war existing between Germany and Great Britain."

The occupying authorities, in face of the resistance which they encountered, were anxious that their orders regarding the requisitions of labour should be obeyed. The measures which they took to this end are just as illegal as the measures taken for the requisition itself. The National Socialist authorities in occupied France proceeded by legislative means. They promulgated ordinances by which sentence of death could be pronounced against persons disobeying requisition orders.

I submit two of these ordinances to the Tribunal as evidence. The first was given in the early months of the occupation, 10th October, 1940. It was published in the "Verordnungsblatt" of France on 17th October, 1940, Page 108.submit it to the Tribunal as Exhibit RF 24, and I read it:

"Ordinance relative to protection against acts of sabotage:

By virtue of the powers which have been conferred upon me by the Fuehrer and Supreme Commander of the Armed Forces, I decree the following:

"(1) Whoever intentionally does not fulfil or fulfils inadequately the tasks of supervision which are conferred upon him by the Chief of the Military Administration in France, or by a service undertaken by the latter, shall be condemned to death."

I will read paragraph 3:

"In less serious cases of infringements mentioned in paragraphs 1 and 2 of the present ordinance and in case of neglect, the offenders may be punished by solitary confinement with hard labour or imprisonment."

The second ordinance of the Military Commander in France to which I refer is dated 31st January, 1942. It was published in the "Verordnungsblatt" of France of 3rd February, 1942, Page 338.submit it to the Tribunal as Exhibit RF 25, and I read:

"Ordinance of 31st January, 1942, concerning the requisitioning of service and requisitioning in kind.

By virtue of the plenary powers which have been conferred on me by the Fuehrer and Supreme Commander of the Armed Forces, I order the following:

(1) Anyone who does not carry out these services or the requisitions in kind which are imposed upon him by the Military Commander

in France or by an authority designated by him, or who performs them in such a manner that the object of the services or requisitions is not fulfilled, shall be punishable by forced labour, imprisonment, or fine. A fine may be fixed in addition to a penalty of forced labour or imprisonment.

(2) In serious cases the death penalty may be inflicted."

These orders called forth a protest by the French authorities. General Doyen protested on several occasions against the first of them, without his protest having any effect.

I refer again to his letter of the 25th May, 1941, which I have just submitted to the Tribunal as Exhibit RF 23, and I read on page of the French translation, Page 4 of the German text:

"... I have been asked to make a formal protest to you against such practices and to beg you to intervene so that an immediate end may be put to them.

From the 16th November, in letter No. 7843/AE, I have already protested against the ordinance that was decreed on the 10th October, 1940, by the Chief of the Military Administration in France, which laid down the death penalty for any person failing to carry out, or carrying out inadequately, the guard duties entrusted to him by the occupation authorities. I protested then that this requirement, as well as its penalty, was contrary to the spirit of the Armistice Convention, having as its object to relieve the French population from any participation in the hostilities.

I had limited myself to this protest in principle because at the time no concrete case of guard duties having been imposed had been called to my attention, but it was not possible to accept, as justifying the ordinance in question, the arguments which you proffered in your letter No. 1361 of 6th March. [Page 398] You pointed out in effect that, at Article 43 of The Hague Convention, the occupying power had the authority to legislate, but the authority to which you refer in this same article is subject to two restrictions: There can be legislation only to establish order, and to make public life secure in as far as possible. On the other hand, the ordinances decreed must"—

**THE PRESIDENT:** Is it not enough to show that General Doyen protested? It is not necessary to read all the argument which was put forward on the one side or the other.

**M. HERZOG:** I shall then stop this quotation, Mr. President.

The German ordinances which I have just read to the Tribunal thus contained formal violations of the general principles of the criminal legislation of civilised nations; they were made in contradiction to Article 102 of the Appendix to the Fourth Convention of The Hague and also in contradiction to Article 43, on which they were supposed to be based. They were, therefore, illegal and they were criminal, since they provided death sentences which no International Law or domestic law justifies.

The system of labour requisition furnishes the first example of the criminal character of the methods pursued by the defendants in the execution of their recruiting plan for foreign labour.

The National Socialist authorities then had recourse to a second procedure to give an appearance of legality to the recruiting of foreign workers. They called upon workers who were so-called volunteers. From 1940 on, the occupation authorities opened recruiting offices in all the large cities of the occupied territories. These offices were placed under the control of a special service instituted to this effect within the general staff of the Commanders-in-Chief of the occupation zones.

The Tribunal knows that these services from 1940 to 1942 functioned under the control of the generals. From 1942 on, and, more precisely, from the day when the defendant Sauckel became the Plenipotentiary of Labour they received their orders directly from the latter. General von Falkenhausen, Commander-in-Chief in Belgium and in the North of France, declared in the testimony which I have just read to the Tribunal that, from the summer of 1942 on, he had become the simple intermediary in charge of transmitting the instructions given by Sauckel to the Arbeitseinsatz.

Thus the policy of the German employment offices set up in the occupied areas was carried out on the sole responsibility of the defendant Sauckel from 1942, under the responsibility of the defendant Sauckel and his immediate superior, the Trustee for the Four Year Plan, the defendant Goering. I ask the Tribunal to take note of this.

The task of the employment offices was to organise the recruiting of workers for the factories and workshops set up in Europe by the Todt organisation and by the Wehrmacht, Kriegsmarine, Luftwaffe and other German organisations. It was also their task to obtain for the German munition factories the amount of foreign labour needed. Workers recruited in this way signed a labour contract; thus they had, theoretically, the status of free workers and were apparently volunteers.

The occupation authorities always made a point of the voluntary nature of the recruiting carried out by the employment offices, but the lines taken by their propaganda systematically took no account of what they were actually doing. In fact, the voluntary character of this recruiting was entirely fictitious: the workers of the areas who agreed to sign German labour contracts were subject to physical and moral pressure.

This pressure took several forms: it was sometimes collective and sometimes individual; in all its forms it was heavy enough to deprive the workers who suffered under it of their freedom of choice.

The nullity of contracts entered into under the reign of violence is a fundamental principle of the common law of civilised nations: it is found just as expressly stated in German law as in the laws of the powers represented in the Court or the States occupied by Germany. The German employment offices forced on the foreign workers labour contracts which had no legal significance, because they were tainted with violence. I make this as a definite statement and I will provide the Court with proof of my assertions.

First of all, I will show that the pressure was premeditated by the Germans. The pressure under which the foreign workers suffered was not the result of sporadic action on the part of subordinate authorities. It came from the deliberate intent, which the National Socialist leaders of Germany formulated into precise instructions.

I submit to the Tribunal Document 1183, which is the Exhibit RF 26; this is a directive dated 29th January, 1942, dealing with the recruiting of foreign workers. This directive comes from a section of the Arbeitseinsatz of the Commissariat for the Four Year Plan. It bears the signature of the Section Chief, Dr. Mansfeld, but it places the executive responsibility directly on the defendant Goering, the Trustee for the Four Year Plan. I read this circular:

"Berlin, S.W. 11, 29th January, 1942.

Saarlandstr. 96.

Subject: Increased mobilisation of manpower for the German Reich from the occupied territories and preparations for mobilisation by force.

The labour shortage which was rendered more acute by the draft for the Wehrmacht and, on the other hand, the increased scope of the armament problem in the German Reich, render it necessary that manpower for service in the Reich be recruited from the occupied territories to a much greater extent than heretofore, in order to relieve the shortage of labour.

Therefore, any and all methods must be adopted which make possible the transportation, without exception and delay, for employment in the Reich of manpower in the occupied territories which is unemployed, or which can be replaced for use in Germany after most careful screening."

I read further on Page 2 of the German text:

"This mobilisation shall as heretofore be carried out on a voluntary basis. For this reason the recruiting effort for employment in the German Reich must be strengthened considerably, but, if satisfactory results are to be obtained, the German authorities who are functioning in the occupied territories must be able to exert any pressure necessary to support the voluntary recruiting of labour for employment in Germany.

Accordingly, to the extent that that may be necessary, the regulations in force in the occupied territories in regard to shifting employment, or concerning the ill will of those refusing work, must be tightened. Supplementary regulations concerning distribution of labour must above all insure that older personnel who are exempt will be exchanged for younger personnel, so that the latter may be made available for the Reich. A far-reaching decrease in the amount of relief granted by public welfare must also be effected, in order to induce labourers to accept employment in the Reich. Unemployment relief must be set so low that the amount in comparison with the average wages in the Reich, and the possibilities there for sending remittances home, may serve as an inducement to the workers to accept employment in Germany. When refusal to accept work in the Reich is not justified, the compensation must be reduced to an amount barely enough for subsistence, or even be cancelled. In this case partial withdrawal of ration cards and an assignment to particularly heavy, obligatory labour may be considered."

I here end the quotation, and. I call to the Tribunal's attention that this circular is addressed to all the services responsible for labour in the occupied areas. Its distribution in Western Europe was: the Reich Commissar for the occupied Norwegian Territories, the Reich Commissar for the occupied Dutch territories, the Chief of the Military Administration of Belgium and Northern France, the Chief of the Military Administration of France, the Chief of the Civilian Administration of Luxembourg, the Chief of the Civilian Administration at Metz, and the Chief of the Civilian Administration at Strasbourg.

It is thus proved that a general common plan existed with a view to compelling the workers of the occupied territories to work for Germany.

I have now to show how this plan was put into practice in the different occupation zones. The machinery of pressure which the National Socialist authorities exerted on the foreign workers can be analysed in the following manner: German labour offices organised intense propaganda in favour of the recruitment of foreign workers. This propaganda was intended to deceive the workers of the occupied areas with regard to the material advantage offered them by the German employment courts. It was carried out by the Press, the radio, and by every possible means of publicity.

It was also carried on as a side-line to official administrative duties by secret organisations which had been given the task of enticing foreign workers and thereby exercising illegal pressure.

These measures proved themselves to be insufficient. The occupation authorities then intervened in the social life of the occupied countries: they strove to produce artificial unemployment there, and at the same time they devoted their energies to making living conditions worse for the workers and the unemployed.

In spite of unemployment and the poverty with which they were threatened, the foreign workers showed themselves insensible to German propaganda. This is why the German authorities finally resorted to direct methods of pressure. They exercised pressure on the political authorities of the occupied countries to make them give support to the recruiting campaign. They compelled employers, especially the organisational committees in France, to encourage their workers to accept the labour contracts of the German employment offices. Finally, they took action by way of direct pressure on the workers, and gradually passed from so-called voluntary recruitment to compulsory enrolment.

The fiction of voluntary enrolment was dispelled when the people saw the individual arrests and collective raids of which the workers of the occupied areas rapidly became the victims.

There are innumerable documents capable of providing proof of the facts which I relate. I shall submit the most important of these to the Tribunal.

The documents which bring the proof of the publicity campaigns made in France by the German administration will be submitted to the Tribunal by Mr. Edgar Faure in the course of his brief on Germanisation and Nazification. By way of example I wish to draw upon a document which in the French classification bears the No. RF-516 and which I submit as Exhibit RF 27.

This is a report of the Prefect of the Department of the Nord to the Delegate of the Minister of the Interior in the General Delegation of the French Government in the occupied territories. This report points out that a German publicity car tours through the community of Lille in order to lure French workers to go to Germany. I quote the report:

"Lille, 25th March, 1942. Prefect of the Nord, Prefect of the Lille Region, to the Prefect, Delegate of the Minister of the Interior with the General Delegation of the French Government in the occupied territories.

Subject: German publicity car.

I have the honour of advising you that for some days a publicity car covered with posters urging French workers to sign up and go and work in Germany has been touring in the Lille area, while a loud speaker plays a whole repertoire of discs of French music, among which are featured the 'Marche Lorraine,' and the song 'Marchal, nous voila.'"

This is the end of my quotation.

**THE PRESIDENT:** I think we will adjourn until 2 o'clock.

*(A recess was taken.)*

**M. HERZOG:** Mr. President, your Honours. I wish this morning to show what the official propaganda was which was given out by the German offices in France in order to persuade volunteers to work in Germany. The effect of this official propaganda was reinforced by the clandestine bureaux of recruitment. Offices for clandestine recruiting were organised by the occupation authorities, apart from the administrative services, whose activities they completed. These employments bureaux were directed by German agents who often succeeded in acquiring local accomplices. In France these bureaus extended their ramifications in the non-occupied as well as in the occupied zone. Several documents attest to their existence. The first among them is a report transmitted on 7th March, 1942, by the Vice-President of the Council of Ministers of the de facto Government of Vichy, to the General Delegate for Franco-German Economic Relations. It is Document 654 of the French archives.

This report is drawn up under the seal of Vice-President of the Council Darlan. It bears the signature of an officer of the latter's General Staff, Commander de Fontaine. I file this report as Exhibit RF 28 and I read it:

"Vichy, 7th March, 1942. Your Honour, the General Delegate, I have the honour of transmitting to you in this letter, for your information, a report on the organisation of recruitment in France of workers for the

*General Friedrich Fromm, two sailors, Albert Speer, Grand Admiral Karl Doenitz and Hans Kehrl sharing a joke in 1942.*
Bundesarchiv, Bild 146-1968-036-13 / Ruge, Willi / CC-BY-SA

German industry."

I now go to Page 2:

"26th of February, 1942. Secret note on the organisation of the recruitment in France of workers for German industry. Excellent source: 1.Organisation of the recruitment of workers in France. One of the main organisations for the recruitment of workers in France for Germany was the Mechanical Society of the Seine, whose seat is in Puteaux, Seine, at 8 Quai Nationale, which was also known as A.M.S.

This society was to function under the secret control of the Kommandantur, and of three engineers; one would have the capacity of chief engineer and the other two would be M. Meyer and M. Schronner. In addition to the work which it was to carry out, this society is particularly entrusted with the re-education of workers recruited in France and sent to Germany at the request of German industrial houses on premium payments. The A.M.S. society is assisted in these operations in the occupied zone by three centres of recruiting which function in Paris and are: the centre of Porte De Vincennes, the centre of Courbevoie, 200 Boulevard St. Denis and the centre of Avenue des Tourelles. These centres are also charged to co-operate with the operations of recruitment in the non-occupied zone. For this zone, the two principal centres are in Marseilles and Toulouse. A third centre will be at Tarbes.

(a) The centre at Marseilles is entrusted with the recruitment in the Mediterranean zone, under the direction of M. Meyer, who is mentioned above. The address of this engineer is not known, but one can get information about him in No. 24 Avenue Kleber, Paris, at the Militarbefehlshaber's.

At Marseilles the A.M.S. office is situated at 85 Rue de Silvabelle. In his task M. Meyer is assisted by M. Ringo, residing in Madrague-Ville, 5 bis Boulevard Bernabo, near the slaughter house."

I here end my quotation. I submit to the Tribunal the correspondence exchanged between the months of December, 1941, and January, 1942, between the Prefect of the Alpes Maritimes and the authorities of the Vichy Government. This is Document 528,, which I file with the Tribunal as Exhibit RF 29. This correspondence emphasises the activity of the German agents in the clandestine recruiting, and particularly of M. Meyer, to whom the report of Commander Fontaine, which I just read, applies. I quote first the letter of the 10th December, 1941, in which the Prefect of the Alpes Maritimes confirmed the report which he had previously made on this question. It is the letter which is on the 5th page of the French text and the 7th page of the German text:

"Nice, 10th December, 1941: The State Counsellor, Prefect of the Alpes Maritimes, to his Honour, the State Secretary of the Interior, General Secretariat of the Police Directorate for Home and Foreign Police. Object: The activity of foreign agents, attending to the enticing away of specialised workers.

Reference: Your telegrams 12,402, and 12,426, of 28th November, 1941. My reports 955 and 986 of 24th November, 1941, and the 6th December, 1941. In my reports referred to I pointed out to you the activity of recruiting agents, who sought to have specialised workers discharged for the benefit of Germany.

I have the honour of giving you, below, some additional information gathered on this subject.

The German engineer Meyer and the French subject, M. Bentz, stopped on the 1st December, 1941, at the Hotel Splendid in Nice, coming from Marseilles."

Now, I go to the third paragraph before the end:

"I permit myself to draw your attention particularly to the fact that in Paris they hired workers to be sent to Germany."

Here I end the quotation.

These documents attest to the activity which the clandestine recruiting offices developed. I am not satisfied merely to point out their existence. I wish to show that these offices functioned under the initiative of the official administration and of the German Office for Labour.

The proof is furnished by a statement which the defendant Sauckel made on the first of March 1944, during the 54th conference of the central office for the Four Year Plan. The stenographic transcript of these conferences has been found. It forms Document R-124, to which my American colleagues have already referred. I submit it again to the Tribunal as Exhibit RF 30, and

I shall read from an extract of the transcript of the session of the 1st March, 1944. This is Exhibit RF 30, in the French text, Page 2, second paragraph; in the German text, Pages 1770 and 1771. I quote the page numbers which are at the bottom and on the right of the German original. I read:

"The most abominable thing done by my adversaries"—this is a declaration of the defendant Sauckel—"is that they pretend that no executive measure has been foreseen in these sectors to recruit in a rational manner the French, the Belgians, and the Italians, and to send them to work. I therefore had begun to employ and train a whole group of French male and female agents who, for adequate remuneration, just as it was done in older times in Shanghai, would hunt for men, using liquor and persuasion...."

**THE PRESIDENT:** I am told that this has been read before by the Prosecutor of the United States.

**M. HERZOG:** I will not insist on it, Mr. President. I go on:

The propaganda of the official offices and that of the clandestine recruiting offices proved to be inefficacious. The National Socialist authorities then had to resort to methods of economic pressure. They tried to give to the workers, who were to go to Germany, the hope of material advantages. I cite in this respect an ordinance of the General Military Commandant in Belgium and in the North of France, which I submit to the Tribunal. It is an ordinance of 20th July, 1942, which appeared in the "Verordnungsblatt" of Belgium. It exempts from tax Belgian workers who work in German factories. I submit it to the Tribunal as Exhibit RF 31.

On the other hand, the occupation authorities sought to lower the living standard of workers who remained in the occupied territories. I said that they had made poverty a factor in their recruiting policy. I am going to prove it by showing how they went about creating artificial unemployment in the occupation zones and deteriorating the material situation of the unemployed.

I wish to recall that the German authorities also practised a policy of freezing salaries. This measure aided the recruiting campaign for labour to go to Germany and had also an economic bearing, and I would like to refer the Tribunal to the explanations which will be given it on this point by M. Gerthoffer.

Unemployment was produced by two complementary measures:

The first was the regulation of the legal length of work;

The second was the concentration and, if need be, the closing of industrial enterprises.

From 1940 the local Feldkommandanten concerned themselves with increasing the duration of work in their administrative zones. In France, initiative taken by the local authorities brought about reactions. The problem became general and was solved on a national plane. Long negotiations were imposed on the representatives of the pseudo-Government of Vichy.

Finally an ordinance of 22nd April, 1942, from the military command in France, reserved for the occupation authorities the right of fixing the duration of work in industrial enterprises. This ordinance appeared in their Verordnungsblatt for France, 1942. I submit it to the Tribunal as Exhibit RF 32 and I quote the first paragraph. First part:

"For establishments and enterprises of all kinds, a minimum of working hours may be imposed. This minimum of the length of work will be decreed for a whole economic region, or for certain economic fields, or for individual enterprises."

In Belgium the length of work was fixed by an ordinance, by a directive, on the 6th October, 1942, which appeared in the "Verordnungsblatt" of Belgium. I submit this ordinance to the Tribunal as Exhibit RF 33. The regulation of the duration of work had not released a sufficient number of workers for the German factories; that is why the National Socialist authorities used a second method: under the pretext of rationalising production, they brought about a concentration of industrial and commercial enterprises, certain of which were closed at their instigation.

I cite in this relation the provisions which were taken or imposed by the Germans in France, in Belgium and in Holland. In France I would like to refer to two texts:

The first is the law of the Vichy Government of 17th December, 1941, which I submit to the Tribunal as Exhibit RF 34;

The second text to which I wish to draw the attention of the Tribunal is the ordinance of 25th February, 1942, issued by the Military Commandant in France. This ordinance appeared in the "Verordnungsblatt des Militarbefehlshabers" in France. I shall read from it to the Tribunal, because this ordinance seems particularly important, as the principle of compulsorily closing certain French enterprises is established by a legislative text of the occupying power. I shall read the first and second paragraphs. The first paragraph:

"If the economic situation, notably the use of raw materials and secondary materials requires it, establishments and economic enterprises may be partly or completely closed."

Second paragraph:

"The closing of these enterprises will be pronounced by the Feldkommandantur by means of a written notification addressed to the establishment or to the industrial enterprise."

**THE PRESIDENT:** That was Exhibit RF 35, was it not?

**M. HERZOG:** Yes, Mr. President.

In Belgium I refer to the ordinance of the Military Commandant, 30th March and 3rd October, 1942, which appeared in the "Verordnungsblatt" in Belgium. I submit to the Tribunal the ordinance of 30th March as Exhibit RF 36.

In Holland the regulating provisions of the occupying authorities were more stringent than elsewhere. I present an ordinance of the Reich Commissar for the territories of occupied Holland, 15th March, 1943.submit it to the Tribunal as Exhibit RF 37.

This ordinance presents a double interest: First it offers precise information which emphasises the method with which the German services executed their recruiting plan. It constitutes, on the other hand, the first document which I shall submit to the Tribunal, accusing the defendant Seyss- Inquart. The policy of Sauckel was carried out in Holland with the collaboration of Reich Commissar Seyss-Inquart. The ordinances regarding compulsory labour in Holland were all issued at the responsibility of Seyss-Inquart, whether they bear, directly or not, his signature. I ask the Tribunal to note this.

The increase of the legal length of work and the closing of industrial enterprises deprived thousands of workers of their jobs. The defendants did not hesitate to use material constraint to incite the unemployed to work on behalf of Germany. They threatened the unemployed that they would do away with their unemployment compensation. This threat was made on several occasions by the local Feldkommandants in Occupied France. I find proof in the protest made 8th March, 1941, by General Doyen, representing the French authorities with the German armistice commission. The document is 282, which I submit to the Tribunal as Exhibit RF 38.

I read the first page, third paragraph of the letter:

"Moreover, the occupation authorities foresee that the workers who refuse the work offered them will see their right to unemployment compensation denied, and may be prosecuted by the war tribunal for sabotage of Franco-German collaboration."

Far from disavowing the initiative of their local authorities, the central office for labour gave them instructions to continue this policy. The proof is furnished by the directive of Dr. Mansfeld, dated 29th January, 1942, which I have just submitted to the Tribunal as Exhibit RF 26, in which instructions were given that the discontinuation of unemployment compensation should be utilised as a means of pressure against workers in foreign countries. The directive of Dr. Mansfeld shows that the blackmail by the National Socialist leaders was exercised not only over the control of unemployment compensation, but also in the issuing of ration cards.

Moreover, the defendants tried to force the inhabitants of the occupied territories to leave for Germany by increasing their difficulties in finding food. The proof of this desire is given in the transcript of the session of 1st March, 1944, of the Conference of the Four Year Plan. This document I referred to a short time ago as Exhibit RF 30. This is a passage which has not yet been read, which the Tribunal will please permit me to read. It is on Page 5 of the French translation.

**THE PRESIDENT:** Exhibit RF 30?

**M. HERZOG:** Yes, Pages 1814, 1815 and 1816 of the German text. The page numbers are at the bottom and on the right. I read on top of Page 5 of the French text. It should be Milch. It is General Milch.

"Milch: 'Would not the following method be better? The German administration should concern itself with the feeding of Italians and say to them: " No one shall receive food unless he works in a protected factory or leaves for Germany.'"

Sauckel: 'It is true that the French workman in France is better fed than the German workman. The Italian workman, even if he does not work at all, is better fed in the part of Italy which we occupy than if he worked in Germany.'"

I end the quotation here.

I have shown the Tribunal that these measures were measures of an economic order—economic-social—which the National Socialist authorities took, to force workers in the occupied territory to accept labour contracts offered by the German authorities.

This indirect duress was strengthened by direct pressure which was simultaneously put on the local governments and the employers and on the workers themselves.

The National Socialist leaders knew that their recruiting policy could be facilitated by the local authorities. That is why they tried to make the pseudo-governments of the occupied territories guarantee or endorse the fiction of voluntary enrolments. I submit to the Tribunal an example of the pressure which the German Services placed on the Vichy Government for that purpose. They first arranged that the State Secretariat of Labour should issue a directive to all Prefects. It is the directive of 29th March, 1941. The German authorities were not satisfied with this directive; they were conscious of the illegality of their recruiting methods and they wished to justify them by an agreement with the de facto government of France. They required that this agreement be made known by public statement. The negotiations were carried out for this purpose in 1941 and 1942. The violence of the German pressure is substantiated by the letters concerning it addressed by Dr. Michel of the Administrative Staff to the General Delegate for Franco-German Economic Relations.

I refer especially to his letters of 3rd March, 1942, and 15th May, 1942, which constitute Exhibits RF 39 and 40. I read first to the Tribunal the letter of 15th May, which is RF 40:

"Paris, 15th May, 1942.

Purpose: The Recruiting of French Labour for Germany.

As the result of the conversations of 24th January, 1942, and after repeated appeals, the first draft of declarations of the French Government concerning recruiting was presented on the 27th; on the German side it was accepted with slight modifications and in written form on 3rd March, on the condition that attention should be directed, at the time of its transmission to the organisational committees, to the fact that the French Government approved expressly the acceptance of labour in Germany.

On 19th March it was recalled that a draft for a memorandum to the organisation committees should be submitted. The draft was afterwards submitted on 27th March. On the 30th March a proposal for modification was delivered to M. Terray, who should take it up with

M. Bichelonne."

I omit the two following paragraphs, and I will read the last paragraph:

"Although no reason appears which explains the unaccustomed and incomprehensible delay, the draft was not presented until this day. More than two months having passed since the first request for the presentation of the memorandum, it is requested that this document be edited anew and presented on 19th May.

For the Military Commandant, Chief of the Administrative Staff.

Signed: Michel."

The Tribunal undoubtedly has observed that Dr. Michel demanded not only the circulation of a public declaration, but also required that the text of this statement be officially transmitted to the organisational committees. The pressure which occupation authorities put upon French industrial enterprises, to stimulate them to facilitate the departure of their workers to Germany, was brought about in fact through the medium of the organisational committees. The German offices for labour acted directly upon the organisational committees. They ordered conferences, in the course of which they dictated their will to the leaders of these committees. They also required that the organisational committees be informed of all the measures which the French authorities were led to take.

The committees might then be associated with these measures in the interests of German policy. The correspondence of Dr. Michel offers numerous examples of the constant efforts of the German authorities to act upon the organisational committees.

I have just offered an example of this to the Tribunal in the document which I read. I now offer another one. In 1941 the Germans requested especially that circulars, especially the directive of 29th March, 1942, addressed to the Prefects, regarding the recruiting of labourers for Germany, should be officially transmitted to the organisational committees. The occupation authorities obtained satisfaction through a circular of 25th April, which I submit to the Tribunal as Exhibit RF 41.

But the terms of this circular did not receive the approval of the German authorities, and on 28th May, 1941, Dr. Michel protested in violent terms to the General Delegate for Franco-German Economic Relations. This protest constitutes Document 522 in the French Archives. I submit it to the Tribunal as Exhibit RF 42, and I shall read:

"Paris, 28th May, 1941.

Purpose: Recruiting of Workers for Germany.

Reference: Your letter No. 192 of 29th April, 1941.

From your explanations I gather that even before my letter of the 23rd April was received, a circular for the organisational committees had been drafted and sent on 25th April.

This circular, nevertheless, does not seem to me adequate to support, in an efficacious manner, the recruiting of workers carried out by Germany. That is why I consider that it is necessary that, in another directive, attention may be drawn to the points which were particularly mentioned by me on 23rd April, and request that you submit to me as soon as possible the appropriate draft.

On the German side an impressive contribution toward the creating of a favourable atmosphere has been made by means of the intended release of an additional large number of prisoners of war, which was considered by you at the time of our conversation of 24th May as a necessary condition for the success of a reinforced recruiting of workers for Germany.

I therefore am probably not wrong in expecting that you will send to the economic organisations a communication so designed that the attitude of waiting, maintained by French economy up to now, will develop also, in the field of the release of labour, into a constructive co-operation. I then expect that you will submit to me your proposals with all possible promptness."

And, finally, the German Services placed direct pressure upon the workers themselves.

**THE PRESIDENT:** Are you reading from the document now?

**M. HERZOG:** No. I am resuming the text of the brief.

Moral pressure at first, the "operation de la releve" (prisoner exchange plan), tried in France in the Spring of 1942, is characteristic. The occupation authorities promised to compensate for the sending of French workers to Germany by a liberation of prisoners of war. The return of a prisoner was to take place upon the departure of a worker. This promise was fallacious, and reality was quite different.

I quote in this connection the report on compulsory labour and the deportation of workers, which I submitted this morning to the Tribunal as Exhibit RF 42.

I quote Page 51, both in the French original and in the German translation. In the French original it is the third paragraph of Page 51 and in the German translation the first paragraph:

"If the Press, inspired by the occupying power, pretends in its commentaries to applaud the replacement plan of one prisoner for one worker, it is undoubtedly done upon order and based on calculation. Also this is the case, it seems, because until 20th June, 1942, two days before the speech cited before"—it was a speech of the chief of the de facto government of France—"it was indeed this proportion which the Germans Michel and Ritter had pretended to accept in their reports to the French administrative services.

The proportion, in fact, of one to five, appears to have been a last minute surprise of which the Press never spoke."

Here I end my quotation.

The pressure of which foreign workers were the victims was also a material pressure. I said that the fiction of voluntary enrolment could not hold water in view of the arrests. I wish to submit a document to the Tribunal which furnished a characteristic example of the German mentality and of the methods utilised by the National Socialist administrations. This is a document which in the French Archives is No. 527, which I submit to the Tribunal as Exhibit RF 43. This is a letter from the delegate of the Reich Labour Minister in the French department of Pas de Calais. This official enjoins a young French workman to depart for Germany as a free agent, under threat of unfavourable consequences. I read the document; this is Exhibit RF 43, third page:

"Sir:

The 26th of March last, in Marquise, I ordered, you to go to work in Germany in your profession. You were to leave with the convoy of the 1st of April for Germany. You took no notice of this summons. I warn you that you must present yourself, furnished with your baggage, next Monday, 28th April, before 19.00 hours, at 51, Rue de la Pomme d'Or in Calais. I call your attention to the fact that you leave for Germany as a free worker, that you will work there under the same conditions, and that you will earn there the same wages as German workers.

In the event of your not presenting yourself, I must tell you that unfavourable consequences may very well follow.

Delegate for the Labour Ministry of the Reich:

Signed: Hannerann."

The proof of the constraint which the German authorities exercised on the workers of the occupied territories, to bring about their allegedly voluntary enrolment, may be continued. The National Socialist authorities did not merely impose labour contracts tainted with violence on foreign workers. They themselves deliberately failed to honour these contracts.

I find proof of this in the fact that they unilaterally prolonged the duration of the enrolments made by foreign workers. This proof is based on several documents. Some ordinances were issued by the defendant Goering in his capacity as Delegate for the Four Year Plan, others by the defendant Sauckel.

I now call the attention of the Tribunal to an order of Sauckel's, dated 22nd March, 1943, which I submit to the Tribunal as Exhibit RF 44. It is an extract from the volume of decrees, Vol. V, Page 203:

"Extension of work contracts, fixed for a period of time, of foreign workers, who during the time of their contract have absented themselves from their work without proper excuse.

The General Plenipotentiary for Employment of Labour decrees: 'The regular carrying out of the clauses of a contract for a fixed period of time, concluded by a foreign worker, necessitates that the worker should put all his energy at the disposal of the enterprise for the whole duration of the contract.

Nevertheless, it happens that foreign workers, as the result of slackness, delay in their return to work from visits to their homes'—and I draw the Tribunal's attention to the following words—'serving of prison terms, internment in a camp of correction ..."

**THE PRESIDENT:** Will you read that again?

M. HERZOG:

"The regular carrying out of the clauses of a contract for a fixed period of time concluded by a foreign worker, necessitates that the worker should put all his energy at the disposal of the enterprise for the whole duration of the contract. Nevertheless, it happens that foreign workers as a result of idleness, delay in their return to work from visits to their homes, serving of prison terms, internment in a camp of correction, or for other reasons, remain absent from their work without just cause, for a longer or shorter period of time. In such cases the foreign workers cannot be authorised to return to their country when the period of time, for which they agreed to work voluntarily in Germany, has elapsed.

Such a procedure would not correspond to the spirit of a work contract for a fixed period of time, whose object is not only the presence of the foreign worker, but also the work accomplished by him."

Kept by force in the German factories which they had entered under force, the foreign workers were neither voluntary nor free workers. The expose of the methods of German recruiting will suffice to show the Tribunal the fictitious character of the voluntary enrolment, on which it was supposed to be based. The foreign workers who agreed to work in the factories of the National Socialist war industry did not act through free will. Their number, however, remained limited. The workers of the occupied territories had the physical courage, the ethical courage, to resist German pressure. This is proved in an admission of the defendant Sauckel, which I take from the minutes of the meeting of 3rd March, 1944, of the conference of the Four Year Plan.

This is from an extract which has already been read by my American colleague, Mr. Dodd, so I will not read it again to the Tribunal. I merely wish to recall that the defendant Sauckel admitted that, out of five million foreign workers who came to Germany, there were not even two hundred thousand who came voluntarily. The resistance of the foreign workers surprised the defendant Sauckel as much as it irritated him. One day he expressed his surprise to a German general, who replied:

"Our difficulties come from the fact that you address yourself to patriots who do not share our ideals."

Indeed, only force could constrain the patriots of the occupied territories to work on behalf of the enemy. The National Socialist authorities resorted to force.

The Germans had, from the first, the possibility of imposing their policy of force on that kind of labour whose particular status guaranteed recruitment and apparent submission: the prisoners of war.

From 1940 on, the German military authorities organised labour Commandos in prison camps. They constantly increased the importance of these Commandos, who were put at the disposal of agricultural economy and the war industry.

The importance of the work required from war prisoners is substantiated by the Report on Forced Labour and the Deportation of Workers which I have filed with the Tribunal as Exhibit RF 22. We find on Page 68 of the French and German texts the following estimates:

There were, at the end of 1942, 1,036,319 French prisoners of war in Germany, 987,687 had been assigned to the work Commandos. Only the surplus, that is, 48,632 prisoners, remained unemployed.

The utilisation of prisoners of war in German factories does not constitute a distinct phenomenon which can be disassociated from the general plan for the recruiting of foreign workers; it is, on the contrary, an integral part of this plan.

The National Socialists have always considered that the obligation to work applied as much to war prisoners as to the civilian workers of the occupied territories. They have on many occasions expressed such a belief. I refer especially to two documents.

The first is the decree of the appointment of the defendant Sauckel, which I have filed with the Tribunal at the beginning of my explanatory remarks.

The second document to which I wish to draw the attention of the Tribunal is the tenth decree of Sauckel, which I submitted sometime ago as Exhibit RF 17. This decree formulates the principle of the obligation to work and applies to war prisoners, according to the terms of its Article 8.

Finally, Sauckel had, in another document, affirmed that the prisoners of war were to be subject to work to the same degree as civilian workers. This is found in the letter which he wrote to the defendant Rosenberg on 24th April, 1942, some days after his appointment, to explain his project to the latter. This is Document 016-PS, which my American colleague, Mr. Dodd, has already submitted to the Tribunal. I present it as Exhibit RF 45. I shall not read from it, but I call to mind that on Page 11 of the German text the problem of compulsory labour is treated in the general heading, entitled: "Prisoners of War and Foreign Workers."

These documents bring a double proof to the Tribunal. First of all, they reveal the willingness of the National Socialists to force prisoners to work on behalf of the German war economy, within the general frame of their recruiting policy. In the second place, these documents establish that the utilisation of prisoners of war was not undertaken only by military authorities; this utilisation was ordered and systematised by a civilian organisation, that of the Arbeitseinsatz. As well as the responsibility of the defendants Sauckel and Keitel, it entails also that of the German leaders who conducted the labour policy: the defendant Sauckel, the defendant Speer, and the defendant Goering.

The Tribunal knows that International Law regulates the conditions under which prisoners of war may be forced to work. The Hague Conventions formulated rules which were clarified by the Geneva Convention in Articles 27, 31 and 32:

> "ARTICLE 27:—Belligerents may use as workers healthy war prisoners, according to their rank and their attitudes, with the exception of officers and assimilated ranks. Nevertheless, if officers, or those of

assimilated rank, ask for suitable work, it will be procured for them as far as possible. The non-commissioned officers who are war prisoners can be forced to work as supervisors only if they expressly request a remunerative occupation.

ARTICLE 31:—The work furnished by the prisoners of war—"

**THE PRESIDENT:** I think we will take judicial notice of these Articles.

**M. HERZOG:** These rules of International Law determine positively the legal powers of the nation having prisoners of war in its custody. It is legal to force prisoners of war to work during the duration of their captivity, but this includes three legal limits:

(1) It is forbidden to require non-commissioned officers, who are prisoners, to work, unless they have expressly requested to do so.

(2) War prisoners must not be used for work which is dangerous.

(3) Prisoners must not be associated with the enemy war effort.

The National Socialist authorities systematically neglected these imperative provisions; they have exercised violent constraint on non-commissioned officers held in captivity, to force them to join labour crews. They have integrated war prisoners as workers in their factories and in the work yards, without considering the nature of the work imposed upon them. The utilisation of war prisoners by National Socialist Germany took place under illegal and criminal conditions. This I declare, and I wish to prove this to the Tribunal.

**THE PRESIDENT:** We will take a recess for 10 minutes.

*(A recess was taken.)*

**M. HERZOG:** Mr. President, your Honours.

Dating from 1941, the Germans exercised direct pressure on non-commissioned officers to force them to engage in productive work for the Reich war economy. This pressure, after the failure of propaganda methods, took the form of reprisals. Non- commissioned officers who refused were the object of ill- treatment; they were sent to special camps, such as Coberczyn where they were subject to a disciplinary regime. Some incurred penal sentences because of their refusal to work. I file, as proof, the report of the Ministry of Prisoners, Deportees, and Refugees of the French Government, Document UK-78-2, which is, in my document book, RF 46. The document is in a white file. I shall read from Page 18 of the French original, Page 10 of the German translation, Page 18, at the bottom of the page:

"Work of the Non-Commissioned Officers.

On this subject the Geneva Convention was explicit: non-commissioned officers who are war prisoners cannot be subjected to work as supervisors, unless they make an express request for a remunerative occupation.

In conformity with this article a certain number of non-commissioned officers refused to work from the beginning of their captivity. The strength of imprisoned non-commissioned officers was, at the end of 1940, about 130,000, and represented later a very important source of labour for the Reich. The German authorities tried, therefore, by every means, to induce to work the greatest possible number of those refusing. To this effect, during the last months of 1941, the non-commissioned officers who did not volunteer for the work were, in most camps, subjected to an alternating regime. For a few days they were subjected to punishments such as the diminution of food rations, doing without beds, the obligation to undergo physical exercises for a number of hours, and particularly the 'pelote' (punishment drill). During another period they were promised work, in conformity with their wishes, and other material advantages, for example, special regulations of insurance, extra letter provisions and higher wages. These methods led a certain number of non-commissioned officers to accept work. The non-commissioned officers who persisted in their refusal to work, were subjected to a very severe disciplinary regime and to arduous physical exercises."

The National Socialist military authorities utilised the prisoners of war for dangerous work. The French, British, Belgian and Dutch prisoners were used to transport munitions, to load bombs or planes, to repair aviation camps, and to construct fortifications. The proof of the use of prisoners of war for the transportation of munitions and for the loading of bombs on planes, is furnished by the affidavits of repatriated French prisoners of war. These affidavits have been assembled in the report of the Ministry of Prisoners, which I have just quoted, and which I shall quote again.

I now quote Page 27 of the French document, Page 14 of the German translation. It is the same document from which I have just quoted, Exhibit RF 46, Page 27:

"(b) The requisition of prisoners for the construction of fortifications and for the transport of munitions, occurs very often in the close vicinity of the line of fire.

The war prisoners, Command 274 of Stalag 2-B, complained, December, 1944, of being employed on Sundays in the construction of anti-tank trenches.

On 2nd February, 1945, the prisoners of Stalag 2-B, evacuated before the advance of the Russian Army, worked, as soon as they arrived at Sassnity, at fortification works and anti-tank works, in particular around the city.

After falling back from Stalag 3-B, the war prisoners were engaged, to the end of April, in doing ditch work, digging trenches, and in transporting aviation bombs.

Kommando 553 at Lebus was obliged to carry out work in the front lines under the fire of Russian artillery.

Numerous comrades, drawn back at Furstenwalde, were employed in loading bombs on German bombers.

In spite of their protests to the International Committee of the Red Cross in Geneva and to the colonel commanding Stalag 3-B, about billeting in barns, very bad hygiene and insufficient food, the latter answered that he was obeying superior orders of the O.K.W., ordering the prisoners to dig trenches."

The National Socialist leaders, for that matter, admitted that they used French and British prisoners of war for military work on aerodromes exposed to allied bombardment.

I offer in proof two notes, the first addressed by the O.K.H. to the War Prisoners Section of the Wehrmacht, and the second by Wilhelmstrasse to the German representative at the Wiesbaden Armistice Commission.

The memorandum of the O.K.H., dated 7th October, 1940, constitutes Document 549. I submit it to the Tribunal as Exhibit RF 47, and I read it in full:

"The protest of the French delegation shall be considered unfounded. The lodging of war prisoners in camps situated in the vicinity of aviation fields is not in contradiction to the rules of the rights of nations.

According to Articles 9 and 4 of the Convention on the Treatment of War Prisoners—of 27th July, 1929—no prisoners of war shall be exposed to the fire of a combat zone. Combat zones in this sense must be understood as the space in which normally a battle between two armies is carried on, thus extending to a distance of about 20 kilometres from the advance line. On the other hand it is possible that the areas exposed to aerial attacks do not belong to combat zones. At this period of air war there no longer exists any sure shelter. The fact of using war prisoners for the construction of a camp and for the repairing of destroyed runways does not seem to lend itself to any controversy.

According to Article 31 of the Convention quoted here above, war prisoners must not be used in works directly related to war activity. The construction of shelters, houses, and camps is not directly a war act. It is recognised that war prisoners may be employed in the construction of roads. Accordingly their utilisation for the reconstruction of aviation camps that have been destroyed is permissible: on the roads, trucks, tanks, ammunition cars, etc. are driven, and on the aviation fields there are planes. It is all the same.

On the other hand, it would be illegal to use war prisoners in loading bombs, munitions, etc. on bombers. Here a work directly related to war activity would be involved.

By reason of the juridical situation expounded here above, the O.K.H. has rejected the idea of withdrawing French prisoners of war employed in work in the aviation camps."

I draw the attention of the Tribunal to this document. It emphasises the ill faith of the leaders of National Socialist Germany, which was two-fold: In the first place, the note of 7th October, 1940, which I have read, acknowledges that it is forbidden by International Law to use prisoners of war for the loading of bombs and ammunition on bombers. But I have just brought proof to the Tribunal that the French prisoners of war were used for this purpose. In the second place, the note of the O.K.H. contests the dangerous character of the work carried out on the aviation fields.

Now, the note of Wilhelmstrasse, to which I shall now refer, and which I submit to the Tribunal as Exhibit RF 48—this note recognises, on the contrary, that prisoners submitted to work on an aviation field incur grave danger because of the military purpose of this work.

I will read to the Tribunal a note of the German Foreign Office dated 14th February, 1941, Exhibit RF 48:

> "Article 87 of the Agreement of 1929 on Prisoners of War provides that, in case of difference of opinion on the subject of the interpretation of the Agreement, the protecting powers shall offer their services to settle the dispute. To accomplish this, any protecting power may propose a meeting of representatives of the belligerent powers. In the relation between Germany and France, protecting powers no longer exist. France herself assumes the responsibilities of a protecting power in questions on prisoners of war."

I shall pass on from this quotation to Page 2 of the same document:

> "As to the point in dispute, it is well to call attention to the following:
>
> The French conception, according to which prisoners of war may not be quartered near air fields and may not be employed in repairing plane runways, cannot be based on the exact content of Articles 9 and 31; but, on the other hand, it is certain that French prisoners of war quartered and employed under these conditions are in a particularly dangerous situation, because the air fields in occupied territories are used exclusively for German military purposes and thus constitute a special objective for enemy aerial attacks.
>
> The American Embassy in Berlin has likewise made a protest against a similar use of British prisoners of war in Germany. Thus far no answer has been made, because a rejection of this protest might result in German prisoners being employed in similar work in England."

The utilisation of war prisoners for the construction of fortifications is substantiated by Document 828-PS, which I file with the Tribunal as Exhibit RF 49. It is a letter of 29th September, 1944, addressed by the Chief of the First Army Corps to the O.K.W., to give an account of work on fortifications accomplished by eighty Belgian prisoners of war. I quote:

> "According to the teletype referred to, it is reported that in the territory of Stalag 1-A, Stablack, Einsatzbereich 2-213, Tilsit-Loten, near Ragnitz, there are forty Belgian prisoners of war, and in Lindbach, near Neusiedel, forty Belgian prisoners of war who were employed in fortification labour."

There remains the task of proving that Allied prisoners, forced to work in Reich armament factories, were associated with the enemy war effort. To this end I first offer Document 1206-PS. This document is a memorandum dated 11th November, 1941. It is a resumé of a report made 7th November, 1941, to the Aviation Minister by the Reichsmarshal. The document, consequently, establishes the direct responsibility of the defendant Goering. The use of Russian war prisoners is treated in a general way in this document, but it deals also with the use of war prisoners of Western European countries. I submit this document to the Tribunal as Exhibit RF 50, and I read:

"Berlin, 11th November, 1941.

Notes on statements made by the Reichsmarshal in a meeting of 7th November, 1941, in the Reich Ministry of Air.

Subject: Employment of Russian labour in the war economy."

**THE PRESIDENT:** Has that already been put in by the United States?

**M. HERZOG:** Yes.

**THE PRESIDENT:** Then perhaps you could summarise it.

**M. HERZOG:** I think, Mr. President, that it was presented by the United States Prosecution. I shall, therefore, simply quote an extract, the fifth and sixth paragraphs of the first page, concerning the employment of French and Belgian war prisoners as individuals in the economy of armament. This use of war prisoners in the Reich munitions factories corresponded to a common plan. It is the result of a systematic policy. The administrative offices for labour deliberately assigned to armament factories all war prisoners who seemed capable of carrying out specialised work. I quote, in this connection, Document 3005-PS. It is a directive addressed, in 1941, by the Ministry of Labour to the Directors of Personnel Procurement concerning the respective use of French and Russian prisoners of war. The document has been submitted and commented upon by my American colleague, Mr. Dodd, shall, therefore, not read it. I simply point out that this circular deals with the employment of all French war prisoners in the armament factories of the Reich.

After the capitulation of Italy, Italian soldiers who had fallen into the hands of the Germans—they were not called prisoners of war, but rather "military internees"—were forced to work. I offer in this connection a directive of the defendant Bormann, of 28th September, 1943, Document 657- PS, which I submit to the Tribunal as Exhibit RV 52.

The Italian military internees are placed in three categories: some ask to continue the struggle on the side of the German Army; others desire to keep a neutral attitude; others have turned their arms against their former allies. The military internees of the second and third categories must, in the terms of the circular, be forced to work. I read:

"Circular No. 55/43 G.R.S., Top secret. Concerns the treatment and putting to work of Italian military internees.

The O.K.W., in connection with the General Plenipotentiary for the Employment of Labour, has regulated the treatment and the putting to work of Italian military internees. The most important general lines of the ordinances of the O.K.W. are the following."

I shall omit the rest of the first page and proceed to Page 2 of the French translation:

"The Italian internees who, when investigated, do not declare themselves ready to continue the struggle under German command, are put at the disposal of the General Plenipotentiary for the Employment of Labour who has already given the necessary instructions for their employment, to the Chiefs of the Regional Labour Offices.

It is to be noted that Italian military internees must not be utilised together with the British and American prisoners of war."

The prisoners of war offered passive resistance to German force. The National Socialist authorities intervened again and again, to attempt to increase their output. I refer to Document 233-PS, which I file with the Tribunal as Exhibit RF 53. It is a directive of the O.K.W. of 17th October, 1944. The purpose is to point out to the war prisoner bureaux, measures capable of increasing the productivity of the prisoners. I read from the document:

"Subject: Treatment of War Prisoners—Increase in Production.

The measures taken until now, in regard to the treatment of war prisoners and the increasing of their productivity, have not given the results that had been hoped for. The offices of the Party, and those of economy, continually complain of the poor labour output of all the war prisoners. Therefore the following directives for prisoners of war are made known, in agreement with all interested offices of the Party and State. Accordingly, all guard companies and their auxiliaries are to be given detailed instructions.

Collaboration with the bearers of sovereignty of the N.S.D.A.P. The co-operation of all officers in charge of war prisoners with the bearers of sovereignty of the Party must be strengthened to an even greater extent. To this end the commanders of the war-prisoner camps shall immediately detail, for all the Kreise in their command, an energetic officer acquainted with all questions concerning prisoners of war, to act as liaison officer to the Kreisleiter. This officer shall have the duty of treating in closest collaboration with the Kreisleiter, according to the instructions of the camp commander, all questions concerning prisoners of war which might become public knowledge. The aim of this collaboration should be:

(a) To increase the labour output of war prisoners;

(b) To solve all difficulties quickly and on the spot;

(c) To organise the employment of war prisoners in the Kreise in such a way that it fulfils the political, military and economic requirements.

The Chancellery of the Party will give the necessary orders to the Gauleiter and the Kreisleiter.

(2) Treatment of the prisoners of war. The treatment of prisoners of war shall be dictated within limits compatible with security, with the sole purpose of increasing, as far as possible, the labour output. In addition to just treatment, the providing of the prisoners with the food due to them according to stipulations, and with proper billets, the supervising of the labour output is necessary to achieve the highest possible results.

Available means must be employed with extreme rigour as regards the lazy and the rebellious."

I shall stop my quotation here. The resistance of war prisoners caused the German Labour Bureaux to use a subterfuge to force them to work. I refer to the operation called the transformation of war prisoners into free workers. It consisted in transforming prisoners of war into so-called free workers, to whom a labour contract was offered. The operation was perfected by the defendant Sauckel in the course of one of his trips to Paris on 9th April, 1943. To Germany it offered the advantage of permitting the use of transformed prisoners in armament factories, without directly violating the Geneva Convention. For the prisoners it presented only a seeming advantage, the decrease of the surveillance to which they were subject. In reality the length and the nature of the work imposed upon them was in no way changed; their housing conditions and the quality of their rations remained unchanged. Moreover, this operation, presented by German propaganda as a measure favourable to war prisoners, brought about a deterioration of their juridical status.

The prisoners of war were not fooled; in most cases they refused to cooperate with this German manoeuvre; some agreed to do it, but a number of these took advantage of the first leave granted them because of their change in status, and fled. The report of the Statistical Institute on Forced Labour which I submitted to the Tribunal this morning as Exhibit RF 22, gives in this connection the following information. I quote it, Page 70 of the French text, Page 70 of the German translation. I shall read the second paragraph:

"The transformation of prisoners into 'free' workers, which was realised or carried out as the second Sauckel act, and which, because of this fact, must be counted in the present list as dating from the 25th of April, 1942, was decided by Sauckel, in the course of a trip to Paris on 9th April, 1943, It was to involve, after the prisoner had signed his contract as a labourer, a leave to go to France—depending on the return of the men who had gone on leave before. Two attempts were made to carry out this plan. On the 24th of April, 1943, out of 1,000 on leave, 43 did not return. In the month of August following, 2,000 out of 8,000 did not return. A last appeal directed to them was published in the Press of 17th August without result. There is no third experiment, and the transformation in practice limited itself to the removal of sentinels and of camp guards, but did not change either the nature or the duration of the work, or the housing conditions or the rations. On the other hand, it entailed loss of rights to receive packages from the International Red Cross and loss of diplomatic protection for prisoners of war."

The forced utilisation of war prisoners did not permit the German authorities to solve the labour problem of the war economy. That is why they applied their policy of force to the civilian populations of the occupied territories.

The National Socialist authorities systematised their policy of force from 1942 on by establishing the Bureau of Compulsory Labour in the different occupied territories. From the end of 1941 it has been verified, that neither the recruiting of voluntary workers nor the utilisation of prisoners, permitted a solution of the problem of labour required for the war economy. The Germans then decided to proceed to the forced enrolment of civilian workers. They decreed a veritable civilian mobilisation, the execution of which characterises their criminal activity.

I refer to a directive of 29th January, 1942, given by Dr. Mansfeld under authorisation of the defendant Goering. I remind the Tribunal that I have filed this document already as Exhibit RF 26. I read the passage from the document where I stopped this morning, Page 2, last paragraph of the French translation, Page 2, last paragraph also of the German original:

> "In order to avoid a damaging of the armament industry, all misgivings must yield to the necessity of filling in, at any rate, the gaps in the labour employment caused by extensive drafting into the Wehrmacht. To this end the forced mobilisation of workers from the occupied territories must not be neglected, if the voluntary recruitment remains unsuccessful. The mere factor of a compulsory mobilisation will, in many cases, make recruiting easier.
>
> Therefore, I ask you to take immediate measures in your district to promote the employment of workers in the German Reich on a voluntary basis. I herewith request you to prepare for publication, regulations making possible the forced mobilisation of labour from your territory for Germany, so that they may be decreed at once in case recruiting on a voluntary basis remains without the success necessary to relieve labour employment in the Reich."

The appointment of the defendant Sauckel may be considered a preparatory measure for the establishment of the Bureau of Compulsory Labour. It was necessary that a central authority be set up in order to co-ordinate the activity of the different labour departments and in order to proceed to the mobilisation of civilian workers. The terms of the exposition of the motives of the decree of appointment are explicit: the mission of the Plenipotentiary for Labour consists in satisfying the labour needs of the German economy through the recruiting of foreign workers and the utilisation of war prisoners. The decree of Sauckel, dated 22nd August, 1942, which I have filed with the Tribunal as Exhibit RF 17, expresses, moreover, the will of the defendant to go about recruiting by means of coercion.

The institution of the office of compulsory labour represents deliberate violation of international conventions. The deportation of workers is forbidden by several contractual regulations which have the value of positive law. I shall quote, first of all, Article 52 of the Annex to the Fourth Convention of The Hague. I have already given a commentary on it to the Tribunal, to demonstrate that the requisitioning of labour effected by the authorities of the occupation was illegal.

All the more, the institution of compulsory labour was prohibited by Article 52, Compulsory labour was imposed upon foreign workers in the interest of the war economy; it was carried out in armament factories of

National Socialist Germany; it deprived the occupied territories of labour necessary for the rational exploitation of their wealth, it therefore is not within the framework of that labour requisition which Article 52 of The Hague Convention authorises.

The prohibition of forced labour is, moreover, affirmed by another international convention. It is a question of the Convention of the 25th of September, 1926, on slavery, of which Germany is a signatory. This treaty makes forced labour equivalent to slavery, in its Article 5.ask the Tribunal to refer to it.

Deportation of workers is the object of a formal prohibition. Forced labour in German war factories was, therefore, instituted in flagrant violation of International Law and of all pledges subscribed to by Germany. The National Socialist authorities transgressed positive International Law; they likewise violated the rights of nations.

The latter guarantees individual liberty, on which the principle of forced recruitment is a characteristic attack.

The violation of treaties and contempt for the rights of individuals are the tenets of National Socialist doctrine. Therefore the defendants proceeded not merely to the mobilisation of foreign workers; they proclaimed the necessity and the legitimacy of forced labour. I shall, first of all, indicate to the Tribunal certain declarations made by the defendants which have the strength of confessions. I shall thereupon indicate how the occupation authorities introduced the service of compulsory work in the different occupied territories. I shall demonstrate, finally, that the Germans took measures of violent coercion in an attempt to assure the execution of the civilian mobilisation, which had been decreed.

The legitimacy of forced enrolment has been upheld by Hitler. The proof of this can be found in the report of the Four Year Plan Conference held on the 10th, 11th and 12th of August, 1942. It is contained in Document R-124, which I presented this morning as Exhibit RF 30.shall not read it to the Tribunal, because my American colleague, Mr. Dodd, has done so during his presentation on forced labour. I recall that the document to which I refer indicates that the Fuehrer agreed to exercise all the necessary constraint in the East as well as in the West, if the question of recruiting foreign labourers could not be regulated on a voluntary basis.

The necessity of the utilisation of compulsory labour was expressed in identical terms by certain of the defendants.

I shall not stress the numerous statements of the defendant Sauckel to which I have already drawn the attention of the Tribunal. The exposition of the motives of his decree of 22nd August, 1942, the programme included in his letter of 24th April, 1942, and the policy advocated in his speech at Posen in February, 1943, reproduce faithfully the determination of the defendant to justify the principle of forced recruiting. I shall not revert to this. I present to the Tribunal the declaration of the defendant Jodl. This declaration is an extract from a long speech made by Jodl on 7th November, 1943, at Munich, before an audience of Gauleiters. This speech is Document L-172. I offer it in evidence to the Tribunal as Exhibit RF 54.I shall read Page 2 of the French translation, second paragraph, Pages 38-39 of the German original:

"This dilemma of manpower shortage has led to the idea of making more thorough use of the manpower reserves in the territories occupied by us. Here, right thinking and wrong thinking are mixed up together. I believe that, in so far as it concerns labour, everything has been done that could be done; but where this is not yet the case, it appeared preferable, from the political point of view, not to have recourse to measures of compulsion, but rather to aim at order and economic relief. In my opinion, however, the time has now come to take steps with remorseless vigour and resolution in Denmark, Holland, France and Belgium, and also to compel thousands of idle persons to carry out the fortification work, which is more important than any other work. The necessary orders for this have already been given."

The German Labour Service had not waited for the appeal of General Jodl to decree the mobilisation of civilian foreign workers. I am going to show the Tribunal how the Bureau of Compulsory Labour was established and organised in France, in Norway, in Belgium, and in Holland.

I should like to remind the Tribunal that in Denmark there was never any legal regulation for forced labour, and that this was carried out as a simple de facto measure.

I also wish to remind the Tribunal that the Bureau of Forced Labour was introduced in a special form in Luxembourg and in the French departments of Alsace and Lorraine. The occupation authorities incorporated the citizens of Luxembourg and the French citizens residing in the departments of Bas-Rhin, Haut-Rhin and Moselle, in the Labour Service of the Reich. This incorporation was carried out by ordinances of Gauleiter Simon and Gauleiter Wagner. The ordinances constitute an integral part of the Germanisation plan for territories of Luxembourg, Alsace and Lorraine. Their consequences surpass those of the measures of forced enrolment which were taken in other occupied territories. That is why I refer the Tribunal, on this point, to the explanation which will be given in the prosecution brief of M. Edgar Faure.

Two German texts of a general nature serve as a foundation for the legislation on forced labour in the occupied territories of Western Europe.

The first is the decree of Sauckel of 22nd August, 1942, to which I have drawn the attention of the Tribunal on several occasions. This decree prescribes the mobilisation of all civilian workers in the service of the war economy. Article 2—of which I remind the Tribunal—prescribes that this decree is applicable to occupied territories. This decree of 22nd August, 1942, thus constitutes the legal charter of the civilian mobilisation of foreign workers. This mobilisation was confirmed by an order of the Fuehrer of 8th September, 1942. It is Document 556-PS-2, which I file with the Tribunal as Exhibit RF 55, and from which I shall read:

"The Fuehrer and Supreme Commander of the Wehrmacht. General

Headquarters of the Fuehrer, 8th September, 1942.

The extensive coastal fortification, which I have ordered to be erected in the area of Army Group West, makes it necessary that, in the occupied territory, all available workers work to the fullest extent of their production capacity. The previous allotment of labour for this work is absolutely insufficient. In order to increase it, I order the introduction of compulsory labour and the prohibition of changing the place of employment without permission of the authorities in the occupied territories.

Furthermore, in the future, the distribution of food and clothing ration cards to those subject to labour draft shall depend on the possession of a certificate of employment. Refusal to accept an assigned job, as well as abandoning the place of work without the consent of the authorities in charge, will result in the withdrawal of the food and clothing ration cards.

The G.B.A., that is, the office of the defendant Sauckel, in agreement with the military commander or the Reich Commissar, will issue the appropriate decrees for execution."

The forced enrolment of foreign workers was preceded by preliminary measures, to which the order of 8th September, 1942, which I just read, refers. I am speaking of the freezing of labour. To carry out the mobilisation of workers it was necessary that the public services exercise strict control over their use in the industrial enterprises of occupied territories. This control had a double purpose: it was to facilitate the census of workers suitable for work in Germany; and also to prevent workers from avoiding the German requisition by alleging a real or fictitious employment.

The National Socialist authorities exercised this control by restricting the liberty of hiring and of discharging, which they had given over to the authorities of the Labour Bureau.

In France, the freezing of labour was brought about by the law of 4th September, 1942. I shall shortly expose to the Tribunal the conditions under which, this law was formulated. I shall, for the moment, simply supply it to the Tribunal as Exhibit RF 56 and ask the Tribunal to take judicial notice of it.

In Belgium the freezing of labour was carried out by the ordinance of the military commandant of the 6th of October, 1942. I submit to the Tribunal Exhibit RF 57, of which I ask the Tribunal to take judicial notice.

Finally, in Holland, where the Bureau of Compulsory Labour was established early in 1941, an ordinance of the Reich Commissar dated 28th February, 1941, which I offer to the Tribunal as Exhibit RF 58, organised the freezing of labour.

The immobilisation of labour was brought about under an economic pretext in all countries. In reality it constituted a preliminary measure for the mobilisation of workers, which the National Socialists immediately proceeded to carry out.

In France, the Bureau of Compulsory Labour was established by the

*Hitler and Speer walking to a meeting at the Führer's Headquarters. March 1942.*
Bundesarchiv, Bild 146-1979-026-23 / Heinrich Hoffmann / CC-BY-SA

legislation of the pseudo-Government of Vichy, but this legislation was imposed upon the de facto French authorities by the defendants, and especially by Sauckel. The action which Sauckel brought against the Government of Vichy, to force it to favour the deportation of workers into Germany, was exercised in four phases: I shall briefly review for the Tribunal the history of these four Sauckel actions.

The first Sauckel action was initiated in the Spring of 1942, soon after the appointment of the defendant as Plenipotentiary for Labour. The German armament industry had an urgent need for workers. The service of the Arbeitseinsatz had decided to recruit 150,000 specialists in France. Sauckel came to Paris in the month of June, 1942. He had several conversations with

French ministers. Otto Abetz, German Ambassador in Paris, presided over these meetings. They brought about the following results:

In view of the reluctance of French authorities to establish forced labour it was decided that the recruiting of the 150,000 specialists would be carried out by a pseudo-voluntary enrolment. This was the beginning of the so-called exchange operation, to which I have already drawn the attention of the Tribunal.

But the Tribunal knows that the exchange operation was a failure and that, despite an intensification of German propaganda, the number of voluntary enrolments remained at a minimum. The German authorities then put the Vichy Government in a position to proceed to forced enrolment. I offer in evidence the threatening letter of 26th August, 1942, addressed by the German, Dr. Michel, Chief of the Administrative Staff, to the General Delegate for Franco-German economic relations. This is French Document 530, which I shall submit to the Tribunal as Exhibit RF 59:

"Paris, 25th August, 1942.

Military Commandant in France, Economic Section, to M. Barnaud, General Delegate for Franco-German Relations, Paris.

President Laval promised Gauleiter Sauckel, General Plenipotentiary for the Employment of Labour, to make every effort to send to Germany, in order to reinforce the German armament economy, 350,000 workers, among them 150,000 metal workers.

The French Government proposed originally to solve this problem by recruitment, in particular of the 'affectes speciaux.' This method has been abandoned and that of voluntary enrolment has been attempted with a view to the liberation of prisoners. The months which have passed have demonstrated that the end in view cannot be achieved by means of voluntary recruiting.

In France, German armament orders have increased in volume and assumed a more marked and urgent character. Besides, the accomplishment of special tasks has been requested, which can be successfully carried only by having a very considerable number of available workers.

In order to assure the realisation of the tasks for which France is responsible in the domain of labour supply, the French Government must be asked, henceforth, to put into execution the following measures:

(1) The publication of a decree, relative to the change of place of work. By virtue of this decree the place of work cannot be changed and labour cannot be hired without the approval of certain specified services.

(2) The institution of a compulsory registration of all persons out of work, as well as of those who do not work during the whole working day, or are not permanently employed.

This compulsory registration will make it possible to determine, as fully as possible, the reserves that are still available.

(3) The publication of a decree for the mobilisation of workers for

important tasks, relating to the policy of State. This decree is to furnish:

(a) the necessary labour for Germany;

(b) the workers necessary in France for the carrying out of orders which have been transferred here for special tasks.

(4) Publication of a decree protecting young specialists. This decree must impose upon French enterprise the obligation of turning out, by means of apprenticeship and systematic education, young workers possessing sufficient qualifications.

For the Military Commandant, the Chief of the Administrative Staff.

(Signed) Dr. Michel."

Dr. Michel's letter forms the basis for the law relative to the utilisation and the orientation of labour. It is the law of 4th September, 1942, which I have filed with the Tribunal as Exhibit RF 56.

In the application of the law all Frenchmen between 18 and 50, who did not have employment for more than 30 hours a week, were forced to state this at their local city hall. A decree of 19th September, 1942, and an enabling directive of 22nd September, provided regulations for the different phases of the statement.

Sauckel's first action was achieved through a legislative plan; the defendant had merely to dip into the labour resources which were established by it. But the resistance of the French workers caused his recruiting plan to fail. This is why Sauckel undertook his second action, beginning in January, 1943.

The second Sauckel action is marked by the setting up of the Service of Compulsory Labour, properly speaking. Until then workers had been the only victims of the policy of force of the defendants. The latter understood the demagogic argument which they could derive from this de facto situation. They explained that it was inadmissible that the working classes of the occupied territory be the only ones to participate in the German war effort. They required that the basis of forced labour be enlarged by the establishment of the Bureau of Compulsory Labour.

This was established by two measures. A directive of 2nd February, 1943, prescribed a general census of all French of masculine sex born between the 1st of January, 1912, and the 1st of January, 1921. The census took place between the 15th and 23rd of February. It had just been put in force when the law and decree of 16th February, 1943, appeared. These regulations established the Bureau of Compulsory Labour for all young men born between the 1st of January, 1920, and 31st of December, 1922. I file them with the Tribunal as Exhibits RF 60 and RF 61, and I ask the Court to take judicial notice of them.

The action carried out by the defendant, to impose the legislation which was not in the domain of common law, is substantiated by numerous documents. I particularly draw the attention of the Tribunal to four of these, which permit us to retrace the activities of the defendant Sauckel during the months of January and February, 1943. On 5th January, 1943, Sauckel transmitted to the different departments of his administration an order of the Fuehrer which the defendant Speer had communicated to him. This is

Document 556-PS-13, which I file with the Tribunal as Exhibit RF 62. I shall read its first paragraph:

"(1) On 4th January, 1943, at 8 o'clock in the evening, Minister Speer telephones from the General Headquarters of the Fuehrer to give the information that, according to a decision of the Fuehrer it will no longer be necessary, when recruiting specialists and assistants in France, to have any particular regard for the French. One may likewise in the said country exercise pressure and use more severe measures to the end of procuring the necessary labour."

On 11th January, 1943, the defendant Sauckel was in Paris. He attended a meeting which brought together, at the Military Commandant's, all responsible officials of the Labour Service. He announced to them that new measures of constraint were to be taken in France. I refer you to the minutes of the meeting which constitutes Document 1342-PS, which I file with the Tribunal as Exhibit RF 63. I shall read from Page 2 of the French translation, Page 1, fourth line of the second paragraph of the German original:

"Gauleiter Sauckel likewise thanks the various services for the successful carrying out of the first action. Now already, at the beginning of the new year, he sees himself obliged to announce new severe measures. There is a great new need of labour for the front as well as for the Reich armament industry."

I pass to the end of the paragraph. I shall read from the next paragraph:

"The situation at the front calls for 700,000 soldiers fit for front line service. The armament industry would have to lose 200,000 key workers by the middle of March. I have received an order from the Fuehrer to find 200,000 foreign specialised workers as replacements, and I shall need for this 150,000 French specialists, while the other 50,000 can be drawn from Holland, Belgium and other occupied countries.

In addition, 100,000 unskilled French workers are necessary for the Reich. The second action of recruitment in France makes it necessary that, by the middle of March, 150,000 skilled workers and 100,000 unskilled workers and women be transferred to Germany."

The defendant Sauckel went back to Germany a few days later. On 15th February he was in Berlin at the meeting of the Central Office of the Four Year Plan. He gave a commentary on the law, which was to appear that very day, and revealed that he was the instigator of it.

I refer once more to the minutes of the conference of the Four Year Plan, included under R-124, which I submitted this morning to the Tribunal as Exhibit RF 30. I shall read an extract from this document, which my American colleagues have not mentioned. It is Page 7 of the French translation of the document, Pages 284-5 of the German original:

"This is the situation in France. Since my collaborators and I succeeded, after difficult discussions, in persuading Laval to establish the law of compulsory labour, this law has been extended, thanks to our pressure, so successfully, that since yesterday three French age-groups have already been called. This is why we are now legally qualified to recruit in France, with the assistance of the French Government, workers of three age-groups, whom we shall be able to employ henceforth in French factories, but among whom we shall be able to choose some for our own needs in Germany, and send them there."

In fact, the defendant Sauckel returned to France on 24th February. I offer in evidence to the Tribunal the letter which he addressed to Hitler before his departure to inform him of his trip. It proves the continuity of the action of Sauckel. The letter constitutes Document 556-PS-25, which I submit to the Tribunal as Exhibit RF 64, and I shall read it:

"General Plenipotentiary for the Employment of Labour to the Fuehrer General Headquarters of the Fuehrer.

My Fuehrer:

I allow myself herewith to take leave of you before undertaking my official trip to France which has already been arranged. The objective of my trip is:

(1) To put at the disposal of the Reich, within the anticipated time, workers replacing German workers of key industries, for the benefit of the Wehrmacht.

May I add that Marshal Keitel and General von Unruh received a communication from me yesterday to the effect that half of these workers intended to replace German workers in the key industries, that is, 125,000 French qualified specialists, have already arrived in the Reich on 1st January, 1943, and that a corresponding number of soldiers has already been drafted. I shall now make sure, in France, that the second half shall arrive in the Reich by the end of March, or earlier if possible. The first French programme was executed by the end of December.

(2) To assure the necessary labour for the French wharves in order to permit the carrying out of the programme undertaken there by Grand Admiral Doenitz and Gauleiter Kauffmann.

(3) To assure the necessary labour for the programme of the Luftwaffe.

(4) To assure the necessary labour for the other German armament programmes which are in process in France.

(5) To prepare supplementary labour in agreement with State Secretary Backe, in view of intensifying French agricultural production.

(6) To have conversations, if necessary, with the French Government on the subject of the carrying out of the labour service, the calling up of age groups, and so forth, with, a view to activating the recruitment of labour for the benefit of the German war economy."

*(The Tribunal adjourned until 19th January, 1946, at 10.00 hours.)*

# The Brief Relating to Forced Labour

## SATURDAY, JANUARY 19TH, 1946

M. HERZOG: Mr. President, your Honours.

At the end of yesterday's session I was expounding to the Tribunal the conditions under which the Compulsory Labour Service was progressively imposed in France. I reached the second action of the defendant Sauckel as set out in the laws of 16th February, 1943.

Sauckel's second action precipitated the enforced enrolment of Frenchmen during the months of February and March, 1943. Several tens of thousands of young men of the 1940 and 1942 classes were deported to Germany by the application of the law of 16th February. The tempo of these deportations slowed down in the month of April, but the Arbeitseinsatz immediately formulated fresh requirements. On 9th April, 1943, the defendant Sauckel asked the French authorities to furnish him with 120,000 workers during the month of May, and 100,000 during the month of June. In June he made it known that he wished to effect the transfer of 500,000 workers up to 31st December.

Sauckel's third action was about to begin. It was to be marked, on 5th June, 1943, by the total mobilisation of the 1942 class. All exemptions provided by the law of 16th February and subsequent texts were withdrawn, and the young men of the 1942 class were hunted all through France.

In reality, Sauckel's third action was especially manifested by a violent pressure on the part of the defendant, envisaging wholesale deportation by forced recruiting. I offer in evidence three documents, which testify to the action taken by Sauckel in the summer of 1943.

The first document is a letter from Sauckel to Hitler, dated 27th June, 1943. Drafted by the defendant upon his return from a trip to France, it contains an outlined plan for the recruiting of French workers for the second half of 1943. Its object was, on the one hand, to secure that one million workers be assigned, in France, to French armament factories and, on the other hand, that 500,000 French workers be deported to Germany. This letter constitutes Document 556-PS- 39, which I submit to the Tribunal as Exhibit RF 65. I quote:

"Weimar, 27th June, 1943.

My Fuehrer:

With your permission I beg to report my return from my official trip to France.

Inasmuch as the free labour reserves in the territories occupied by the German Armed Forces have been, numerically, absorbed to saturation point, I am now carefully examining the possibilities of mobilising additional labour reserves in the Reich and the occupied territories to work on German war production.

In my reports of 20th April, I was allowed to point out that intensive and careful utilisation must be made of European labour forces in territories submitted to direct German influence.

It was the precise purpose of my recent stay in Paris to investigate the possibilities still existing in France for the recruitment of labour (Arbeitseinsatz). My task was accomplished by extensive conferences and my own personal investigation. On the basis of a carefully established balance sheet I have come to the following decision:

(1) Assuming that war economy measures in France are carried out which would at least prove partially effective, or approximately approach, in efficacy, the measures carried out in Germany, then—until the 31st of December, 1943—a further million workers, both men and women, could be assigned to the French war and armament industries for work on German orders and assignments. In this case it should prove possible to place additional German orders in France.

(2) In consideration of these measures, and given a careful study of the subject, together with the co-operation of our German Armament Services and the German Labour Recruiting Offices, it should be possible to transfer a further 500,000 workers, both men and women, from France to the Reich between now and the end of the year.

The prerequisites which I have established for the realisation of this programme are as follows:

(1) Closest possible collaboration between all German agencies, especially in dealing with the French agencies.

(2) A constant check on French economy by joint commissions, as already agreed upon by the Reich Minister of Armaments and Munitions, Party Member Speer and myself.

(3) Constant, skilful and successful propaganda against the cliques of de Gaulle and Giraud.

(4) The guarantee of adequate food supplies to the French population working for Germany.

(5) An emphatic insistence on this urgency before the French Government, in particular before Marshal Petain, who still represents the main obstacle to the further recruiting of French women for compulsory labour (Arbeitseinsatz).

(6) A pronounced increase in the programme which I have already introduced in France, for re-education in trades essential to war production."

I omit the next and read the last paragraph:

"I consequently beg you, my Fuehrer, to approve my suggestion of freeing one million Frenchmen and Frenchwomen for German war production in France proper, in the second half of 1943, and, in addition, of transferring 500,000 Frenchmen and Frenchwomen to the

Reich before the end of the current year.

Yours faithfully and obediently,

(Signed) Fritz Sauckel."

The document to which I would now like to call the Tribunal's attention proves that the Fuehrer gave his approval to Sauckel's programme. A note drawn up on 28th July, 1943, by Dr. Stothfang, under the letter-heading of the Plenipotentiary General for Manpower Utilisation (Arbeitseinsatz), gives a report on a discussion between Sauckel and the Fuehrer. It is Document 556-PS-41, which I submit to the Tribunal as Exhibit RF 66. I shall limit myself to reading the last paragraph.

"(d) The transfer envisaged for the end of the year of 1,000,000 French workers to the war industries in France, and the transportation of 500,000 other French workers to the interior of the Reich has been approved by the Fuehrer."

A document finally establishes that the defendant Sauckel, on the strength of Hitler's approval, attempted to realise his programme by working on the French Government. This document is a letter from Sauckel to Hitler. It is dated 13th August, 1943, upon the defendant's return from a trip to France, Belgium and Holland. It is Document 556-PS-43. I shall read it to the Tribunal. It is Exhibit RF 67:

"Weimar, 13th August, 1943.

My Fuehrer:

With your permission I beg to report my return from my official trip to France, Belgium and Holland. In the course of tough, difficult and tedious negotiations, I have imposed upon the occupied Western territories, for the last five months of 1943, the programme set forth below, and have prepared very detailed measures for realising it: in France—with the Military Commander, the German Embassy and the French Government; in Belgium—with the Military Commander, and in Holland with the offices of the Reich Commissar.

The programme provides:

(1) In France, the transfer of one million French workers, both men and women, from the civilian to the German war industries in France. This measure should render possible a new important shifting of work on German orders to France.

(2) Soliciting and recruiting of 500,000 French workers for work in Germany. This figure should not be made public abroad.

(3) In order to render void any passive resistance from large groups of French officials, I have ordered, in agreement with the Military Commander in France, the introduction of labour recruiting commissions for each two French departments, and placed them under the supervision and direction of the German Gau offices. Only in this manner can the complete recruitment of the French labour potential and its intensive utilisation be made possible. The French Government has given its approval."

If the Tribunal will allow me, I shall quote the rest of this letter; the following paragraphs concern Belgium and Holland. It will allow me to refer to this document later without reading it again.

"(4) A programme was secured in Belgium for the employment of 150,000 workers in the Reich, and with the approval of the Military Commander in Belgium an organisation for compulsory labour, corresponding to that in France, has been established."

I pass to the fifth paragraph.

"(5) A programme has likewise been prepared for Holland, providing for the transfer of 150,000 workers to Germany and of 100,000 workers, men and women, from Dutch civilian industries to German war production."

Such was Sauckel's programme in 1943. His plan was partly thwarted by the resistance of officials and patriotic workers. Proof of this is furnished by a statement of the defendant. I am referring to the report on a conference of the Central Office for the Four Year Plan held on 1st March, 1944. I submitted this document to the Tribunal yesterday as Exhibit RF 30. I shall read from the first page of the French translation, second paragraph-German text 1768-1769.

"Last autumn, as far as foreign manpower is concerned, the labour recruiting programme has been severely battered. I do not wish to elaborate the reasons here. They have been discussed at length; all I have to say is: the programme has been wrecked."

Sauckel, however, was not discouraged by the difficulties encountered in 1943. In 1944 he attempted to realise a new programme by the trick of the fourth action. The National Socialist authorities decided to secure, in 1944, the transfer of four million foreign workers to Germany. This decision was made on 4th January, 1944, during a conference at the Headquarters of the Fuehrer and in his presence. The report on this conference constitutes Document 1292-PS. I submit it herewith to the Tribunal as Exhibit RF 68, and I read from Page 3 of the French translation—Page 6 of the German original, last paragraph:

"Final results of the conference:

(1) The Plenipotentiary General for Manpower Utilisation shall produce at least four million new workers from the occupied territories."

The details concerning the contingents demanded from each occupied territory must have been determined on 16th February, 1944, during a conference of the Central Office for the Four Year Plan. Yesterday I submitted the report of this session at the outset of my explanations, under Exhibit RF 20. I am quoting the conclusions today. They will be found on the first page of the translation, second page of the German original:

"Results of the 53rd session of the Office for Central Planning."

Labour recruiting (Arbeitseinsatz) in 1944.

(1) About 500,000 new workers can be mobilised from among the

German home reserves."

I omit the rest.

(2) Recruiting of Italian labour to the number of 1,500,000; of these—1,000,000 at the rate of 250,000 per month from January to April and 500,000 from May to December.

(3) Recruiting of 1,000,000 French workers at equal monthly rates from 1st February to 31st December, 1944 (approximately 9 1,000 per month).

(4) Recruiting of 250,000 workers from Belgium.

(5) Recruiting of 250,000 workers from the Netherlands."

I abstain from quoting further, since the other paragraphs concern the Eastern European countries.

The Tribunal has seen that France was called upon to furnish a large contingent of workers. After the 15th of January Sauckel went to Paris to inflict his demands on the French authorities.

The fourth Sauckel action consisted of two distinct measures: the adoption of the procedure known as the combing of industries, and the publication of the law of 1st February, 1944, which widened the sphere of application of compulsory labour. The system of combing the industries led the labour administration to carry out direct recruiting in the industrial enterprises. Mixed Franco-German commissions were set up in each department. They determined the percentage of workers to be deported. They proceeded to requisition and transfer them.

The practice of combing the industries represents the realisation of the projects elaborated by defendant Sauckel since 1943. In the documents which I have read to the Tribunal Sauckel announced, in fact, his intention of creating mixed labour commissions.

The law of 1st February, 1944, marked the culminating point of Sauckel's actions in the field of legislation. It extends the scope of application of the law of 4th September, 1942. As from February, 1944, all men between the ages of 16 and 60, and all women between the ages of 18 and 45 were subject to compulsory labour.

I submit to the Tribunal the law of 1st February, 1944, as Exhibit RF 69, with the request to take judicial note of it.

The proof of the pressure that Sauckel exerted on the French authorities in order to impose on them the publication of this law is furnished by a report of the defendant to Hitler. This report is dated the 25th of January, 1944. It was, therefore, drafted during the negotiations which characterised the fourth Sauckel action. It constituted Document 556-PS-55, which I submit to the Tribunal as Exhibit RF 70. I shall read this document:

"My Fuehrer:

On the 22nd of January, 1944, the French Government, together with Marshal Petain, accepted the majority of my demands for increasing the working week from 40 to 48 hours, as well as for extending the compulsory labour law in France and utilising French manpower in

Germany.

The Marshal did not agree to the compulsory work of women in the Reich, but he did agree to the compulsory work of women inside France, to be limited to women between the ages of 26 and 45. Women between 15 and 25 are to be employed only at their place of residence.

Since this, nevertheless, represents appreciable progress in comparison with the extremely difficult negotiations which I had to conduct in Paris, I approved this law, in order to save further loss of time, on condition that the German demands were energetically met and carried out.

The French Government likewise accepted my demand that French officials sabotaging the enforcement of the Compulsory Labour Law should be punished by severe penalties, including the death penalty. I have left them in no doubt that further and more rigid measures would be adopted, should the demands for the manpower required not be fulfilled.

Your ever obedient and faithful, Fritz Sauckel."

I draw the attention of the Tribunal to the problem of compulsory labour of women, referred to in the two preceding documents. For a long time the French authorities categorically opposed the introduction of female labour. The defendant Sauckel did not cease to exercise violent activity.

On the 27th June, 1943, in a letter to Hitler, he suggested that an energetic statement of German interests be made before the French Government. I have already quoted this letter to the Tribunal, Exhibit RF 65. I shall not revert to it, but I emphasise the fact that the law of 1st February did not satisfy Sauckel and did not in the least appease his demands. His dissatisfaction and his determination to pursue his policy of compulsion become apparent from a report of 26th April, 1944, bearing his signature; that the report was forwarded is certified by Berk, one of his assistants.

This report—there actually were four reports submitted jointly—constitutes Document 1289-PS. I submit them to the Tribunal as Exhibit RF 71, and I quote from the second page:

"France (1). The problem of women.

At the time of the promulgation of the French Compulsory Labour Law, the French authorities (Marshal Petain in particular) have urgently desired that women be exempted from performing compulsory labour in Germany. In spite of serious objections the G.B.A. approved of this exemption. The reservation was made, however, that the approval was given on condition that the contingencies imposed were met; or else the G.B.A. would retain the right of taking further measures. Inasmuch as the contingencies are far from being met, the demand must be addressed to the French Government of extending the compulsory labour service to women also."

The fourth Sauckel action, therefore, was directed in such a manner as to utilise all of France's manpower. The French resistance and the development of the military operations hindered the execution of the Sauckel plan. The defendant, in the meantime, had contemplated such extraordinary measures as would have to be taken on the day the Allied Armies landed. I quote again Document 1289-PS, Exhibit RF 71, and I read on Page 3:

"Measures concerning compulsory labour in the case of invasion:

To some extent precautions have been taken to evacuate the population of those areas invaded and to protect valuable manpower from being seized by our enemies. In view of the actual situation of labour utilisation in Germany, it is necessary to induct efficient workers to the greatest extent possible into efficacious employment within the Reich. Orders to this effect on the part of the Wehrmacht are indispensable for carrying out these measures.

The following text is proposed for an order by the Fuehrer..."

I shall not read the text of the order proposed by Sauckel.

The Allied victory, however, came so quickly that Sauckel did not have the chance to realise fully his plan of mass deportation. All the same, he started to carry it out, and deportations of workers went on up to the day of liberation of the territory. Several hundred thousand French workers were finally stationed in Germany as a result of the various Sauckel actions. Will the Tribunal, please, bear this in mind.

The compulsory labour service was introduced in Norway in the same manner as in France. The defendants imposed upon the Norwegian authorities the publication of a law instituting the compulsory registration of Norwegian citizens, and ordering their enrolment by force. I quote in this respect the preliminary report on the crimes of Germany against Norway, a report prepared by the Norwegian Government and submitted to the Tribunal as U.K. 79. I now submit it as Exhibit RF 72, and I quote from the first page, third paragraph:

"The result of Sauckel's order in Norway was the promulgation of the Quisling law of 3rd February, 1943, concerning the compulsory registration of Norwegian men and women for the so-called national labour effort.

Terboven and Quisling openly admitted that the law had been promulgated to enable the Norwegian people to utilise its manpower for the benefit of the German war effort.

In a speech of 2nd February Terboven incidentally declared that he himself and the German Reich supported this law with their authority, and he threatened to use force against any one attempting to oppose its application."

In Belgium and in the Netherlands the German authorities used a direct procedure. The compulsory labour service was organised by decrees of the occupying power.

In Belgium these were decrees of the Military Commander, and in the Netherlands decrees of the Reich Commissar. I remind the Tribunal of the fact that the authority of the Military Commander in Belgium extended to the North of France.

A decree of 6th March, 1942, established the principle of compulsory labour in Belgium. It was published in the Belgian "Verordnungsblatt" of 1942, Page 845. I submit it to the Tribunal as Exhibit RF 73, and I ask the Tribunal to take judicial notice of it.

The decree of 6th March excluded the possibility of forced deportation of workers to Germany. However, such deportation was ordered by a decree of 6th October, 1942, which was published in the Belgian "Verordnungsblatt" of 1942, Page 1060. I submitted it to the Tribunal as Exhibit RF 57 in the course of my explanations.

The German activities in Belgium gave rise to interventions and protests by leading Belgian personalities, among others the King of Belgium and Cardinal van Roey.

The decrees instituting compulsory labour in Belgium and the North of France bore the signature of General von Falkenhausen, but the latter proclaimed his decree of 6th October on the order of Sauckel. I refer once more to the testimony of General von Falkenhausen, which I submitted to the Tribunal yesterday as Exhibit RF 15. I ask your permission to quote the following passages, first page, fifth paragraph:

"Q. On 6th October, 1942, a decree was published which instituted compulsory labour in Belgium, and in the Departments of Northern France, for men between the ages of 18 and 50 years, and for single women between the ages of 21 and 25 years.

A. I was Commander-in-Chief for Northern France and Belgium.

Q. Does the witness recall having promulgated this decree?

A. I do not remember exactly the text of this decree because it was issued following a long dispute with the labour deputy Sauckel.

Q. Did you have any trouble with Sauckel?

A. I was fundamentally opposed to the establishment of compulsory labour, and consented to promulgating the decree only after receiving orders.

Q. Then this decree was not issued on the initiative of von Falkenhausen?

A. On the contrary.

Q. Who gave instruction in this matter?

A. I suppose that at that time Sauckel was already responsible for manpower and that at that time he gave me all instructions on Hitler's orders."

I take up the quotation again on Page 3 of the French translation, fourth paragraph:

Q. Since you were opposed to the idea of compulsory labour, did you not protest when you received these instructions?

A. There were unending quarrels between Sauckel and myself. In the end this contributed greatly to my discharge."

The violence of the pressure exerted by the defendant Sauckel in Belgium, in order to impose his plan of recruitment by force, is also demonstrated by the document which I have just submitted to the Tribunal as Exhibit RF 67. The Tribunal will remember that it is the report addressed on the 13th August, 1943, by Sauckel to Hitler on his return from France, Belgium and Holland.

Finally, I have to deal with the introduction of compulsory labour in the Netherlands. I request the Tribunal to charge the defendant Seyss-Inquart, as well as the defendant Sauckel, with the institution of compulsory enrolment in the occupied Dutch territories.

As a matter of fact, the deportation of the Dutch workers was organised by decrees of the Reich Commissar. They established all the more the responsibility of the defendant, who, in his quality as Reich Commissar, derived his powers directly from the Fuehrer.

The defendant Seyss-Inquart introduced the compulsory labour service in the Netherlands by a decree of 28th February, 1941, published in the Dutch "Verordnungsblatt" of 1941, No. 42. I referred to this decree as Exhibit RF 58 in the course of my explanation yesterday, and asked the Tribunal to take judicial notice of it.

As in Belgium the compulsory labour service could originally be enforced in the interior of the occupied countries only, but, just as in Belgium, it was soon extended in order to permit the deportation of workers to Germany. The extension was made effective by a decree of Seyss-Inquart of 23rd March, 1942, which appeared in No. 26 of the "Verordnungsblatt." I submit it to the Tribunal as Exhibit RF 74, and I ask the Tribunal to add it to the record.

The defendant Seyss-Inquart had thus paved the road on which the defendant Sauckel was to be enabled to proceed to action. Sauckel actually utilised all the human potential of the Netherlands. New measures were soon necessary, measures which Seyss-Inquart adopted.

A decree dated 6th May, 1943, "Verordnungsblatt," 1943, Page 173, ordered the mobilisation of all men from 18 to 35 years of age. I submit this decree to the Tribunal as Exhibit RF 75.

Moreover since the 19th of February, 1943, Seyss-Inquart had issued a decree which permitted his services to take all measures in the utilisation of manpower which he considered to be opportune.

This decree, which appeared in the "Verordnungsblatt" of 1943, has been submitted to the Tribunal as Exhibit RF 76.

The extent of deportation from Holland in 1943 is attested to by a letter of 16th June, 1943, from Sauckel's representative in the Netherlands. This letter, which bears the French document number 664, is submitted to the Tribunal as Exhibit RF 77. I quote:

> "In conformity with the census decree of 7th May, the 1920 to 1924 classes have been registered on filing cards. Although this involved very much work it was nevertheless possible to send 22,986 workers to the Reich, and, in addition, the prisoners of war put at our disposal. During the month of June the deficiency of the month of May will be made up.
>
> These classes include, according to the Statistical Service of the Kingdom of Holland, 80,000 each. It is from these classes that transfers

to the Reich have been made so far. 446,493 persons have been transferred to the Reich up to 1st June, 1943, and a number of them have returned from there. The figures as per index are as follows:

1921 class, 43,331;
1922 class, 45,354;
1923 class, 47,593;
1924 class, 45,232.

As up to 80 per cent. have been deferred, it is now imperative to begin transporting entire classes to the Reich. The Reich Commissar has given his agreement to this action. The other authorities involved, of Economy, Armament, Agriculture, and the Armed Forces, pressed by necessity, have given their approval."

At the end of the year 1944, the German authorities increased their pressure on the Netherlands. During that period tens of thousands of persons were arrested within two days in Rotterdam. Systematic raids took place in all the larger cities of Holland, sometimes improvised, sometimes after the population had been publicly summoned to appear in places named. I submit to the Tribunal various proclamations of this kind. They form Document 1162-PS, and have already been submitted to the Tribunal by Mr. Dodd. I shall not read them again. I use them in support of my argument and submit them as Exhibit RF 78.

These documents do not reveal isolated facts; they show a systematic policy which the defendants were to pursue up to 5th May, 1945, when the capitulation of Germany brought liberation to the Netherlands.

I still owe the Tribunal a supplementary explanation. The defendants did not stop at introducing compulsory labour service in the occupied territories. I declare that they proceeded to criminal coercion in order to ensure that the mobilisation of foreign workers was carried out. I am going to prove this fact.

The measures taken by the National Socialist authorities to guarantee the forced enlistment of foreign workers cannot be dissociated from the procedures they applied to ensure the so-called voluntary enlistment. The pressure was more violent, but it sprang from the same spirit. The method was to deceive, and, where this proved unsuccessful, to use coercion. The defendants very soon realised that no kind of propaganda would lend the cloak of justice to compulsory labour in the eyes of its victims. If they had any doubts in this respect, these would have been dissipated by the reports of the occupation authorities. The latter were unanimous in their reports of the political trouble provoked by this compulsory enlistment and of the resistance encountered by them. That is why the defendants once again used force in their attempt to ensure that the civilian mobilisation decreed by them was carried out.

First in line among the coercive measures to which the Germans had recourse, I mention the withholding of the ration cards of defaulters. The Tribunal knows from the circular letter of Dr. Manfeld, submitted as Exhibit RF 26, that this measure had been proposed since January, 1942, and will recall that by decree of the Fuehrer of 8th September, 1942, which I submitted as Exhibit RF 55, this measure was put into effect. This order provided that food and clothing ration cards were not to be issued to persons incapable of proving that they were working, nor to those who refused to do compulsory work.

Hitler's order was put into effect in all occupied territories. In France, circulars by the occupation authorities prohibited the renewal of ration cards of those French people who had eluded the census of 16th February, 1943. In Belgium, the forfeiture of ration certificates was regulated by an order of the Military Commander. It is the order of 5th March, 1943, published in the "Verordnungsblatt" for Belgium, which I submit to the Tribunal as Exhibit RF 79.

General von Falkenhausen, the signatory of this order, admitted its grave significance during the interrogation, which I have submitted to the Tribunal as Exhibit RF 15, and to which I refer again. General von Falkenhausen declared that the defendant Sauckel was the originator of this order, and that he had refused to grant an amnesty proposed by the General. I quote, Page 4 of the French translation, fifth paragraph:

"Q. Does the witness remember an order of 5th March, 1943, by which those refusing to enter the compulsory labour service had their ration cards withdrawn?

A. I do not remember. At the time when the order was issued for men from 18 to 50 years old, the implementing orders were not given by myself but by my offices, and I am not conversant with the details of the application of reprisals. I was not the executive head of the administration. I was above it.

Q. But at that time you were informed of the means of pressure and manner of treatment which the authorities thought fit to employ?

A. I do not wish to deny my responsibility for everything for, after all, I was aware of many things. I remember in particular the order regarding ration cards, because on various occasions I proposed that an amnesty be declared for persons who were obliged to live illegally, and who did not have a ration card.

Q. To whom was this proposal made?

A. To Sauckel, with the consent of President Revert.

Q. What was the attitude taken by Sauckel at that time?

A. He refused to grant such an amnesty."

In Holland likewise the renewal of ration certificates which did not bear the stamp of the labour office was prohibited.

The defendants, however, used a method of coercion which was even more criminal than the forfeiture of ration cards. I refer to the persecution directed against the families of those who refused to do compulsory labour. I call this method criminal, because it is based on the concept of family responsibility, which is contrary to the fundamental principles of the penal law of civilised nations. It was, nevertheless, sanctioned by several legislative texts issued or imposed by the National Socialists.

In France, I quote the law of 11th June, 1943, which I submit to the Tribunal as Exhibit RF 80, with the request that it take judicial notice thereof.

In Belgium, I refer to the order of the Military Commander of 30th April, 1943, and particularly to paragraphs 8 and 9. I submit this order to the Tribunal as Exhibit RF 81, with the request that it take judicial notice thereof.

Judicial action by the defendants was likewise directed against the employers and against the officials of the employment bureaux. In France, the action was initiated by two laws of 1st February, 1944. I emphasise that these laws were issued on the same day as the Compulsory Labour Law, and I confirm that they were imposed at the same time. In support of my statement, I submit the admission of the defendant Sauckel, in his letter of 25th February, 1944, which I read a little while ago to the Tribunal as Exhibit RF 70. I submit to the Tribunal the laws of 1st February, 1944, as Exhibit RF 82, with the request that it be added to the record.

There were still other measures of coercion. One of these, for instance, was the closing of the faculties and schools to defaulting students. It was decreed in Belgium on 28th June, 1943; in France, on 15th July, 1943. In Holland the students were victims of a systematic deportation from February on. I quote in this connection a letter of 4th May, 1943, from the Higher Chief of the S.S. and Police. This is Document 665, which I produce as Exhibit RF 83.

**THE PRESIDENT:** Perhaps this is a good time to break off.

*(A recess was taken.)*

**M. HERZOG:** Mr. President, your Honours. At the suspension of the session I was about to read to the Tribunal the letter of 4th May, 1943, which gives evidence of the action taken in Holland towards a systematic deportation of the students. I quote Exhibit RF 83, Document 665 in the document book:

"Subject: Action against Students.

The action will start on Thursday morning. As it is now too late to have this published in the Press today, an announcement by the Higher Chief of the S.S. and Police will be made over the radio, beginning tomorrow at 7 o'clock; it will be published tomorrow in the morning and the evening papers. Besides that, we will follow the directives given in yesterday's telegram."

Following is the text of the proclamation:

"Ordinance on the Registration of Students."

I will omit the first paragraph and I quote:

"1. All persons of the male sex who have attended a Dutch university or academy during the years 1942-43, and have not yet finished their studies according to the curriculum (referred to below as 'students'), are to report between 10.00 and 15.00 hours on 6th May, 1943, to the commander of the sector of the S.S. and the Security Police competent for their respective residence, for the purpose of their induction into the compulsory labour service."

I omit paragraphs 2 and 3 and quote:

"4.(1) Persons violating this ordinance, or trying to circumvent it, particularly such persons who do not comply with their duty to register, or either intentionally or through negligence state any false data, will be punished by imprisonment and/or unlimited fines, unless other laws providing a more severe penalty are applicable.

(4) Those exercising paternal authority or guardianship over the students are co-responsible for their reporting as prescribed. They are subjected to the same penalties as the offenders themselves.

5. This ordinance becomes effective on promulgation.

(Signed) The Higher Chief of the S.S. and Police with the Reich Commissar for the Occupied Dutch Territories."

Since no measures whatsoever succeeded in intimidating the workers in the occupied territories, the defendants, finally, resorted to their police forces to ensure the arrest of those workers destined for deportation to Germany.

This intervention by the police had been demanded by the defendant Sauckel. I submit two documents in evidence. The first consists of the minutes of a conference which took place on 4th January, 1944, at the Headquarters of the Fuehrer. I have just submitted this document to the Tribunal as Exhibit RF 68. I quote, French translation, Page 2, last paragraph; German original, Page 4, in the middle of the page:

"The Plenipotentiary General for Manpower Utilisation (G.B.A.) Sauckel, declared that he would try with fanatical determination to obtain this manpower. Up to now he had always kept his promises regarding the number of workers to be provided; with the best will in the world, however, he was not in a position to make a definite promise for 1944. He would do everything possible to provide the manpower required for 1944. The success would depend mainly on the number of German police put at his disposal. If he had to rely on the police of the countries concerned his project could not be carried out."

I refer now to the statements made by Sauckel at the conference of the Central Office for the Four Year Plan on 1st March, 1944. It is Exhibit RF 30, to which I repeatedly have called the attention of the Tribunal. The passage which I am about to quote has not yet been referred to before the Tribunal. Page 3 of the French Translation—German text, Page 1775 ff.—15th line from the bottom, Page 3 of the French translation:

"The term 'S-factory' (S-Betrieb) in France is actually nothing else but a protection against Sauckel's grasp. That is how the French look at it, and they certainly cannot be expected to think differently. They are Frenchmen, in the first place, who are faced with a German point of view and German actions different from theirs. It is not up to me to decide whether the protected factories (Schutzbetriebe) are useful and necessary. I have only described the situation from my point of view. Nevertheless, I still hope to succeed eventually by using my old organisation of agents on the one hand and, on the other hand, by those measures which I have fortunately been able to wrest from the French Government.

In the course of negotiations, lasting five to six hours, I obtained from M. Laval the concession that the death sentence may be imposed on officials who sabotage the recruitment of labour and other measures. Believe me, it was very difficult. I had to fight hard to succeed, but I did succeed. I am requesting, especially of the Armed Forces that, in case the French Government does not really put its mind to it, most drastic action now be taken by the Germans in France. Please do not resent my following remark: Several times, when in the company of my assistants, I have faced situations in France which caused me to ask: 'Is there no respect in France for the German Lieutenant and his ten men? For months on end everything I said was paralysed by the reply: 'What do you want, Herr Gauleiter? Do you not know that we have no police forces at our disposal? We are powerless in France.' This was the reply given over and over again. How, in the face of these facts, am I to achieve labour recruitment in France? The German authorities must co-operate, and if the French, despite all their promises, do not remedy the situation, we Germans must make an example of one case, and on the provisions of this law, put some prefect or mayor against the wall if he does not co-operate, or else not a single Frenchman will go to Germany."

By such means, finally, the deportation of workers to Germany was achieved by arresting them, and by the threat of reprisals. It was a logical consequence of the National Socialist system, that the policy of recruiting foreign workers was accomplished by police terror.

I have told the Tribunal that the resistance offered by the prisoners of war and by the workers of the occupied territories, against the activities of the defendants, which were in turn insidious or brutal, wrecked the plan for the recruitment of foreign workers. The defendant Sauckel encountered the greatest difficulty in carrying out the programme which he had persuaded Hitler and the defendants Goering, Speer and Funk to accept.

From this it does not follow that Nazi Germany did not succeed in carrying out mass deportations of foreign workers. The number of native workers from the occupied territories of Western Europe who were deported into Germany was very high. More numerous still were those workers compelled to work at home in factories and workyards under the control of the occupation authorities.

I shall give the Tribunal statistical information which will enable it to verify my statements. These statistics are fragmentary. They are excerpts from reports compiled by the Governments of the occupied countries after their liberation, and from reports sent during the war by the Arbeitseinsatz office to its superiors.

These statistics of Allied origin are incomplete. The records on which they are based have been partially destroyed. Further, the administration of the occupied territories are in possession of second-hand information only, whenever the requisition of workers was made directly by the occupation authorities. As to the German statistics, they are also incomplete, since the Allied authorities have not yet discovered all the records of the enemy.

It is, however, possible to give to the Tribunal an exact evaluation of the extent of the deportations effected by Germany. This evaluation will furnish proof that the violations of International Law committed by the defendants did not remain in the tentative stage, characterised by a beginning only, though reprehensible even as such. They brought about such social disorder as, under penal law, constitutes the perpetration of the crime.

I shall first submit to the Tribunal the statistics furnished by the reports of the French Government. The French Government's report has been published by the Institute of Market Analysis. It contains numerous statistical tables from which I quote the total figures. The figures are as follows:

> 738,000 workers were pressed into compulsory labour service in France.
> 875,952 French workers were deported to German factories.
> 987,687 prisoners of war were utilised for the Reich war economy.

Thus, a total of 2,601,639 workers of French citizenship were pressed into work serving the war effort of National Socialist Germany.

From the official report of the Belgian Government it appears that 150,000 persons were pressed into compulsory labour; and the report of the Dutch Government gives a figure of 431,000 persons; but it should be noted that this figure does not take into account the systematic raids undertaken during November, 1944, nor the deportations carried out in 1945.

I am submitting to the Tribunal exact figures which cover all the stages of the policy of recruiting foreign labour. These figures are taken from the reports of the defendant Sauckel himself, or of various administrative offices concerned with the deportation of labour. The extent of labour utilised in the occupied territories is demonstrated by the statistics concerning workers who were used in constructing fortifications of the so-called Atlantic Wall, as part of the Organisation Todt, which I recall was directed by the defendant Speer after the death of its founder. These statistics are to be found in a teletype message sent to Hitler by the defendant Sauckel on 17th May, 1943. It is Document 556-PS-33, which I submit to the Tribunal as Exhibit RF 84. I quote:

> "The Mandatory of the Four Year Plan—the Plenipotentiary General for Manpower Utilisation, Berlin, to the Fuehrer, Headquarters of the Fuehrer.
>
> My Fuehrer! I beg to submit to you the following figures on the manpower employed in the Todt Organisation:
>
> In addition to the manpower assigned to the entire German industry by the 'Manpower Utilisation' since I took office, fresh workers have also been constantly supplied to the Todt Organisation. The total figure of the workers employed by the Todt Organisation was as follows:

>End of March, 1942-270,969.
>
>End of March, 1943-696,003.

>It should be noted that the 'Manpower Utilisation' has, with great speed and energy, assigned workers preferably to the Todt Organisation in the West for the purpose of completing the work on the Atlantic Wall. This is all the more remarkable because (1) in France, Belgium and Holland..."

I omit a few lines and quote from Page 2:

>"Despite the difficulties involved, the manpower strength of the Todt Organisation in the West was increased from 66,701 workers at the end of March, 1942, to 248,200 workers at the end of March, 1943."

The number of foreign workers deported to Germany by 30th September, 1941, is furnished by a report which was found in the archives of the O.K.W. It is Document 1323-PS, which I submit as Exhibit RF 85. According to this document, 1,226,686 workers were employed in Germany on the 30th September,1941. Of that number, 483,842 came from the occupied Western territories. I quote from the document the number of labour deportees by country of origin. I shall confine myself to the columns of interest to the Western States, since the statistics of workers deported from the East of Europe come within the province of my Soviet colleague.

>"Denmark, 63,309.
>
>Holland, 134,093.
>
>Belgium, 212,903.
>
>France, 72,475.
>
>Italy, 238,557."

Finally, on 7th July, 1944, Sauckel, in one of his last reports, informed the National Socialist Government of the results of his campaign during the first half of 1944. I quote the document, which bears the No. 208-PS, and which I submit to the Tribunal as Exhibit RF 86. I read from the second page—

>"C. The foreigners came from:
>
>France, except the North, 33,000.
>
>Belgium, including the North of France, 16,000.
>
>Netherlands, 15,000.
>
>Italy, 37,000."

This is the fresh manpower put at the disposal of German industry during the period of 1st January to 30th June,1944.

I have furnished the proof I owed to the Tribunal. The Tribunal will, moreover, remember Sauckel's admission at the 43rd conference of the Four Year Plan, which I have read to you previously. Sauckel admitted that there were 5,000,000 foreign workers in Germany, of whom 200,000 were actually volunteers.

The enormity of the crime exposed is established by the circumstances of its perpetration, and by the multitude of the victims affected. To prove the gravity of its effect, I have but to recall the treatment to which foreign workers were subjected in Germany.

*Hermann Göring, Adolf Hitler and Albert Speer in August 1943.*
*Bundesarchiv, Bild 146-1977-149-13 / Heinrich Hoffmann / CC-BY-SA*

German propaganda always claimed that foreign workers deported to Germany were treated on an equal basis with German workers; the same living conditions, the same labour contracts and discipline. This contention, as such, is not conclusive. My American colleagues have furnished proof of the blows which the National Socialist conspirators have dealt to the dignity and decency of the life of the German worker. But the actual facts were different. Foreign workers did not enjoy the treatment in Germany to which they were entitled as human beings. I affirm this and I shall try to prove it to the Tribunal.

But, before going into that, I wish to call its attention to the significance of the next crime which I am denouncing. It does not only make the crime of deportation complete, but provides its true meaning also. I said that the policy of the defendants in the occupied territories could be summed up as follows:

Utilisation of the productive forces and extermination of the unproductive forces. This is the principle representing one of the favourite concepts of National Socialism, on the basis of which the treatment inflicted on foreign workers by the defendants should be judged. The Germans have exploited the human potential of the occupied countries to the extreme limit of the strength of the individuals concerned. They showed some consideration for foreign workers only in so far as they wished to increase their output. But as soon as their capacity for work decreased, the foreign workers shared the common lot of deportees.

I shall prove my argument by expounding to the Tribunal the working and living conditions and rules of discipline which were imposed on foreign workers deported to Germany.

I request the Tribunal to charge the defendant Sauckel with the acts I am going to denounce. He was put in charge of the working conditions for foreign workers, following an agreement to which he readily consented. The text of this agreement, made with Ley, the Chief of the German Labour Front, on 2nd June, 1943, was published in the "Reichsarbeitsblatt," 1943, Part 1, Page 588. I submitted this to the Tribunal at the beginning of my presentation as Exhibit RF 18.

This agreement shows that the treatment of foreign workers was subject to control by the inspection department of the "Manpower Utilisation" (Arbeitseinsatz). The defendant Sauckel could, therefore, not ignore the mistreatment to which foreign workers were subjected. If not prescribed, it was tolerated by him.

The working conditions of workers deported to Germany provided the first evidence of the determination of the defendants to exploit the human potential of the occupied territories to the extreme limit of its strength.

First, I call the attention of the Tribunal to the working hours imposed on foreign workers. The working hours were legally set at 54 hours per week by Sauckel's decree of 22nd August, 1942. Actually, most foreign workers were subjected to still longer working hours. Rush work, which necessitated overtime, was mostly assigned to foreign workers. It was not unusual for the latter to be forced to work 11 hours a day—that is, 66 hours a week—provided they had one day off per week.

For this purpose, I quote the report of the Minister for Prisoners, Deportees and Refugees, Document U.K. 783, which I submit as Exhibit RF 87:

"Working Hours." I quote paragraph 2:

The average number of working hours was 11 and sometimes 13 a day in certain factories, e.g. Maschinenfabrik, Berlin 31. In Berlin-Spandau, the Alkett factory, imposed 10 1/4 hours' work on dayshift and 12 hours on nightshift. At Konigsberg, the caterpillar treads factory, Krupp, imposed 12 hours a day."

The work of foreign workers was remunerated by wages identical with those of the German workers.

I call the attention of the Tribunal to the illusory character of this equality. The policy of freezing wages was a permanent element of the wage and price policy pursued by the National Socialist Government; consequently, the wages of the workers employed in Germany remained limited. They were, moreover, heavily burdened with rates and taxes. Finally, they were encroached upon by fines which the German employers had the right to impose upon their workers. These fines could reach the amount of the weekly wage for slight breaches of discipline.

I submit in evidence Document D-182. These are two drafts of speeches to foreign civilian workers. One of them is intended for Russian and Polish workers. I leave this to be dealt with by my Soviet colleagues. I submit the other to the Tribunal as Exhibit RF 88, and I quote:

"Draft of an address to foreign civilian workers: Maintenance of Labour Discipline, January, 1944. I must inform you of the following: The increase in lack of punctuality and in absenteeism has caused the competent authorities to issue stricter regulations to ensure labour discipline, whereby the competence of the employers to impose penalties has been extended. Violations of labour discipline, such as repeated unpunctuality, being absent without cause or excuse, leaving a job without authorisation, will in future be punished by fines up to the average daily wage. In more serious cases—e.g., repeated absences without cause or excuse, or insubordination, fines up to the average weekly salary will be imposed. In such cases, moreover, the additional ration cards may be taken away for a period up to four weeks.... "

The precariousness of wages, which, after these various cuts, were actually received by the foreign workers, did not allow them to raise their standard of living in the places to which they had been deported. I maintain that this standard was insufficient, and that the attitude of the Arbeitseinsatz in this matter constitutes a characteristic violation of the elementary principles of the rights of man. I will confirm this by submitting to the Tribunal proof of the inadequacy of food and medical care to which the foreign workers were entitled.

The German Propaganda Services issued, in France, illustrated pamphlets in which the accommodation for foreign workers were represented as being comfortable. It was quite different in reality.

I will not dwell on this point. Mr. Dodd, my American colleague, has already submitted and commented upon Document D-288, an affidavit by Dr. Jaeger, chief medical officer in charge of the working camps in the Krupp factories. I will not read this document again to the Tribunal, but I would like to repeat that in it Dr. Jaeger stated that French prisoners of war working in the Krupp factories had been billeted for more than half a year in kennels, urinals, unused ovens; the kennels were three feet high, nine feet long and six feet wide, and the men had to sleep there, five in a kennel. I submit this document, in support of my argument, as Exhibit RF 89.

Often to this unsanitary accommodation, inadequate food was added. In this respect I wish to explain the following to the Tribunal:

I do not claim that the foreign workers deported to Germany were systematically exposed to starvation; but I do maintain that the leading principle of National Socialism found its expression in the food regulations for foreign workers. They were decently fed only in so far as the "Manpower Utilisation" wished to maintain or to increase their capacity for work. They were put on a starvation diet the moment when, for any reason whatsoever, their industrial output diminished. They then entered that category of unproductive forces, which National Socialism sought to destroy.

On 10th September, 1942, the defendant Sauckel declared, to the First Congress of the Labour Administration of Greater Germany: "Food and remuneration of foreign workers should be in proportion to their output and their good will." He developed this point of view in documents which I am offering in evidence to the Tribunal.

I refer, in the first place, to the letter from Sauckel to Rosenberg, which is Document 016-PS, and which I shall not read since it has already been read to the Tribunal by my American colleagues. I wish, however, to draw the Tribunal's attention to the second paragraph, Page 20 of this document, which concerns the work of prisoners of war and foreign workers:

> "All these people must be fed, lodged and treated in such a way that they may be exploited to the maximum with a minimum of expense."

I ask the Tribunal to remember this formula. The aim to exploit the foreign manpower to the maximum at a minimum of expense. It is the same concept which I find in a letter of Sauckel of 14th March, 1943, addressed to all Gauleiter. It is Document 633-PS, which I submit to the Tribunal as Exhibit RF 90.

> "Subject: Treatment and Care of Foreign Labour.
>
> Not only our honour and reputation and, still more than that, our National Socialist ideology, which is opposed to the methods of plutocrats and Bolshevists, but also cool common sense in the first place demand proper treatment of foreign labour, including even Soviet-Russians. Slaves who are underfed, diseased, resentful, despairing and filled with hate, will never yield that maximum of output, which they might achieve under normal conditions."

I pass now to the next to the last paragraph:

> "But since we will need foreign labour for many years, and the possibility of replacing it is very limited, I cannot exploit them on a short-term policy nor can I waste their working capacity."

The criminal concept revealed by these documents is particularly manifest in the establishment of the food sanctions which were inflicted on the deported workers. I refer to Document D-182, which I have just submitted as Exhibit RF 88, and I remind the Tribunal that it provides the possibility of inflicting on recalcitrant workers the penalty of a partial suppression of food rations. Moreover, the foreign workers, who were all the more exposed to diseases and epidemics, since they were poorly lodged and fed, did not enjoy proper medical care.

I submit in evidence a report made on 15th June, 1944, by Dr. Fevrier, Head of the Health Service of the French Delegation with the German Labour Front. It is Document 536. I submit it as Exhibit RF 91, and I quote from Page 15 of the French original, Page 13 of the German translation, the last paragraph at Page 15 of the French original:

> "At Auschwitz, in a very fine camp of 2,000 workers, we find, going about free, tubercular people, who were recognised as such by the local German doctor of the Arbeitsamt, but this doctor, out of hostile indifference, neglects to repatriate them. I am now taking steps to obtain their repatriation.
>
> In Berlin, in a clean hospital, well lighted and ventilated, where the

chief doctor, a German, makes the rounds only once in three weeks, and a female Russian doctor every morning distributes uniformly the same calming drops to every patient, I have seen a dozen tuberculars, three of them transformed prisoners. All of them except one have passed beyond the extreme limit at which treatment might still have had some chance of proving effective."

No statistics have been made of foreign workers who died during their deportation. Professor Henri Desaille, Medical Inspector General of the Labour Ministry, estimates that 25,000 French workers died in Germany during their deportation. But not all of them died of diseases. To slow extermination was added swift extermination in concentration camps.

The disciplinary regime over the foreign workers was, in fact, of a severity contrary to the rights of man. I have already given some examples of penalties to which the deported workers were exposed. There were still more. The workers who were deemed recalcitrant by their supervisors were sent to special reprisal camps, the "Straflager"; some disappeared in political concentration camps.

I remind the Tribunal that I have already, indirectly, proved this fact. In the course of my presentation I submitted as Exhibit RF 44, the ordinance of Sauckel of 22nd March, 1943, which extends the term of the labour contracts by the length of time which the workers spent in prison or in internment camps.

I will not dwell on this point. Mr. Dodd, my American colleague, has submitted to the Tribunal the documents which prove the shipment of labour deportees to concentration camps. For the rest, I take the liberty of referring the Tribunal to the presentation which M. Dubost will deliver to the Tribunal within a few days.

I emphasise, however, the significance of this persecution of foreign workers. It completes the crime of their deportation and renders proof of the coherence of the German policy of extermination.

I have already reported to the Tribunal the events which marked the civilian mobilisation of foreign workers for the service of National Socialist Germany. I have shown how the device of compulsory labour was inserted into the general framework of the policy of German domination. I have denounced the methods employed by the defendants to enforce the recruitment of foreign manpower. I have emphasised the importance of the deportations undertaken by the Arbeitseinsatz, and I have recalled how the deported workers were treated and ill-treated.

The policy of compulsory labour encompasses all the infractions under the jurisdiction of the Tribunal: Violation of international conventions, violation of the rights of man and crimes against Common Law.

All the defendants bear official responsibility for these infractions. It was the Reich Cabinet which set up the principles of the policy of enforced recruitment; the High Command of the German Armed Forces tried to carry them out in the workshops of the Wehrmacht, the Navy, and the Air

Force; the civilian administration made use of it to support the German War production.

I recall more particularly the guilt of certain of the defendants: Goering, Plenipotentiary for the Four Year Plan, co-ordinated the planning and the execution of the plans for the recruitment of foreign workers. Keitel, Commander-in-Chief of the Armed Forces, co-signatory of Hitler's decrees, integrated compulsory labour with his manpower policy. Funk, Reich Minister of Economics, and Speer, Minister of Armament, based their programme of war production on compulsory labour. Sauckel, finally, Plenipotentiary General for the Utilisation of Manpower, proved to be the resolute and fanatical agent—to use his own words—of the policy of compulsory enrolment which, in Holland, was promoted and carried out by Seyss-Inquart.

The Tribunal will appreciate their respective responsibility; I demand the Tribunal to condemn the crime of mobilisation of foreign workers. I ask the Tribunal to restore the dignity of human labour which the defendants have attempted to destroy.

# Individual Responsibility of the Defendant

## WEDNESDAY, 6TH FEBRUARY, 1946

M. MOUNIER: Mr. President, your Honours, Gentlemen of the High Tribunal, we have the honour of appearing before your high jurisdiction in order to submit the conclusions of the French prosecution in connection with the responsibility individually incurred by the defendants brought before this bar of justice. In pursuance of the allotment of the various tasks incumbent on each of the four nations resulting both from the Indictment presented in compliance with the Charter of 8th August, 1945, and the agreements reached between the four delegations, the French prosecution, in its presentation, has particularly applied itself to the study of the War Crimes under the Third Count of the Indictment, i.e., the crimes committed by the defendants in France and in the countries of Western Europe during hostilities and during the German occupation.

It follows quite naturally that, in the explanations about to be presented, the case of some of the defendants will be set aside, although their responsibility will already have been established by the other delegations who are, if I may say so, more interested in the crimes committed by the defendants: which correspond to the First, Second and Fourth Counts of the Indictment. The French prosecution, nevertheless, intends to join in the accusations raised by the other delegations against those of the defendants who concern them directly, especially against the defendants von Neurath and von Ribbentrop. The French delegation associates itself with the statement presented against them by Sir David Maxwell Fyfe. The same holds good as far as the defendants Hess, Kaltenbrunner, Frank, Bormann, Funk, Schacht, von Papen, Baldur von Schirach, Streicher, Raeder, Doenitz and Fritzsche are concerned.

Moreover, Mr. President, your Honours, we should like, in this brief presentation, slightly to deviate from the order of priority in which the defendants appear, both in the Indictment and in the dock, in order to clarify certain points. As a matter of fact, it would appear desirable, when presenting some of the Chiefs of the National Socialist conspiracy, as viewed from the angle of crimes committed in the West, to show how they implemented their philosophical, political economic and, finally, their military conceptions. Consequently, this order will determine the order in which we shall present the case of the defendants.

On the other hand the defendants, in pursuance of the rule governing the proceedings which the Tribunal follows in this trial, have not yet given their oral explanations before the Court, and the hearing of the majority of the witnesses, or at least of the more important witnesses, has not yet taken place.

That is why the French prosecution, with the permission of the Tribunal, reserves the right of completing, at a later date, its statement regarding the individual defendants on the one hand, and the groups accused, according to the expression used by my eminent friend, prosecutor Boissary, of "International Indignity," on the other hand.

Needless to say, the concluding phase of our presentation will be as brief as possible, since the French Delegation is anxious to avoid any unnecessary prolongation of the proceedings.

An imposing number of documents has been submitted to the Tribunal. Their reading, presented in the first instance for the information of the Tribunal, then for the information of the defence, and finally, be it said, for that of universal public opinion, has already taken up a very considerable time. That is why, with the permission of the Tribunal, we shall abstain, as far as possible, from presenting the Tribunal with still more copious documents. Sufficient written evidence has already been furnished by the American, British and French prosecutions, when added to those still to be submitted by the prosecution of the Union of Soviet Socialist Republics, to convince the Tribunal of the defendants' guilt.

We shall therefore content ourselves, in general, with quoting documents already produced, in order to correlate the facts which we shall bring forward with the evidence already supplied. I should like, however, Mr. President, before approaching the case of the defendants, whom I wish to accuse individually, to make a statement of a very general nature. It would be idle to pretend that a certain part of this public opinion—and not the least enlightened part at that—in the Old as well as in the New World, has not evinced surprise in seeing that this Indictment, which is the basis of the present proceedings, collectively denounces the criminal character of certain organisations, i.e., the Reich Cabinet, the Leadership Corps of the National Socialist Party, the S.S. including the S.D., the Gestapo, the S.A., the General Staff, and the High Command.

In this connection the Tribunal has been good enough to invite the various delegations to present written memoranda in order to establish the validity of the allegations contained in the Indictment. But may I be allowed, before a more complete memorandum is handed to you, to present a few ideas which appear to me to be considered. It appears, as a matter of fact, that this concept of a collective responsibility of the various groups goes hand in hand with the concept of conspiracy constituting the other governing idea of the Indictment.

There is no doubt, as far as this idea of a conspiracy is concerned, as defined in the Indictment, that one finds, in the first instance, in the acts of the defendants, that mystery which generally accompanies any conspiracy, whatever its nature, and that the various documents already supplied to the Tribunal are sufficient to confirm the existence of all the elements which render it possible for me to state that the defendants, their partners and their accomplices had, in fact, conceived and realised the foul agreement which has to enable them to commit crimes against the peace of the world by means contrary to the laws of war, to International Law, and to international morality.

There is no particle of doubt that the Nazi leaders had invested all their meetings with a cloak of secrecy, whether these meetings were regular and administrative, or whether they were of a casual or of an informal kind. This secrecy, in itself, would be an abnormal thing if it could be isolated from all the other elements in the case. But, when added to them, it clearly shows the guilty intent of the conspirators, for this secrecy alone made possible the employment of criminal means, as we shall emphasise.

I shall, however, remind the Tribunal that very often, when orders transmitted were concerned, certain paragraphs were erased so as to leave no trace. The defendant Hermann Goering admitted this in the course of the interrogations. Consequently this fact proves the intent not only to act in the greatest secrecy, but also the intent of doing away with every trace of whatever had happened.

If I may transpose an expression used during the war of 1914-18, an expression applied to the sinking of certain ships of friendly or Allied nations, I should say, where this particular paragraph is concerned, that it was a case of "Spurlos Versenkt," i.e., sunk without trace.

On the other hand, the proof of this foul agreement is evident from the eminently and evidently criminal nature of the decisions taken in these secret councils.

**THE PRESIDENT:** It is just 1 o'clock now. Would it be convenient for counsel to break off at this time?

**M. MOUNIER:** I am at the disposal of the Court.

**THE PRESIDENT:** Very well.

*(A recess was taken.)*

**THE PRESIDENT:** M. Mounier, owing to technical difficulties we will not be able to continue the sitting this afternoon, because these difficulties, we are advised, cannot be remedied for some hours, and under those circumstances, the Tribunal thinks it better to adjourn now. But the Tribunal hopes that you will be able to conclude the case on behalf of the French prosecution tomorrow, and that the case against the defendant Hess will be presented on behalf of the British prosecution.

**M. MOUNIER:** I understand, Mr. President, and I will get in touch with the British prosecution and we will arrange to conclude that part of the case tomorrow.

**THE PRESIDENT:** Sir David Maxwell Fyfe, do you wish to say anything?

**SIR DAVID MAXWELL FYFE:** No, My Lord. We are ready to go on with the presentation against the defendant Hess, and we think that it should take two and a half hours, approximately.

*(Whereupon at 15.30 hours the Tribunal adjourned until 10.00 hours on 7th February, 1946.)*

# THURSDAY, 7TH FEBRUARY, 1946

M. MOUNIER: Mr. President, your Honours, before the adjournment yesterday I had begun to explain to you very briefly the relation which, in our eyes, exists between two of the main themes in the Indictment, to wit, the accusation of conspiracy brought against certain groups designated in the Indictment and which I enumerated yesterday, on the one hand; and, on the other hand, the various acts which enable us to form our conclusions as to the criminal character of the activity of the National Socialist conspirators.

I told you, to begin with, that what appeared to us to be at the bottom of this criminal activity was the profound mystery, the absolute mystery surrounding their meetings, both official and unofficial, a fact which is corroborated by statements made by certain of the defendants in their interrogations from which it frequently emerged that orders emanating from high places were to be suppressed in part or in toto, so as to leave no trace.

We consider, likewise, that proof of the fraudulent collaboration which existed among the conspirators is afforded by the criminal character of the decisions made at these secret councils, which aimed at the conquest of neighboring countries through wars of aggression.

Finally, proof of this fraudulent collaboration is afforded—in our eyes—by the way in which these criminal plans were carried out by the employment of all kinds of means, condemned both by international morality and by the letter of the law. For example: in international and diplomatic spheres the most cynical plots, the use in foreign countries of what is known as the "Fifth Column," financial camouflage, the exertion of improper pressure, backed by demonstrations of violence, and finally, when these methods no longer proved effective, the waging of a war of aggression.

As for those individuals who regularly and of their own free will took part in meetings of groups and organisations, such as those denounced in the Indictment, their voluntary membership in these groups, or the live and deliberate part which they took in their activities, suffice to show that they had every intention of giving their active co-operation to these groups in a way which admits of no possible doubt. In view of the aims pursued and the means adopted, this intention could only be a guilty one.

In the eyes of the Prosecution, engaged in seeking the elements constituting the crime, it would appear that this suffices to prove what we call the consilium fraudis, and to enable us to verify the causal link between this will to evil, on the one hand, and the criminal deed on the other, and to make it possible to reassert the criminal character of the understanding between the conspirators, and thereby the criminal character of their individual acts.

Could the Trustee of the Four Year Plan, when he ordered the Plenipotentiary for Manpower to recruit 1,000,000 foreign workers for the Reich, forget that this act was contrary to international conventions, and leave out of consideration the tragic consequences which the execution of this murderous action would entail—and has in fact entailed—for these people and for their families?

Could the Minister of Armaments who set up, in agreement with or by order of the Chief of the Air Force, underground aircraft factories in the internment camps—could he, I say, fail to be aware that using prisoners who were already exhausted under such conditions was equivalent to causing their premature death?

Could the diplomat who, on various pretexts, treated diplomatic instruments intended to assure the stability and the peace of the world as scraps of paper—could he lose sight of the fact that these acts would plunge the civilized world into catastrophe?

Whether their conscience was at that moment disturbed by the feeling, more or less obscure, that they were infringing human and divine laws is a question which need not be asked on the juridical plane on which you will be working. But even assuming that we should consider it our moral duty to put this question to ourselves on the psychological plane, we should then have to remember two essential concepts: The first is that the German, as a French writer puts it, at times combines in himself the identity of contraries. Consequently, it is possible that in certain cases he may consciously do evil while remaining convinced that his act is irreproachable from the moral point of view. The second concept is that, according to the law of National Socialist ethics sometimes put into words by certain National Socialist leaders, that which promotes the interests of the Party is good; that which does not promote the interests is evil.

And yet, our personal impression on the occasion of the masterly speech given by M. Francois de Menthon, was that some of his words, striking in their accent of deep humanity, had stirred some consciences. Even today, after so many accumulated proofs, we may wonder whether the defendants admit their responsibility as chiefs, as men, as representatives of the incriminated organisations. This will perhaps be revealed in the course of the proceedings.

Mr. President, your Honours, I should like now to summarise the activity of the defendant Speer, for as regards France and the Western countries the defendant Speer incurs responsibilities of the same nature as those of the defendant Sauckel. Like the defendant of whom I have just spoken, he permitted violations of the laws of war, violations of the laws of humanity, in working towards drafting and carrying out of a vast programme of deportation and enslavement of the occupied countries.

Speer, Mr. President, first took part in working out the programme of forced labor and collaborated in its adoption. In the course of his interrogation and, he stated under oath: First, that he took part in the discussion at which the decision to use forced labor was made. Second, that he collaborated in the execution of this plan. Third, that the basis of this programme was the removal to Germany by force of foreign workers on the authority of Sauckel, Plenipotentiary for Allocation of Labor under the Four Year Plan.

The Tribunal will kindly refer to Exhibit USA 220, submitted by the United

States delegation on 12 December 1945, which I quote as Exhibit RF 1411 of our documentation.

As regards France in particular, Hitler and the defendant Speer held a conference on 4 January 1943, in the course of which it was decided that more severe measures should be taken to expedite the recruiting of French civilian workers without discrimination between skilled and unskilled workers. This is made clear by a note to which I would ask the Tribunal to refer. That is a note signed by Fritz Sauckel himself. It has already been presented by the American prosecution as Document 556-PS, and I submit it as Exhibit RF 1412.

The defendant Speer knew that the levies for forced labor in the occupied territories were obtained by violence and terror. He approved the continuation of these methods from September, 1942, onward. He knew, for instance, that workers were deported by force from the Ukraine to work in the Reich. He knew, likewise, that the great majority of workers in the occupied regions of the West were sent to Germany against their will. He even declared before the American magistrate who was questioning him that he considered these methods regular and legal.

The defendant Speer, knowing that the foreign workers were recruited and deported for forced labour in Germany, made specific demands for foreign workers and provided for their employment in the various branches of activity placed under his direction.

The preceding paragraphs summarise all the declarations made by the defendant in the course of the interrogation already mentioned and to which I have just referred.

I beg to remind you that Speer, in addition, was a member of the Central Planning Board. On account of this, and in common with Field Marshal Milch, only Hitler and Goering were superior to him as far as demands for labour were concerned. He likewise took part, in this capacity, in discussions which took place with Hitler to settle the numbers of foreign workers required. He knew that most of these were obtained by means of deportation, through coercion and enslavement of the occupied countries. Proof of this is furnished by various passages of the minutes of the Central Planning Board and from Speer's conferences with Hitler.

I refer to Documents 124R and 125R which have been submitted as Exhibit USA 179 on 12 December 1945 (Exhibit RF 1414).

Speer did not hesitate to resort to methods of terrorism and brutality as a means of achieving a peak output from this forced labour. He found justification for the action of the S.S. and of the police and for the use of concentration camps to subdue recalcitrants.

I beg to recall to the Tribunal Document 124R, relating to the minutes of the 21st meeting of the Central Planning Board, 30th October, 1942, Page 1059, already quoted. This is the document quoted previously, Exhibit USA 179, on 12 December 1945.

The defendant Speer likewise bears responsibility for the use of prisoners of war in military operations directed against their countries, for in his capacity as chief of the Todt Organisation, he forced citizens of the Allied nations to work for this organisation, particularly, in the building of fortifications and, among other things, the famous West Wall. He likewise forced Frenchmen, Belgians, Luxembourgers, Dutchmen, Norwegians, and Danes to manufacture arms to be utilised against the allies of the countries to which they themselves belonged.

Finally—and this is a very important point regarding the responsibility of the defendant Speer—he participated directly in the use of prisoners from the concentration camps. He proposed the use of prisoners from the concentration camps in the armament factories. Now, in view of the wretched physical condition of the prisoners, no profit, but only the extermination of the prisoners could be expected from this measure. The use of prisoners from concentration camps in the factories had the effect of increasing the demand for this type of labour; and this demand was satisfied in part, at least, by sending to the concentration camps persons who, in ordinary times, would never have been sent there.

Speer went so far as to establish, near the factories, concentration camps which served solely to provide labour.

He knew the Mauthausen Camp. The Spanish witness, Boix, whom the Tribunal heard a few days ago, attested under oath that he had with his own eyes seen the defendant Speer visit the camp at Mauthausen and congratulate the leaders of this camp. Boix even declared that he had worked on the preparation of photographs of this scene. Consequently this visit to the camp cannot be questioned. Speer, therefore, saw for himself the barbarous conditions in which the prisoners lived. Nevertheless, he persisted in utilising labour from the Camp of Mauthausen in the factories under his authority.

I have concluded the case against Speer. I am at the disposal of the Tribunal to continue.

**THE PRESIDENT:** We will adjourn now for 10 minutes.

*(A recess was taken.)*

# The Case for Albert Speer

## WEDNESDAY, 19TH JUNE, 1946

THE PRESIDENT: I call on counsel for the defendant Speer.
DR. FLAECHSNER (on behalf of the defendant Speer):
Mr. President, gentlemen of the Tribunal:
Perhaps the High Tribunal will recall the fact that, when we were discussing the material evidence which I had suggested for presentation in this case, I dispensed with the testimony of witnesses and stated that I would limit myself to the use of interrogatories and to the questioning of witnesses outside of the court-room.

I had hoped I should thus be able to produce my entire evidence. However, I am not in possession of all the interrogatories I sent out. I have only received part of them. I will use those replies which are at my disposal to the best of my ability in the examination of the defendant so that a special presentation of those interrogatories and of the protocol will be superfluous. Despite everything, I hope to conduct the examination-in-chief of the defendant in such a manner that, in my estimation, I shall be finished in seven hours or, at the most, in a day.

Now, with the permission of the High Tribunal I should like to call the defendant Speer to the witness box.
THE PRESIDENT: Yes.
(ALBERT SPEER, a witness, took the stand and testified as follows):
BY THE PRESIDENT:
Q. Will you state your full name, please?
A. Albert Speer.
Q. Will you repeat this oath after me:
I swear by God, the Almighty and Omniscient, that I will speak the pure truth and will withhold and add nothing.
*(The witness repeated the oath.)*
THE PRESIDENT: Sit down.
DIRECT EXAMINATION BY DR. FLAECHSNER:
Q. Herr Speer, will you please tell the Tribunal about your life up until the time you were appointed minister?
A. I was born on 19th March, 1905. My grandfather and my father were successful architects. At first I wanted to study mathematics and physics but studied architecture, more because of tradition than inclination. I attended the universities at Munich and Berlin and at the age of 24, in 1929, I was the first assistant at the technical college in Berlin.

At the age of twenty-seven, in 1932, I went into business for myself until 1942.

In 1934 Hitler noticed me for the first time. I became acquainted with him and, from that period of time onwards, I followed my profession with joy and enthusiasm, for Hitler was quite fanatical on the subject of architecture and I received many important constructional contracts from him. In addition to putting up a new Reich chancellery in Berlin and the various buildings on the Party grounds in Nuremberg, I was entrusted with the re-planning of the cities of Berlin and Nuremberg. I had draughted plans for buildings which would have been among the largest in the world, and the carrying through of these plans would have cost no more than two months of Germany's war expenditure. Through this predilection which Hitler had for architecture, I had a close personal contact with him. I belonged to a circle which consisted of other artists and his personal staff. If Hitler had had any friends at all, I certainly would have been one of his close friends.

Despite the war, this peaceful constructional work was carried on until December 1941, when the catastrophe in Russia put an end to it. The German personnel of the manpower was furnished by me for the reconstruction of the destroyed railway installations in Russia.

Q. The prosecution, in Document 1435-PS, which is Exhibit USA 216, has quoted a remark from your first speech as a minister, dated February 1942, in which you state that, at that time, you had placed ten thousand prisoners of war at the disposal of the armament industry.

DR. FLAECHSNER: Mr. President, this remark may be found in my document book on Page 4 of the English text and Page 1 of the French text.

BY DR. FLAECHSNER:

Q. Herr Speer, what do you have to say to us about this document?

A. At that time, in my capacity as an architect, I had nothing to say as to whether these workers were to be taken into armaments or not. They were put at the disposal of the prisoner-of-war organisation of the OKW. I took it as a matter of course that they would be utilised in the armament industry.

Q. Herr Speer, did you ever participate in the planning and preparation of an aggressive war?

A. No. Since I was active as an architect up until the year 1942, there can be no question about that whatsoever. The buildings which I constructed were completely representative of peacetime activities. As an architect, I used up material, manpower and money in considerable amounts for this purpose. This material, in the last analysis, was lost to armaments.

Q. Were you—

A. One moment, please.

The carrying out of these large building plans which Hitler sponsored was, actually and especially psychologically, the antithesis to armament.

Q. The prosecution asserts you had been a Reichsleiter.

A. No, that is a mistake on the part of the prosecution.

Q. You wore the Golden Party Emblem. When and why did you receive it?

A. I received the Golden Party Emblem from Hitler in 1938. It was because I had completed the plans for a new building programme in Berlin. Besides myself, five other artists received this Golden Party Emblem at the same time.

**Q.** Were you a member of the Reichstag?

**A.** In 1941 I was made a member of the Reichstag by Hitler, that is, without being elected, as replacement for a member who had left the Reichstag. Hitler At that time said that he wanted me in the Reichstag as representative of the artists.

**Q.** Did you ever receive a donation?

**A.** No.

**Q.** How did your activity as a minister start?

**A.** On 8th February, 1942, my predecessor, Dr. Todt, was killed in an aeroplane crash. Several days later, Hitler declared I was to be his successor in his many offices. At that time I was thirty-six years of age. Up until that time, Hitler considered the main activity of Todt to be in the building sphere, and that is why he called me to be his successor. I believe that it was a complete surprise to everyone when I was appointed as minister.

Immediately upon my assuming office, it was plain that not building but armament production was to be my main task. Because of the heavy losses of material in the battles in Russia during the winter of 1941-1942, Hitler called for considerable intensification of armament production.

**Q.** When you assumed office, did you find the Reich Ministry for Munitions well and completely organised?

**A.** No, Dr. Todt had neglected this function of his up to that time, and in addition, in the autumn of 1941, Hitler had issued a decree according to which the armament of the army was to take second place to the armament of the air force. At that time he foresaw a victorious outcome of the war in Russia and had decreed that armament was to be concentrated on the imminent war against England, and was to be converted to that end. Because of this unbelievable optimism of his, the rescinding of that order was postponed until January 1942, and only from that date onward, for a month—that is, during the last month of his life—did Dr. Todt start to build up his organisation. Therefore, I had the difficult task, first of all, to make myself acquainted with a completely new field of activity; secondly, at the same time to create all organisational prerequisites for my task; and thirdly, to increase armament production for the army, and to increase production generally as much as possible within the next few months. As is very well known today, I succeeded in doing that.

**Q.** What promises did you receive from Hitler about the duration of your task and about your staff of collaborators?

**A.** Hitler promised me that I should consider my task only as a war task and that after the war I might once more resume my profession of architect.

**DR. FLAECHSNER:** At this point I should like to mention a passage from Document 1435 which deals with a speech delivered by Speer on 24th February, 1942, ten days after he assumed office. This document shows that he was very reluctant about changing his profession of architect for that of a minister. I quote:

> "Finally, I can say for myself that my personal contribution is a very large one. Up until very recently I lived in a world of pure ideals."

In Document 1520-PS, which is Exhibit GB 156, which is on Page 2 of my Document Book; Page 5 of the English text and Page 2 of the French and Russian texts, on 8th May, 1942, Hitler stated, and I quote:

> "The Fuehrer thereupon stated several times that the Reich Ministry Speer would be dissolved on the day when peace was concluded."

I should further like to submit Speer Document 43, which is a memorandum from Speer to Hitler, dated 20th September, 1944. Mr. President, this may be found on Page 6 of the English text, Page 3 of the French and Russian texts. From this document you can see that Speer was considered hostile to the Party ("parteifremd" and "parteifeindlich") by Bormann and Goebbels because of his circle of collaborators. Speer writes in his memorandum, and I quote:

> "The task which I have to fulfil is a non-political one. I was content in my work, as long as I personally and my work were evaluated only according to professional achievements and standards. I do not feel strong enough to carry out successfully and without hindrance the technical work to be accomplished by myself and my co-workers if it is to be measured by Party political standards."

**BY DR. FLAECHSNER:**

Q. Herr Speer, can you describe the fundamental principles according to which you built up your ministry?

**THE PRESIDENT:** What exhibit number are you giving that?

**DR. FLAECHSNER:** Exhibit No. 1, Mr. President.

**BY DR. FLAECHSNER:**

Q. Herr Speer, can you describe the fundamental principles which you followed in building up your ministry?

A. I personally was no expert, and I did not want to act as an expert. Therefore, I selected the best possible experts to be found in Germany as my co-workers. I believed that these men were to be found within industry itself. Therefore, I made up my ministry of honorary industrial co-workers. This was done in the United States in a similar way during the war in matters of production. Professional civil servants were lacking in my ministry and you cannot really consider my ministry as one set up on normal lines.

In June 1944 I delivered a speech in Essen about the fundamental principles upon which I founded my ministry and its work, to defend myself against the various attacks on my system in Party circles.

**DR. FLAECHSNER:** Mr. President, I believe that the High Tribunal is not yet in possession of my Document Book containing the interrogatories. I would have been glad to point out that the statements given by witnesses Sauer and Schieber in this connection are summed up in this answer. Now I shall submit—

**THE PRESIDENT:** If you will give us the reference—give us the names of the witnesses. We can take notice of them afterwards. What are their names?

DR. FLAECHSNER: The witness Sauer, and we are dealing with his answers to Points 4, 5 and 8 of the interrogatory; the witness Schieber gives a statement regarding this matter under Point 12 of his interrogatory.

Now I should like to submit the speech given by Speer on 9th June, 1944, as Exhibit No. 2. It confirms the testimony which the defendant has made about the organisation of his ministry and the staffing of it with honorary industrial co-workers. I shall quote it. I am sorry to say that this speech is also not contained in your Honour's supplementary volume. I am very sorry. I will just have to read it, and I quote:

"These honorary co-workers drawn from industry—"

THE PRESIDENT: Dr. Flaechsner, it is a little bit inconvenient to the Tribunal not to have these documents before them. You could not possibly postpone dealing with the particular documents that you have not got here until tomorrow morning? Shall we have the supplementary volume then?

DR. FLAECHSNER: The promise was given me that it would be at my disposal by this afternoon.

THE PRESIDENT: Yes, well, then, would it be convenient to leave those parts which are contained in the supplementary volume over until tomorrow?

DR. FLAECHSNER: In the supplementary volume No. 5 we find a document, very short in part, with which I shall not concern myself today. Only this one speech which I am mentioning now is—

THE PRESIDENT: Very well.

DR. FLAECHSNER: I quote:

"These honorary co-workers, drawn from industry, carry the responsibility to the last detail for what is manufactured in the various enterprises and industries and for how it is manufactured."

Then a few lines farther down:

"Among your main tasks, next to the assigning of contracts to these industries, is to supervise the restriction of the types and specialisation of these industries; under certain circumstances, to close certain enterprises, to further rationalisation from the point of view of raw materials, construction and production, as well as unconditional exchange of experience, without regard to 'Schutzrechte' (patents)."

From various passages of this document it can be seen clearly that Speer considered his office an improvised instrument which made use of the existing authorities of the Reich for the fulfilment of his tasks without burdening his office with administrative duties. The decree of 10th August, which is mentioned in the speech of Speer, shows that he expressly prohibited his offices from turning into administrative offices. The defendant did not want the bureaucratic system in his ministry.

THE PRESIDENT: What speech of Speer are you referring to? You said the decree of 10th August.

DR. FLAECHSNER: It is still the same speech, Mr. President, which I just mentioned.

The decree is mentioned therein.

**THE PRESIDENT:** I did not get what the year was when you began. What was the year?

**DR. FLAECHSNER:** The year was 1942, 10th August, and the speech was given in, the year 1944. Therefore, he was referring to a decree which had been in force for some time.

Just how important it was to the defendant to have non-bureaucratic new forces in his ministry is shown in a passage from his speech which I would like to quote now:

> "Any organisation which is to last for some period of time and which exceeds a certain size has a tendency to become bureaucratic. Even though, in one of the first large attacks on Berlin, large numbers of the current files of the ministry were burned and therefore, for some time, we were lucky enough to have unnecessary ballast taken from us, we cannot expect occurrences of that sort will continuously bring new vigour into our work."

BY **DR. FLAECHSNER:**

**Q.** Herr Speer, so far as the Tribunal wishes, will you please briefly supplement these statements about the tasks of your ministry from the technical point of view?

**A.** I shall try to be very brief.

**THE PRESIDENT:** Well, you, Dr. Flaechsner, you read us the speech.

**DR. FLAECHSNER:** The speech, yes—

**THE PRESIDENT:** It seems to be very remote to every issue, even as it is, and why you should want to supplement it, I do not know.

**DR. FLAECHSNER:** I thought it might be of interest to the High Tribunal to hear about the sphere of activity which the defendant had in his capacity as a minister. This speech was made to experts and is, therefore, really only of interest to an expert. I assumed that the High Tribunal would wish to know just what the task of the production ministry of Herr Speer was. I am under the impression that the prosecution thinks its sphere of activity to have been considerably greater than it actually was.

**THE PRESIDENT:** If you want to know what he says about the tasks of his ministry, you can ask him. But you have just been reading his speech, and we do not want to—

**DR. FLAECHSNER (interposing):** No, no, I do not want that either. He is just going to give us briefly some of the technical tasks of his ministry. That is what I wanted to know.

**THE PRESIDENT:** You do not seem to be hearing me accurately. Would it not be better if you put your earphones on?

What I said was that you had read the speech and we did not want to hear any more argument upon the speech from the defendant. If you want to ask the defendant what the tasks of his ministry were, ask him. What you asked him was: "Do you wish to supplement the speech?"

BY **DR. FLAECHSNER:**

**Q.** Herr Speer, will you please tell us what the tasks were which your ministry had to carry out, and please do not refer to the things that I mentioned in the speech.

A. I believe the tasks of a production ministry are well known in all industrial States. I just wanted to summarize briefly which functions I had to concern myself with in detail in this ministry.

For one, we had to surmount the deficiency in raw materials, metals and steel. Then, through an introduction of the Fliessbandarbeiten (assembly line work), which is customary in the United States, but was not yet very current in Germany, the work was systematised and thus machinery and space were used to the utmost. Also, it was necessary to amplify the production programme, for example, for fine steel, aluminium, and for individual parts like ball bearings and cog-wheels.

One of the most important tasks was the development of new weapons and their mass production; and then, beginning with 1943, repairing of the damage caused by the extraordinarily rapid bombing attacks, which forced us to work with improvised means and methods.

Q. What was the importance of this activity in the sphere of your ministry?

A. It is to be taken as a matter of course that this sphere of activity was the most important in our country, if only because it included providing equipment for the army. I claimed that during the war the rest of the economy would have to be regulated according to the exigencies of armament. In times of war, at home, there are only two tasks which count: Furnishing soldiers for the front, and supplying weapons.

Q. Why was the task of your ministry purely a war function?

A. Because during peace-time the giving of orders is normally regulated according to supply and demand, but in war time this regulating factor is lacking.

Q. Therefore it was one of the main tasks of your ministry to exercise a State control over the distribution of orders?

A. Yes.

Q. Then, at first, you had responsibility only for armament production for the army, but at the end of 1944 you were responsible for the entire field of armament and war production. Can you briefly tell me the stages of this development, and how thereby the extent of your task grew?

A. It would be best for me to tell you about the development by dealing with the number of workers I had.

In 1942 I took over the armament and construction programmes with altogether 2,600,000 workers. In the spring of 1943, Doenitz gave me the responsibility for naval armament as well, and at this period I had 3,200,000 workers. In September of 1943, through an agreement with the Minister of Economics, Herr Funk, the production task of the Ministry of Economics was transferred to me. With that I had 12,000,000 workers working for me.

Finally, I took over the air armament from Goering on 1st August, 1944. With that the total production was marshalled under me with 14,000,000 workers. The number of workers applies to the Greater German Reich, not including the occupied countries.

**Q.** How was it possible to have a task of that magnitude directed by a ministry that consisted almost exclusively of honorary members who, moreover, had no practical routine experience in purely administrative matters?

**A.** The administrative departments in the various armament offices retained their tasks. In that way, for example, in the army, the Heereswaffenamt—the Army Weapon Office—with a staff of several thousands, gave the orders, supervised the carrying out of these orders, and saw to it that delivery of the orders and payments were carried out in a proper manner. Only in that way did I succeed in having the entire armament production—which amounted to three to four billion marks a month—carried through with an honorary co-worker staff of six thousand people.

**Q.** Were all armament enterprises subordinate to you?

**A.** No. There was a small group of enterprises, which were run directly by the Wehrmacht branches with their own workers, not controlled by me; and also the enterprises of the SS were excluded from my domain as well.

**Q.** The prosecution makes the charge that you shared the responsibility for the recruiting of foreign workers and prisoners of war, and took manpower from concentration camps. What do you say to this?

**A.** In this connection, neither I nor the ministry were responsible for this. The ministry was a new establishment, which had a technical problem to deal with. It took no competence in any field away from an existing authority. The conditions of work were still handled through the old existing authorities. The Food Ministry, and the various offices connected with it, were responsible for the food supply, and the trade supervising agencies in the Reich Ministry were responsible for the maintenance of safe, liveable conditions at the places of work; the Trustees of Labour, working under the Plenipotentiary for Labour Commitment, were responsible for the salaries and the quality and quantity of work done; and the Health Office of the Reich Ministry of the Interior was responsible for health conditions. The Justice Department and the Police Department dealt with violations against labour discipline, and finally, the German Labour Front was responsible for representing the interests of the workers.

The centralisation of all of these authorities lay in the bands of the Gauleiter as Reich Defence Commissioner. The fact that the SS put itself and its concentration camp internees outside the control of State departments was not a matter with which I or my ministry were concerned.

**Q.** Your co-defendant Sauckel testified to the effect that with the carrying out of the recruiting of workers for the industries his task was finished. Is that correct in your opinion?

**A.** Yes, certainly, as far as the recruiting of workers is concerned, for one of the subjects of dissension between Sauckel and me was that the suitable employment of workers in the industry itself was a matter for the judgement of the man in charge of the industry, and that this could not be influenced by the Labour Office. It applied, however, only to the recruitment of labour, and not to the observing of conditions of labour. In this latter connection, the office of Sauckel was partly responsible as supervising authority.

**Q.** To what extent could the works manager carry out the decrees of Sauckel as to labour conditions, etc.?

**A.** The decrees issued by Sauckel were unobjectionable, but the works managers did not always find it possible to carry out the orders for reasons which were beyond their control. The bombing attacks brought about difficulties, such as disorganised transportation or destroyed living quarters. It is not possible to make the managers responsible for the observing of these decrees under circumstances which often took on catastrophic proportions after the summer of 1944. These were times of crises, and it was a matter for the Reich authorities to determine just how far it was possible to carry through these decrees, and it was not right to push this responsibility on to the shoulders of the works manager.

**Q.** How far was the factory manager responsible to your ministry in this regard?

**A.** Within the framework of the above-mentioned responsibility which industry enjoyed, the armament factory managers had received an equal State responsibility from me. This, of course, applied only to technical tasks.

**Q.** Were there any industries making secret items which were not permitted to be inspected by the Gauleiters? I recall evidence given here where this, was reported.

**A.** There were some industries which concerned themselves with secret matters, but in such cases the sectional manager of the Labour Front was represented, and the representative could report to the Gauleiter on conditions in the factory through the Gauobmann (Chief of the Labour Front of a Gau).

**Q.** Did you approve of the punishment of people who were unwilling to work?

**A.** Yes, I considered it right that workers who violated labour discipline should be punished, but I did not demand supplementary measures in this regard. As a matter of principle, I represented the view that a satisfactory output on the part of fourteen million workers could be achieved in the long run only through the good will of the workers themselves. This is a bit of experience which applies generally, causing every employer in the world to do all in his power to make his workers satisfied.

**Q.** Did you support the efforts made by Sauckel to improve the social conditions of the workers, and if so, why?

**A.** Naturally I supported them, even though I did not have any jurisdiction in that sphere, for the reasons which I have just mentioned. For our experience proved that when labour was content and satisfied, there was much less loss in materials. This for me was very important, because of our deficiency in raw materials. Moreover it is obvious that the better quality which is produced by satisfied labourers is of special importance in time of war.

**Q.** In the records of your discussions with Hitler, there are various directives made by Hitler dealing with the care and the treatment of foreign workers.

Did you cause Hitler to give these directives?

**A.** Yes.

**DR. FLAECHSNER:** In this connection, I should like to submit three pieces of evidence—first of all, Speer Document 11. Mr. President, this is found on Page 10 of the English text, Page 7 of the French text. In this document, upon Speer's request, in March 1942, it was put down and I quote:

> "That the Russians under all circumstances were to receive sufficient food and that Russian civilians were not to be put behind barbed wire and be treated as prisoners of war."

As my next piece of evidence, which will be Exhibit 4, I would like to submit Speer Document 13.

According to this document, in May 1943, Hitler decided, at the suggestion of Speer, that the German as well as Russian miners should receive a substantial amount of supplementary rations; it is also particularly specified there that the Russian prisoners of war are to receive rewards in the form of tobacco and similar items, for special efforts and achievements.

The next piece of evidence is Speer Exhibit 5 and it is Document 9. Mr. President, this is found on Page 12 of the English text and Page 9 of the German text in the Document Book. According to this document the food supply in Italian armament plants is to be raised to about the level of the German rations. In this connection it is important to note that Speer at the same time issued directives that also the families of these workers receive equivalent care.

I had other documents of this type at my disposal, but, in order to save the time of the translation department, I did not include them in my Document Book.

**BY DR. FLAECHSNER:**

**Q.** Herr Speer, to whom did the bonuses of the armament industry go, and of what did they consist?

**A.** We gave out many millions of packages to armament plants. They contained additional food, chocolate, cigarettes, and so forth, and these bonuses were given in addition to all the extra food rations which were allowed by the Food Ministry for those who worked longer hours or who did heavy work. In the industries, these bonuses were given to all workers without distinction, including the foreign workers, prisoners of war and the workers from concentration camps.

**Q.** I shall again refer to the fact that these bonuses were also given to armament workers from concentration camps later on when discussing another document.

In what form did your ministry put its demands to the industries?

**A.** It is important to note that the demands put to industries were only in the manner of production schedules. It was up to the industries to make their requests as to manpower, machinery and material on the basis of these schedules.

**Q.** Was there often an unusual increase in working hours in industry, and how did this happen?

A. In theory, working time should remain uniform in modern assembly line production during the entire month. But due to the bombing attacks, delays in supplying tools and raw materials set in. As a result the number of hours in industry varied from eight to twelve a day. The average, according to our statistics, was 60 to 64 hours a week.

Q. What were the working hours of the factory workers who came from concentration camps?

A. They were exactly the same as for all the other workers in the industry, for the workers from concentration camps were on the whole only a part of the workers employed, and these workers were not called upon to do any more work than the other workers in the factory.

Q. How is that shown?

A. There was a demand on the part of the SS that the inmates of concentration camps should be kept in one part of the factory. The supervisors consisted of German foremen and specialists. The working hours, for organisational reasons, had to be co-ordinated with those of the entire industry.

Q. It is shown unequivocally from two documents, which I shall submit in another connection, that also the workers from concentration camps employed in army, naval, and air armament branches worked on the average 60 hours per week.

Herr Speer, were special KZ Camps, the so-called work camps, established next to the industries?

A. The work camps were established so that long trips to the factories could be avoided and so enable the workers to arrive at the factories fresh and ready for work.

Furthermore, the additional food which the Food Ministry had granted for all workers, including the workers from concentration camps, would not have been received by these men if they had come directly from big concentration camps; for then this additional food would have been used up in the concentration camp. In this way, those workers who came from concentration camps received in full measure bonuses which were granted in the industry, such as cigarettes, or additional food.

Q. Did you know, during your activities, that the workers from concentration camps had advantages if they worked in factories?

A. Yes. My co-workers called my attention to this fact, and I also heard it when I inspected the industries. Of course, a wrong impression should not be created about the number of concentration camp inmates who worked in German industry. In toto one per cent of the labour personnel came from concentration camps.

Q. When you inspected establishments, did you ever see concentration camp inmates?

A. Of course, when on inspection tours of industries I occasionally saw inmates of concentration camps, who, however, looked well fed.

**DR. FLAECHSNER:** Concerning the report which Herr Speer made about concentration camps and the treatment which the inmates received in factories, I refer to a confidential letter from the Office Chief Schieber to Speer, dated 7th May, 1944. I submit it as Speer Document 44, Exhibit 6.

Mr. President, I am sorry, this will also be found in the second Document Book which has not yet been submitted. But it would be a pity if I were not to discuss it at this time, for it fits so well into this pattern. Therefore, I should like to quote briefly from it.

The Office Chief Schieber writes to his minister as follows:

**THE PRESIDENT:** Dr. Flaechsner, the Tribunal thinks it would be much more helpful to them to have the document before them.

We are told that the book will be ready tomorrow afternoon, and that it will not be ready before tomorrow afternoon.

**DR. FLAECHSNER:** Mr. President, I believe that I did everything possible at the time to see that the documents were put at the disposal of the translation department in good time. The difficulty must have arisen from the fact that the interrogatories did not come back in time. I assume that is what happened.

The quotation from this document is not long, Mr. President. I believe I might as well quote from it now. Or do you wish that—

**THE PRESIDENT:** No; go on, if it is more convenient to you. I do not mind. You may go on.

**DR. FLAECHSNER:** Thank you very much.

The Office Chief Schieber writes to his minister:

"Owing to the care of the workers from camps by our factory managers in spite of all the difficulties, and the generally decent and humane treatment which foreign and concentration camp labourers received, both the Jewesses and concentration camp labourers work very efficiently, and do everything in order not to be sent back to the concentration camps.

These, facts really demand that we transfer still more concentration camp inmates into armament industries."

And a few lines farther down:

"I have discussed this whole matter in great detail with the delegate of Obergruppenfuehrer Pohl, Sturmbannfuehrer Maurer, and especially pointed out that, by a decentralisation of concentration camp labourers, it might be possible to fully utilise their working strength and at the same time give them better nourishment and care."

Then he goes on to say:

"Moreover, Maurer especially points out—"

**THE PRESIDENT:** You need not make such long pauses as you are making.

**DR. FLAECHSNER:**

"Moreover, Maurer especially points out that Obergruppenfuehrer Pohl stated the food situation of concentration camp inmates working in factories is being improved constantly, and, because of special bonuses in the form of food and constant medical attention, there had been a marked increase in their weight, and, because of these things, better work was being achieved."

In another document, No. 46, we see that the using of concentration camp workers in armament industries is recommended in that it brings advantages to these workers and that for this reason concentration camp inmates are glad to work in armament industries.

I refer, in this connection, to Document 1992-PS, which may be found on Page 11 of the Document Book. It is Page 14 in the English text. This document shows that already in 1937 inmates of concentration camps were being employed in workshops and that this employment was quite popular.

**BY DR. FLAECHSNER:**

Q. Herr Speer, what do you know about the working conditions in subterranean factories?

A. The most modern equipment and the most modern weapons were installed and stored in subterranean factories. This equipment required perfect conditions of work, air which was dry and free from dust, good lighting facilities, big fresh air installations, so that the conditions which applied to such a subterranean factory would be about the same as those for night shifts in ordinary factories.

I should like to add that contrary to the impression which has been created here in court, these subterranean factories, almost without exception, were staffed with German workers, because we had a special interest in having these modern installations manned by the best workers who were at our disposal.

Q. Can you tell us about how many of these factories there were?

A. It was an insignificant number at the end of the war. We were using 300,000 square metres for subterranean factory buildings, and we had planned for 3,000,000 square metres.

Q. Herr Speer, in the year 1943, you visited the concentration camp at Mauthausen? Why did you visit this camp?

A. I learned, when I inspected industries at Linz, that along the Danube, near the camp at Mauthausen, a large harbour installation and numerous railway installations were being erected, and that the stone coming from the quarry at Mauthausen was to be transported to the Danube. This was purely a peace-time matter which I could not tolerate at all, for it violated all the decrees and directives which I had issued. I gave short notice of an impending visit, for I wanted to ascertain on the spot whether this construction work was an actual fact, and if so, to demand a stoppage of the work. This is an example of giving directives in a field within the economic administrative sphere of the SS. I stated on that occasion that it would be more judicious to have these workers employed during war time in a steel plant at Linz rather than in peace-time construction.

Q. Will you describe the visit to the camp?

A. My visit ostensibly followed the prescribed programme as already described by the witness Blaha. I saw the kitchens, laundry, and living quarters of the barracks. These barracks were made of massive stone, and were models as far as modern equipment is concerned. Since my intention of visiting had only been announced a short time before my arrival, in my opinion it is out of the question that big preparations could have been made before my visit. Nevertheless, the camp, or the small part of the camp which I saw, appeared to me to be very clean. But I did not see any of the workers, any of the camp inmates, since at that time they were all engaged in work. The entire inspection lasted perhaps forty-five minutes, as I had very little time at my disposal for a matter of that kind, and I had a repugnance to visiting such a camp where prisoners were being kept.

**Q.** The main purpose of your visit, then, was to request the stoppage of the work which you considered non-essential to the war effort?

**A.** Yes.

**Q.** On your visit, were you able to learn about the working conditions in the camp?

**A.** No, I couldn't do that since no workers were to be seen in the camp and the harbour installations were so far from the street that I could not see the men who were working there.

**Q.** Did you learn, on your visit to Mauthausen or on another occasion, about the cruelties which took place at this concentration camp and at other concentration camps?

**A.** No.

**Q.** Now, I should like to conclude my questions on the utilisation of workers by asking you:

Did you have any interest in the fact that a healthy and sufficiently trained labour supply should be at your disposal?

**A.** Naturally, I had the utmost interest in this matter even though labour supply was not within my province. Beginning in 1942, we had mass production, and this system with assembly line workers demands an extraordinarily large percentage of skilled workers. Because of conscription for military service, these skilled labourers had become especially important, so that any loss of a worker or the illness of a worker meant a big loss for me.

Since a skilled worker needed an apprenticeship of six to twelve weeks, and even after that training for a period of about six months, the loss in production is considerable, for it takes about that much time before work of quality can be expected. Thus it is evident that the care of skilled workers in industry was a matter of considerable anxiety to me.

**Q.** The prosecution has mentioned the so-called extermination by work. Could a change of personnel, arising from extermination by work, be tolerated at all by an industry?

**A.** No. A change in the workers in the way in which it was described here would not be tolerated in any industry. It is out of the question that, in any German industry, anything like that could have taken place without my hearing about it; and I never heard anything of that sort.

**Q.** Herr Speer, the prosecution asserts that you used methods of terror and brutality to increase to the utmost the output of the compulsory workers—

**A.** No

**Q.** Just a moment. I have not finished. The prosecution is of the opinion that you used SS and police against recalcitrant workers and favoured and recommended the use of concentration camps for the same. Is that correct?

**A.** No, not in that form, for that was against my interests. There were efforts in Germany to bring about increased productivity through very severe compulsory measures. These efforts did not meet with my approval. It is quite out of the question that 14,000,000 workers can be forced to produce satisfactory work through coercion and terror, as the prosecution maintains.

**DR. FLAECHSNER:** In this connection, please refer to Page 7 of the English text, Page 4 of the French text. I should like to quote from Speer Document 143. It says there:

"I do not believe that the second system which might be applied in our economy—the system of compulsion by Industrial Commissioners, and punishment when output is insufficient—can lead to success."

Now, Mr. President, I have come to the end of my first part.

**THE PRESIDENT:** The Court will adjourn.

*(The Tribunal adjourned until 20th June, 1946, at 1000 hours.)*

## THURSDAY, 20TH JUNE, 1946

**THE PRESIDENT:** I have an announcement to make. In the first place, supplementary witnesses will be heard at the end of the case for the defendants.

Secondly, interrogatories and other documents received by that time must be offered in evidence then. Thirdly, interrogatories and other documents allowed before the end of the evidence, but received at a later date, will be received and considered by the Tribunal up to the end of the trial. That is all.

**ALBERT SPEER RESUMED**
**DIRECT EXAMINATION BY DR. FLAECHSNER:**

**Q.** Yesterday we finished talking about the utilisation of labour in industry, and now we shall turn to the question of how industry was supplied with manpower: that is to say, the question of special demands made for workers.

Herr Speer, you stated in your testimony of 18th October, 1945, first that you demanded further supplies of labour from Sauckel, and secondly, that you knew that among these workers there would be foreigners; thirdly, that you had known that some of these foreign workers were working in Germany against their will. Please comment on this statement.

**A.** This voluntary statement is quite correct. During the war I was very grateful to Sauckel for every labourer I got through him. Many a time I held him responsible for the fact that through lack of workers the armament industry did not achieve the results it might have done, but I always emphasised the credit due to him because of his activity on behalf of the armament industry.

Q. Now, when, in your testimony of 18th October, 1945, and in your testimony here, you refer to workers, do you mean all labour in general, including German workers, foreigners from occupied countries, and foreigners from friendly or annexed States, and also prisoners of war?

A. Yes. Beginning with the middle of 1943, I was in disagreement with Sauckel over questions of production and about the insufficient availability of reserves of German labour. But that has nothing to do with my fundamental attitude toward Sauckel's work.

Q. What percentage of the total number of assigned workers was Sauckel obliged to furnish upon your demands?

A. You mean of the total labour supply, not foreigners?

Q. Yes.

A. Up to August, 1944—that is, up till the time when I took over the air armament as well—perhaps thirty to forty per cent of all workers who were at our disposal. Of course, the largest number of them were German workers. When, in August, 1944, I took over the air armament I had no appreciable demand for workers because the bomber attacks on the transportation system in the Reich resulted in a steady decline of armament production.

Q. Was your need for labour excessive?

A. No. The volume of armament production, and also of our entire production with a corresponding need for labour, was governed by our raw material supply.

Q. That means, your need was restricted by the amount of raw materials available?

A. My need for labour was limited by the amount of raw materials.

Q. You achieved a marked increase in production figures for armament. In order to achieve this increase, did the workers employed increase proportionally?

A. No. Comparison with the 1942 figures of production shows that in 1944 seven times as many weapons were manufactured, five and a half times as many armoured vehicles, and six times as much ammunition, yet the number of workers in these branches had increased by only thirty per cent. This success was not brought about through a higher exploitation of labour, but rather through the abolition of obsolete methods of production and through an improved system of controlling the production of armaments.

Q. What do you mean by the term "war production," "Kriegsproduktion"?

A. The term which is frequently used here, "war production," is nothing else but the ordinary term: production. It comprises everything which is manufactured industrially, including essential things for civilians.

Q. What did you mean in Germany by the term "armaments"? What did that include?

A. The term "armaments" was in no way limited to that meaning laid down in the Geneva Prisoner-of-War Agreement. The modern concept of "armaments" is a much more comprehensive one. It includes a much wider sphere of activity. In our concept of armaments, we were guided by no basic principles. The characteristic of an armament factory was that the Armament Inspectorate took care of it and watched over it. In Germany, for instance, the entire production of raw steel belonged to armament, all rolling- mills, foundries and forges; the production of aluminium and modern synthetic materials, the chemical production of nitrogen or fuel or synthetic rubber, the production of synthetic wool, the manufacture of individual items, the use of which in armament cannot be predicted at the time of their manufacture, such as ball-bearings, gears, valves, engine pistons and so forth; or the production of tool machinery; the setting up of chain production systems; similarly the manufacture of motor cars and the construction of locomotives, of commercial ships; also the output of textile concerns, and concerns manufacturing leather goods and so on.

In the interrogatories which I sent to my witnesses, I tried to obtain estimates as to what percentage of the German armament industries produced armaments as defined by the Geneva Convention, and I should like to give you the figures. My co-workers agree unanimously that between 14 and 20 per cent. of our armament programme was concerned with the production of weapons, armoured cars, planes or warships or the general equipment which the various branches of the Wehrmacht required. The bulk of the material, therefore, was not armament production in the sense of the Geneva Convention. The reason for the expansion of the term armament to cover a wider field of production was the preferential treatment given to armament industries, a treatment which resulted in numerous industries pressing to be called armament industries.

**DR. FLAECHSNER:** Mr. President, in the questionnaires which have not yet been submitted to the Tribunal because the document book is not yet ready, the witness Sauer, under figures 7 and 10, the witness Schieber under figures 6 to 9, and the witness Kehrl under figures 4 to 7, concern themselves with the definition of the meaning of the term "armament."

**THE PRESIDENT:** What was the last name?

**DR. FLAECHSNER:** Kehrl.

**BY DR. FLAECHSNER:**

Q. Herr Speer, by way of example, you know the works of Krupp at Essen. How far did this concern produce armament equipment in the sense of the Geneva Prisoner-of-War Agreement, that is, weapons, munitions, and objects which are necessary for the direct conduct of war?

A. The Krupp concern is an excellent example of the fact that an armament firm often only devotes a fraction of its productive capacity to war equipment. Of course, I must point out the fact that the Krupp organisation was one of those armament firms which, amongst others, was responsible for the smallest production of armaments, on a percentage basis.

The Krupp concern was mainly interested in mining and with three large works producing highly tempered steel. The manufacture of locomotives and products for the chemical industry were specialities of Krupp's.

*The Krupp Works in Essen was bombed by the Allies, and fell to the 17th U.S. Airborne Division in April 1945.*

On the other hand, the actual armament speciality of Krupp's—the construction of armoured turrets for warships, and special guns of large calibre—was not at all exploited during this war. Only in 1944 did Krupp erect the first big factory for the production of guns near Breslau. Up to that time, Krupp was mainly concerned with the invention of new weapons, and then, for this production other firms were licensed.

All in all, one can say that at Krupp's 10 to 15 per cent of the personnel were engaged in armament equipment in the sense of the Geneva Prisoner-of-War Agreement, even though the entire works were classified as armament works.

**Q.** What did you and your Ministry have to say as to whether an industry should be supplied with German or foreign workers?

**A.** My Ministry had no influence in that direction at all. The need for workers was reported to my Ministry by the industries which were subordinate to me. They reported a total figure of workers needed, and there were no specifications as to whether foreign workers, prisoners of war, or German workers were wanted. This total figure was forwarded to the General Plenipotentiary for Labour. Sauckel refused to accept detailed demands, and he was quite right in this respect, for he could not issue detailed directives to the offices subordinate to him concerning the percentage of German or foreign workers who were to be allocated locally to the various industries.

The ultimate distribution of workers to industries was taken care of by the labour offices without any intervention of my offices or agencies. Therefore, here, too, we did not exert influence as to whether Germans, foreigners or prisoners of war were to be allocated to any industry. The industry then had to report back to us about the number of workers newly received. In this report only a lump figure was given, so that I could not tell whether any or what number of foreign workers or prisoners of war were included in the total figure. Of course, I knew that foreigners worked on armament equipment, and I quite agreed to that.

**DR. FLAECHSNER:** Mr. President, to facilitate matters for the Tribunal, I would like to remark that figures 7 and 17 of the questionnaire of the witness Schmelte, and also figures 1 and 8 of the same questionnaire deal with this matter; and in the questionnaire of Schieber, numbers 10, 11, 30 and 31. Furthermore, in the questionnaire of Kehrl relevant material is contained in the answers to questions 8 and 9.

**BY DR. FLAECHSNER:**

Q. Herr Speer, who sent in to the Plenipotentiary General for Labour Commitment the demands for manpower needed for armament production?

A. The demands for workers were placed by various sectors, according to the different economic branches. There were approximately 15 different sectors which placed their demands. I placed demands for army and navy armament and for construction, and beginning with September of 1943, for the sectors chemistry, mining, and other production. Air armament had its special labour assignment department, and their demands were made by the Reich Air Ministry.

**DR. FLAECHSNER:** In their questionnaires, the witness Schmelte has dealt with this matter in his answer to question 2; the witness Schieber in his answers to 2, 3, and 5, and the witness Kehrl to 2 and 3.

**BY DR. FLAECHSNER:**

Q. Weren't the demands for labour for the three branches of the Wehrmacht centralised in your Ministry?

A. No. Of course, beginning with March, 1942, I had nominally taken over the Armament Office under General Thomas from the German High Command, and this armament office was a joint office of all three Wehrmacht branches where labour assignment problems were discussed, too. Through an agreement between Goering and me, it was decided that air armament, independently of me, should look after its own interests.

This agreement was necessary since first of all I, as Minister for Armament, had a biased interest, and, therefore, did not want to make decisions regarding the demands for labour of a unit that was not subordinate to me.

Q. To what extent were you responsible for the employment of prisoners of war in armament production in contravention of the Geneva Convention?

A. I did not exert my influence to have prisoners of war employed contrary to the directives given out by the German High Command. I knew the point of view held by the German High Command according to which the Geneva regulations were to be strictly observed. Of course, I knew as well, that these Geneva regulations did not apply to Russian prisoners of war and Italian military internees. I could not exert any influence on the allocation of prisoners of war to the various industries. This allocation was determined by the Labour Office in conjunction with the officials of the Chief Office for Prisoner-of-War Affairs.

Q. In this connection I should like to refer to the questionnaire of the witness Schmelte, to his reply to question 14.

Herr Speer, who was the competent officer of the lower level under the OWK?

A. The supervision of the proper assignment of prisoners of war was carried out through the military economy officer (Wehrwirtschaftsoffizier) as the intermediary authority. He was incorporated into the organisation of the military area commander who was under the jurisdiction of the army.

Q. The prosecution has submitted an affidavit by Mr. Deuss, who is an American statistics expert. This is Document 2520-PS.

According to this affidavit, four hundred thousand prisoners of war were employed in the production of war equipment. These figures are supposed to originate from statistics in your Ministry. Will you comment on this figure?

A. The figures are well known to me through my activity as a Minister and they are correct. This figure of four hundred thousand prisoners of war covers the total number of them employed in armament production.

A wrong conclusion is drawn from this affidavit if it is assumed that all these prisoners of war were connected with the production of armament equipment as specified in the Geneva Convention. Statistics of the number of prisoners of war employed in those industries which produced armaments according to the meaning of the term in the Geneva Prisoners-of-War Agreement were not kept by us, and therefore no such figure can be compiled from my documents.

Apart from that, in this figure of four hundred thousand prisoners of war, two to three hundred thousand Italian military internees are included, all of whom were brought into my production field at that time. This affidavit does not prove, therefore, that prisoners of war were employed in the production of armaments in contravention of the Geneva agreement.

Q. The Central Planning Board has been mentioned here frequently. You were a member of this Board. Can you describe in detail the origin of the Central Planning Board and its sphere of activity?

A. When in 1942 I assumed my office, it was urgently necessary to centralise the allocation and distribution of various materials to the three branches of the Wehrmacht and to guarantee the proper direction of the war economy for a long time to come. Up to that time this matter had been taken care of by the Ministry of Economics and partly by the German High Command. Both these agencies were much too weak to prevail against the three Wehrmacht branches.

On my suggestion, in March, 1942, the Central Planning Board was established by the Trustee for the Four-Year Plan. Its three members, Milch, Koerner and myself, were entitled to make decisions joint decisions only which, however, could always be reached without any difficulty. It is obvious that, through my predominant position, I was the decisive factor in this Central Planning Board.

The tasks of the Central Planning Board were clearly outlined and laid down in Goering's decree which I had drafted.

To make statistics of the demands for labour or of the allocation of workers was not a matter which was laid down in this decree. This activity was not carried out systematically by the Central Planning Board, in spite of the evidence of documents presented here. As far as decisions regarding demands and allocation of labour were concerned, I tried to have them made by the Central Planning Board since this was an essential factor in the directing of the entire economy. This, however, always met with Sauckel's refusal because he considered it as interfering with his rights.

**DR. FLAECHSNER:** I submit the decree of Goering regarding the establishment of a Central Planning Board. It was published on 25th April, 1942, and this will be Speer Document 42, Exhibit 7.

Mr. President, the text may be found on Page 17 of the English document book.

The sphere of activity of the Central Planning Board—

**THE PRESIDENT:** Wait a minute. What number are you giving to it? On the document here it has got Speer 142.

**DR. FLAECHSNER:** No, that must be a typographical error. It should be 42, Mr. President, it may be found—

**THE PRESIDENT:** What is the exhibit number?

**DR. FLAECHSNER:** Speer Exhibit 7.

**THE PRESIDENT:** What does 42 mean? What is the point of putting 42 on it if its Exhibit number is 7?

**DR. FLAECHSNER:** Mr. President, that is the number according to which the document was admitted when we compiled the document book. However, the exhibit number 7 is the decisive number in this case.

**THE PRESIDENT:** Very well.

**DR. FLAECHSNER:** It is only meant to facilitate reference to it in the document book. It is on Page 17 of the English text; and I might be allowed to call the attention of the High Tribunal to clause three of the decree. According to this the Central Planning Board had to decide on all the necessary new industrial projects for the increase in the production of raw materials, and their distribution, as well as on the co-ordination of the demands on the transport system. This decree does not provide for any regulation of the labour problem.

**BY DR. FLAECHSNER:**

Q. Herr Speer, how did it come about that in spite of this latter fact, labour demands were discussed in the Central Planning Board?

A. These minutes of all, the sixteen meetings of the Central Planning Board, which took place from 1942 until 1945, are contained in the stenographic records. These five thousand typed pages give a clear report on the activities carried out and the tasks of the Central Planning Board. It is quite obvious to any expert that there was no planning with regard to manpower allocation, for it is clear that a plan regarding labour allocation would have to be revised at least every three months, just as we did for raw materials. In fact, three to four meetings took place in the Central Planning Board which were concerned with labour. These three or four discussions were held for the following reasons:

In the years 1942 and 1943—that is, before I took over the management of the total economy—when soldiers were being recruited for the Wehrmacht, I had reserved for myself the right to determine the various recruitment quotas in the different sectors of production. At a meeting this allocation of quotas was determined by the Central Planning Board as a neutral assembly. At this meeting, of course, there was a representative of the General Plenipotentiary for Labour, since at the same time the problem of replacements had to be dealt with. Another problem which was discussed by the Central Planning Board was the distribution and allocation of coal for the following year. Just as in England, coal was the decisive factor in our entire war production. At these discussions we had to determine at the same time how the demands for labour supply for the mines could be satisfied by the General Plenipotentiary for Labour because only in agreement with him could proper plans be made for the following year. From these discussions resulted the assignment of Russian prisoners of war to mines, a matter which has been mentioned here.

Furthermore, two meetings took place at which the demands for labour supplies put forward by all interested parties were actually discussed, and in such a way as corresponds to some extent with the suggestion of the prosecution as to the activities of the Central Planning Board in such matters. These two meetings took place in February and March, 1944, and no others were held either before or after. Besides, these two meetings took place during my illness. At that time already it was not quite clear to me why, just when I was ill, Sauckel first complied with my wish to have the Central Planning Board put under my Ministry and then later on opposed the suggestion.

**DR. FLAECHSNER:** The prosecution has submitted various extracts dealing with meetings of the Central Planning Board.

**BY DR. FLAECHSNER:**

Q. As far as you know, are these extracts taken from the stenographic records, or are they taken from the minutes?

A. They are taken from the stenographic records. Besides these stenographic records, minutes were made on the results of the meetings. These minutes are the official records of the results of the meetings. No material from the actual minutes has so far been submitted by the prosecution. The contents of the stenographic records are, of course, of remarks and debates which always take place when matters of such importance are dealt with, even when the authorities involved are not directly responsible for some of the matters which come up for discussion, such as those relative to labour commitments.

Q. Therefore, do these quotations which have been heard here concern decisions made by the Central Planning Board or by you?

**A.** I have already answered that.

**Q.** I would like to put one more question to you. You had another special position in the Four-Year Plan? What about that?

**A.** I was the Armaments Plenipotentiary for the Four-Year Plan. In March, 1942, Goering, giving heed to my proposal, created the post of Armaments Plenipotentiary in the Four-Year Plan, and I was appointed Armaments Plenipotentiary. This was purely a matter of form. It was generally known that Goering had quarrelled with my predecessor, Todt, since armaments problems had not been put under his, Goering's, control. In assuming this post as Armaments Plenipotentiary, I had subordinated myself nominally to Goering. In fact, the Armaments Plenipotentiary never achieved any influence. I issued no directives whatsoever in that capacity. As Minister I had sufficient authority, and it was not necessary for me to use any authority I had under the Four-Year Plan.

**DR. FLAECHSNER:** For the benefit of the High Tribunal, when dealing with the question of the Central Planning Board, perhaps I might refer to the fact that statements were made relative to it by the witness Schieber in his questionnaire under figures 4 and 45, and by the witness Kehrl in his questionnaire under figure 2.

Now I shall turn to the problem of the responsibility for the number of foreign workers in. general.

**BY DR. FLAECHSNER:**

**Q.** Herr Speer, the prosecution charges you with co-responsibility for the entire number of foreign workers who were transported to Germany. Your co-defendant Sauckel has testified in this connection that principally he worked for you in this matter so that his activity was primarily determined by your needs. Will you please comment on this?

**A.** Of course, I expected Sauckel to meet all the demands of war production, but it cannot be maintained that he primarily took care of my demands, for, beginning with the spring of 1943, I received only a part of the workers I needed. If my requirements had been the principal care of Sauckel, I should have received all the workers I asked for. But this was not the position. For example, some two hundred thousand Ukrainian women were made available for housework, and it is quite certain that I was of the opinion that they could have been put to better use in armaments production.

It is also clear that the German labour reserve had not been fully utilised. In January, 1943, these German reserves were still ample. I was interested in having German workers—and, of course, women—and this non-utilisation of German reserves indicates that I cannot be held solely responsible for demanding foreign workers to meet my labour requirements.

**DR. FLAECHSNER:** I should like to point out that the following witnesses have made statements in connection with this problem in their respective questionnaires: The witness Schmelte in answer to questions 12, 13 and 16; the witness Schieber to 22; the witness Roland to 1 and 4, and the witness Kehrl to 9.

**BY DR. FLAECHSNER:**

Q. Herr Speer, if you or your office demanded workers, then, of course, you knew that you would receive foreign workers amongst them. Did you need these foreign workers?

A. I needed them only for part of my production. For instance, the coal mines could not be fully operated without Russian prisoners of war. It would have been quite impossible to employ German reserves, which consisted mainly of women, in these mines. There were, furthermore, special assignments for which it was desirable to have foreign experts, but the majority of the needs could be met by German workers, even German female workers. The same principle was followed in the armament industries in England and America, and certainly in the Soviet Union, too.

THE PRESIDENT: Can you not go on, Dr. Flaechsner? There is no need to wait.

DR. FLAECHSNER: Yes. In my documentary evidence I shall return to this point in more detail.

**BY DR. FLAECHSNER:**

Q. Herr Speer, I should like to go back to your testimony of 18th October, 1945 In it you stated several times that you knew that the workers from occupied countries were being brought to Germany against their will. The prosecution alleges that you approved of the use of force and of terror. Will you comment on that?

A. I had no influence on the method by which workers were recruited. If the workers were being brought to Germany against their will that means, as I see it, that they were obligated by lawful measures to work for Germany. Whether these legal measures were justified or not, that was a matter I did not check at the time. Besides, this was no concern of mine. On the other hand, by application of force and terror I understand police measures such as raids and arrests and so on. I did not approve of these violent measures, which may be seen from the attitude I took at the discussion I had on this question with Lammers on 11th June, 1944.

At that time I held the view that neither an increase in police forces, nor raids, nor violent measures were correct. In this document I am, at the same time, referred to as one of those who expressed their objections to the violent measures which had been proposed.

THE PRESIDENT: Where is the document?

DR. FLAECHSNER: Mr. President, that is Document 3819-PS, which the prosecution submitted in the cross-examination of, I believe, the defendant Keitel and of the defendant Sauckel. I did not include it in my document book.

**BY DR. FLAECHSNER:**

Herr Speer, why were you against such violent measures?

A. Because through violent measures of that kind, a regular flow of manpower supply in the occupied countries would not have been possible in the long run. I wanted production to be regulated and orderly in the occupied countries. Measures of violence meant to me a loss of manpower, because people, in increasing numbers, fled to the woods so as not to have to go to Germany and strengthened the ranks of the resistance movement. This led to increased acts of sabotage and that, in turn, to a decrease of production in the occupied countries.

Therefore, time and again the military commanders, and the commanders-in-chief of the army groups, as well as myself, protested against these proposed large-scale measures of violence.

Q. Were you especially interested in the recruiting of workers from various countries, and if so, why?

A. Yes. I was especially interested in the labour recruitment from France, Belgium and Holland—that is, countries in the West—and from Italy, because, beginning with the spring of 1943, the General Plenipotentiary for Labour Commitment had decreed that mainly the workers from these regions were to be assigned for war production. On the other hand, the workers from the East were mainly to be used for agriculture, for forestry, and for the building of railways.

This decree was repeatedly stressed to me by Sauckel, even as late as 1944.

**DR. FLAECHSNER:** In this connection, I should like to refer to Document 3072-PS, which is Exhibit USA 790. This document is found on Page 79 of the English text, and Page 76 of the French text of my document book. I quote from the conference of the Economic Inspectorate South in Russia:

Peukert—the delegate for Sauckel in Russia—states here, and I quote: "Provisions have been made for employing workers from the East principally in agriculture and in the food economy while the workers from the West, especially those skilled workers required by Minister Speer, are to be made available to the armament industry."

Document 7289-PS, which is Exhibit RF 77, may be found on Page 42 of the English text of my document book and Page 39 of the French and German texts. Here we are concerned with a remark by Sauckel, on 26th April, 1944, and I quote:

"Only by a renewed mobilization of reserves in the occupied Western territories can the urgent need of German armament for skilled workers be satisfied. For this purpose the reserves from other territories are not sufficient either in quality or in quantity. They are urgently needed for the requirements of agriculture, transportation, and construction. Up to 75 per cent of the workers from the West have always been allocated to armament."

**THE PRESIDENT:** Dr. Flaechsner, speaking for myself, I do not know what the problem is that you are trying to solve, or what argument you are putting forward in the very least. I do not know what relevance this has at all. What does it matter whether they came from the West or whether they came from the East? I understand your argument, or the defendant's argument, that the armament industry, under the Geneva Convention, does not include a variety of branches of industry which go eventually into armament, and it only relates to things which are directly concerned with munitions. But when you have placed that argument before us, what is the good of referring us to this sort of evidence?

I mean, I only want to know because I do not understand in the least what you are getting at.

**DR. FLAECHSNER:** Mr. President, this is to prepare for the problem to which we are now turning, and that is the problem of the blocked or protected industries (Sperr Betriebe). By setting up these blocked industries, Speer, if I may put it that way, wanted to put an effective stop to the transfer of workers from the West to Germany. Therefore I first have to show that up to that time his workers, the labour for his industries, mainly came from the West. I want to establish that—

**THE PRESIDENT (interposing):** Supposing he did want to stop them from coming from the West, what difference does it make?

**DR. FLAECHSNER:** Mr. President, Speer is being charged with actively having taken part in the deportation of workers from the West, workers who were used in his armament industries. Now, the date is important here.

He says that beginning with the year 1943, he followed a different policy. Before that time, as may be seen from the evidence, the workers who had come to Germany had, to a large extent, been voluntary workers.

**THE PRESIDENT:** Of course, if you can prove that they were all voluntary workers it would be extremely material, but you are not directing evidence to that at all.

**DR. FLAECHSNER:** Mr. President, this is the final reason for my evidence. I should like to carry it through, if possible, to the end.

**THE PRESIDENT:** I am only telling you that I do not understand what the end is. Go on; do not wait any further.

**BY DR. FLAECHSNER:**

Q. Herr Speer, the General Plenipotentiary for Labour designated Italy and the occupied Western countries as the countries from which foreign workers would mainly be recruited for armament purposes.

How far did you endorse Sauckel's measures in these countries?

A. Up to the spring of 1943 I completely endorsed them. Up to that time no obvious disadvantages had resulted for me. However, beginning with the spring of 1943, workers from the West refused, in ever-increasing numbers, to go to Germany. That may have had something to do with our defeat at Stalingrad and with the intensified air attacks on Germany.

Up to the spring of 1943 to my knowledge, the labour commitments were met with more or less good will. However, beginning with the spring of 1943, frequently only part of the workers who had been called up came to report at the recruiting offices.

Therefore, approximately since June, 1943, I established the so-called blocked industries, through the Military Commander-in-Chief in France. Belgium, Holland and Italy soon after also introduced the system of blocked industries. The important feature was that every worker employed in these blocked industries was automatically excluded from assignment to Germany; and any worker who was recruited for Germany was free to go into a blocked industry in his own country without the labour assignment authorities having the power to take him out of this blocked industry.

Q. What consequences did this have on the recruitment of labourers in the occupied Western countries?

A. After the establishment of the blocked industries, the labour commitment from the occupied countries in the West to Germany decreased to a fraction of what it had been. For instance, before that, eighty to a hundred thousand workers came from France to Germany every month. After the establishment of the blocked industries, this figure decreased to the insignificant number of three to four thousand a month, as is evident from Exhibit RF 22.

It is obvious, and we have to state the facts, that the decrease in these figures was also due to the resistance movement which began to expand in the West at that time.

Did you and your offices endorse the policies followed by Sauckel at that time?

A. No. At that time the first serious differences arose about the "blocking" of these workers for labour commitments in Germany. This came about through the fact that the loss of my workers employed in industry in the occupied countries was larger than the number of workers who came to Germany from the occupied countries of the West.

This may be seen from Exhibit RF 22. According to it about four hundred thousand workers were transported from France to Germany in 1943. Industrial workers in France, however, decreased by eight hundred thousand, and the French workers in France who worked for Germany decreased by four hundred and fifty thousand workers.

Q. Why did you demand to take over the entire German production from the Ministry of Economics in the summer of 1943?

A. According to my opinion, there was still a considerable labour reserve latent in Germany, because the German peace economy had not been converted into a war economy on a sufficiently large scale. Here was, in my opinion, next to the German women workers, the largest reserve of the German labour supply.

Q. What did you do when the total economy was handed over to you by the Ministry of Economics?

A. At that time, I had already worked out the following plan. A large part of the industry in Germany produced so-called consumer goods. Consumer goods are, for instance, shoes, clothing, furniture, and other articles necessary for the armed forces and for civilian requirements. In the occupied Western territories, however, the industries which supplied these products were kept idle, as the raw materials were lacking.

My plan was to deprive German industries of the raw materials which were produced in Germany, such as synthetic wool, and send them to the West. Thereby, in the long run, a million workers were to be supplied with work in the occupied Western territories, and thus I would have freed one million German workers in Germany for armament production.

**Q.** Did you not want to increase armament production or help it along in France as well?

**A.** No. However, all these plans failed. Before the outbreak of war, the French Government did not succeed in building up armament production in France, and I also failed, or rather my agencies failed, in this task.

**Q.** What were your intentions with this new plan? What advantages did you gain?

**A.** I will comment on it quite briefly. Through this plan I could close down numbers of industries in Germany and in that way free not only workers, but also factories and administrative personnel for armament production. I also saved electricity and transport. Apart from that, since these industries had never been of importance for the war effort, they had hardly received any foreign workers; and thus I almost exclusively obtained German workers for the German production—workers, of course, who were more valuable, much more valuable than any foreign workers.

**Q.** Did such a plan not entail dangers and disadvantages for the German industrial development?

**A.** The disadvantages were considerable, since any closing down of an industry meant the taking out of machinery, and at the end of the war a re-conversion to peace-time production would take at least six to eight months. At that time, at a Gauleiter meeting at Posen, I said that if we wanted to be successful in this war, we would have to be those who made the greater sacrifices.

**Q.** How was this plan put into reality?

**THE PRESIDENT:** Dr. Flaechsner, what has the Tribunal got to do with the details of these plans? What do we care whether his plans were efficient or whether they were inefficient? The only question this Tribunal has got to decide is whether they were legal in accordance with the Charter of International Law. It does not matter to us whether his plans were good plans or bad plans, or what the details of the plans were, except in so far as they are legal or illegal.

**DR. FLAECHSNER:** Yes, Mr. President.

**THE PRESIDENT:** It is a mere waste of our time to go into the details of these plans.

**DR. FLAECHSNER:** I wanted to show that the tendencies, or rather the tendency followed by the defendant in his policy was to employ foreigners in their own country and to use the German reserves solely for his own purpose; that is, for armament proper. Thus everything which—

**THE PRESIDENT:** But, Dr. Flaechsner, that is a question of efficiency, not of legality. What he is saying is that he had a lot of German workers, good workers, and they were producing consumer goods instead of producing armament goods. He thought it better to transfer certain industries so that the workers could remain in France or the other Western countries.

What have we got to do with that? If they were forced to work there, it is just as illegal as if they had been brought to Germany to be forced to work. At least, that is the suggestion that is made by the prosecution.

**DR. FLAECHSNER:** Yes, but I thought and believed—

**THE PRESIDENT (interposing):** We will adjourn now.

*(A recess was taken.)*

**THE PRESIDENT:** The Tribunal will hear defendant's counsel at two o'clock tomorrow afternoon on the question of the apportionment of time for the defendants' counsel's speeches.

**BY DR. FLAECHSNER:**

Q. Herr Speer, please tell us briefly how you and Mons. Bichelonne, the French Minister of Economics, agreed on your programme; but, please be concise.

A. Immediately after taking over production in September, 1943, I agreed with Bichelonne that a large-scale programme of shifting industry from Germany to France should be put into operation, according to the system I already described. In an ensuing conference, Bichelonne stated that he was not authorised to talk about labour assignment with me for Minister Laval had expressly forbidden him to do so. He had to point out, he said, that a further recruitment of workers on the present scale would make it impossible to adhere to the programme which we had agreed upon. I was of the same opinion. We agreed, therefore, that the entire French production, beginning with coal, right up to the finished products, should be declared as "blocked industries." In this connection, both of us were perfectly aware of the fact that this would almost stop the recruitment of workers for Germany, since, as I have already explained, every Frenchman was free to enter one of these blocked industries, once he had been called up for work in Germany. I gave Bichelonne my word that I should adhere to this principle for a lengthy period, and, in spite of all difficulties which occurred, I kept my promise to him.

**DR. FLAECHSNER:** Mr. President, in connection with this I should like to quote from Document R-124, which is Exhibit USA 179. It is on Page 37 of the English document book. It is a speech of Sauckel's before the Central Planning Board which has been mentioned frequently. I quote:

"When I came to France the next time my agencies in France stated: Minister Bichelonne has concluded an agreement with Minister Speer according to which only French workers are to be considered for employment in France and none of them need go to Germany any more."

**BY DR. FLAECHSNER:**

Q. Herr Speer, what were the consequences of this change-over of labour commitment from Germany to France?

A. I have already mentioned that. Beginning with 1st October, recruitment of labour almost came to a complete standstill.

**DR. FLAECHSNER:** Later on I shall comment in detail on the documentary evidence of the effect of this Speer-Bichelonne plan and on the policy pursued by Speer in connection with the various attempts to carry out this principle at a later date. At this moment I shall, therefore, discontinue the questions on the subject and I shall confine myself to quoting from the official French Document, RF 22, Page 20 of the English text of my document book, Page 17 of the German and French texts: I quote:

> "Finally, a real hostility arose between Sauckel and Speer who was commissioned with the organisation of forced labour in the occupied territories."

And then a few lines farther on:

> "The superiority of the first mentioned over the latter which made itself felt more and more during the course of the occupation facilitated to a large degree the resistance against the removal of workers."

The text shows that—

**THE PRESIDENT:** That is all cumulative; that's what you have been proving three or four times already.

**DR. FLAECHSNER:** Very well, I shall not continue with it.

**BY DR. FLAECHSNER:**

Q. I only want to rectify a mistake, Herr Speer. It is mentioned in the document that you had something to do with organising forced labour in France; is that true?

A. No, the organisation of labour in France was not under my control.

Q. You have already mentioned that this Verlagerungsprogramm (shifting of labour commitment) was not only confined to France. Will you tell me to which other countries that also applied?

A. The programme was extended to Belgium, Holland, Italy and Czechoslovakia. The entire production in these countries was also declared blocked, and the labourers in these blocked industries were given the same protection as in France; even after the meeting with Hitler on 4th January, 1944, during which the new programme for the West for 1944 was agreed upon, I adhered to this policy. The result was that during the first half of 1944 only 33,000 workers came from France to Germany of the five hundred thousand planned for at that conference; and from other countries, too, only about ten per cent of the proposed workers were taken to Germany.

Q. What about the figures applying to workers from the Protectorate?

A. Everywhere only a fraction of the numbers proposed were sent.

Q. A Document 1739-PS, Exhibit RF 10, has been submitted by the prosecution. It is on Page 23 of the English text of my document book and it is a report by Sauckel, dated December, 1942; furthermore, there is Document 1290-PS, on Page 24 of the English text, which has also been submitted. These documents appear to show that, according to Sauckel's personal assertions, from the beginning of his activities until March, 1943, there was an excess supply of labour. Is that true?

A. Yes, that is true.

Document 16-PS, Exhibit USA 168, which is on Page 25 of the English text of my document book, also shows that Sauckel was not in favour of using German women in the armament industry, but in the summer of 1942 he had several hundred thousand Ukrainian girls placed at the disposal of German householders.

These three documents, in their entirety, show that Speer, in his Ministry, cannot be held responsible for the total figure of workers who came to Germany.

I should also like to present, Mr. President, Document 02 in the document book, Speer Exhibit 8, and it is on Page 26 of the English text. It refers to a meeting of the Central Planning Board.

**THE PRESIDENT:** Dr. Flaechsner, you are not stating the exhibit numbers of any of these documents, so that you are not offering them properly in evidence at all. I mean you are referring now to 02, which is some numbering which we have got nothing whatever to do with.

**DR. FLAECHSNER:** May I then present this document as Exhibit 8?

**THE PRESIDENT:** What about the one before? Oh, that is already in. Perhaps it would be well to submit a list afterwards, giving the proper exhibit numbers for all these documents you are referring to.

**DR. FLAECHSNER:** Yes, Mr. President, I shall be glad to do that. I should like to quote—this is a remark made by Speer:

> "For this it is necessary to supply the industries with new German workers, even unskilled labour, because I cannot replace with foreigners all those whom we have to give up as soldiers. The German supply is simply becoming too scanty. Already today we are having one case of sabotage after another and we do not know their origin. Cases of sabotage will increase. The measures which will have to be taken in order to switch at least one million Germans over to the armament industry are extremely hard and will, in my opinion, lower the entire living standard of the upper classes. Therefore, it means that, roughly speaking, we are all going to be proletarians for the duration of the war. This matter has to be considered coolly and soberly. There is no other alternative."

This opinion and project of Speer, namely, to exploit ruthlessly the labour reserve within Germany, was not realised until the summer of 1944. And this was a subject for argument between Speer on one side and Sauckel and the Gauleiter on the other. The testimony of the witnesses in the questionnaires will deal with it. To assist the Tribunal I should like to state that with Schieber it is the answer to question 22; with Roland, to 1 and 4; with Kehrl, to 9; and in the case of Schmelte, answers to 13 and 16. Unfortunately, I cannot give the pages in the English book, Mr. President, because I have not yet seen it.

**THE PRESIDENT:** What was the document you were referring to?

**DR. FLAECHSNER:** Mr. President, the filled-in questionnaires in the supplement volume of my document book, which I hope is now in the hands of the Tribunal.

**THE PRESIDENT:** Yes, it is.

DR. FLAECHSNER: Besides, I should like to reserve the right to submit these documents in toto at the end of my examination. I am only taking the liberty of referring to the points in which the witnesses have dealt with this question.

THE PRESIDENT: Very well.

DR. FLAECHSNER: Furthermore, we are informed about the different opinions presented by Sauckel and Speer through a conference of Speer's during a meeting of the Central Planning Board on 21st December, 1943. I refer to Page 27 of the English text of my document book and it will be my Exhibit 9. I quote—

THE PRESIDENT: You do not need to quote it, Dr. Flaechsner. I thought I had made it clear to you that we are not concerned with the efficiency or the inefficiency of these plans.

BY DR. FLAECHSNER:

Q. Herr Speer, there is an important document submitted by the prosecution. It is the minutes of a meeting with Hitler on 4th January, 1944. It has been submitted as Document 1292-PS, Exhibit USA 225. I refer to Page 28 of the English text of my document book. How was this meeting arranged?

A. It was called by request of Hitler.

Q. For what reason?

A. To settle the arguments between Sauckel and myself.

Q. And what was Hitler's decision?

A. His decision was a useless compromise, as was often the case with Hitler. These blocked industries were to be maintained, and for this purpose Sauckel was given the order to obtain three and a half million workers from the occupied territories. Hitler gave strictest instructions through the High Command of the Armed Forces to the military commanders, that Sauckel's request should be met by all means possible.

Q. Did you agree to this decision?

A. No, not at all; for it meant that my programme of shifting the labour commitment to the West would collapse.

Q. And what action did you take after that?

A. Contrary to the Fuehrer's decision during that meeting, I informed the military commander of the way I wanted it so that, in connection with the expected order from the High Command of the Armed Forces, the military commander would have two interpretations of the result of the meeting in his hands. Since the military commander was agreeable to my interpretation, it could be expected that he would follow my wish.

DR. FLAECHSNER: In this connection, may I present a document which is on Page 29 of the English text of my document book, Page 26 of the German and French texts. This is a teletype message from Speer to General Studt in Paris. It will be Exhibit 10. Two things appear from this letter. One, Speer wrote, and I quote:

"Gauleiter Sauckel will start negotiations with the appropriate agencies with regard to the occupied Western territories, in order to

*Speer inspecting the new medium German Panzer V (the Panther). This tank was developed to fight off the Russian T34.*
*Bundesarchiv, Bild 183-2005-0103-502 / Ruge, Willi / CC-BY-SA*

achieve clarity on the manner and possibility of the execution—"

**THE PRESIDENT:** What is the point in reading that, Dr. Flaechsner?

**DR. FLAECHSNER:** Mr. President, the prosecution has submitted this document, 1292-PS, to prove—

**THE PRESIDENT:** The defendant just told us what is in the document. He has told us the substance of the whole affair. We quite understand what the difference of opinion between Sauckel and Speer was.

**DR. FLAECHSNER:** Very well. This document shows the reaction on the part of the defendant, namely, what he did so that Hitler's decision, as such, would be nullified or at least modified. In this letter the defendant said to General Studt—

**THE PRESIDENT:** Dr. Flaechsner, the Tribunal has given you the clearest possible indication of the view which they take about these matters of different plans and differences of view between Sauckel and Speer. Why do you not pass on to some other part of your case if there is any other part of it?

**DR. FLAECHSNER:** Mr. President, I do not wish to discuss the argument between these two. I am trying to show the actions taken by Speer so as to put his point of view into practice. This is not referring to—

**THE PRESIDENT:** Yes, but that is irrelevant. As I said just now, the defendant has told us what he did. It is not necessary to read it all out to us again.

**DR. FLAECHSNER:** Very well. In that case, may I go on to present a document which is on Page 30 of the English text of my document book, Page 27 of the German and French texts. It is a letter from Speer to Sauckel, dated 6th January, 1944, and it is shown in this letter that, for the French industrial firms working in France, 400,000 workers were to be reserved at once and another 400,000 workers during the following months, who, therefore, would not be deported.

**BY DR. FLAECHSNER:**

Q. What results did these two letters have, Herr Speer, with reference to Hitler's order that one million workers should be taken from France to Germany?

A. I should like to summarize the entire subject and say a few words about it. We had a system of dealing with inconvenient orders from Hitler which enabled us to by-pass them. Jodl has already said in his testimony that he had developed such a technique, too. And so, of course, the letters which are being submitted here are only clear to the expert, as to their meaning and the results they would produce.

From the document which is being presented now, from Sauckel's speech on 1st March, 1944, it is evident, too, what the results were in regard to the labour assignment in the occupied territories. The result is clear and I have already described it here, and I think we can therefore pass to Page 49.

Q. Herr Speer, can you give me a description of the results of the air attacks on the occupied Western territories?

A. Yes. In this connection I should again like to summarize a few points.

The invasion was preceded by heavy air attacks on the transport system in the occupied Western territories. As a result of that, beginning with May and June, 1944 production in France was paralysed and one million workers were unemployed. With that, the idea of shifting production (Verlagerung) had collapsed as far as I was concerned, and according to normal expectations of the French officials, too, the impression was general that a large-scale attack on Germany would now commence.

I gave the order that in spite of this shutting down of the entire French industry, the blocked industries should be kept up, although I knew as an expert that their rehabilitation, considering the damage to the transport system, would not be possible in less than nine to twelve months, even if the air attacks should cease. I was, therefore, acting against my own interests here.

The French prosecution has confirmed this in Document RF 22. The corresponding passages are indicated in the document book.

Between 19th and 22nd June I had a conference with Hitler and I obtained a decree according to which the workers in the occupied territories had to remain on the spot no matter what happened. Seyss-Inquart has already testified that a similar decision was applied to Holland. Upon my orders, the workers in these blocked industries even continued to receive their wages.

**DR. FLAECHSNER:** In this connection I submit Speer Exhibit 12. It is an extract from the Fuehrer conference from 19th to 22nd June, 1944, and I beg the Tribunal to take judicial notice of it. The document is on Page 22 of the English text of my document book.

**BY DR. FLAECHSNER:**

**Q.** Herr Speer, you must have been aware of the fact that, because of this decision of yours, at least one million workers would be unemployed in all the Western territories and be unproductive for quite a long time. How could you justify such a decision?

**A.** I have to admit quite frankly that this was my first decision which I considered justified by the war situation which had deteriorated so catastrophically. The invasion was a success. The heavy air attacks on production were showing decisive results. An early end of the war was foreseeable and all this altered the situation as far as I was concerned. How the consequences arising from this situation affected me will become apparent through various other examples which I shall put forward in the course of the trial.

Of course, Hitler was not of the same opinion during that period. On the contrary, he believed that everything ought to be done in order to utilise the last reserves of manpower.

**Q.** Please describe briefly your attitude towards the meeting of 11th July, 1944, to which we have already referred once before. This was Document 3819-PS. Please be very brief.

**A.** During this meeting of 11th July, I maintained my point of view. Once again I pointed to Germany's reserves, as is shown in the minutes, and I announced that the transport difficulties should not be allowed to influence production, and that the blocked industries were to be kept up in these territories. Both I and the military commanders of the occupied territories were perfectly aware of the fact that with this, the well-known consequences for these blocked industries would be the same as before, that is, the transfer of labour assignment from the occupied Western territories to Germany would continue.

Q. The French prosecution has presented a certain order, Document 833. It presented it during the session of 30th May, if I remember correctly. It came up during the cross-examination of co-defendant Sauckel.

According to this order, troops were to round up workers in the West. Please give a brief statement on that. So as to refresh your memory, I want to say that reference is made in this telegram to the meeting of 11th July.

A. The minutes of the meeting show, as I said before, that I opposed the measures of coercion. I did not see Keitel's actual order.

Q. No. 1824 is another document submitted by the French prosecution on the same subject. It is a document of General von Kluge's, dated 25th July, 1944. It refers to the telegram from Keitel which has been previously mentioned. Do you know anything about it, whether that order was ever actually carried out?

A. I know that the order was not carried out. To understand the situation, it is necessary to become familiar with the atmosphere prevailing during the time around the 20th July. At that time, not every order of the Fuehrer was carried out. As the investigations after the 20th July proved, even at that time in his capacity as Commander-in-Chief in the West, Kluge was planning negotiations with the Western enemies for a capitulation and, probably, he made his initial attempts at that time. That, incidentally, was the reason for his suicide after the attempt of the 20th July had failed. It is out of the question—

THE PRESIDENT: You gave the number 1824. What does that mean?

DR. FLAECHSNER: Mr. President, 824 is the number which the French prosecution has given to this Document. That is the number under which it has submitted it. Unfortunately, I cannot ascertain the exhibit number. I have made inquiries, but I have not had an answer yet.

I am just given to understand that it is Exhibit RF 1515.

THE PRESIDENT: Thank you.

A. (continuing): It is out of the question that Field-Marshal Kluge, in the military situation in which he found himself and considering his views, should have given orders for raids and measures of coercion at that moment. The release of the Sauckel-Laval agreement, which was mentioned in this document, has no practical significance, since the blocked industries were kept up, and thus this agreement could not become effective.

This was well known to the officials in France, and the best proof for this fact, namely that the order was not carried out, is Document RF 22 of the French prosecution, which shows that in July, 1944, only 3,000 workers came to Germany from France. If the military authorities had used measures of coercion, it would have been a simple matter to send a very much larger number of workers than these 3,000 from France to Germany.

**Q.** Did you use your influence to stop completely the allocation of labour from occupied territories to Germany?

**A.** No. I have to tell you quite frankly that although I did use my influence to reduce the recruitment of labour or to put an end to measures of force and raids, I did not use it to stop the assignment of labour completely.

**Q.** I shall now pass to another problem.

The prosecution has touched- upon and mentioned the Organisation Todt. Can you briefly explain the tasks of the Organisation Todt to the Tribunal?

**A.** Here, again, I shall give a little summary. The tasks of the Organisation Todt were exclusively technical ones, that is to say, they had to carry out technical construction work; in the East mainly road and rail construction, and in the West, the construction of concrete dug-outs which became known as the so-called Atlantic Wall. For this purpose the Organisation Todt used foreign workers to a disproportionate degree. In the West there were about twenty foreigners to one German worker; in Russia there were about four Russians to one German. This could only be carried out in the West if the Organisation Todt could use local construction firms and their work-yards to a considerable extent. They supplied the technical staffs and recruited their own workers, it being obvious that these firms had no possibility to recruit by force.

Accordingly a large number of workers of the Todt Organisation were volunteers. But it is clear that constantly a certain percentage was working in the Todt organisation under the calling-up system.

The Organisation Todt has been described here as part of the armed forces, and it is merely necessary to state in this connection that foreign workers did not, of course, belong to it, but only German workers who, of course, in occupied territories, had to become members of the armed forces in some way or other. The prosecution holds a different opinion on this matter.

Apart from the Organisation Todt, there were certain transport units attached to my Ministry which were working in occupied territories, and, for a certain reason, I am anxious to state that they were principally recruited as volunteers. The prosecution has alleged that the Organisation Todt was the comprehensive organisation for all military construction work in the occupied territories. That is not the case. They only had to carry out one quarter to one fifth of the construction programme.

In May, 1944, the Organisation Todt was taken over by the Reich and from that time was made responsible for some of the large-scale construction programmes and for the management of the organisation of the General Plenipotentiary for construction work in the Four-Year Plan. This General Plenipotentiary for construction work distributed the contingents coming from the Central Planning Board and he was responsible for other directive tasks, but he was not responsible for the carrying out, and for the supervision of, the construction work itself. For these purposes there were the different state authorities in the Reich, and in particular the SS Building Administration who had their own responsibility for the building programmes which they carried out.

**Q.** The prosecution has alleged that you had caused the employment of concentration camp inmates in the armament industry and has submitted Document RF 24, Exhibit USA 179.

**DR. FLAECHSNER:** Mr. President, this document is on Page 47 of the English text in my document book. It is about a conference with Hitler in September, 1942.

**BY DR. FLAECHSNER:**

**Q.** How did that conference come about, Herr Speer?

**A.** When in February, 1942, I took over the armament department of the armed forces, there were demands for considerable increases in production and, to meet them, it was necessary to construct numerous new factories. For this purpose Himmler offered his concentration camps, both to Hitler and to me. It was his plan that some of these necessary new constructions with the requisite machinery should be erected within the concentration camps and be operated there under the supervision of the SS. The chief of the armament department of the armed forces, General Fromm, was against this plan, and so was I. Apart from general reasons for this, the first point was that uncontrolled arms production on the part of the SS should be prevented. Secondly, this would certainly entail my being deprived of the technical management in these industries. For these reasons, when planning the large extension programme of armament production in the spring of 1942, I ignored these demands by the SS. Himmler went to see Hitler and the minutes of this conference, which are available here, show the objections to my plans which Hitler put to me upon Himmler's suggestions.

**DR. FLAECHSNER:** Mr. President, in this connection I should like to draw your attention to Page 44 of the German text, which is Page 47 of the English text. It is point 36 of a Fuehrer protocol. There it says

**THE PRESIDENT:** It is Page 47 of the English text.

**DR. FLAECHSNER:** Yes, that is correct.

There it says, and I quote:

"... beyond a small number of workers it will not be possible to organise armament production in the concentration camps."

**THE PRESIDENT:** Dr. Flaechsner, the witness has just given us the substance of it, has he not?

**BY DR. FLAECHSNER:**

**Q.** Herr Speer, according to this document you proposed that factories should be staffed entirely with internees from concentration camps. Did you carry that out?

**A.** No, this proposal was not carried out in full because it soon became clear that it was Himmler's intention to exercise his influence over these industries and in some way or other he would undoubtedly have succeeded in getting these industries under his control. For that reason, as a basic principle, only a part of the industrial staff consisted of internees from concentration camps, so as to counteract Himmler's efforts. And so it happened that the labour camps were attached to the armament industries. But Himmler never received his share of five to eight per cent of arms which had been decided upon. This was prevented due to an agreement with the general of the Army Staff in the High Command of the Armed Forces, General Buhle.

This document also confirms the statement of the defendant Speer that inmates of concentration camps were paid premiums if they proved themselves particularly useful; furthermore, it shows on the last page that on average the working hours of all internees were 240 hours per month, which would correspond to sixty working hours per week.

I also refer to a document which has already been mentioned yesterday, it is number 44, and has already been submitted by me as Exhibit 6; it is in the second volume of my document book. Mr. President, it is the first document book in the appendix volume.

This document shows clearly how much the extension of the SS industries was a matter determined by the ambition of Himmler and Pohl. The document also states, and I quote:

> "The monthly working hours contributed by concentration camp inmates did not even amount to 8,000,000 hours, so that most certainly not more than about 32,000 men and women from concentration camps can be working in our armaments industries. This number is constantly diminishing."

Mr. President, this sentence is on Page 90, at the bottom. You will find it there in the English text.

The letter also shows that the author computes nearly the same number of working hours as is mentioned by Pohl in his letter; namely, 250 hours per month, which is approximately 63 hours per week.

**BY DR. FLAECHSNER:**

Q. Herr Speer, through this letter you got knowledge of the fact that workers, particularly foreigners, were not returned to their old places of work when, for certain acts, they fell into the hands of the police, but that they were taken to concentration camps. What steps did you take then?

A. Here again I should like to summarize several points. I received the letter on or about 15th May, in Berlin, when I returned after my illness. Its contents greatly upset me because, after all, this was nothing else but kidnapping. I had an estimate submitted to me about the number of people' thus being removed from the economic system. The number, quoted without guarantee of accuracy, was 30,000 to 40,000 per month.

The result was I got in touch with the Central Planning Board on 22nd May, 1944, and demanded that these workers should be returned to their old industries at once. This demand was not practical, but I wished to express through it that workers had to be returned to their own places of work. This demand to the Central Planning Board has been submitted by the prosecution.

Immediately after the meeting of the Central Planning Board I went to see Hitler, and there I had a conference on 5th June, 1944. The minutes of the Fuehrer conference are available. I stated that I would not stand for any such procedure, and I cited many arguments based entirely on reason, since no other arguments would have been effective. Hitler declared, as the minutes show, that these workers had to be returned to their former work at once, and that, after a conference between Himmler and myself, he would once again communicate this decision of his to Himmler.

**DR. FLAECHSNER:** I submit Exhibit 13, which is an extract from the Fuehrer conference of 3rd and 5th June, 1944; you will find this document on Page 92 of the document book.

**THE WITNESS:** Immediately after this conference I went to see Himmler and communicated to him Hitler's decision. He told me that no such number had ever been arrested by the police. But he promised me that he would immediately issue a decree which would correspond to Hitler's demands; namely, that the SS would no longer be permitted to detain these workers.

I informed Hitler of this result, and I asked him once more to get in touch with Himmler about it. In those days I had no reason to suspect Himmler's promise, because, after all, it is not customary for Reich Ministers to distrust each other so much. But anyhow, I did not have any further complaints from my assistants concerning this affair. I must emphasize that the settling of the entire matter was not really my affair, but the information appeared so incredible to me that I intervened at once.

Had I known that already eighteen months before Himmler had started a very similar action, and that in this letter—a letter which has been submitted here—

**DR. FLAECHSNER:** Mr. President, this is Document 1063-PS, and it is Exhibit USA 219. It is on Page 51 of the English text of my document book. That is the document to which the witness is now referring.

**BY DR. FLAECHSNER:**

How far did your efforts go to get workers for the armaments industry from concentration camps?

A. I want to make a brief statement to the document.

Had I known of this letter, I would never have had enough confidence in Himmler to expect that he would correctly execute the order as given by Hitler. For this letter shows quite clearly that this action was to be kept secret from other offices. These other offices could only be the office of the General Plenipotentiary for Labour or my own office.

Finally, I want to say in connection with this problem that it was my duty as Minister for Armament to use as many workers as were possibly available for armaments production or for any other production. I considered it proper, therefore, that workers from concentration camps, too, should work in war production or armament industries.

The main accusation by the prosecution, however, that I deliberately increased the number of concentration camps or caused them to be increased is by no means correct. On the contrary, I wanted just the opposite, regarding the matter from the point of view of production.

**DR. FLAECHSNER:** May I refer in this connection to the answers of the witness Schmelte to questions 9 and 35 in the questionnaire which was submitted to him, and to the answer of the witness Schieber to No. 20.

**BY DR. FLAECHSNER:**

**Q.** Herr Speer, Document R-124, Exhibit USA 179, which was submitted by the prosecution, contains several remarks you made during the meetings of the Central Planning Board.

**DR. FLAECHSNER:** Mr. President, may I draw your attention to Page 53 of the English text of my document book.

**BY DR. FLAECHSNER:**

**Q.** Herr Speer, what do you want to say about your remark concerning "idler" in the meeting of 30th October, 1942?

**A.** I made the remark as reproduced by the stenographic record. However, I have had here an opportunity to read all the shorthand notes of the Central Planning Board and I see that this remark was not followed up in any way and that no measures were demanded of me.

**DR. FLAECHSNER:** On the same page of the document book, Mr. President, there is a statement from a meeting on 22nd April, 1943.

**BY DR. FLAECHSNER:**

**Q.** Herr Speer, what do you have to say in connection with that remark regarding Russian prisoners of war?

**A.** It can be elucidated very briefly. This is proof of the fact that the conception of armaments must be understood in the way I have explained, because of the 90,000 Russians employed in armaments according to this document, 29,000 were employed in the iron, steel and metal industries and 63,000 in the industries constructing engines, boilers, vehicles and apparatus of all sorts.

**Q.** Herr Speer, the prosecution has also mentioned a remark made by you on 25th May, 1944. That, too, can be found on Page 53 of the English text of the document book. There you said at a conference with Keitel and Zeitzler that, in accordance with Hitler's instructions, the groups of auxiliary volunteers were to be dissolved and that you would effect the transfer of the Russians from the lines-of-communications area.

**A.** In this case also I have read through the shorthand notes. The matter can be explained briefly. The "HIWI" mentioned in the document are the so-called auxiliary volunteers who had joined the troops fighting in Russia. As the months went by, they had grown to a great number, and during the retreat they kept with the troops, as they would probably have been treated as traitors in their own country. These volunteers, however, were not, as I desired it, put into industry, since the conference which was planned did not take place.

**Q.** Please make a brief statement concerning Sauckel's memorandum, Document 556-PS, submitted by the prosecution, concerning a telephone call on 4th January, 1943, which refers to labour commitment.

A. After this telephone call, further measures were to be taken in France to increase the number of workers available for assignment. Minutes of a Fuehrer conference which I found recently, namely, those of the meeting of 3rd [sic] to 5th January, 1943, show that, at that time, Hitler's statement of opinion referred to increased employment of French people in France for the local industry and economy.

DR. FLAECHSNER: Mr. President, I shall submit this document later because up to now I have not yet had the opportunity to—

THE PRESIDENT: Can you tell the Tribunal how long you are going to be, Dr. Flaechsner?

DR. FLAECHSNER: I hope, Mr. President, that I shall be through before five o'clock this afternoon.

THE PRESIDENT: You will not lose sight of what I have said to you already about the relevance of the argument and evidence you have been adducing up to date?

DR. FLAECHSNER: Very well, Mr. President.

THE PRESIDENT: The Tribunal will adjourn now.

*(A recess was taken until 1400 hours.)*

BY DR. FLAECHSNER:

Herr Speer, this morning we stopped at a discussion of Sauckel's telephone message of 4th January, 1943, regarding the matter of labour commitments. As you have already stated, the Fuehrer protocol of 3rd to 5th January, which I shall submit to the Tribunal later on, is connected with this. Will you please make a brief statement on the subject of that discussion?

A. As the record shows, measures were to be taken to raise economy in France to a higher level. It contains stern injunctions from Hitler concerning the ways and means that were to be used to this end. It states that acts of sabotage were to be punished in the most rigorous manner and that humanitarian considerations were not to be tolerated.

This record also shows that at that time I asked Hitler to transfer the control of production questions in France to me, a step which was actually taken several months later.

I mention this only for the purpose of making it clear, while I am still in a position to testify as a witness, that I did not carry out Hitler's policy of abandoning all humanitarianism in France.

My attention was drawn to one case in which ten hostages were to be shot as a reprisal for acts of industrial sabotage committed in the Meurthe-et-Moselle district. At that time I managed to prevent the sentence from being carried out. Rochling, who was in charge of iron production in the occupied Western regions, is my witness in this case.

That is the only case in which I was informed that hostages were to be shot on account of sabotage in production.

I can also prove that, through a decision by Hitler dated September, 1943, I was responsible for providing a supplementary meal, in addition to the existing rations, for factory workers employed in France. In a letter which I sent to the General Plenipotentiary for Manpower in December, 1943, I strongly urged the necessity, not only of paying wages to the workers in the occupied Western regions, but also of making available to them a corresponding quantity of consumer goods a line of policy which doubtless does not accord with the policy of plundering the Western regions, on which so much stress has been laid by the French prosecution.

All three documents are in my possession and they can be produced.

I only mention these facts to show that I neither approved of nor followed the very harsh policy laid down by Hitler in the records of 3rd to 5th January.

**Q.** I now turn to another point, Herr Speer; what did you produce in France, that is, on the basis of your programme?

**A.** We have already discussed this at sufficient length. No armaments were manufactured; only spare parts and consumer goods.

**Q.** Very well. I merely wanted to get that clear.

The prosecution has submitted to you a Fuehrer protocol, Document 124-R, dated March, 1944, and containing a statement that you discussed with Hitler the Reichsmarschall's proposal to deliver prisoners of war to France.

What can you say to that?

**A.** This record dates back to 3rd March, 1944. From January until May, 1944, I was seriously ill, and the discussion took place without me. A member of my staff was in charge of this discussion—a man who enjoyed the confidence of Hitler to an unusually high degree. In any case, the proposal was not carried out.

**Q.** Herr Speer, you attended the session of 30th May, at which the question of how the office of General Plenipotentiary for Manpower came to be established was discussed. Will you comment briefly on that point?

**A.** I should like to say briefly that I wanted a delegate to deal with all labour problems connected with my task of military armament production. My chief concern in the commitment problem, at the beginning of my term of office, was with the Gauleiter, who carried on a policy of Gau preferentialism. The non-political offices of the Labour Ministry could not proceed against the Gauleiter and the result was that manpower inside Germany was frozen. I suggested to Hitler that I should have a Gauleiter whom I knew for this delegate—a man named Hancke. Goering, by the way, had already supported the suggestion. Hitler agreed.

Two days later, Bormann made the suggestion that Sauckel be chosen.

I did not know Sauckel well, but I was quite ready to accept the choice. It is quite possible that Sauckel did not know anything about the affair, and that he assumed—as he was entitled to do—that he was chosen at my suggestion.

The office of the Plenipotentiary for Labour was created in the following way:

Lammers declared that he could not issue special authority for a partial labour sector, as that would be a doubtful procedure from an administrative point of view, and for that reason the whole question of manpower would have to be put into the hands of a plenipotentiary. At first it was contemplated to do this by a Fuehrer decree. Goering protested on the grounds that it was his task under the Four-Year Plan. A compromise was made, therefore, in accordance with which Sauckel was to be the General Plenipotentiary within the framework of the Four-Year Plan, but that he would be appointed by Hitler.

This was the only arrangement of the kind under the Four-Year Plan. In that way, Sauckel was in effect subordinated to Hitler; and he always looked upon it in that way.

**Q.** You have heard that Sauckel, in giving his testimony on 30th May, said that Goering participated in the meetings of the Central Planning Board. Is that true?

**A.** No, that is in no way correct. I would not have had any use for him, for after all, we had to carry out practical work.

**Q.** The prosecution has submitted a statement by Sauckel dated 8th October, 1945, according to which arrangements for his deputies to function in the occupied territories were supposed to have been made by you. Is that true?

**A.** No. In 1941 I had not yet anything to do with armaments, and even later, during the period of Sauckel's activity, I did not employ these deputies and did not do much to promote their activities. That was a matter for Sauckel to handle; it was within his jurisdiction.

**Q.** The French prosecution quoted from the record of Sauckel's preliminary interrogation on 27th September, 1945, and according to this quotation, you gave a special order for transport trains carrying foreign workers.

**A.** I believe it would be to the purpose to deal at the same time with all the statements made by Sauckel which apply to me, that will save time.

**Q.** Please go ahead.

**A.** Arrangements for transport trains were made by Sauckel and his staff. It is possible that air raids or a sudden change in the production programme made it necessary for my office to ask for transport trains to be re-routed; but the responsibility for that always rested with the General Plenipotentiary for Manpower.

Sauckel also testified here that, after Stalingrad, Goebbels and I started on the total war effort. But that is not correct in this form. Stalingrad was January, 1943, and Goebbels started on his total war effort in August, 1944. After Stalingrad, a great re-organisation programme was to be carried out in Germany in order to free German workers. I myself was one of those who demanded this. Neither Goebbels nor I, however, were able to carry out this plan. A committee of three, Lammers, Keitel and Bormann, was formed; but, owing to their lack of technical knowledge, they were unable to carry out this task.

My manpower department was mentioned by Sauckel in his testimony. This worked as follows: Every large factory and every employer of labour had a manpower department, which, naturally came under mine, and did not encroach in the slightest degree on Sauckel's interests. Their sphere of activity was not very great, as may be seen from the fact that my manpower department was one of 50 or 60 departments coming under my office. If I had attached very much importance to it, it would have been one of my six or eight special branches.

Sauckel further mentioned the Stabsleiter discussions which took place in his office. A representative of my manpower department for military and naval armament and for building attended these conferences. At these meetings which were attended by about fifteen people who were in need of labour, the question of priority was settled on the basis of Sauckel's information as to the state of economy generally.

This was the function erroneously ascribed here to the Central Planning Board.

In addition, it was asserted that I promoted the transport of foreign workers to Germany in April, 1942; and that I was responsible for the fact that foreign workers were brought to Germany at all. That, however, is not true. I did not need to use any influence on Sauckel to attain that. In any case, it is evident from a document in my possession—a Fuehrer decree of 4th May, 1943—that the introduction of compulsory labour in the Western region was approved by the Fuehrer at Sauckel's suggestion.

I can further quote a speech which I delivered on 18th April, 1942, showing that at that period I was still of the opinion that the German building industry, which employed approximately 1,800,000 workmen, should be reduced considerably so that workers could be diverted to the production of armaments. This speech which I made to my staff, in which I explained my principles and also discussed the question of manpower, does not contain any mention of the planning of a foreign labour draft. If I had been the active instigator of such a plan, surely I would have mentioned the subject in this speech.

Finally, in connection with Sauckel's testimony, I must correct the chart of the organisation submitted here. It is not correct in that the separate sectors enumerated in it are classified under various Ministries. In reality, these sectors of employers of labour were classified under various economic branches, independently of the Ministries. Only in the case of my own Ministry and that of the Air Ministry were sectors concerned classified under their relative Ministry.

The chart is also incorrect in stating that the building industry was represented in the Ministry of Economics. That came under my jurisdiction. From 1943 on, the chemical and mining industries, both of which are listed under the Ministry of Economics, were under my jurisdiction. To my knowledge, these branches were represented through plenipotentiaries in the Four-Year Plan, even prior to September, 1943, and stated their requirements to Sauckel direct, independently of the Ministry of Economics.

This chart is further incorrect in stating that the demands of these workers and individual employers went directly to Hitler. It would have been impossible for Hitler to settle disputes between 15 employers. As I have already said, the latter attended the Stabsleiter conferences, over which Sauckel presided.

Q. Herr Speer, what did you do with your documents at the end of the war?

A. I felt bound to preserve my documents so that the necessary transition measures could be taken during reconstruction. I refused to allow these documents even to be looked at. They were turned over in their entirety to the Allied authorities, here in Nuremberg, where I had a branch archive. I handed them over when I was still at liberty in the Flensburg Zone. The prosecution is thus in possession of all my documents to the number of several thousands, as well as all public speeches, Gauleiter speeches, and other speeches dealing with armament and industry; some 4,000 Fuehrer decisions, 5,000 pages of stenographic records of the Central Planning Board, memoranda and so forth. I mention this only because these documents show conclusively to what extent my task was a technical and economic one.

Q. In your documents, as far as you remember, did you ever make statements regarding ideology, anti-Semitism, etc.?

A. No; I never made any statements of the kind, either in speeches or memoranda. I assume that otherwise the prosecution would be in a position to produce some evidence of such statements.

Q. Herr Speer, your name appears as Armament Minister on the list of members of the new Government drawn up by the men responsible for the Putsch of 20th July. Did you participate in the attempted assassination of 20th July?

A. I neither participated in it, nor was I informed of it in advance. At that time I was against assassinating Hitler.

DR. FLAECHSNER: Mr. President, this point is mentioned in interrogatories by the witness Kempf (Point 9) and the witness Stahl (Point 1).

BY DR. FLAECHSNER:

What was the reason why you—as the only Minister from the National Socialist regime—were on the opposition list?

A. At that period, I was working in collaboration with Army experts of the General Staff and the Commander-in-Chief of the home defence forces. Both staffs were the nucleus of those involved in the attempt of 20th July.

I had particularly close relations with General Fromm, the leader of the home defence forces, and also with General Zeitzler, the chief of the Army General Staff. After 20th July, Fromm was hanged and Zeitzler was dismissed from the Army. A close contact developed through this collaboration, and these circles recognised my technical achievements. I assumed at that time that that was why they wanted to retain me.

Q. So political reasons did not play any part in that connection?

A. Certainly not directly. Of course, it was well known that for a long time I had spoken my mind emphatically and in public regarding the abuses of power by members of Hitler's immediate circle. As I found out later, I shared the opinions of the men of 20th July on many points of principle.

Q. What were your relations with Hitler in regard to your work?

A. My closest contact with him, in my capacity of architect, was probably during the period from 1937 to September, 1939; after that, the relationship was no longer so close, on account of the circumstances of the war. After I was appointed successor to Todt, a closer but much more official working relationship was established. Because of the heavy demands made upon me by industry, I had very little opportunity to go to headquarters. I only visited the Fuehrer's headquarters about once in two or three weeks. My four months' illness in spring, 1944, was exploited by many people interested in weakening my position, and after 20th July, the fact that I had been nominated for the Ministry undoubtedly occasioned a shock to Hitler—a fact which Bormann and Goebbels used to stress in their open fight against me. The details are shown by a letter which I sent to Hitler on 20th December, 1944, and which has been submitted as a document.

Q. Were you able to carry on political discussions with Hitler?

A. No, he regarded me as a purely technical Minister. Attempts to discuss political or personal problems with him always failed because of the fact that he was unapproachable. From 1944 on, he was so averse to general discussions, and particularly discussions of the war situation, that I set down my ideas in memorandum form, which I handed to him. Hitler knew how to confine every man to his own speciality. He himself was therefore the only co-ordinating factor. This was far beyond his strength and also his capacity. A unified political leadership was lacking in consequence. So also was an expert military office for making decisions.

Q. Then, as an expert Minister, do you wish to limit your responsibility to your sphere of work?

A. No, I should like to say something of fundamental importance here. This war has brought inconceivable catastrophe to the German people and has started a world catastrophe. Therefore, it is my unquestionable duty to assume my share of responsibility for this misfortune before the German people. This is all the more my obligation, all the more my responsibility since the head of the late government has evaded responsibility before the German people and before the world. I, as an important member of the leadership of the Reich, therefore share in the total responsibility, beginning with 1942. I will state my arguments in this connection in my final remarks.

Q. Do you assume responsibility for the affairs covered by the extensive sphere of your assignments?

A. Of course, as far as is possible according to the principles generally applied and with regard to actions taken according to my directives.

Q. Do you wish to refer to Fuehrer decrees in this connection?

A. No. In so far as Hitler gave me orders and I carried them out, I assume the responsibility for them. I did not, of course, carry out all the orders which he gave me.

DR. FLAECHSNER: Mr. President, I turn now to a second part of my evidence in the case of the defendant. This presentation is not meant to exonerate the defendant from those charges brought against him by the prosecution which apply to his actual sphere of activity.

This part concerns itself with those accusations raised by the prosecution against the defendant as a member of the so-called joint conspiracy. This second part is relatively brief, and I assume that I shall be able to conclude my entire presentation of evidence within an hour.

In this matter, we are concerned with Speer's activity in his attempts to prevent Hitler's destructive intentions in Germany and the occupied countries, and with the measures he took and the attempts he made to shorten a war which he believed already lost.

I assume that the High Tribunal will agree to my presentation.

**BY DR. FLAECHSNER:**

Q. Herr Speer, up to what time did you devote all your powers to obtaining the strongest possible armament and thus continuing the war?

A. Up to the middle of January, 1945.

Q. Had not the war been lost before that?

A. From a military point of view, and as far as the general situation was concerned, it was certainly lost before that. It is difficult, however, to consider a war as lost and personally come to final decisions if one is faced with unconditional surrender.

Q. Long before that, did not considerations arising out of the production situation, of which you were in a position to have a comprehensive view, force you to regard the war as lost?

A. From the armament point of view, not until the autumn of 1944, for I succeeded up to that time, in spite of bombing attacks, in maintaining a constant rise in production. If I may express it in figures, this was so great that in the year 1944 I could completely re-equip 130 infantry divisions and 40 armoured divisions. That involved new equipment for two million men. This figure would have been thirty per cent higher had it not been for the bombing attacks. We reached our production peak for the entire war in August, 1944, for munitions; in September, 1944, for aircraft; and in December, 1944, for ordnance and the new U-boats. The new weapons were to be put into use a few months later, probably in February or March of 1945. For example, the jet planes which had already been announced in the Press, the new U-boats and the new anti-aircraft installations, etc. Here, too, however, bombing attacks retarded the mass production of these new weapons, which in the last phase of the war might have changed the situation to a great extent, so that they could not be used against the enemy in large numbers. All attempts at mass attacks were fruitless, however, since from 12th May, 1944, on, our fuel plants became targets for concentrated attacks from the air.

This was catastrophic. Ninety per cent of the fuel was lost to us from that time on. The success of these attacks meant the loss of the war as far as production was concerned, for our new tanks and jet planes were of no use without fuel.

Q. Did you tell Hitler about the effect on production of the bombing attacks?

**A.** Yes, I told him of this in great detail, both orally and in writing. Between June and December, 1944, I sent him twelve memoranda, all with catastrophic news.

**DR. FLAECHSNER:** Mr. President, in this connection, I should like to submit to the Tribunal a document which deals with a memorandum sent by Speer on 30th June, 1944. It is reproduced on Page 56 of the English Document Book and will be Exhibit 14. I should like to quote from this. Speer writes to Hitler:

> "But in September of this year the quantities required to cover the most urgent needs of the Wehrmacht cannot possibly be supplied any longer, which means that from that time on there will be a deficiency which cannot be made good and which must lead to tragic consequences."

Speer informed Hitler in another memorandum, dated 30th August, 1944, on the situation in the chemical industry and the fuel production industry. This is on Page 62 of the English text, Exhibit 15. I quote only one sentence:

> "So that these are shortages in important categories of those materials necessary for the conduct of modern warfare."

**BY DR. FLAECHSNER:**

**Q.** Herr Speer, how was it possible that you and the other co-workers of Hitler, despite your realization of the situation, still tried to do everything possible to continue the war?

**A.** In this phase of the war, Hitler deceived all of us. From summer of 1944 on, he circulated through his agent, Hebel, of the Foreign Office, definite statements to the effect that discussions connected with foreign policy had been started. General Jodl has confirmed this to me here in Court. In this way, for instance, the fact that several visits were paid to Hitler by the Japanese Ambassador was interpreted to mean that through Japan we were carrying on conversations with Moscow; or else Ambassador Neubacher, who was here as a witness, was reported to have initiated conversations in the Balkans with the United States; or else the former Soviet Minister in Berlin was alleged to have been in Stockholm for the purpose of initiating conversations.

In this way he raised hopes that, like Japan, we would start negotiations in this hopeless situation, so that the people would be saved from the worst consequences. To do this, however, it was necessary to stiffen resistance as much as possible. He deceived all of us by holding out to the military leaders false hopes as to the success of diplomatic moves, promising the political leaders new victories through the use of new troops and new weapons; and systematically spreading rumours to encourage the people to believe in the appearance of a miracle weapon—all for the purpose of keeping up resistance. I can prove by a speech I made during this period and from letters which I wrote to Hitler and Goebbels how unedifying and disastrous I considered this policy of deceiving the people by promising them a miracle weapon.

**Q.** Herr Speer, were orders given to destroy industry in Belgium, Holland and France?

A. Yes. In case of occupation by the Allies, Hitler had ordered a far-reaching system of destruction of war industries in all these countries; according to planned preparations, coal and mineral mines, power plants and industrial premises were to be destroyed.

Q. Did you take any steps to prevent the execution of these orders?

A. Yes.

Q. And did you prevent them?

A. The Commander-in-Chief of the West was responsible for carrying out this decree, since these orders were to be carried out in his operational zone. But I informed him that, as far as I was concerned, this destruction had no sense and no purpose, and that I, in my capacity of Armament Minister, did not consider this destruction necessary. Thereupon no order to destroy these things was given.

Q. When was that?

A. By this, of course, I made myself responsible to Hitler for the fact that no destruction took place.

Q. When was that?

A. About the beginning of July, 1944.

Q. How could you justify your position?

A. All the military leaders whom I knew said at that time that the war was bound to end in October or November, since the invasion had been successful.

I myself was of the same opinion in view of the fuel situation. This may be clearly seen from the memorandum which I sent to Hitler on 30th August, in which I told him that in view of this development in the fuel situation, no operational actions by the troops would be possible by October or November. The fact that the war lasted longer than that can be ascribed only to the halt of the enemy offensive in 1944. This made it possible to decrease our fuel consumption and to give the Western Front new. supplies of tanks and ammunition. In these circumstances I was perfectly willing to accept responsibility for abandoning the industries in the Western countries to the enemy in an undamaged condition, for they could be of no use to them for at least nine months, the transport system having been destroyed beforehand. This memorandum coincides with the protection of the unemployed workers in the blocked industries—a matter which I dealt with this morning.

Q. Did Hitler sanction these measures?

A. He could not sanction these measures for he knew nothing about them. It was a period of such hectic activity at Headquarters that he never thought of checking up on the measures taken for destruction. Later, in January, 1945, reports appeared in the French Press on the rapid reconstruction of their undestroyed industries. Then, of course, serious charges were raised against me.

Q. The French prosecution has submitted a document, RF-132. This is a report by the Field Economic Officer attached to the Wehrmacht Commander for the Netherlands. According to this report, a decree by the Commander-in

Chief for the West was still in existence in September, 1944. This said that destructive measures were to be taken only in the coastal towns and nowhere else, and the Field Economic Officer for the Netherlands stated, as may be seen from the document, that the order issued by the Commander-in-Chief for the West was obsolete, and that he himself had therefore decreed, on his own initiative, that the industries in Holland should be destroyed. How was this possible and what did you do about it?

A. As a matter of fact, over-enthusiasm on the part of some of the junior officers caused the basic decrees not to destroy in the West to be ignored. Our means of ensuring that orders were carried out had been destroyed through bombing attacks. Seyss-Inquart had drawn my attention to the fact that destruction was to take place in Holland. He has already testified that I authorised him not to take destructive measures. This was in September, 1944. In addition, in order to prevent such destruction on 5th September, 1944, acting on my own initiative, I directed the managers of the coal and iron production and the chief of the civilian administration in Luxembourg to prevent destruction in the Minette ore mines, in the Saar coal mines, and the coal mines of Belgium and Holland, etc. In view of the hopeless war situation at that time, I, as the person responsible for supplying electric current, continued to furnish current to the undertakings on the other side of the front so that the pumping stations in the coal mines would not have to stop working, because, if these pumping stations had stopped, the mines would have been flooded.

DR. FLAECHSNER: In this connection, I am submitting a copy of a letter from Speer to Gauleiter Simon at Koblenz. This is Speer Exhibit 16—Page 57 of the English text in my Document Book.

**BY DR. FLAECHSNER:**

Q. Herr Speer, with regard to the other occupied countries—those outside France, Belgium and Holland—did you use your influence to prevent destruction?

A. From August, 1944, in the industrial installations in the General Government, the ore works in the Balkans, the nickel works in Finland; from September, 1944, the industrial installations in Upper Italy; beginning with February, 1945, in the oil fields in Hungary and the industries of Czechoslovakia. I should like to emphasize in this connection that I was supported to a great extent by General Jodl, who quietly tolerated this policy of non-destruction.

Q. What were Hitler's intentions with regard to the preservation of industry and means of existence for the German population at the beginning of September, 1944, when enemy troops approached the frontiers of the Greater German Reich from all sides?

A. He had absolutely no intention of preserving industry. On the contrary, he ordered the scorched earth policy with special application to Germany. That meant the ruthless destruction of all installations on the approach of the enemy. This policy was backed by Bormann, Ley and Goebbels, while the

*Speer sitting on a stair in the snow, date unconfirmed, c1942-44.*
*Bundesarchiv, Bild 183-1984-1206-511 / CC-BY-SA*

various branches of the Wehrmacht and the competent Ministries opposed it.

**DR. FLAECHSNER:** As these efforts by Speer to prevent the application of destructive measures—measures which had been considerably intensified—also applied to areas then considered part of the German Reich—such as Polish Upper Silesia, Alsace and Lorraine, Austria, Poland, the Protectorate of Bohemia and Moravia—I should like to have this matter admitted as part of my evidence.

**BY DR. FLAECHSNER:**

Q. Herr Speer, did the Commanders-in-Chief of the Army in the greater German Reich, in the areas that I have just defined, have executive powers to carry out orders of destruction?

A. No. As far as industries were concerned, those executive powers were vested in me. Bridges, locks, railway installations, etc., were the affair of the Wehrmacht.

Q. In your measures for the protection of industry, did you differentiate between the territories of the so-called old Reich and those which were added after 1933?

A. No. The industrial region of Upper Silesia, the remaining districts of Poland, Bohemia and Moravia, Alsace Lorraine and Austria, of course, were protected against destruction in the same way as the German areas. I made the necessary arrangements by personal directives on the spot-particularly in the Eastern territories.

Q. What steps did you take against the "scorched earth" policy?

A. I returned from a trip to the Western Front on 14th September, 1944, and found the decree awaiting me that everything was to be destroyed ruthlessly. I immediately issued a counter-decree officially prescribing the protection of all industrial installations. At that time, I was very much upset about the fact that industries were now to be destroyed in Germany, especially as the war situation was hopeless, and I was all the more upset because I thought I had succeeded in saving the industries in the occupied Western countries from destruction.

**DR. FLAECHSNER:** I should like to submit a document in this connection—a decree by Speer dated 14th September, 1944, for the protection of industries. It is on Page 58 of the English text of my Document Book—Exhibit 17.

**BY DR. FLAECHSNER:**

Q. Herr Speer, did you succeed in getting this order carried out?

**THE PRESIDENT:** What is the date of it? The 14th of September, did you say?

**DR. FLAECHSNER:** 14th September, Mr. President, 1944.

**THE PRESIDENT:** What page is it?

**DR. FLAECHSNER:** It is Page 58 of the English text.

**BY DR. FLAECHSNER:**

Q. Did you succeed in carrying out this order of yours, Herr Speer?

A. The scorched earth policy was officially proclaimed in the Volkischer Beobachter at the same time, in an official article by the Reich Press Chief, so that I realised quite clearly that my counter-decree could not be effective for any length of time. In this connection I used a method which is, perhaps, typical of the means employed by members of Hitler's immediate circle. In order to dissuade him from the "scorched earth" policy, I made use of the faith which he instilled into all his co-workers, that the lost territories would be recaptured. I made him decide between the two situations: firstly, if these industrial areas were lost, my armament production would drop if they were not recaptured; and secondly, if they were recaptured, they would be of value to us only if we had not destroyed the factories and other industrial installations.

Q. You thereupon addressed a letter to Bormann.

DR. FLAECHSNER: I should like to submit this letter as Exhibit 18, Mr. President—Page 59 of the English text of the Document Book. This teleprint—

WITNESS: I think we can dispense with the quotation.

BY DR. FLAECHSNER:

Q. Yes. You sent this teleprint message to Bormann before you discussed the contents with Hitler?

A. Yes. I should like to summarize

THE PRESIDENT (interposing): Would you give the French page as well so that the French members may have it.

DR. FLAECHSNER: It is Page 56 of the French text of the Document Book.

A. (continuing): Hitler approved of the text which I suggested to him, in which I gave him alternatives, either of considering the war as lost or of leaving the areas intact. For the time being, there was in any case no danger, because the fronts remained stable. Hitler demanded the destruction of the Monet mines in France, but in this case too, I was successful, as may be seen from the document, in preventing the destruction of these mines—again by exploiting Hitler's hopes of a successful counter attack.

DR. FLAECHSNER: Mr. President, the document to which the defendant has just referred is an extract from the Fuehrer decree of 18th-20th August, 1944, and I submit it as Speer Exhibit 19. It is reproduced in the supplement of my Document Book—Page 101.

BY DR. FLAECHSNER:

Q. Herr Speer, how did this order originate?

A. I have already told you.

Q. The term "paralysis" frequently occurs in your document in connection with industrial installations, etc. Will you tell the Tribunal just what you mean by the use of this term?

A. I can only say briefly that this concerns the removal of essential parts, which put the plant temporarily out of commission; but these parts were not destroyed, they were merely concealed.

Q. You emphasized a few minutes ago that, up to January, 1945, you tried to achieve the highest possible degree of armament. What were your reasons for giving up the idea after January, 1945?

A. From January, 1945, onward, a very unpleasant chapter begins, namely, the last phase of the war, and the realization that Hitler had identified the fate of the German people with his own. From March, 1945, onward, I further realised that Hitler intended deliberately to destroy the means of life for his own people if the war were lost. I have no intention of using my actions during that phase of the war to help me in my personal defence, but this is a matter of honour which must be defended, and for that reason I should like to tell you briefly about this period of time.

**Q.** Herr Speer, what was the production situation in the various areas under your jurisdiction at the end of January, 1945?

**A.** The fuel production had been quite inadequate since the beginning of the attacks on fuel plants in May, 1944, and the situation did not improve afterwards. The bombing of our transportation centres had eliminated the Ruhr area as a source of raw material for Germany as early as November, 1944, and with the successful Soviet offensive in the coal areas of Upper Silesia, most of our supply of coal from that region had been cut off since the middle of January, 1945.

Thus we could calculate precisely when the economic set-up must collapse. We had reached a point at which, even if there were a complete cessation of operations on the part of the enemy, the war would soon be lost, since the Reich, because of its lack of coal, was on the verge of an economic collapse.

**DR. FLAECHSNER:** In this connection, I submit a memorandum which Hitler received from Speer on 11th December, 1944. Mr. President, you will find an extract on Page 64 of the English Document Book—Page 61 of the German and French books. It states:

> "In view of the whole structure of the Reich economy, it is obvious that the loss of the Rhenish-Westphalian industrial area will, in the long run, spell ruin for the whole German economy, and of any chance of further successful prosecution of the war. This would mean, in fact, the total loss of the Ruhr territory as far as the German economy is concerned. It is superfluous to discuss the consequences resulting for the whole German Reich if it is deprived of the Ruhr territory."

On 15th December, 1944, in connection with the Ardennes offensive which was then imminent, Speer pointed out to Hitler in detail the consequences entailed by a possible loss of Upper Silesia.

In this connection I submit Speer's memorandum—Page 102 of the supplementary volume of my Document Book, English text, and the same page in the French text. This is an extract from a memorandum addressed to the Chief of the Army General Staff, dated 15th December, 1944—Exhibit 21.

**THE WITNESS:** This memorandum was addressed to Hitler as well.

**DR. FLAECHSNER:** It is not necessary to quote from this memorandum. It points out that a possible loss of Upper Silesia would make fighting impossible even after a few weeks and that the armed forces could in no way be supplied with armaments. A large part of Upper Silesia was actually lost shortly afterwards. On 30th January, 1945, Speer again sent a memorandum to Hitler—Page 67 of the English text of the Document Book—Page 64 in the French text. I submit this document as Exhibit 22, and I quote only the following:

> "After the loss of Upper Silesia, the German armament production will

no longer be in a position to cover even a fraction of the requirements of the front as regards munitions, weapons and tanks, losses on the front and equipment needed for new formations."

By way of special emphasis, there follows this sentence:

"The material superiority of the enemy can therefore no longer be counterbalanced, even by the bravery of our soldiers."

**BY DR. FLAECHSNER:**

Q. Herr Speer, what did you mean by the last sentence I quoted?

A. At that time Hitler issued the slogan that in defence of the Fatherland the soldiers' bravery would increase tremendously, and that—vice versa—the Allied troops, after the liberation of the occupied territories, would have less will to fight. That was also the main argument employed by Goebbels and Bormann to justify the use of all means to intensify the war.

Q. Herr Speer, did others advise Hitler in the same way that you yourself did?

A. Guderian, the Chief of Staff of the Army, reported through Ribbentrop at that time to Hitler that the war was lost. Hitler then told Guderian and myself at the beginning of February that pessimistic statements of the nature of those contained in my memorandum, or the step I had taken in regard to the Reich Minister for Foreign Affairs, would in future be considered as high treason and punished accordingly. In addition, some days later, in a situation report, he forbade his other close collaborators to make any statements about the hopelessness of the situation, and warned us that anyone who disobeyed would be shot without regard for position or rank and his family would be arrested.

The statements which Guderian and I made to Hitler about the hopelessness of the war situation had precisely the opposite effect to that which we desired. Early in February, a few days before the beginning of the Yalta Conference, Hitler sent for his Press expert and instructed him in my presence to announce in the entire German Press, and in the most uncompromising terms, the intention of Germany not to capitulate. He declared at the same time that he was doing this so that the German people would in no case receive any offer from the enemy. The language used would have to be so strong that statesmen of the hostile nations would lose all hope of driving a wedge between himself and the German people.

At the same time Hitler once again proclaimed to the German people the slogan "Victory or Collapse." All these events took place at a time when it should have been clear to him and every intelligent member of his circle that the only thing that could happen was collapse.

At a meeting of Gauleiter in the summer of 1944 Hitler had already stated— and Schirach is my witness for this—that if the German people had to be defeated in the struggle it must have been too weak, it had failed to stand its trial before history and was destined only to collapse. Now, in the hopeless situation existing in January and February, 1945, Hitler made remarks which showed that these earlier statements had not been mere flowers of rhetoric.

During this period he attributed the outcome of the war in an increasing degree to the failure of the German people; but he never blamed himself. He criticised severely this alleged failure of our people, who made so many brave sacrifices in this war.

Q. General Jodl has already testified before the Tribunal that both Hitler and his co-workers saw quite clearly the hopelessness of the military and economic situation.

Was no unified action taken by some of Hitler's closer advisers in this hopeless situation to demand the termination of war?

A. No. No unified action was taken by the leading men in Hitler's circle. A step like this was quite impossible, for these men considered themselves either as pure specialists, or else as people whose job it was to receive orders, or merely resigned themselves to the situation. No one took over the leadership in this situation for the purpose of bringing about at least a discussion with Hitler on the possibility of avoiding further sacrifices. And of course, there was an influential group which tried, with all the means at its disposal, to intensify the struggle.

That group consisted of Goebbels, Bormann, Ley, Fegelein and Burgdorf. This group was also behind the move to induce Hitler to withdraw from the Geneva Convention. At the beginning of February, Dr. Goebbels handed to Hitler a very sharp memorandum demanding our withdrawal from the Geneva Convention. Hitler had already agreed to this proposal, as Naumann, who was State Secretary to Goebbels had told me. This step meant that the struggle was to be carried on with all available means and without regard for international agreements. This was the sense of the memorandum addressed by Goebbels, to Hitler.

It must be said that this intention of Hitler and Goebbels failed on account of the unanimous resistance offered by the military leaders, as Naumann told me later.

Q. Herr Speer, the witness Stahl said in his written interrogatory that, about the middle of February, 1945, you had demanded from him a supply of the new poison gas in order to assassinate Hitler, Bormann and Goebbels, Why did you intend to do this then?

A. I thought there was no other way out. In my despair I wanted to take this step as it had been obvious to me since the beginning of February that Hitler intended to go on with the war at all costs, ruthlessly and without consideration for the German people. It was obvious to me that in the loss of the war he connected his own fate with that of the German people, and that in his own end he saw the end of the German people as well. It was also obvious that the war was lost so completely that even unconditional surrender would have to be accepted.

Q. Did you mean to carry through this assassination yourself and why did it fail?

A. I do not wish to testify to the details here. I could only carry it through personally because, since 20th July, only an intimate circle had access to

Hitler. I met with various technical difficulties ....

**THE PRESIDENT:** The Tribunal would like to hear the particulars, but will hear them after the adjournment.

*(A recess was taken.)*

**BY DR. FLAECHSNER:**

Q. Herr Speer, will you tell the Tribunal what circumstances hindered you in your undertaking?

A. I am most unwilling to describe the details, because there is always something repellent about such matters. I do it only because it is the Tribunal's wish.

Q. Please do.

A. In those days, Hitler, according to the military situation, often had conversations in his shelter with Ley, Goebbels, and Bormann, who were particularly close to him then because they supported and co-operated in his radical course of action.

Since the 20th of July, it was no longer possible even for Hitler's closest associates to enter his shelter without their pockets and briefcases being examined by the SS for explosives. As an architect, I knew this shelter intimately. It had an air-conditioning plant similar to the one installed in this courtroom.

It was not difficult to introduce the gas into the ventilator of the air-conditioning plant, which was in the garden of the Reich Chancellery. It was then bound to disperse through the entire shelter in a very short time. Thereupon, in the middle of February, 1945, I sent to Stahl, the head of my department for munitions, with whom I had particularly intimate relations, since I had worked in close co-operation with him during the war years. I frankly told him of my intention, as his testimony shows. I asked him to procure some of the new poison gas for me from the munitions production. He inquired of one of his associates, Lieut.-Col. Soyka, of the Army Ordnance Branch, as to how to get hold of this poison gas; it turned out that this new poison gas was only effective when made to explode, as a high temperature was necessary to render it effective. I am not sure whether I am going too much into detail.

An explosion was not possible, however, as this air-conditioning plant was made of thin sheets of tin, which would have been torn to pieces by the explosion. Thereupon, I had conferences with Hanschel, the chief engineer of the Chancellery, starting in the middle of March, 1945, and I managed to arrange that the anti-gas filter should no longer be switched on continuously. In this way I would have been able to use the ordinary type of gas. Naturally, Hanschel had no knowledge of the purpose for which I was conducting the talks with him. When the time came, I inspected the ventilator in the garden of the Chancellery, along with Hanschel, and there I discovered that on Hitler's personal order this ventilator had recently been surrounded by a chimney four metres high. That can still be ascertained today. Due to this it was no longer possible to carry out my plan.

**Q.** I shall now come to another problem. Herr Speer, you have heard the testimony of the witnesses Riecke and Milch in this courtroom, and they have testified as to your activities, after the middle of February, 1945, to secure the food position. What have you yourself to say in regard to your work in that direction?

**A.** I can say quite briefly that the system of preferential food supplies which I finally put into effect was arranged at the time for the purpose of planned re-conversion from war to peace. This was at the expense of armaments, which I personally represented. The tremendous number of measures which we introduced would be too extensive to describe here. All of the relevant decrees are still available. It was a system of arranging, contrary to the official policy, that shortly before their occupation by the enemy, large towns should be sufficiently supplied with food; and of arranging that, despite the catastrophe in transportation, the 1945 crops should be ensured by sending seed in good time, which was a burning problem just then. Had the seeds arrived a few weeks late, then the crops would have been extremely bad. These measures had, of course, a direct disadvantageous effect on armament production. We were only able to maintain production of armaments through stock reserves until the middle of March, after which there was no armament production worth mentioning. This was owing to the fact that we only had 20 to 30 per cent of the transport capacity at our disposal which I mainly used for the transport of food. Therefore, transport of armaments was, practically speaking, out of the question.

**Q.** Was it possible to carry out such measures, which were openly against the official war plans of "Resistance to the Last," on a large scale? Were there any people at all who were prepared to approve such measures as you suggested, and to put them into practice?

**A.** All these measures were not so difficult and they were not so dangerous as one might perhaps imagine, because in those days—after January, 1945—any reasonable measure could be carried out in Germany against the official policy. Any reasonable man welcomed such measures and was satisfied if anyone would assume responsibility for them. All of these conferences took place amongst a large circle of specialists. Every one of these participants knew the meaning of these orders, without explanations being given. During those days I also had close contacts with reference to other similar measures with the Secretary of State of the Ministry of Transport, the Ministry of Food, the Ministry of Propaganda, and later, even with the State Secretary of the Party Chancellery, that is, Bormann himself. They were all old Party members, and in spite of that, they did their duty to the nation at that time differently from the way in which many leading men in the Party were doing it. I kept them currently informed, in spite of Hitler's prohibition, of the developments in the military situation, and in that manner there was much that we could do jointly to stop the insane orders of those days.

**Q.** In which sectors did you see a danger for the greater mass of the German people through the continuation of the war?

A. In the middle of March 1945, the enemy troops were once more on the move. It was absolutely clear by then that quite soon those territories which had not yet been occupied would be occupied. That included the territories of Polish Upper Silesia and others outside the borders of the old Reich. The ordered destruction of all bridges during retreat was actually the greatest danger because a bridge blown up by engineers is much more difficult to repair than a bridge which has been destroyed by an air attack. A planned destruction of bridges amounts to the destruction of the entire life of a modern State. In addition, beginning with the end of January, radical circles in the Party were making demands for the destruction of industry, and it was also Hitler's opinion that this should be so. In February, 1945, therefore, I stopped production and delivery of the so-called industrial dynamiting materials. The intention was that the stocks of explosives in the mines and in private possession should be diminished. As a witness of mine has testified, these orders were actually carried out. In the middle of March, Guderian and I tried once more to stop the ordered destruction of bridges or to reduce it to a minimum. A suggested order for the stoppage was submitted to Hitler, which he refused bluntly, and demanded, on the contrary, intensified orders for the destruction of bridges. Simultaneously, on the 18th of March, 1945, he had eight officers shot because they had failed to do their duty in connection with the destruction of a bridge. He announced this fact in the Armed Forces Bulletin so that it should serve as a warning for future cases. Thus it was extremely difficult to disobey orders for the destruction of bridges. In spite of this, I sent a new memorandum to Hitler on the 18th of March, 1945, the contents of which were very clear and in which I did not allow him any further excuses for the measures he had planned. The memorandum was brought to the attention of several of his associates.

**DR. FLAECHSNER:** The Tribunal will find extracts from that memorandum on Page 69 of the English text of the Document Book.

**BY DR. FLAECHSNER:**

Q. Will you continue, please? A. I shall quote something more from that memorandum on Page 69, Mr. President:

"The enemy air force has concentrated further on traffic installations. Economic transportation has thereby been considerably reduced. In four to eight weeks, the final collapse of German economy must therefore be expected with certainty. After that collapse, the war cannot even be continued militarily. We at the head have the duty to help the nation in the difficult times which must be expected. In this connection, we must soberly, and without regard for our fate, ask ourselves the question as to how this can be done even in the more remote future. If the enemy wishes to destroy the nation and the basis of its existence, then he must do the job himself. We must do everything to maintain, even if perhaps in a most primitive manner, a basis of existence for the nation to the last."

Then there, follow a few of my demands, and I shall summarize them briefly.

I quote:

"It must be guaranteed that, if the battle advances farther into the territory of the Reich, nobody has the right to destroy industrial plants, coal mines, electric plants, and other supply facilities, or traffic facilities and inland shipping routes, etc. The blowing up of bridges to the extent which has been planned would mean that traffic facilities would be more thoroughly destroyed than the air attacks of the last weeks have been able to achieve. Their destruction means the removal of any further possibility for existence of the German nation."

Then, I shall quote briefly from the end of the memorandum:

"We have no right, at this stage of the war, to carry out destructions on our part which might affect the life of the nation. If the enemies wish to destroy this nation, which has fought with unique bravery, then this historical shame shall rest exclusively upon them. We have the obligation of leaving to the nation all possibilities which, in the more remote future, might be able to insure for it a new reconstruction."

This expressed clearly enough something which Hitler would have to know in any case, because there was not the need for much economic insight to realize the results of such destruction for the future of the nation.

On the occasion of the handing over of the memorandum, Hitler knew of the contents since I had discussed it with some of his associates. Therefore, his statements are typical of his attitude towards this basic question.

I would not have uttered the severe accusation which I have made here by saying that he wanted to draw Germany into the abyss with him, if I had not confirmed his statements in that respect in the letter of 29th March, 1945.

**THE PRESIDENT:** Are you meaning May or March?

**THE WITNESS:** March, 1945, Mr. President.

**DR. FLAECHSNER:** Mr. President, you will find this document on Page 75 of the English text of the Document Book, and it is Page 72 in the French text. I submit it as Exhibit 24. It is Speer's letter to Hitler, dated the 29th of March, 1945.

**BY DR. FLAECHSNER:**

Q. Will you continue, please?

**THE PRESIDENT:** Ought you not to read this letter?

**DR. FLAECHSNER:** The defendant wants to read it himself.

**BY DR. FLAECHSNER:**

Q. Will you read it?

A. I quote:

"When on 18th March I transmitted my letter to you, I was of the firm conviction that the conclusions which I had drawn from the present situation for the maintenance of our national power would find your unconditional approval, because you yourself had once determined that it was the task of the Government to preserve a nation from a heroic end if the war should be lost. However, during the evening you made declarations to me, the tenor of which, unless I misunderstood you, was clearly as follows: If the war is lost, the nation will also perish. This fate is inevitable. There is no necessity to take into consideration the basic requirements of the people for continuing a most primitive existence. On the contrary, it would be wiser to destroy these things ourselves, because this nation will have proved to be the weaker one and the future belongs solely to the stronger Eastern nation. Besides, those who remain after the battle are only the inferior ones; for the good ones have fallen."

I go on to quote:

"After these words I was profoundly shaken, and when on the next day I read the order for destruction, and shortly after that the strict order of evacuation, I saw in this the first steps towards the realization of these intentions."

**DR. FLAECHSNER:** Mr. President, may I in this connection submit as a "Speer document" the destruction order of Hitler, dated 19th March, 1945, which the Tribunal will find on Page 73 of the French and Page 76 of the English text of the Document Book.

I also submit to the Tribunal the order for the traffic and communication systems which you will find on Page 78 of the English text, and Page 75 of the French text. They become Speer Exhibit 26.

Then there is the order for destruction and evacuation by Bormann dated 23rd March, 1945, which is contained on Page 102 of my Document Book. The latter document is Speer Exhibit 27.

**BY DR. FLAECHSNER:**

**Q.** Herr Speer, since these are orders with technical expressions, will you please summarize the contents briefly for the Tribunal?

**THE PRESIDENT:** You said that last one was at Page 102 of the second volume. In my copy that is a document of General Guderian of December 13, 1944.

**DR. FLAECHSNER:** Mr. President, I beg to apologise, I have made a mistake.

It is not Page 102, it is Pages 93 and 94. I beg to apologise. I have only just received the document today.

**BY DR. FLAECHSNER:**

**Q.** Herr Speer, will you briefly elucidate these orders?

**A.** I can summarize them very briefly. They gave the order to the Gauleiter to carry out the destruction of all industrial plants, all important electrical facilities, water works, gas works, and so on, and also the destruction of all food and clothing stores. My jurisdiction had specifically been excluded, by means of that order, and all my orders for the maintenance of industry had been cancelled.

The military authorities had been given the order to destroy all bridges, all railway installations, postal systems, communication systems in the German railway, also the waterways, all ships, all freight cars and all locomotives.

The target was, as is stated in one of the decrees, the creation of a traffic desert.

The Bormann decree aimed at bringing the population to the centre of the Reich, both from the West and the East, and the foreign workers and prisoners of war were to be included. These millions of people were to be sent upon their trek on foot. No provisions for their existence had been made, nor was it possible to do so in view of the situation.

The carrying out of these orders alone would have resulted in an unimaginable hunger catastrophe. Add to this that on the 19th of March, 1945, there was a strict order from Hitler to all army groups and all Gauleiter, that the battle should be conducted without consideration for our own population.

With the carrying out of these orders, Hitler's pledge of the 18th of March would be kept, namely, that it would not be necessary to consider the basis which the nation would need to continue its existence, even on a most primitive scale, on the contrary, it would be better to destroy these things ourselves. Considering the discipline which existed in Germany in connection with every order, no matter what its contents, it was to be expected that these orders would be carried out. These orders also applied to those territories which had been included in the Greater German Reich.

Now, during journeys into the most endangered territories, and by means of discussions with my associates, I quite openly tried to stop the carrying out of these orders. I ordered that the high explosives which were still available in the Ruhr should be dropped down the mines, and that the stores of high explosives which were on the building sites should be hidden.

We distributed automatic pistols to the staffs of the most important plants so that they could fight against destruction. All this, I know, sounds somewhat theatrical, but the situation at the time was such that if a Gauleiter had dared to approach the coal mines in the Ruhr and there had been a single automatic pistol available, then it would have been fired.

I tried to convince the local army commanders of the nonsensical character of the task of destroying bridges which had been given to them, and furthermore, by talking to the local authorities, I succeeded in stopping most of the evacuation which had been ordered. In this connection the secretary of the Party Chancellery, Klopper, deserves credit in that he held up the evacuation orders which were to be sent to Gauleiter.

When I came back from this journey, I was called before Hitler at once. This was on the 29th of March, 1945. I had intentionally resisted his orders so openly, and I had discussed the lost war with so many of his Gauleiter that my insubordination must have become known to him. With regard to this period, witnesses are available who know that this is what I wanted to achieve.

I did not want to betray him behind his back. I wanted to put the alternative before him. At the beginning of the conference, he stated that he had had reports from Bormann to the effect that I considered the war as lost, and that I had openly expressed this view contrary to his prohibition. He demanded that I should make a statement to the effect that I did not consider the war lost, and I replied, "The war is lost." He gave me twenty-four hours to think, and it was during those twenty-four hours that the letter was written from which the extract has been quoted, and which has been submitted to the Tribunal in full.

After this period of reflection, I intended to hand him this letter as my reply. But he refused to accept it. Thereupon, I declared to him that he could rely on me in the future, and in that way I was able to get him to hand over to me once more the carrying out of the destruction work.

**DR. FLAECHSNER:** In this connection, may I submit Hitler's order dated 30th March, 1945, which the Tribunal will find on Pages 83 of the English text and 79 of the French text in the Document Book? It will be Exhibit 28.

**BY DR. FLAECHSNER:**

Q. Then, what did you do on the strength of this new order which you had?

A. I had the text of it drawn up and it gave me the possibility of circumventing the destruction which had been ordered. I issued an order at once re-establishing all my old orders for the protection of industry. In this connection, I did not submit this new order of mine for Hitler's approval, although he had expressly made this proviso in his order.

Contrary to the promise which I had given him, namely, that I would stand behind him unconditionally, I left the following day to see Seyss-Inquart, who has testified to that here, and two Gauleiter to tell them, too, that the war was lost, and to discuss the consequences with them.

On that occasion I found Seyss-Inquart very understanding. Both my decrees for the prevention of destruction, as well as my discussion, were contrary to the promise I had given Hitler on the 21st of March. I considered that this was my natural duty.

**DR. FLAECHSNER:** I submit as Speer Exhibit 29 the instructions issued by Speer on the 30th of March for carrying out the order which has already been mentioned. In the French and German texts of the Document Book they appear on Page 81, and in the English Document Book on Page 85.

**THE WITNESS:** In spite of this, the orders for the destruction of bridges still remained in force, and everywhere in Germany, Austria and Poland and elsewhere you can see the result today. I made numerous journeys to the front, and had many conferences with the commanders of the front-line troops. Perhaps that may have brought about relief in some form or other. Finally, I succeeded in persuading the Commander-in-Chief of the Corps of Signals, on the 3rd of April, 1945 to forbid at least the destruction of the signals, postal, railway and wireless installations by means of a new order.

Finally, on the 5th of April, I issued six OKW orders under the name of General Winter, who has been a witness in this courtroom. These orders were to ensure the preservation of important railway lines. The orders are still in existence.

I issued these orders through my command channels and the channels of the Reich railways, and considering the tremendous confusion of orders at the time, such orders, which I was not empowered to give, had at least a distracting effect.

**BY DR. FLAECHSNER:**

Q. Herr Speer, a number of attempts on your part to shorten the war became known to the Press. Could you please describe summarily to the Tribunal the problem which has been hinted at in the Press.

A. I do not want to spend too much time on things which did not succeed. I tried repeatedly to exclude Himmler and others from the Government and to force them to make themselves responsible for their deeds. To carry that and other plans out, eight officers from the front joined me, all of whom had received high decorations. Among them were the two best-known pilots in Germany, Galland and Baumbach. The Secretary of State of the Propaganda Ministry made it possible for me on the 9th of April to speak briefly over the entire German radio system. All preparations were made, and at the last moment Goebbels heard about it and demanded that Hitler should approve of the text of my speech. I submitted to him a very modified text. But he forbade the broadcasting even of this very modified version.

On the 21st of April, 1945, an opportunity was offered me to record a speech at the broadcasting station at Hamburg. This was to be broadcast as the instructions for the final phase. The recording officials, however, demanded that this speech should be broadcast only after Hitler's death, which would relieve them of their oath of allegiance to him.

Furthermore, I was in contact with the chief of staff of an army group in the East, the Army Group Weichsel. We were both aware that a fight for Berlin ought not to take place, and that contrary to their orders the armies should by-pass Berlin. To begin with, this was carried out, but later there were several persons empowered with special authority by Hitler and sent outside Berlin who succeeded in leading some divisions into Berlin. The original intention, however, that entire armies should be led into Berlin, was, therefore, not carried through. The Chief of Staff with whom I had these conferences was General Kinsler.

Q. Were these attempts still of any avail at the beginning of April, and later on?

A. Yes. We expected that the war would last longer, because Churchill, too, predicted at the time that the end of the war would come at the end of July, 1945

Q. You have described here how much you did to preserve industrial plants and other economic installations. Did you also act on behalf of the foreign workers?

A. My responsibility was the industrial sector. I felt it my duty, therefore, to hand over my sector undamaged. As regards the foreign workers in Germany, several of my actions were in their favour. For example, these foreign workers and prisoners of war, through the steps which I had taken to secure the food situation, were quite obviously the beneficiaries of my work during the last phase.

Secondly, through local discussions, I prevented a certain amount of destruction, contrary to the evacuation orders which had been received from the Party. I also made it possible for the foreign workers and prisoners to remain where they were. Such discussions took place on the 18th of March in the Saar district, and on the 28th of March in the Ruhr district. At the beginning of March, I made the proposal that five hundred thousand foreigners should be transferred from the Reich to the territories which we still held; that is to say, the Dutch to Holland, the Czechs to Czechoslovakia. The railways, however, refused to take responsibility for their transportation, since the traffic system had already been so destroyed that the carrying out of this plan was no longer possible. Finally, in the speech I intended to deliver over the German broadcasting system on the 9th of April, and in the one I had hoped to broadcast from Hamburg on the gist of April, I pointed out the duties which we had towards the foreigners, the prisoners of war and the prisoners from concentration camps during this last phase.

**DR. FLAECHSNER:** Mr. President, may I draw your attention to Page 88 of the English text in this connection; it is Page 84 of the French and I submit it as Speer Exhibit 30.

**BY DR. FLAECHSNER:**

Q. Herr Speer, you have described to us how much during the last phase of the war you were opposed to Hitler and his policies. Why did you not resign?

A. I had the possibility to resign on three occasions; once in April, 1944, when my powers were considerably limited; the second time in September, 1944, when Bormann and Goebbels were in favour of my resignation; and the third time on the 29th of March, 1945, when Hitler himself demanded that I should go on permanent leave, which was equivalent to resignation. I turned down all these possibilities because, from July, 1944, I thought it was my duty to remain at my post.

Q. There has been testimony in this courtroom to the effect that the last phase of the war, that is, from January, 1945, was tactically justified from the point of view that the nation was, in reality, spared unnecessary sacrifices. Were you of that same opinion?

A. No. It was said that military protection in the East was necessary to protect great numbers of refugees until they reached Germany. In reality, until the middle of April, 1945, the bulk of our last reserves of armoured vehicles and munitions was used for the fight against the West. The tactical principle, therefore, was different from the one it would have been if the fight had been carried on with those aims which have been stated here. The destruction of bridges in the West and the destruction orders against the foundations of life of the nation show the opposite. The sacrifices which were made on both sides after January, 1945, were senseless. The dead of this period will be the accusers of the man responsible for the continuation of that fight, Adolf Hitler, and the ruined cities which, in this last phase, lost tremendous cultural values and in which a colossal number of dwellings were destroyed. Many of the difficulties under which the German nation is suffering today are due to the ruthless destruction of bridges, traffic installations, trucks, locomotives and ships. The German people remained faithful to Adolf Hitler until the end. He betrayed them knowingly. He finally tried to throw them into the abyss. Only after the 1st of May, 1945, did Doenitz try to act with reason, but it was too late.

**DR. FLAECHSNER:** I have one last question.

**BY DR. FLAECHSNER:**

**Q.** Was it possible for you to reconcile your actions during the last phase of the war with your oath and your conception of loyalty to Adolf Hitler?

**A.** There is one loyalty which everyone must always keep and that is loyalty towards one's own people. That duty comes before everything. If I am in a leading position and if I see that acts are being committed against the interests of the nation, I must oppose them. That Hitler had broken faith with the nation must have been clear to every intelligent member of his circle, certainly at the latest in January or February, 1945. Hitler had been given his mission by the people; but he had no right to gamble away the destiny of the people with his own. Therefore, I fulfilled my natural duty as a German. I did not succeed in every way, but I am proud today that with my achievements I was able to render one more service to the workers in Germany and the Occupied Territories.

**DR. FLAECHSNER:** Mr. President, I have now reached the end of my examination of the defendant Speer.

May I perhaps draw the attention of the Tribunal to the fact that statements have been made on the theme which was the subject of this afternoon's session, by the witness Kehrl in his interrogatory under 10 and 12; Rohland under 5, 6, and 8; witness Schieber under 25; witness Guderian under 1 to 3, 7 to 9, and on point 6; the witness named by Speer, Stahl under points 1 and 2 of his testimony; the witness Kempf under 10 of her testimony.

Still outstanding are the interrogatories of the witness, Malzacher, and, which is most important to the defence, of the witness von Poser, since he was the liaison officer between the General Staff of the Army and Speer's Ministry. These will be handed in when received. Furthermore, still outstanding is the interrogatory of General Buhle, who was the Chief of the Army Staff, and that of Colonel Baumbach, who was the commander of a bomber wing. The remaining documents I shall submit to the Tribunal at the end of the final examination of the defendant Speer.

**THE PRESIDENT:** Do any of the other defendants' counsel want to ask any questions?

**DR. SERVATIUS:** Dr. Servatius, counsel for Sauckel.

**BY DR. SERVATIUS:**

**Q.** Witness, during the negotiations which Sauckel had in 1943 and 1944 with Laval in Paris, were there representatives present who came from your department and did they support Sauckel's demands?

**A.** During these conferences, representatives from my departments were sometimes present. They were present for the purpose of protecting the blocked industries, and also to see to it that there were no encroachments on the production interests for which I had provided protection.

**Q.** So that these representatives were therefore not acting to support Sauckel's demands, but they were against them?

**A.** It was not the task of these representatives to act for or against Sauckel's demands because Sauckel stated his demands in such definite language that a smaller official was not in a position to speak either for or against these demands in any way. This would have been a task which I would have had to carry out myself.

**Q.** So that these representatives did not fulfil any task?

**A.** My representatives were the representatives from the armament, from the heavy armament and war production in the Occupied Territories and as such, they had their special tasks.

**Q.** Witness, did you in 1943, acting independently and without consultation with Sauckel, transfer fifty thousand French OT (Organisation Todt) workers to the Ruhr district?

**A.** Yes, that is true. After the attack on the Mone Dam and the Eder Dam in April-May, 1943, I went there and during that visit I ordered that a special group from the Todt Organisation should take over the restoration of these plants. I did this because I wanted the necessary machinery and technical staff at once. This special group of the Todt Organisation, without consulting me, brought the French workers along. This had tremendous repercussions for us in the West, because the workers on the building sites on the Atlantic Wall, who had up to that time felt safe from Sauckel's reach—

**Q.** Witness, we are not interested in hearing what was done. I am only interested in the fact that these 50,000 OT workers were obtained without Sauckel's agreement and by yourself independently, and that you have confirmed, have you not?

**A.** Yes, that is true.

**Q.** Sauckel was responsible for the ruling on working hours in these plants. Do you know that the ten-hour day was later on ordered by Goebbels in his capacity as Plenipotentiary for Total Warfare, applicable to both Germans and foreign workers?

**A.** That is probably true. I do not directly recollect it, but I assume it is right.

**Q.** Then you have stated that the Geneva Convention was not applied to Soviet prisoners of war and Italian civilian internees?

**A.** Yes.

**Q.** Do you know that the Geneva Convention, although it was not recognized for Soviet prisoners of war, was nevertheless applied as far as its regulations were concerned and that there were orders to that effect?

**A.** I cannot give you any information about that because that was too much of a detail and was dealt with by my department directly. I should like to confirm it for you.

**DR. SERVATIUS:** I shall later on submit to the Tribunal a document which

*Hitler presenting Speer with an Organisation Todt ring in a casket for his efforts at increasing the production of weapons and armaments in May 1943.*
*Bundesarchiv, Bild 146-1979-026-22 / Hoffmann, Heinrich / CC-BY-SA*

confirms this.
**BY DR. SERVATIUS:**
**Q.** Do you know that Italian civilian internees, that is, those who came from the Italian Armed Forces, were transferred to free working conditions and therefore did not come under the Convention?

**A.** Yes, that is true and it was done on Sauckel's request.

**Q.** The factory managers were responsible for carrying out Sauckel's orders in the firms. Is that right?

**A.** As far as they could be carried out, yes.

**Q.** And you have said that if, on account of special events, such as air attacks, it was not possible to carry them out, the supreme authorities in the Reich took them over?

**A.** Yes.

**Q.** Which authorities in the Reich do you mean?

**A.** The General Plenipotentiary for Labour.

**Q.** That would be Sauckel?

**A.** Yes. And the German Labour Front, which was responsible for accommodations and working conditions.

**Q.** Which organisation did Sauckel have at his disposal to stop abuses? After all, this was a matter for co-operative assistance then, was it not?

**A.** No, I think you have misunderstood me. The catastrophic conditions were conditions which were brought about by bombing. Nobody could remedy them, with the best will in the world, because every day there were new air attacks. But, as Sauckel has testified, one cannot blame the factory manager either for the fact that these conditions could not be alleviated. I wanted to indicate that in such emergencies, all the leaders had to get together and decide whether conditions were still bearable or not. In that connection, it was the special duty of Sauckel, as the official who made the reports and gave the orders, to recommend such meetings.

Q. To whom then was he supposed to make such recommendations?

A. To the Fuehrer.

Q. Witness, you have explained your own administrative organisation and you have said that you were an opponent of a bureaucratic administration. You introduced self-administration for the firms, and on the professional side you formed agencies and above them committees, directed by you?

A. Yes.

Q. And it was a closed administration which could not be penetrated from the outside by other authorities?

A. Yes, I would not have allowed that.

Q. Then you were actually the representative of these firms to the higher authorities.

A. Only as far as the technical tasks were concerned, as I have stated here.

Q. You limited yourself to the technical tasks, is that correct?

A. Well, otherwise I would have been responsible for food conditions or health conditions or matters which affected the police, but that was expecting too much.

Q. Witness, did you not refer earlier to the fact that, particularly as far as food was concerned, you had given instructions which would benefit the workers, and are you not in that way confirming my view, that you bore the entire responsibility for that sector?

A. Not in the least. I believe that I took such action during the last phase within my general responsibility, but not as the individual responsible for that sector.

Q. Then, witness, you spoke about the responsibility of the Gauleiter as Reich Defence Commissioners with reference to the armament industries. Could you describe in more detail the scope of that responsibility, because I did not understand it.

A. From 1942, responsibility was transferred to the Gauleiter as Reich Defence Commissioners to an ever-increasing degree. This was mostly the effort of Bormann—

Q. What tasks did they have.

A. Just a minute—who desired the centralisation of all the forces of the State and the Party in the Gauleiter. This state of centralisation had almost been achieved in full after 1943, the only exception which still existed being my armament offices, the so-called Armament Inspectorates. These, since they had previously come under the OKW, were military establishments which were staffed by officers, and that made it possible for me to remain outside the jurisdiction of the Gauleiter. But the Gauleiter was the centre of authority in his Gau and he assumed the right to give orders though he did not have the right. The situation in our case was, as you very well know, that it did not make much difference who had the powers; it was a question of who assumed the right to give orders. In this case, most Gauleiter did assume all the rights, by which means they became the responsible and centralised departments.

Q. What do you mean by "centralised departments"?

Perhaps I may put something to you: The Gauleiter, as Reich Defence Commissioner, only had the task of centralising the offices if a decision was necessary in the Gau. For instance, after an air attack, regarding the removal of the damaged parts, construction of a new plant, necessitating that representatives from various departments should be brought to one conference table; but he did not have the authority to give orders or make decisions. Is that right?

A. No; I should like to recommend to you that you should talk to a few Gauleiter who will tell you how it was.

Q. In that case, I will drop the question. You then went on to say, witness, that during a certain period there was a surplus of labour in Germany. Was this due to the fact that Sauckel had brought too many foreign workers into Germany?

A. There may be an error here. My defence counsel has referred to two documents, according to which, during the time from April, 1942, until April, 1943, Sauckel had supplied more labour to the armament sector than armament had requested. I do not know if that is the passage you mean.

Q. I can only remember that you said that there had been more workers than were required.

A. Yes.

Q. You do not want to say, therefore, that this had been caused by the fact that Sauckel had brought too many workers in from foreign countries?

A. No. I wanted to prove by that answer that, even according to Sauckel's opinion, at the time it was not necessary to try to bring the maximum numbers of workers from France to Germany because of the demands for labour. For if, in a report to Hitler, he asserts that he brought more workers to the armament sector than I demanded, which is what you can see from the letter, then it is clear that he did more than I asked him to do. Actually, it was quite different. In actual fact, he did not supply these workers at all, and we had a heated argument because it was my opinion that he had supplied a far smaller number than the figure given in his report to Hitler.

Q. You have just pointed out also that there was an argument between you and Sauckel as to whether there were sufficient labour reserves in Germany, and if I have understood you rightly, you said that if workers had been brought to work in the manner used by England and the Soviet Union, one would not have needed any foreign workers at all. Is that true?

A. No, I did not say that.

Q. Well, then, how am I to understand it?

A. I have expressed quite clearly enough that I considered Sauckel's labour policy of bringing foreigners into Germany to be correct. I did not try to dodge that responsibility, but there were considerable reserves of German labour, and that again is only proof of the fact that I was not responsible for the demands which were made, and that was all I wanted to prove.

Q. Are the laws known to you according to which German women and youth were used to a very considerable degree?

A. Yes.

Q. Do you also know that officers' wives or the wives of high officials also worked in factories?

A. Yes, beginning in August, 1944.

Q. Well, then, where were these labour reserves of which you are speaking?

A. I was talking about the period 1943. In 1943 I demanded, in the Central Planning Board, that the German labour reserves should be drawn upon, and in 1944 during the conversation of the 4th of January with Hitler, I urged the same thing. Sauckel at that time stated—and that can be seen from his speech of the 1st of March, 1944, which has been submitted as a document—that there were no longer any reserves of German workers.

Q. Yes.

A. But at the same time he also testified here that he had succeeded, in 1944, in mobilising a further 2,000,000 workers from Germany, but at a conference with Hitler on the 1st of January, 1944, he considered that to be completely impossible. He himself has proved here that at a time when I desired the use of internal labour, he did not think there was any, but that he was later forced, through circumstances, to mobilize these workers in Germany after all; therefore my statement at the time was right.

Q. Witness, these two million workers you have mentioned, were they people who could be employed in industry?

A. Yes, of course.

Q. Were they employed directly as skilled workers in industry?

A. No, they had to be trained first.

Q. Did they first of all have to go through complicated transfers to be released from one firm to another?

A. Only partly, because we were able to use them in the fine mechanical industry and other kinds of work, because, as everyone who is familiar with American and British industry knows, these modern machines are perfectly suitable to be worked by women, even for difficult work.

**THE PRESIDENT:** The Tribunal is not interested in all these details, Dr. Servatius.

**DR. SERVATIUS:** Mr. President, I am very interested in the basic question, whether workers were obtained from foreign countries in superfluous numbers and if, therefore, there was no necessity for the State to have them. That question is of the greatest importance from the point of view of International Law, especially with regard to the point whether foreign workers can be recruited. That is what I wish to clarify.

I have two more questions, and perhaps I may put them now.

**THE PRESIDENT:** Yes, you can put two more questions, but not on those details.

**DR. SERVATIUS:** No, they are questions on other points.

**BY DR. SERVATIUS:**

Witness, you have stated that your attempt to subordinate yourself to Sauckel failed. Did you not achieve that subordination in practice by the fact that in the final test of authority, Sauckel's Gau labour exchanges had to do what your armament commissions ordered?

**A.** No. That is a matter into which I shall have to go in greater detail. If you want an explanation ...

**Q.** But you have said no

**A.** Yes. But these are entirely new conceptions which should first be explained to the Tribunal, but if "no" is sufficient for you

**Q.** There is no need for any lengthy statement, because if you clearly say no, the matter is settled.

Witness, one last question. You said that Sauckel decided the question of distributing labour with his staff.

**A.** Yes.

**Q.** He himself says that the Fuehrer made certain decisions. In this connection, must not one differentiate between the long-term planning of the programme for the distribution of labour and the distribution which was carried out currently, according to the needs of the programme?

**A.** According to my recollection, and also from having read the records I received of the conferences which I had with the Fuehrer, there are two phases to be differentiated. The first one ending October, 1942, during which there were frequent joint conferences with Sauckel which I attended. During these conferences, the distribution of labour for the following months was discussed in detail. After that time, there were no longer any conferences with Hitler at which I was present dealing with such details. I only know of the conferences of January, 1944; and then there was another conference in April or May, 1944, which has not yet been mentioned here. During those conferences, there was only a general discussion and the distribution was then carried out in accordance with directives, as Sauckel says.

**Q.** But that is just what I am asking you. These were general demands based on a programme, concerning which decisions of policy were made. Two million workers were to be obtained from foreign countries, and the subsequent distribution was carried out by Sauckel.

**A.** Yes, that's right, and I can confirm Sauckel's testimony, that he always got his orders from Hitler with reference to the occupied territories, since he needed Hitler's authority to assert himself in foreign countries.

**DR. SERVATIUS:** In that case, Mr. President, I have no further questions.

**THE PRESIDENT:** The Tribunal will adjourn.

*(The Tribunal adjourned until 21st June, 1946, at 1000 hours.)*

# FRIDAY, 21ST JUNE, 1946

THE PRESIDENT: Have you finished, Dr. Servatius?
DR. SERVATIUS: Yes.
THE PRESIDENT: Very well. Do any other defendants' counsel want to ask any questions?
BY DR. KRAUS (counsel for the defendant Schacht):
Q. Witness, on the 25th of January, 1946, you handed two statements to my client here in the prison at Nuremberg. During his examination Dr. Schacht made mention of these and for the sake of brevity I should like the Tribunal to allow me to read out the statement which the defendant gave me that day so that its truth may be confirmed. It is very brief. The first statement reads as follows:

"I was on the terrace of the Berghof on the Obersalzberg waiting to submit my building plans—this was in the summer of 1937—when Schacht appeared at the Berghof. From where I was on the terrace I could hear a loud argument between Hitler and Schacht in Hitler's room. Hitler's voice grew louder and louder. At the end of the discussion Hitler came out on the terrace and, visibly excited, he told the people around him that he could not collaborate with Schacht, that he had had a terrible argument with him, and that Schacht's finance policy was going to upset his plans."

Now, that is the first statement. Is it correct?
A. Yes, it is.
Q. It is correct. The second statement deals with the events after the 20th of July. It reads as follows:

"It was on about the 22nd of July that Hitler said in my presence to a fairly large group of people..."

THE PRESIDENT (interposing): What year?
DR. KRAUS: 1944, your Lordship.
Q (continuing):

"...that Schacht, as one of the opponents of the totalitarian system, should be one of those to be arrested. Hitler went on to speak harshly of Schacht's activities and of the difficulties which he, Hitler, had experienced through Schacht's economic policy as regards rearmament. He said that actually a man like Schacht ought to be shot for his hostile activities before the war."

The last sentence of the statement says:

"After the harshness of these remarks, I was surprised to meet Schacht here alive."

Is this statement correct, too?
A. Yes, it is.
THE PRESIDENT: Do any of the other defendants' counsel want to ask questions?

Then, does the prosecution wish to cross-examine?
**CROSS-EXAMINATION BY MR. JUSTICE JACKSON:**
Defendant, your counsel divided your examination into two parts, the first being relative to your personal responsibilities, and the second concerned with the political part of the case, and I will follow the same plan.

You have stated a good many of the matters for which you were not responsible, and I want to make clear just what your sphere of responsibility was.

You were not only a member of the Nazi Party after 1932, but you held high rank in the Party, did you not?

**A.** Correct.

**Q.** And what was the position which you held in the Party?

**A.** I have already mentioned that in my pre-trial interrogations.

Temporarily in 1934 I became a departmental head in the German Labour Front and dealt with the improvement of labour conditions in German factories. Then I was in charge of public works on the staff of Hess. I gave up both these activities in 1941. Notes of the conference I had with Hitler about this are available. After the 8th of February, 1942, I automatically became Todt's successor in the Central Office for technical matters in the Reich Directorate of the NSDAP.

**Q.** And what was your official title?

**A.** Party titles had just been introduced, and they were so complicated that I cannot tell you at the moment what they were. But the work I did there was that of a chief of a department in the Reich Directorate of the NSDAP. My title was Hauptdienstleiter or something of the kind.

**Q.** In the 1943 directory it would appear that you were the "Hauptamt fur Technik."

**A.** Yes.

**Q.** And your rank appears to be "Oberbefehlsleiter"?

**A.** Yes, that is quite possible.

**Q.** ... which as I understand corresponds roughly to a lieutenant general in the army.

**A.** Well, compared to the other tasks I had, it was a very small one.

**Q.** And you attended Party functions from time to time and were informed in a general way as to the Party programme, were you not?

**A.** Before 1942 I joined in the various Party rallies here in Nuremberg because I had to take part in them as an architect, and, of course, I was generally present at official Party meetings or Reichstag meetings.

**Q.** And you heard discussed, and were generally familiar with, the programme of the Nazi Party in its broad outlines, were you not?

**A.** Of course.

**Q.** You ... There is some question as to just what your relation to the SS was. Will you tell me whether you were a member of the SS?

**A.** No, I was not a member of the SS.

**Q.** You filled in an application at one time, or one was filled in for you, and you never went through with it, I believe, or something of that sort.

**A.** That was in 1943, when Himmler wanted me to get a high rank in the SS. He had often wanted it before when I was still an architect. I got out of it by saying that I was willing to be an ordinary SS man under him because I had already been an SS man before. Thereupon, Group Leader Wolff filled in a questionnaire, a temporary one, and wanted to know what my previous SS activities had been in 1933. It came up during his inquiries that in those days I was never put down as a member of the SS and, because of this, they never insisted on my membership as I did not want to become a new member then.

**Q.** And why did you not want to be a member of the SS, which was after all one of the important Party formations?

**A.** I became well known for turning down all these honorary ranks. I did not want them because I felt that one should only hold a rank when one had responsibility.

**Q.** And you did not want any responsibility in the SS?

**A.** I had very little contact with the SS, and did not want any responsibility in that connection.

**Q.** Now there has been some testimony about your relation to concentration camps, and, as I understand it, you have said to us that you did use and encourage the use of forced labour from the concentration camps.

**A.** Yes, we did use it in the German armament industry.

**Q.** And I think you also recommended that persons in labour camps who were slackers should be sent to the concentration camps, did you not?

**A.** That was the question of the so-called idlers or slackers (Bummelanten), and under that name we understood workers who did not get to their work on time or who pretended to be ill. Severe measures were taken against such workers during the War, and I approved of these measures.

**Q.** In fact, at the 30th October, 1942, meeting of the Central Planning Board, you brought the subject up in the following terms, did you not:

> "We must also discuss the slackers. Ley has ascertained that the sick list decreased to one fourth or one fifth in factories where doctors on the staff examined the sick men. There is nothing to be said against SS and police taking drastic steps and putting those known as slackers into concentration camps. There is no alternative. Let it happen several times and the news will soon go around."

That was your recommendation?

**A.** Correct.

**Q.** In other words, the workmen stood in considerable terror of concentration camps, and you wanted to take advantage of that to keep them at their work, did you not?

**A.** It is certain that concentration camps had a bad reputation with us, and the transfer to a concentration camp or threat of such a possibility was bound to reduce the number of absentees in the factories right from the beginning. But at that meeting, as I already said yesterday; there was nothing further said about it. It was one of those remarks one makes in war time when one is upset.

**Q.** However, it is very clear—and if I misinterpret you I give you the chance to correct me—that you understood the very bad reputation that the concentration camps had among the workmen and that the concentration camps were regarded as being much worse places to be in than labour camps.

**A.** That is correct. I knew that. I did not know, of course, what I have heard during this trial, but that was a generally known fact.

**Q.** Well, it was known throughout Germany, was it not, that the concentration camps were pretty tough places in which to be put?

**A.** Yes, but not to the extent which has been revealed during this trial.

**Q.** And the bad reputation of the concentration camp, as a matter of fact, was useful in making people afraid of being sent there, was it not?

**A.** No doubt concentration camps were a means, a menace used to keep order.

**Q.** And to keep people at work?

**A.** I would not like to put it that way. I would say that a great number of the foreign workers in our country did their work quite voluntarily once they had come to Germany.

**Q.** Well, we will take that up later. You used the concentration camp labour in production on the agreement that you were to divide the proceeds of the labour with Himmler, did you not?

**A.** That I did not understand.

**Q.** Well, you made an agreement finally with Himmler that he should have five per cent, or roughly five per cent, of the production of the concentration camp labour while you were to have 95 per cent?

**A.** No, that is not quite true.

**Q.** Well, tell me how it was. That is what the documents indicate, if I read them aright.

**A.** Yes, it is put that way in the Fuehrer record, but I should like to explain the meaning to you. Himmler, as I said yesterday, wanted to build factories of his own in his concentration camps. Then he would have been able to produce arms without any outside control, which Hitler, of course, knew. The five per cent arms production which was to have been handed to Himmler was to a certain extent a compensation for the fact that he himself gave up the idea of building factories in the camps. From the psychological point of view it was not so simple for me to get Himmler to give up this idea when be kept on reminding Hitler of it. I was hoping that he would be satisfied with the five per cent arms production we were going to give him. Actually this five per cent of the production was never handed over. We managed to arrange with the Operation Staff of the OKW and with General Buhle so that he never got the arms at all.

**Q.** Well, I am not criticising the bargain, you understand. I do not doubt you did very well to get 95 per cent, but the point is that Himmler was using, with your knowledge, concentration camp labour to manufacture arms, or was proposing to do so, and you wanted to keep that production within your control?

A. Could the translation come through a bit clearer? Would you please repeat that?

Q. You knew at this time that Himmler was using concentration camp labour to carry on independent industry and that he proposed to go into the armament industry in order to have a source of supply of arms for his own SS?

A. Yes.

Q. You also knew the policy of the Nazi Party and the policy of the Government towards the Jews, did you not?

A. I knew that the National Socialist Party was anti-Semitic, and I knew that the Jews were being evacuated from Germany.

Q. In fact, you participated in that evacuation, did you not?

A. No.

Q. Well, I gather that impression from Document 156-L, Exhibit RF 1522—a letter from the Plenipotentiary for Manpower, which is dated 26th March, 1943, which you have no doubt seen. You may see it again, if you wish. In which he says—

A. I know it.

Q. "At the end of February, Reich Leader SS, in agreement with myself and the Reich Minister for Armaments and Munitions, for reasons concerning the security of the State, removed from their places of work all Jews who were still working freely and were not in camps, and either transferred them to a labour corps or collected them for removal."

Was that a correct representation of your activity?

A. No.

Q. Will you tell me what part you had in that. There is no question that they were put into labour corps or collected for removal, is there?

A. That is correct.

Q. Now you say you did not do it, so will you tell me who did? A. It was a fairly long business. When, in February, 1942, I took over my new office, the Party was already insisting that Jews who were still working in armament factories should be removed from them. I objected at the time and managed to get Bormann to issue a circular letter to the effect that these Jews should go on being employed in armament factories and that Party offices should be prohibited from accusing the heads of these firms on political grounds because of the Jews working there. It was the Gauleiter who made such political accusations against the heads of concerns, and it was mostly in the Gau of Saxony and in the Gau of Berlin. So, after this the Jews could remain in these plants.

Without having any authority to do so, I had had this circular letter from the Party published in my news sheet for heads of factories and had sent it to them so that I should receive their complaints if Party members should not obey the instruction.

After that the problem was left alone until September or October of 1942.

At that time a conference with Hitler took place, at which Sauckel also was present. At this conference Hitler insisted emphatically that the Jews must now be removed from the armament firms, and he gave orders for this to be done—this is to be seen from a Fuehrer protocol which has been kept.

In spite of this, the Jews managed to get kept on in factories and it was only in March, 1943, as this letter shows, that resistance gave way and the Jews finally did have to get out.

I must point out to you that as far as I can remember it was not a question yet of the entire Jewish problem, but, in the years 1941 and 1942, Jews had gone to the armament factories to do important war work and have an occupation of military importance, and through this occupation of military importance they were able to escape the evacuation which at that time was already in full swing. They were mostly occupied in the electrical industry, and Geheimrat Buecher of AEG and Siemens no doubt lent a helping hand in order to get the Jews taken on there in greater numbers. These Jews were still completely free and their families were still in their homes.

The letter you have before you, of course, was not given me by Gauleiter Sauckel; and Sauckel himself says that he had not seen it. But it is certainly true that I knew about it before action was taken; I knew because the question had to be discussed as to how one should get replacements. It is equally certain, though, that I also protested at the time at having experts removed from my armament industries because, apart from other reasons, it was going to make things difficult for me.

Q. That is exactly the point that I want to emphasise. As I understand it, you were struggling to get manpower enough to produce the armaments to win a war for Germany.

A. Yes.

Q. And this anti-Semitic campaign was so strong that it took trained technicians away from you, and made your task more difficult. Now, isn't that the fact?

A. I did not understand the meaning of your question.

Q. Your problem of producing armaments to win the war for Germany was made very much more difficult by this anti-Jewish campaign which was being waged by others of your co-defendants.

A. That is a fact; and it is equally clear that if the Jews who were evacuated had been allowed to work for me, it would have been a considerable advantage to me.

THE PRESIDENT: Mr. Justice Jackson, has it been proved who signed that Document 156-L? It has got a signature apparently on it.

MR. JUSTICE JACKSON: There is a signature on it. I believe it is that of the Plenipotentiary General for Manpower.

THE PRESIDENT: Perhaps the defendant could tell what the signature is.

*(A document was submitted to the witness.)*

THE WITNESS: I do not know the man. Yes, he must be one of the minor officials in the offices of the Plenipotentiary for Manpower, because I knew alt the immediate associates of Sauckel personally .... No. I beg your pardon, the document comes from the Regierungs-Praesident in Koblenz, as I see here. He was an assistant in the Government District of Koblenz of whom, of course, I did not know.

**BY MR. JUSTICE JACKSON:**

Q. In any event, there is no question about the statement as you have explained it?

A. No.

Q. Now I want to ask you about the recruiting of forced labour. As I understand it, you know about the deportation of 100,000 Jews from Hungary for subterranean aeroplane factories, and you told us in your interrogation of 15th October-18th October, 1945, that you made no objection to it. That is true, is it not?

A. That is true, yes.

Q. And you told us also, quite candidly, on that day, that it was no secret to you that a good deal of the manpower brought in by Sauckel was obtained by illegal methods. That is also true, is it not?

A. I took great care at the time to notice what expression the interrogating officer used; he used the expression "they came against their wish"; and that I confirmed.

Q. Did you not say that it was no secret to you that these workers were brought in in an illegal manner? Did you not add that yourself?

A. No, no. That was certainly not so.

Q. Well, in any event, you knew that at the Fuehrer conference in August of 1942 the Fuehrer had approved of all coercive measures for obtaining workers if they couldn't be obtained on a voluntary basis, and you knew that that policy of coercion was carried out. You, as a matter of fact, you did not give any particular attention to the legal side of this thing, did you? You were after manpower; is not that the fact?

A. That is absolutely correct.

Q. And whether legal or illegal means were used did not worry you?

A. I consider that in the light of the whole war situation and of our views in general on this question it was justified.

Q. Yes, it was in accordance with the policy of the Government, and that satisfied you at the time, did it not?

A. Yes. I am of the opinion that at the time I took over my office, in February, 1942, all the violations of International Law, which later ... which are now brought up against me, had already been committed.

Q. And you do not question that you share a certain responsibility for that policy, whether it is a legal responsibility or not, of bringing in workers against their will? You do not deny that, do you?

A. The workers were brought to Germany largely against their will, and I had no objection to their being brought to Germany against their will. On the contrary, during the first period, until the autumn of 1942, I certainly used all my energy to see that as many workers as possible should be brought to

Germany in this manner.

**Q.** You had some participation in the distribution of these workers, did you not, among different plants, different industries that were competing for labour?

**A.** No. That would have to be explained in detail—I do not quite understand.

**Q.** Well, you finally entered into an agreement with Sauckel, did you not, in reference to the distribution of the workers after they reached the Reich?

**A.** That was arranged according to the so-called priorities. I had to tell Sauckel, of course, in relation to my programme where labour was needed most urgently. But that sort of thing was dealt with by general instructions.

**Q.** In other words, you determined the priorities of the different industries with regard to the distribution of the workers when they came to the Reich.

**A.** That was a matter of course; naturally that had to be done.

**Q.** Yes. Now, as to the employment of prisoners of war, you—whatever disagreement there may be about the exact figures, there is no question, is there, that prisoners of war were used in the manufacture of armament?

**A.** No, only Russian prisoners of war and Italian military internees were used for the production of arms. As for the use of French and other prisoners of war in this production, I had several conferences with Keitel on the subject. And I must tell you that Keitel always adopted the view that these prisoners of war could not be used, as it would mean a violation of the Geneva Prisoner-of-War Agreement of the Geneva Convention. I can claim that, on the strength of this fact, I no longer used my influence to obtain these prisoners for employment in the armament industries in violation of the Geneva Convention.

The conception, of course, of the expression "armament production" is very much open to argument. It depends, it always depends what position one takes, whether you have a wide conception of armaments or a narrow one.

**Q.** Well, you succeeded to Dr. Todt's organisation, and you had all the powers that he had, did you not?

**A.** Yes.

**Q.** And one of his directives was dated 31st October, 1941, a letter from the OKW, which is in evidence here as Exhibit 214, Document 194-EC, which provides that the deputies of the Reichsminister for Armament and Munitions are to be admitted to prisoner-of-war camps for the purpose of selecting skilled workers. That was among your powers, was it not?

**A.** No. That was a special action which Dr. Todt introduced on the strength of an agreement with the OKW. It was dropped later, however.

**Q.** Now, on the 22nd of April, 1943, at the 36th meeting of this Planning Board, you made this complaint, did you not, Herr Speer? I quote:

> "There is a statement showing in what sectors the Russian PW's have been distributed, and this statement is quite interesting. It shows that the armament industry only received 30 per cent. I always complained about that."

That is correct, is it not?

**A.** I believe that has been wrongly translated. It should not say "ammunitions industry"; it should say, "the armament industry received 30 per cent."

**Q.** I said "armament."

**A.** Yes. But then, this is still no proof that these prisoners of war were employed in violation of the Geneva Prisoner-of-War Agreement, because in the sector of the armament industry there was ample room to use these workers for producing articles which, in the sense of the Geneva Prisoner-of-War Agreement, were not armament products. In spite of that, I believe that in the case of the Russian prisoners of war there was not the same value attached to a strict observance of the Geneva Convention as in the case of prisoners from Western countries.

**Q.** Is it your contention that the prisoners were not used—I now speak of French prisoners of war—that French prisoners of war were not used in the manufacture of materials which directly contributed to the war, or is it your contention that although they were used it was legal under the Geneva Convention?

**A.** As far as I know, French prisoners of war were not used contrary to the rules of the Convention. I cannot check that, because my office was not responsible for controlling the conditions of their employment. During my numerous visits to factories, I never noticed that any prisoner of war from the Western territories was working directly on armament products.

**Q.** Just explain exactly what French prisoners of war did do ... by way of manufacture. What were they working on?

**A.** That I cannot answer. I already explained yesterday that the allotment of prisoners of war, or foreign workers, or of German workers to a factory was not a matter for me to decide. But the allotment was carried out by the Labour office together with the Stalag (other ranks prisoner-of-war camps), when it was a question of prisoners of war. I received only a general survey of the total number of workers who had gone to the factories and so I could get no idea as to what type of work they were doing in each individual concern. So I cannot give a satisfactory answer to your question.

**Q.** Now let us take the 50,000 skilled workers whom, you said yesterday, you removed and put to work in a different location, of which Sauckel complained. What did you put them to work at?

**A.** They were not prisoners of war, you know.

**Q.** Let us take up those workers. What were you doing with them?

**A.** Those workers had been working on the Atlantic Wall. From there they were transferred to the Ruhr to repair the two dams which had been destroyed by an air attack. I must say that the transfer of these 50,000 workers took place without my knowledge, and the consequences of bringing 50,000 workers from the West into Germany were a catastrophe for us on the Atlantic Wall, because more than a third of all the workers engaged on the Atlantic Wall went away because they, too, were afraid they might have to go to Germany. That is why we rescinded the order as quickly as possible, so that the French workers on the Atlantic Wall should keep their confidence in us. This fact will show you that the French workers we had working for the Todt Organisation were not employed on a coercive basis, otherwise they could not have left in such numbers when they realised that under certain circumstances they, too, might be sent to Germany. So that this taking of the 50,000 workers from the Todt Organisation in France was only a temporary action and was cancelled later. It was one of those mistakes which can happen if a minister gives an urgent directive and his subordinates begin to carry it out by every means at their disposal.

**Q.** Are you familiar with Document 60-EC, which states that the Todt Labour Organisation had to recruit its manpower by force?

**A.** At the moment I cannot recollect it.

**Q.** I beg your pardon?

**A.** At this moment I cannot recollect it. Could I see the document?

**Q.** Yes, if you would like to. I just remind you that the evidence is contrary to your testimony on that subject.

Page 42, the paragraph which reads:

"Unfortunately the assignments for the Todt Organisation on the basis of Article 52 of the Hague Convention on Land Warfare have for some time decreased considerably, because the larger part of the manpower allocated does not turn up. Consequently further compulsory measures must be employed. The Prefect and the French Labour Exchanges co-operate quite loyally, it is true, but they have not sufficient authority to carry out these measures."

**A.** I think that I have perhaps not been understood correctly. I do not deny that a large number of the people working for the Todt Organisation in the West had been called up and came to work because they had to, but we had no means whatsoever of keeping them by force. So if they did not want to work, they could leave again, and then they either joined the resistance movement or went into hiding.

**Q.** Very well. But this calling-up system was a system of compulsion, was it not?

**A.** It was the calling up of French workers for duty in the Reich or in France. But here again I must add something. This report is dated June, 1943. In October, 1943, the whole of the Todt Organisation was declared a blocked industry and thereby received the advantages which other blocked industries had. I explained that sufficiently yesterday. Because of this, the Todt Organisation made great demands for workers who went there voluntarily, unless, of course, you see direct coercion in the pressure arising from their fear of being transferred to Germany, and which drove them to the Todt Organisation or other blocked industries.

**Q.** Were they kept in labour camps?

**A.** That was the custom in the case of such building work. The building sites were far away from any villages, and so workers' camps were set up to accommodate the German and the foreign workers. But some of them

*Speer climbing out of a Russian T34 tank, June 1943.*
Bundesarchiv, Bild 183-J14589 / Willi Kobierowski / CC-BY-SA

were also accommodated in villages as far as it was possible to accommodate them there. I do not think that on principle they were only meant to be accommodated in camps, but I cannot tell you that for certain.

The document—

**THE PRESIDENT:** Has this been introduced before?

**MR. JUSTICE JACKSON:** I was just going to give it to you. The document from which I have quoted is Exhibit USA 892.

**BY MR. JUSTICE JACKSON:**

**Q.** Now, leaving the question of the personal participation in this—

THE PRESIDENT: Is it new, Mr Justice Jackson?

MR. JUSTICE JACKSON: No, it has been in.

THE PRESIDENT: It has been in before?

MR. JUSTICE JACKSON: I am told that I am wrong about that, and that it is new. 892 is a new number.

**BY MR. JUSTICE JACKSON:**

Q. Leaving the part of your personal participation in this programme—

THE PRESIDENT: Could you tell us what the document is and where it comes from? I see it is 60-EC; so it must be captured. But ...

MR. JUSTICE JACKSON: It is one of the economic documents. It is a very large document.

THE PRESIDENT: Could you tell us what it is or who signed it? It is a very long document, apparently, is it?

MR. JUSTICE JACKSON: It is a long document, and it is a report of the Oberfeldkommandant L-I-L-L-E is the name of the signer.

**BY MR. JUSTICE JACKSON:**

Q. Now, coming to the question—

THE PRESIDENT: Let me look at the document, will you?

You see, Mr Justice Jackson, my attention has been drawn to the point that as far as the record is concerned, we have only this extract which you read. We have not got the date, and we do not have the signature, if any, on the document.

MR. JUSTICE JACKSON: I was merely refreshing his recollection to get out the facts, and I was not really offering the document for its own sake. I will go into more detail about it, if your Honour wishes. There is a great deal of irrelevant material in it.

THE PRESIDENT: If you do not want to offer it, then we need not bother about it.

MR. JUSTICE JACKSON: A great part of it is not relevant.

THE PRESIDENT: Yes.

MR. JUSTICE JACKSON: The quotation is adequately verified.

THE PRESIDENT: In that case, you may refer to it without the document being used. Then we need not have the document identified as an exhibit.

**BY MR. JUSTICE JACKSON:**

Q. Leaving the questions of your personal participation in these matters and coming to the questions dealt with in the second part of your examination, I want to ask you about your testimony concerning the proposal to denounce the Geneva Convention.

You testified yesterday that it was proposed to withdraw from the Geneva Convention. Will you tell us who made the proposal?

A. This proposal, as I already testified yesterday, came from Dr. Goebbels.

It was made after the air attack on Dresden, but before this, from the autumn of 1944 on, Goebbels and Ley had often had conversations to the effect that the war effort should be increased in every possible way, so that I had the impression Goebbels was merely using the attack on Dresden, and the excitement it created, as an excuse to renounce the Geneva Convention.

**Q.** Now, was the proposal at that time to resort to poison gas warfare, was the proposal made at that time?

**A.** I was not able to make out from my own direct observations whether gas warfare was to be started, but I knew from various associates of Ley and Goebbels that they were discussing the question of using our two new combat gases, Tabun and Sarin. They believed that these two gases would be of particular efficacy and they did in fact produce the most frightful results. We made these observations as early as the autumn of 1944, when the situation had become critical, and many people were seriously worried about it.

**Q.** Now, will you tell us about these two gases and about their production and their effects, their qualities, and the preparations that were made for gas warfare?

**A.** I cannot tell you that in detail. I am not enough of an expert. All I know is that both these gases had a quite extraordinary effect, and that there was no protection against them that we knew of either by respirator or other means, so that the soldiers would have been unable to protect themselves against this gas in any way. For the manufacture of these gases we had about three factories, all of which were undamaged and which, until November, 1944, were working at full capacity. When rumours reached us that gas might be used, I stopped its production in November, 1944. I stopped it by the following means. I blocked the so-called preliminary production, that is the chemical supplies for the making of gas. So that the gas-production, as the Allied authorities themselves ascertained, after the end of December or the beginning of January, actually did run down and finally came to a standstill. First of all, with the letter you have that I wrote to Hitler in October, 1944, I tried to obtain his permission for these gas factories to stop their production. The reason I gave him was that for air raids the preliminary products, mostly Zian, were needed urgently for other purposes. Hitler informed me that the gas production would have to continue whatever happened, but I gave instructions for the preliminary products not to be supplied any more.

**Q.** Can you identify others of the group who were advocating gas warfare?

**A.** In military circles there was certainly no one in favour of gas warfare. All the sensible army people opposed gas warfare as being utterly insane, for, in view of the enemy's superiority in the air, it would not have been long before it brought the most terrible retribution upon German cities which were completely unprotected.

**Q.** The group that did advocate it, however, consisted of the politicians most intimate with Hitler, did it not?

**A.** A certain circle of political people, very limited in number. It was mostly Ley, Goebbels and Bormann, always the same three, who by every possible means wanted to increase the war effort, and a man like Fegelein certainly belonged to a group like that, too. Of Himmler I would not be too sure for, at that time, Himmler was a little out of favour with Hitler because he indulged himself in the luxury of running an army group, although he knew nothing about such a task.

**Q.** Now, one of these gases was the gas which you proposed to use on those who were proposing to use it on others, and I suppose your motive was—

**A.** I must say quite frankly that my reason for this plan was the fear that under certain circumstances gas might be used, and the thought that we might get the idea of using it ourselves led me to make the whole plan.

**Q.** And your reasons, I take it, were the same as those of the military, that is to say, it was certain Germany would get the worst of it if Germany started that kind of warfare. That is what was worrying the military, was it not?

**A.** No, not only that. It was because at that stage of the war it was perfectly clear that under no circumstances should any international crimes be committed which could be held against the German people after they had lost the war. That was what decided the matter.

**Q.** Now, what about the bombs, after the war was obviously lost, aimed at England day after day; who favoured that?

**A.** You mean the rockets?

**Q.** Yes.

**A.** From the point of view of their technical production, the rockets were a very expensive affair for us, and their effect, compared to the cost of their output, was negligible. In consequence we had no particular interest in developing their production. The person who kept urging it was Himmler. He gave Obergruppenfuehrer Tammler the task of firing off these rockets over England. In army circles they were of the same opinion as I, namely, that the rockets were too expensive; and in air force circles, the opinion was the same, because with the outlay for one rocket one could build a fighter plane. It is quite clear that it would have been much better for us if we had not gone in for this nonsense.

**Q.** Going back to the characteristics of this gas, was one of the characteristics of this gas an exceedingly high temperature? When it was exploded it created exceedingly high temperature so that there could be no defence against it?

**A.** No, that is an error. Actually, ordinary gas evaporates at a normal atmospheric temperature. This gas would not evaporate until very high temperatures were reached and such very high temperatures could only be produced by an explosion; in other words; if the explosives detonated a very high temperature was set up and the gas evaporated. The solid substance turned into gas but the effects had nothing to do with the high temperature.

**Q.** Experiments were carried out with this gas, were they not, to your knowledge?

**A.** That I cannot tell you. Experiments must certainly have been carried out with it.

**Q.** Who was in charge of the experiments with the gases?

**A.** As far as I know it was the research and development department of the OKH in the Army Ordnance Office. I cannot tell you for certain.

**Q.** And certain experiments were also conducted and certain researches made with regard to atomic energy, were they not?

A. We had not got as far as that, unfortunately, because the finest experts we had in atomic research had emigrated to America, and this had thrown us back a great deal in our research, so that we still needed another one to two years in order to achieve any results in the splitting of the atom.

Q. The policy of driving people out who did not agree with the German Government had not produced very good dividends, had it?

A. Just in this sphere it was a great disaster to us.

Q. Now, certain information has been placed in my hands of an experiment which was carried out near Auschwitz, and I would like to ask you if you ever heard about it or knew about it. The purpose of the experiment was to find a quick and complete way of destroying people without the delay and trouble associated with shooting and gassing and burning, the methods being used. This was the experiment, as I am advised. A village, a small village was provisionally erected, with temporary structures, and in it approximately twenty thousand Jews were put. By means of this newly invented weapon of destruction, these twenty thousand people were eradicated almost instantaneously, and there was no, trace left of them; the explosive used developing temperatures of from four to five hundred degrees centigrade.

Do you know about that experiment?

A. No, and I consider it utterly improbable. If we had had such a weapon under preparation I would have known about it. But we did not have such a weapon. It is clear that in the chemical field experiments were made and research work carried on by both sides in attempts to develop all possible weapons, because one did not know which side would start chemical warfare first.

Q. The reports, then, of a new and secret weapon were exaggerated for the purpose of keeping the German people in the war?

A. That was the case mostly during the last phase of the war. From August on ... June or July, 1944, rather, I very often went to the front. I visited about forty front divisions in their sectors and could not help seeing that the troops, just like the German civilian population, were given hopes of a new weapon coming, new weapons even, and miracle weapons which, without requiring the use of soldiers, without military forces, would achieve victory. In this belief lies the secret why so many people in Germany continued to sacrifice their lives, although common sense told them that the war was over. They believed that within the near future this new weapon would arrive. I wrote to Hitler about it and tried in different speeches, even before Goebbels's propaganda leaders, to counteract these hopes. Both Hitler and Goebbels told me, however, that it was not propaganda, but that it was a belief which had grown up amongst the people. Only in the dock here in Nuremberg did I learn from Fritzsche that this propaganda was spread systematically amongst the people through certain channels, and that SS Standartenfuehrer Berg was responsible for it. Many things have become clear to me now because this man Berg as a representative of the Ministry of Propaganda had often taken part in meetings, in big sessions of my Ministry, as he was writing articles about these sessions. There he heard of our future plans and then used this knowledge to tell the people about them with more fantasy than truth.

**Q.** When did it become apparent that the war was lost? I take it that your attitude was that you felt some responsibility for getting the German people out of the war with as little destruction as possible. Is that a fair statement of your position?

**A.** Yes, but I did not only have that feeling with regard to the German people. I knew quite well that one should equally avoid destruction in the occupied territories. That was just as important to me from a realistic point of view for I said to myself that, after the war, the responsibility for all these destructions would not only fall on us, but on the next German Government, and the coming German generations.

**Q.** Where you differed with the people who wanted to continue the war to the bitter end was that you wanted to see Germany have a chance to restore her life. Is that not a fact? Whereas, Hitler took the position that, if he could not survive, he did not care whether Germany survived or not?

**A.** That is true, and I would never have had the courage to make this statement before this Tribunal if I had not been able to prove it on the strength of some documents, because such a statement is so monstrous. But the letter which I wrote to Hitler on the 29th of March, and in which I confirmed this, shows that he said so himself.

**Q.** Well, if I may comment, it was not a new idea to us that that was his viewpoint. I think it was believed in most of the other countries that that was his attitude.

Now, were you present with Hitler at the time he received the telegram from Goering suggesting that Goering take over power?

**A.** On the 23rd of April I flew to Berlin in order to take leave of several of my associates, and—as I frankly admit—after all that had happened, also in order to place myself at Hitler's disposal. Perhaps this will sound strange to you, but the conflicting feelings I had about the action I wanted to take against him, and about the way he had of doing things, still did not give me any clear grounds or any clear inner conviction as to what my relations should be to him, so I flew over to see him. I did not know whether he knew of my plans, and I did not know whether he would order me to remain in Berlin. But I felt that it was my duty not to run away like a coward, but to stand up to him again. It was on that day that Goering's telegram to Hitler arrived. This telegram ... not to Hitler, but from Goering to Ribbentrop. I mean, it was Bormann who submitted it to Hitler.

**Q.** Submitted it to Hitler?

**A.** Yes, to Hitler.

**Q.** What did Hitler say on that occasion?

**A.** Hitler was unusually excited about the contents of the telegram, and said quite plainly what he thought about Goering He said that he "had known for some time that Goering had failed him, that he was corrupt, and that he was a drug addict." I was extremely shaken, because I felt that if the head of the State had known this for such a long time, then it showed a lack of responsibility on his part to leave such a man in office, when the lives of countless people depended on him. It was typical of Hitler's attitude towards the entire problem, however, that he followed his statement up by saying: "But he can negotiate the capitulation all the same."

**Q.** Did he say why he was willing to let Goering negotiate the capitulation?

**A.** No. He said in an off-hand manner: "It does not matter anyway who does it." In the manner he said this, he expressed all his disregard for the German nation.

**Q.** That is, his attitude was that there was nothing left worth saving, so let Goering work it out. Is that a fair statement of his attitude?

**A.** That was my impression, yes.

**Q.** Now this policy, of driving Germany to destruction after the war was lost, troubled you so much that you became a party to several plots, did you not, in an attempt to remove the people who were responsible for the destruction, as you saw it, of your country?

**A.** Yes. But I want to add—

**Q.** There were more plots than you have told us about, were there not?

**A.** During that time it was extremely easy to start a plot. One could accost practically any man in the street and tell him what the situation was, and get him to say, that is insane; and if he had any courage he would place himself at your disposal. Unfortunately, I had no organisation behind me which I could call upon and give orders to do this or that. That is why I had to depend on personal conversations to put me in contact with all kinds of people. But I do want to say that it was not as dangerous as it looks here because, actually, the unreasonable people who were still left only amounted perhaps to a few dozens. The remaining eighty millions were perfectly sensible as soon as they knew what the situation really was.

**Q.** Perhaps you had a sense of responsibility for having put the eighty millions completely in the power of the Fuehrer principle. Did that occur to you, or does it now as you look back on it?

**A.** May I have the question repeated, because I didn't understand its sense.

**Q.** You have eighty million sane and sensible people facing destruction; you have a dozen people driving them on to destruction and they, the eighty million, are unable to stop it. And I ask if you have a feeling of responsibility for having established the Fuehrer principle, which Goring has so well described to us, in Germany?

**A.** I, personally, when I became minister in February, 1942, placed myself at the disposal of this Fuehrer principle. But I admit that in my organisation I soon saw that the Fuehrer principle was in many ways defective and so I tried to weaken its effect. The tremendous danger of the totalitarian system, however, only became really clear at the moment when we were approaching the end. It was then that one could see what the principle really meant, namely, that every order should be carried out without criticism. Everything that has become known during this trial, especially with regard to orders which were carried out without any consideration, has proved how evil it was in the end. In such cases for example as the carrying out of the order to destroy the bridges in our own country, a mistake or consequence of this totalitarian system. Quite apart from the personality of Hitler, on the collapse of the totalitarian system in Germany, it became clear what tremendous dangers there are in a system of that kind. The combination of Hitler and this system has brought about these tremendous catastrophes in the world.

Q. Well, now—Hitler is dead—I assume you accept that?—and we ought to give the devil his due. Is it not a fact that in the circle around Hitler there was almost no one who would stand up and tell him that the war was lost except yourself?

A. That is correct to a certain extent. Amongst the military leaders there were many who, each in his own sphere, told Hitler quite clearly what the situation was. Many commanders of army groups, for instance, made it clear to him how catastrophic developments were, and there were often fierce arguments during the discussions on the situation. Men like Guderian and Jodl, for instance, often talked quite openly about their sectors in my presence, and Hitler could see quite well what the general situation was like. But I never observed that those who were actually responsible in the group around Hitler ever went to him and said: "The war is lost." Nor did I ever see these people who had responsibility attempt to join together to undertake some joint step against Hitler. I did not attempt it either because it would have been useless. During this particular phase, Hitler had so terrified his closest associates that they no longer had any will of their own.

Q. Well, let us take the number two man who has told us that he was in favour of fighting to the very finish. Were you present at a conversation between Goering and General Galland in which Goering, in substance, forbade Galland to report the disaster that was overtaking Germany?

A. No, in that form, that is not correct. That was another conference.

Q. Well, tell us what you know about General Galland's conversation with Goering.

A. It was at the Fuehrer headquarters in East Prussia in front of Goering's train. Galland had reported to Hitler that the enemy fighter planes were already accompanying bombing squadrons as far as Luttich and it was to be expected that in the future the bombing units would travel still farther from their bases accompanied by fighters. After a discussion with Hitler on the military situation, Goering upbraided Galland and told him with some excitement that this could not possibly be true, that the fighters could not go as far as Luttich. He said that from his experience as an old fighter pilot he knew this perfectly well. Thereupon Galland replied that the fighters were being shot down, and were lying on the ground near Luttich. Goering, would not believe that this was true. Galland was an outspoken man who told Goring his opinion quite clearly and refused to allow Goering's excitement to influence him. Finally, Goering, as Commander-in-Chief of the Air Force, expressly forbade Galland to make any further reports on this matter. It was impossible, he said, that enemy fighters could penetrate so deeply into Germany, and so he ordered him to accept that as being true. I continued to discuss the matter afterwards with Galland, who was later relieved of his duties as a General of the Fighter Command by Goering, Up to that time Galland had been in charge of all the fighter units in Germany. He was the General in charge of all the fighters within the High Command of the Air Force.

**THE PRESIDENT:** What is the date of that?

**MR. JUSTICE JACKSON:** I was going to ask.

**THE WITNESS:** It must have been towards the end of 1943.

**THE PRESIDENT:** Mr Justice Jackson, perhaps we had better adjourn now.

*(A recess was taken.)*

Q. Was it known, in the days when you were struggling to obtain adequate manpower to make armaments for Germany, that Goering was using manpower to collect and transport art treasures for himself. Was that known to you at the time?

A. He did not need any workers for that purpose.

Q. Well, even a few were very valuable, were they not?

A. The art treasures were valuable, not the workers.

Q. To him?

A. Yes.

Q. Well, let me ask you about your efforts in producing, and see how much difficulty you were having. Krupp's was a big factor in the German armament production, was it not?

A. Yes.

Q. The biggest single unit, would not you say?

A. Yes, to the extent I said yesterday. It produced few guns and armaments, but it was a big concern, one of the most respected ones in the armament industry.

Q. But you had prevented, as far as possible, the use of resources and manpower for the production of things that were not useful for the war, is not that true?

A. That is true.

Q. And the things which were being created, being built by the Krupp company whether they were guns or other objects, were things which were essential for carrying on the national economy or for conducting the war? That would be true, would it not?

A. Generally speaking one can say that, in the end, every article which in war time is produced in the home country, whether it is a pair of shoes for the workers, or clothing or coal, is helping the war effort. That has nothing to do with the old conception, which has long since died out, and which we find in the Geneva Prisoner-of-War Agreement.

Q. Well, at the moment I am not concerned with the question of the application of the Geneva Convention. I want to ask you some questions about your efforts to produce essential goods, whether they were armament or not armament, and the conditions that this regime was imposing upon labour and adding, as I think, to your problem of production. I think you can give us some information about this. You were frequently at the Krupp plant, were you not?

A. I was at the Krupp plant five or six times.

Q. You were well informed as to the progress of production in the Krupp plant as well as others?

A. Yes, when I went to visit these plants, it was mostly after air raids, and then I got full information of the production. As I worked hard, I knew a lot about these problems, right down to the details.

Q. Krupp also had several labour camps, did they not?

A. Of course Krupp had labour camps.

Q. Krupp was a very large user of both foreign labour and prisoners of war.

A. I cannot give the percentage, but no doubt Krupp did employ foreign workers and prisoners of war.

Q. Well, I may say to you that we have investigated the Krupp labour camps, and from Krupp's own charts it appears that in 1943 they had 39,245 foreign workers and 11,234 prisoners of war, and that these numbers steadily increased until in September, 1944, Krupp had 54,990 foreign workers and 18,902 prisoners of war.

Now, would that be somewhere near what you could expect from your knowledge of the industry?

A. I do not know the details. I do not know the figures of how many workers Krupp employed at all. I am not familiar with them at the moment. But I believe that the percentage of foreign workers at Krupp's was about the same as in other plants and in other armament concerns.

Q. And what would you say that percentage was?

A. That varied a great deal. The older industries which had their old regular personnel had a much lower percentage of foreign workers than the new industries, which had just grown up and which had no old regular personnel. The reason for this was that the young age groups were drafted into the Wehrmacht and, therefore, the concerns which had a personnel of older workers still kept a large percentage of the older workers. Therefore the percentage of foreign workers in the general armament industry, if you take it as a whole and as one of the older industries, was lower than the percentage of foreign workers in the air armament industry because that was a completely new industry which had not old workers. However, I cannot give you the percentage.

Q. Now, the foreign workers who were assigned to Krupp—let us use Krupp as an example—foreign workers that were assigned to Krupp were housed in labour camps and under guard, were they not?

A. I do not believe that they were under guard, but I cannot say. I do not want to avoid giving information here, but I had no time to worry about such things on my visits. The things I was concerned about when I went to a factory were in an entirely different sphere. In all my activities as Armament

Minister I never once visited a labour camp, and cannot, therefore, give any information about them.

**Q.** Well, now, I am going to give you some information about the conditions in the labour camp at Krupp's, and then I am going to ask you some questions about them. I am not attempting to say that you were personally responsible for these conditions. I merely give you the indications as to what the regime was doing and I am going to ask you certain questions as to the effect of this sort of thing on your work of production.

Are you familiar with Document 288-D, which is Exhibit USA 202, the affidavit of Dr. Jaeger who was brought here as a witness?

**A.** Yes, but I considered that somewhat exaggerated.

**Q.** You do not accept that?

**A.** No.

**Q.** Well, you have no personal knowledge of the conditions. What is the basis of your information that Dr. Jaeger's statement is exaggerated?

**A.** If such conditions had existed, I should probably have heard of them, as when I visited plants the head of the plant naturally came to me with his biggest troubles. These troubles occurred primarily after air raids when, for example, both the German workers and foreign workers had no longer any proper shelter. This state of affairs was described to me, so that I know that what is stated in the Jaeger affidavit cannot have been a permanent condition. It can only have been a condition caused temporarily by air raids, for a week or a fortnight, and which was improved later on. It is well known that after a severe air raid on a city, all the sanitary installations, the water supply, gas supply, electricity, and so on, were often put out of order and severely damaged so that temporarily there were very difficult conditions.

**Q.** I remind you that Dr. Jaeger's affidavit relates to the time of October, 1942, and that he was a witness here. And, of course, you are familiar with his testimony.

**A.** Yes.

**Q.** Well, now, I call your attention to a new document which is 361-D, and is Exhibit USA 893, a document signed by the office chief of the Locomotive Construction Works, describing conditions of his labour supply, foreign workers.

And I am not suggesting—I repeat I am not suggesting that this was your responsibility. I am suggesting it is the responsibility of the regime. I should like to read this despite its considerable length. "I received—" This is dated at the Boiler Making Shop, the 25th of February, 1942, addressed to Hupe by way of Winters and Schmidt.

"I received the enclosed letter of the 18th of this month from the German Labour Front, sent to my private address, inviting me to the office of the German Labour Front"—giving its address and date. "I tried to find out by telephoning the reason for the request. The answer from the German Labour Front was that the matter was very important and demanded my personal appearance. Thereupon I asked Herr

Jungerich of the Department for Social Labour Matters whether I had better go. He answered, 'You probably don't have to, but it would be better if you went.' About 9.50 I went round to Room 20 at this place and met Herr Prior.

The following event provided the cause for this conversation, which Herr Prior carried on in a very lively manner, and which lasted about half an hour:

"On the 16th, 23 Russian prisoners of war were assigned to No. 23 Boiler Shop. The people came in the morning without bread and tools. During both breaks the prisoners of war crept up to the German workers and begged for bread, pitifully pointing out their hunger. At the first midday break, the workers had the opportunity of distributing the food which remained over from the French prisoners of war amongst the Russians. In order to alleviate these conditions, I went to the Weidkamp kitchen on the 17th, on instructions from Herr Theile, and talked to the head of the kitchen, Fraulein Block, about the provision of the midday meal. Fraulein Block promised me the food immediately and also lent me the 22 sets of eating utensils which I asked for.

At the same time I asked Fraulein Block to give any food left over by the 800 Dutchmen messing there to our Russian prisoners of war at midday until further notice. Fraulein Block promised to do this, too, and the following midday she sent down a container of milk soup as an extra. The following midday the ration was short in quantity. Since a few Russians had collapsed already, I telephoned Fraulein Block and asked for an increase in the food as the special ration had ceased from the second day onwards. As my telephone conversation was unsuccessful, I again visited Fraulein Block personally. Fraulein Block refused in a very abrupt manner to give any further special ration.

Now, regarding the discussion in detail, Herr Prior, two other gentlemen of the DAF and Fraulein Block, head of the Weidkamp kitchen, were present in the room. Herr Prior started by accusing me, gesticulating in a very insulting manner, of openly taking the part of the Bolsheviks. He referred to the laws of the Reich Government forbidding this. I was unfortunately not clear about the legal position, otherwise I would have left the conference room immediately. I then tried to make it clear to Herr Prior, with special emphasis, that the Russian prisoners of war were assigned to us as workers and not as Bolsheviks; the people were starved and not in a position to perform the heavy work with us in boiler making which they were required to do; and that sick people were a liability to us and not a help to production. To this remark Herr Prior stated that if one was worth nothing, then another was; that the Bolsheviks were a soulless people, and if 100,000 of them died, another 100,000 would replace them. On my remarking that, with such a coming and going, we would not attain our goal, namely the delivery of locomotives to the Reich railways, which were continually cutting down the time limit for delivery, Herr Prior said, 'Deliveries are only of secondary importance in this case.'

My attempts to get Herr Prior to understand our economic needs were not successful. In closing, I can only say that as a German I know our relations to the Russian prisoners of war exactly, and in this case I acted only on behalf of my superiors and with the object of increasing the production which is demanded of us."

It is signed, "Soehling, Office Chief, Locomotive Construction Works." And there is added this letter as a part of the communication, signed by Theile:

"I have the following to add to the above letter: After the Russian prisoners of war had been assigned to us on the 16th of this month by Labour Supply, I got into touch with Dr. Lehmann immediately about their food.

I learned from him that the prisoners received 300 gr. of bread each between 4 a.m. and 5 a.m. I pointed out that it was impossible to last until 1800 hours on this ration of bread, whereupon Dr. Lehmann said that the Russians must not be allowed to get used to the Western European feeding. I replied that the prisoners of war could not do the work required of them in the Boiler Construction Shop on that food, and that it was not practical for us to have these people in the works any longer under such conditions. At the same time I demanded that if the Russians continued to be employed, they should be given a hot midday meal and that, if possible, the bread ration should be split so that one half was distributed early in the morning and the second half during our breakfast break. My suggestion has already been carried out by us with the French prisoners of war and has proved to be very practical and good.

Unfortunately, however, Dr. Lehmann took no notice of my suggestion and, on this account, I naturally had to take matters into my own hands and therefore told Herr Soehling to get the feeding of the Russian prisoners of war organised on exactly the same lines as the French, so that the Russians could, as soon as possible, carry out the work they were supposed to do. For the whole thing concerns an increase in production such as is demanded from us by the Minister of Armament and Munitions and by the DAF."

Now, I ask you, if the action of the Chief of the locomotive construction works was not entirely a necessary action in the interests of production?

A. It is clear that a worker who has not enough food cannot achieve a good output. I said yesterday that every head of a plant, and I too at the top, was naturally interested in having well-fed and satisfied workers, because badly fed, dissatisfied workers make more mistakes and produce poor results.

I should like to comment on this document. The document is dated 25th February, 1942. At that time there were official instructions that the Russian prisoners of war and also the Russian civilian workers who came to the Reich should be treated worse than the Western prisoners of war and the Western civilian workers. I learned of this through complaints from the heads of concerns. In my document book which dates from the middle of March, 1942—that is three or four weeks after this document—there is a Fuehrer protocol, resulting from my calling Hitler's attention to the fact that the feeding both of Russian prisoners of war and of Russian workers was absolutely inadequate and that they would have to be given an adequate diet and that, moreover, the Russian workers were being kept behind barbed wire like prisoners of war and that that would have to be stopped also. The protocol shows that in both cases I succeeded in getting Hitler to agree that conditions should be changed and they were changed.

I must say furthermore that it was a real service on the part of Sauckel that he now fought against this policy and did everything he could to have the foreign workers and prisoners of war treated better and given adequate food.

Q. Well, we will deal with the conditions later. Because I am going to ask you, if you were not responsible and Sauckel was not responsible, who was responsible for these conditions, and you can keep it in mind that that is the question I am leading up to.

I will show you a new document, 398-D, Exhibit USA 894A, a statement taken by the British-American representatives during their investigation of this labour camp at Krupp's.

Well, Document 321-D. I can use that just as well. We will use Document 321-D, which becomes Exhibit USA 894.

**THE PRESIDENT:** 894 was the last number you gave us. What number is this document that you are now offering?

**MR. JUSTICE JACKSON:** Document 398 was Exhibit 894. 321 will be 895.

**BY MR. JUSTICE JACKSON:**

Q. Now, this relates to an employee of the Reich Railways. None of our investigation, I may say, is based upon the statements of the prisoners themselves.

"I, the undersigned, Adam Schmidt, employed as Betriebswart on the Essen West Railway Station and residing"—stating his residence—"make the following statement voluntarily and on oath:

I have been employed by the Reich Railway since 1918 and have been at Essen West Station since 1935. In the middle of 1941 the first workers arrived from Poland, Galicia and Polish Ukraine. They came to Essen in goods wagons in which potatoes, building materials and also cattle had been transported, and were brought to work at Krupp's. The trucks were crammed full with people. My personal view was that it was inhuman to transport people in such a manner. The people were squashed closely together and they had no room for free movement. The Krupp overseers prided themselves on the speed with which the slave workers were got in and out of the trucks. It was enraging for every decent German who had to watch this, to see how the people were beaten and kicked and generally maltreated in a brutal manner. In the very beginning when the first transports arrived we could see how inhumanly these people were treated. Every truck was so overcrowded that it was incredible that such a number of people could be crammed into one. I could see with my own eyes that sick people who could scarcely walk (they were mostly people with foot trouble, or with injuries and people with internal trouble) were nevertheless taken to work. One could see that it was sometimes difficult for them to move. The same can be said of the Eastern workers and prisoners of war who came to Essen in the middle of 1942."

He then describes their clothing and their food. In the interest of time, I will not attempt to read the entire thing.

Do you consider that that, too, is an exaggerated statement?

**A.** When the workers came to Germany from the East, their clothing was no doubt bad, but I know from Sauckel that whilst he was in office a lot was done to get them better clothes, and in Germany many of the Russian workers experienced much better conditions than they had previously known in Russia. The Russian workers were quite satisfied in Germany. If they arrived here in rags, that does not mean that that was our fault. We could not use ragged workers with poor shoes in our industry, so conditions were improved.

**Q.** Well, now, I would like to call your attention to Document 398-D.

**THE PRESIDENT:** Well, before you pass from that, what do you say about the conditions of the transports? The question you were asked was whether this was an exaggerated account. You have not answered that except in reference to clothing.

**THE WITNESS:** Mr. President, I cannot give any information about this transport matter. I received no reports about it.

**BY MR. JUSTICE JACKSON:**

**Q.** Well, I will ask you about Document 398-D, which becomes Exhibit USA 894. This is a statement by Hofer, living in Essen. He says:

"From April, 1943, I worked with Lowenkamp every day in the armour building shop No. 4. Lowenkamp was very brutal to the foreigners. He confiscated food which belonged to the prisoners of war and took it home. Every day he mishandled Eastern workers, Russian prisoners of war, French, Italian, and other foreign civilians. He had a steel box built which was so small that one could hardly stand init. He locked up foreigners in the box, women too, for 48 hours at a time without giving the people food.

They were not released even to relieve nature. It was forbidden for other people to give any help to the persons locked in, or to release them.

Whilst clearing an unofficial camp, he fired on escaping Russian civilians without hitting any of them.

One day, whilst distributing food, I saw how he hit a French civilian in the face with a ladle and made his face bleed. Further, when Russian girls gave birth he never bothered about the babies. There was never any milk for them so the Russians had to feed the children with sugar water. When Lowenkamp was arrested he wrote two letters and sent them to me through his wife. He tried to make out that he never hit people ...."

There is a good deal more of this, but I will not bother to put it into the record.

Is it your view that this is exaggerated?

**A.** I consider this affidavit a lie. I should like to say that among German people such things do not happen, and if such individual cases occurred they were punished. It is not possible to drag the German people in the dirt in such a way. The heads of concerns were decent people too and took interest in their workers. If the head of the Krupp plant heard about such things, he certainly took steps immediately to put a stop to them.

**Q.** Well, what about the steel boxes? Or do you not believe the steel-box story?

**A.** No, I do not believe it, I do not believe it is true. After the collapse in 1945 a lot of affidavits were drawn up, which certainly do not correspond to the truth. That is not your fault. It is the fault of ... well, after a defeat, it is quite possible that people do make false statements like that.

**Q.** Well, I would like to have you examine Document 258 and I attach importance to this as establishing the SS as being the guards:

> "The camp inmates were mostly Jewish women and girls from Hungary and Roumania. The camp inmates were brought to Essen at the beginning of 1944 and were put to work at Krupp's. The accommodation and feeding of the camp prisoners were of a low standard. At first the prisoners were accommodated in simple wooden huts. These huts were burned down during an air raid and from that time on the prisoners had to sleep in a damp cellar. Their beds were made on the floor and each consisted of a straw-filled sack and two blankets. In most cases it was not possible for the prisoners to wash themselves daily, as there was no water. There was no possibility of having a bath.
>
> I could often observe from the Krupp factory, during the lunch break, how the prisoners boiled their underclothing in an old bucket or container over a wood fire, and cleaned themselves. A trench served as an air-raid shelter, whilst the SS guards went to the Humboldt shelter, which was bomb-proof.
>
> Reveille was at 5 a.m. There was no coffee or any food served in the morning. They marched off to the factory at 5.15 a.m. They marched for three-quarters of an hour to the factory, poorly clothed and badly shod, some without shoes, and covered with a blanket, in rain or snow. Work began at 6 a.m. The lunch break was from 12 to 12.30. Only during the break was it at all possible for the prisoners to cook something for themselves from potato peelings and other garbage.
>
> The daily working period was one of ten to eleven hours. Although the prisoners were completely undernourished, their work was very heavy

physically. The prisoners were often ill-treated at their work benches by Nazi overseers and female SS guards. At 5 or 6 in the afternoon they were marched back to camp. The accompanying guards consisted of female SS who, in spite of protests from the civilian population, often ill-treated the prisoners on the way back, kicking and hitting them and abusing them in foul language. If often happened that individual women or girls had to be carried back to the camp by their comrades owing to exhaustion. At 6 or 7 p.m. these exhausted people arrived back in camp. Then the real midday meal was distributed. This consisted of cabbage soup. This was followed by the evening meal of watery soup and a piece of bread which was for the following day. Occasionally the food on Sundays was better. As long as it existed there was never any inspection of the camp by members of the firm of Krupp. On 13th March, 1945, the camp prisoners were brought to Buchenwald Concentration Camp, from there some were sent to work. The camp commandant was SS Oberscharfuehrer Rick."

The rest of it does not matter. In your estimation that, I suppose, is also an exaggeration?

**THE WITNESS:** From the document—

**DR. FLAECHSNER:** Mr. President.

**THE PRESIDENT:** May I hear the answer. I thought the defendant said something.

**DR. FLAECHSNER:** May I call the attention of the Tribunal to the document itself, of which I have only a copy? It is headed "Before a Military Court, under oath," and there is an ordinary signature under it. It does not say that it is an affidavit or a statement in lieu of oath, or any other such thing, it says only "Further inquiries must be made," and it is signed by Hubert Karden. That is apparently the name of the man who was making the statement.

Then there is another signature, "Kriminalassistent on probation." That is a police official who may later have the chance of becoming a candidate for the criminal service. He has signed it. Then there is another signature, "C.E. Long, Major President."

There is not a word in this document to the effect that any of these three people want to vouch for the contents of this as an affidavit. I do not believe this document can be considered an affidavit in that sense, or can be used as such.

**THE PRESIDENT:** Yes, Mr. Justice Jackson? Do you wish to say anything?

**MR. JUSTICE JACKSON:** The document speaks for itself. As I have pointed out to this witness, I am giving him the result of an investigation. I am not accusing him of personal responsibility for these conditions. I intend to ask him some questions about responsibility for conditions in the camp.

**THE PRESIDENT:** Well, there is a statement at the top of the copy that I have got, "Sworn on oath before a Military Court."

**MR. JUSTICE JACKSON:** Yes, it was taken in Essen during this investigation. And of course, if I was charging this particular defendant with the responsibility there might be some argument about it. It comes under the provision of the Charter which authorises the receipt here of proceedings of other courts.

THE PRESIDENT: Have you got the original document here?

MR. JUSTICE JACKSON: Yes.

*(A document was submitted to the Tribunal.)*

THE PRESIDENT: The Tribunal sees no objection to the document being used in cross-examination.

Did you give it an exhibit number?

MR. JUSTICE JACKSON: I should have; it is Exhibit USA 896.

THE PRESIDENT: Yes.

BY MR. JUSTICE JACKSON:

Q. I now want to call your attention to Document 382-D.

A. I wanted to comment on the document.

THE PRESIDENT: Mr. Justice Jackson, there are some photographs which have been put before us. Are they identified and do they form part of an exhibit?

MR. JUSTICE JACKSON: They form part of the exhibit which I am now offering.

THE PRESIDENT: I see.

MR. JUSTICE JACKSON: But the witness desires to comment on the last document, and I will listen to that before we go ahead.

BY MR. JUSTICE JACKSON:

Q. Yes.

A. First I should like to say, as you have so often mentioned my non-responsibility, that if in general these conditions had been true, on the basis of my statement yesterday I should consider myself responsible. I do not want to evade responsibility. But the conditions were not what they are said to have been here. These are only individual cases which are quoted.

As for this document, I should only like to say from what I have seen of it that it seems to be a question of a concentration camp, one of the small concentration camps near the factories. The factories could not inspect these camps. That is why the sentence is quite true where it says that no factory representative ever saw the camp.

The fact that there were SS guards also shows that it was a concentration camp.

If the question which you asked me before, as to whether the labour camps were guarded—those for foreign workers—if that refers to this document, then your conclusion was wrong. As far as I know, the other labour camps were not guarded by SS or by any other organisations. My position is such that I feel it is my duty to protect the heads of plants from any injustice which might be done them. The head of a concern could not bother about the conditions in such a camp.

I cannot say whether conditions were as described in this camp. We have seen so much material on conditions in concentration camps during the trial.

Q. Now I will ask to have you shown Exhibit 382-D—I should say Document 382-D—which will be Exhibit USA 897. Now that is the statement of several as to one of those steel boxes which stood in the foreign workers' camp in the grounds of No. 4 Armour Shop, and of those in the Russian camp. I do not think that it is necessary to read the complete descriptions.

Is that merely an individual instance, or what is your view of that circumstance?

A. What is pictured here is quite a normal locker as was used in every factory. These photographs have no value as evidence.

Q. Very well. I will ask to have you shown Document 230-D which is an inter-office record of the steel switches, and the steel switches which have been found in the camp will be shown to you, 80 of them, distributed according to the reports.

A. Shall I comment on this?

Q. If you wish.

A. Yes. Those are nothing but replacements for rubber truncheons. We had no rubber; and for that reason, the guards probably had something like this. *(Indicating).*

Q. That is the same inference that I drew from the document.

A. Yes, but the guards did not immediately use these steel switches any more than your police use their rubber truncheons. But they had to have something in their hands. It is the same thing, all over the world.

Q. Well, we will not argue that point.

A. I am not an expert. I only assume that that was the case. I cannot testify on oath that that was the case. That was only an argument.

**THE PRESIDENT:** Did you give an exhibit number to that?

**MR. JUSTICE JACKSON:** Exhibit USA 898, your Honour.

**BY MR. JUSTICE JACKSON:**

Q. Now, Exhibit 899 would be our Document 283, which is a 1943 report from the Krupp hospitals taken from the files of Krupp's. The subject:

"Cases of Deaths of Eastern Workers."

"Fifty-four Eastern workers have died in the hospital in Lazarettstrasse, four of them as a result of external causes and fifty as a result of illnesses.

The causes of death in the case of these fifty Eastern workers who died of illnesses were the following:

Tuberculosis: 38

Malnutrition: 2

Internal haemorrhage: 1

Disease of the bowels: 2

Typhus: 1

Pneumonia: 3

Appendicitis: 1

Liver trouble: 1

Abscess of the brain: 1

*Hitler, Speer and Wilhelm Keitel (far left) watching a demonstration of new weaponry, April 1943.*
Bundesarchiv, Bild 146-1971-016-25 / Heinrich Hoffmann / CC-BY-SA

This list therefore shows that four-fifths died of tuberculosis and malnutrition."

Now, did you have any reports from time to time as to the health conditions of the workers who were engaged on your production programme?

A. First I should like to comment on the document. The document does not show the total number of workers employed when these people died, so that one cannot say whether that is an unnaturally high proportion of illness. In an account of a session of the Central Planning Board which I read here, I observed it was said that amongst the Russian workers there was a high rate of tuberculosis. I do not know whether you mean that. That was a remark which Weiger made to me. But presumably through the health offices we tried to alleviate these conditions.

Q. There was an abnormally high rate of deaths from tuberculosis; there is no doubt about that, is there?

A. I do not know whether that was an abnormal death rate. But there was an abnormally high rate of tuberculosis at times.

Q. Well, the exhibit does not show whether the death rate itself was abnormally high, but it shows an abnormal proportion of deaths from tuberculosis among the total deaths, does it not? Eighty per cent deaths from tuberculosis is a very high percentage, is it not?

A. That may be. I cannot say from my own knowledge.

Q. Now I would like to have you shown—

**THE PRESIDENT:** Did you give that an exhibit number? That would be 899, would it not?

**MR. JUSTICE JACKSON:** 899, your Honour.
**BY MR. JUSTICE JACKSON:**

Q. Now, let me ask you to be shown Document 335. This is a report from the files of Krupp dated at Essen, the 12th of June, 1944, directed to the "Gau Camp Doctor Herr Dr. Jaeger," and signed by Stinnesbeck:

"In the middle of May I took over the medical supervision of the P.O.W. Camp 1420 in the Noggerathstrasse. The camp contains 644 French P.O.W.s. During the air raid on 27th April of this year most of the camp was destroyed and at the moment conditions are intolerable.

315 prisoners are still accommodated in the camp. 170 of these are no longer in huts but in the tunnel in Grunertstrasse on the Essen-Muhlheim railway line. This tunnel is damp and is not suitable for accommodation of human beings. The rest of the prisoners are accommodated in ten different factories in Krupp's works.

Medical attention is given by a French military doctor who takes great pains with his fellow-countrymen. Sick people from Krupp's factories must be brought to the sick parade, too. This parade is held in the lavatory of a burned-out public-house outside the camp. The sleeping accommodation of the four French medical orderlies is in what was the urinal. There is a double tier wooden bed available for sick bay patients. In general, treatment takes place in the open. In rainy weather it has to be held in the small room.

These are insufferable conditions. There are no chairs, tables, cupboards or water. The keeping of a register of sick people is impossible. Bandages and medical supplies are very scarce, although people badly hurt in the works are often brought here for first aid and have to be bandaged before being taken to the hospital. There are many strong complaints about food, too, which the guard personnel confirm as being justified.

Illness and loss of manpower result from these conditions.

The construction of huts for the accommodation of the prisoners and the building of sick quarters for the proper treatment of patients is urgently necessary.

Please take the necessary steps.

(Signed) Stinnesbeck."

A. That is a document which shows what conditions can be after a severe air raid. The conditions were the same in these cases for German and foreign workers. There were no beds, no cupboards, and so forth. That was because the camp in which these things had been provided had been burned down. That the food supply was often inadequate in the Ruhr district during this period was due to the fact that attacks from the air were centred on communication lines, so that food transport could not be brought into the Ruhr to the necessary extent. These were temporary conditions which we were able to improve when the air raids ceased for a time. When conditions became even worse after September or October of 1944, or rather after November of 1944, we made every effort to give food supplies the priority for the first time over armament needs, so that in spite of these disasters the workers would be fed.

**Q.** Well, then, you did make it your business to get food for and concern yourself about the conditions of these workers? Do I understand that you did it, that you took steps?

**A.** It is true that I did so and I am glad that I did even if I am to be reproached for it now. For it is a universal human obligation when one hears of such conditions to try to alleviate them, even if it is somebody else's responsibility. But the witness Riecke testified here that the whole of the food question was under the direction of the Food Ministry.

**Q.** And it was an essential part of production, was it not, to keep workers in proper condition to produce? That is elementary, is it not?

**A.** No. That is wrongly formulated.

**Q.** Well, you formulate it for me as to what the relation is between the nourishment and production of workers.

**A.** I said yesterday that the responsibility for labour conditions was divided between the Food Ministry, the Health Office in the Reich Ministry of the Interior and the labour trustee in the office of the Plenipotentiary for Labour Employment and so on. There was no comprehensive authority in my hands. In the Reich, because of the way in which our State machine was built up, we lacked a comprehensive authority in the form of a Reich Chancellor, with power to convene conferences of the heads of departments for joint discussions.

But I, as the man responsible for production, had no responsibility in these matters. However, when I heard complaints from factory heads or from my deputies, I did everything to remove the cause of the complaints.

**Q.** The Krupp works—

**THE PRESIDENT:** Shall we break off now?

**MR. JUSTICE JACKSON:** Any time you say, sir.

*(A recess was taken until 1400 hours.)*

**THE PRESIDENT:** The Tribunal wishes to hear from defendants' counsel what arrangements they have found it possible to make with reference to the apportionment of time for their speeches.

**DR. NELTE:** I should like first of all to point out that the defendants' counsel, with whom the Tribunal discussed the question of final defence speeches during an earlier closed session, did not inform the other defendants' counsel, since they were under the impression that the Tribunal would not impose any restrictions on the defence in this respect. I personally, when I raised my objections, had no knowledge of this discussion, as my colleagues, who conferred with you earlier, have authorized me to explain.

On the suggestion of the Tribunal, counsel for the individual defendants have discussed the decision announced in the session on 13th June, 1946, and I am now, submitting to the Tribunal the outcome of the discussion; in doing so, however, I shall have to make certain qualifications, since some of my colleagues are either not present or differ in their opinion on the apportionment of time.

The defendants' counsel are of the opinion that only the conscientious sense of duty of each counsel can determine the form and length of the final defence pleas in this unusual trial. Their view does not affect the generally recognised right of the Tribunal, as part of its responsibility for controlling the proceedings, to prevent a possible misuse of the freedom of speech. They also believe that, in view of this fundamental consideration and in view of the usual practice of international courts, the Tribunal will understand and approve that the defendants' counsel voice their objections to a measure for restriction of the just right of freedom of speech, for a misuse on their part must not be taken as a foregone conclusion. This fundamental attitude is, of course, in accord with the readiness of the defence to comply with the directives and the wishes of the Tribunal as far as is reconcilable with a proper and right conception of the defence in each case. The individual defendants' counsel have been asked to make their own estimates of the probable duration of their final pleas. The result of these estimates shows that, despite the limitations counsel have imposed upon themselves, and with due respect to the wishes of the High Tribunal, a total duration of approximately twenty full days in court is required by the defence.

**THE PRESIDENT:** Dr. Nelte, the Tribunal asked defence counsel for an apportionment of the fourteen days between them.

**DR. NELTE:** I believe, Mr. President, my statement makes clear that it appears impossible to accept that limitation. If the Tribunal considers that the apportionment of fourteen full days is indisputable, then the entire defence will submit to that decision. But so far as I know, it will be quite impossible, under such circumstances, to obtain agreement among the defence counsel, and considerable danger therefore exists that counsel who make their pleas later will be handicapped in their defence by lack of adequate time.

**THE PRESIDENT:** Yes, I think the Tribunal probably fully understands that you think 14 days—you and your colleagues consider that 14 days is too short, but, as I say, what the Tribunal asked for was an apportionment of the time, and there is nothing in what you have said to indicate that you have made any apportionment at all, either of the fourteen days or of the twenty days which you propose.

**DR. NELTE:** The period of twenty days was arrived at when each defendant's counsel had stated the duration of his speech. It would, therefore, be perfectly possible to say that, if the Tribunal would approve the duration of twenty days, then we could agree on the apportionment of time for the individual speeches. But it is impracticable to apportion the time if the total number of days is only fourteen. You can rest assured, Mr. President, that we have all gone into the question conscientiously and that we have also decided on the manner in which individual subjects can be divided among defendants' counsel; but the total number of about twenty days appears to us,, without wanting to quote a maximum or minimum figure, to be absolutely essential for an apportionment. It is perfectly possible, Mr. President, that in the course of the speeches.

**THE PRESIDENT:** Dr. Nelte, as I have indicated to you, what the Tribunal wanted to know was the apportionment, and presumably you have some apportionment which adds up to the twenty days which you say is required, and the Tribunal would like, if you have such an apportionment, that you should let them see it, or if you have no such apportionment, then they would wish to hear from each individual counsel how long he thinks he is going to take. If you have got a list, it seems to the Tribunal that you could hand it in.

**DR. NELTE:** The figures are available and they will be handed to the Tribunal, but some of my colleagues have said that their estimates are only valid on the assumption that only a specific number of days is to be granted. That is the point of view to which I referred earlier as being slightly at variance with mine, but we all thought that the decision of the Tribunal was only a suggestion and not a maximum to be apportioned. I hope, Mr. President, that your words now are also to be understood in that way, and that the Tribunal will still consider whether the proposed period of fourteen days could not be extended to correspond with the time which we consider necessary.

**THE PRESIDENT:** What the Tribunal wants is an apportionment of the time as between the various counsel.

That is what it asks for, and that is what it wants; and I ask you to give it to us in writing now, or, alternatively, each one of you to state how long you anticipate you will take in your speech.

**DR. NELTE:** I think that I may speak on behalf of my colleagues and say that we shall submit our estimates to the Tribunal in writing.

**THE PRESIDENT:** Dr. Nelte, the Tribunal feels that it would like to have the apportionment now. It gave notice before, yesterday I think it was, that it was desirous to hear defendants' counsel upon the question of the apportionment this afternoon at 2 o'clock, and the Tribunal, therefore, would like to have that apportionment now.

**DR. NELTE:** In that case, I can only ask that the Tribunal hear each individual counsel, since naturally I cannot state from memory what each estimate was.

**THE PRESIDENT:** You could have had it written down, but if you have not got it written down, no doubt you cannot remember. But perhaps you had better give us what you would take.

**DR. NELTE:** I estimated seven hours. My colleague Horn, for Ribbentrop, just tells me he requires six hours.

**THE PRESIDENT:** We will take each counsel in turn, if you please.

Yes, Dr. Stahmer?

**DR. STAHMER:** Seven hours.

**THE PRESIDENT:** Dr. Sauter?

**DR. HORN:** May I, on behalf of Dr. Siemers and Dr. Kranzbuehler, ask to allot each of them eight hours?

**DR. SAUTER:** For the case of Funk, six hours, and for the case of von Schirach, six hours.

**DR. SERVATIUS:** For Sauckel, five hours.

**THE PRESIDENT:** Wait a minute.

I cannot write as quickly as all this. Who was it that Dr. Horn wished to represent? Siemers and who else? And how many hours was it?

**DR. HORN:** Dr. Siemers and Dr. Kranzbuehler, eight hours each.

**DR. SERVATIUS:** For Sauckel, five hours.

**DR. KAUFFMANN:** For Kaltenbrunner, approximately four to five hours.

**DR. MARX:** For Streicher, four hours.

**DR. SEIDL:** For Hess and Frank, eleven hours together.

**DR. PANNENBECKER:** For Frick, five hours. I remember from the list that Dr. Bergold wants three hours for Bormann. Dr. Bergold is not present, but I remember that the list said three hours.

**DR. DIX:** For Schacht, five hours.

**DR. EXNER:** For Jodl, five hours.

**DR. KUBUSCHOK:** For Papen, approximately five hours.

**DR. STEINBAUER:** For Dr. Seyss-Inquart, five hours.

**DR. FLAECHSNER:** For Speer, four hours.

**DR. VON LUEDINGHAUSEN (counsel for von Neurath):** For myself, Mr. President, eight hours. For Professor Jahrreiss, who, before the final pleas, will deal with a technical subject, four hours.

**THE PRESIDENT:** What will Professor Jahrreiss speak about?

**DR. VON LUEDINGHAUSEN:** About a subject approved by the Tribunal, namely the general question of International Law.

**DR. SEIDL:** The defence counsel for the defendant Rosenberg said that he would require eight hours.

**DR. FRITZ (counsel for Fritzsche):** Mr. President, I would ask the Tribunal to take into consideration that the case of Fritzsche has not yet been presented and that therefore I cannot give exact information; but I estimate approximately four hours.

**THE PRESIDENT:** Now, Dr. Nelte, the Tribunal would like to know first of all whether counsel proposes to write down and then read their speeches. Can you hear what I am saying?

**DR. NELTE:** Yes. As far as I have been informed, all defence counsel will write down their speeches before delivery. Whether they will actually read every word of the text, or whether they will read parts of it and submit other parts, is not yet certain.

**THE PRESIDENT:** Have they considered whether they will submit them for translation, because, as the Tribunal has already pointed out, it would be much more convenient for the members of the Tribunal who do not read German to have a translation before them. It would not only greatly assist the Tribunal, but the defendants themselves if they do that.

**DR. NELTE:** This question has not yet been settled. We discussed it, but have so far not come to a final conclusion. We think that the short time now available may perhaps make it impossible to translate the manuscripts into all four languages.

**THE PRESIDENT:** The defendants' counsel, of course, understand that the speeches, if they are submitted for translation, will not be communicated to anybody until they are actually made. So they will not be given beforehand either to the Tribunal or the prosecution or anything of that sort, so that the speeches will remain entirely private until they are made. And the second thing is that, of course, the delivery of a great number of the speeches of counsel will be delayed by the counsel who precede them and, therefore, there will be very considerable time during either the 14 days or some longer period, if such a longer period is given, which will enable the speeches to be translated, and defence counsel will appreciate that if their speeches are written down they can tell exactly how long they will take to deliver, or almost exactly. And there is one other thing I want to bring to their attention.

There are 20 or 21 defendants, and naturally, there are a variety of subjects which are common to them all, and there ought to be, therefore, an opportunity, so it appears to the Tribunal, for counsel to divide up the subjects to some extent between them and not each one to deal with subjects which have been dealt with already, any more than they ought to have been dealt with in evidence over and over again, and I do not know whether counsel for defence have fully considered that in making this estimate of the time they laid before us.

Anyway, the Tribunal hopes that they will address their minds to these three matters: first of all, as to whether they can submit their speeches for translation in order to help the Tribunal; secondly, whether they will be able, when they have got their speeches written down, to assess the time accurately; and thirdly, whether they cannot apportion the subjects to some extent among themselves so that we shall not have to listen to the same subjects over and over again.

I do not know whether the prosecution would wish to say anything. The Tribunal has said, I think, in the order which we made with reference to this question of limitation of time, that they anticipated that the prosecution would take only three days. Perhaps it would be convenient to hear from the prosecution whether that is an accurate estimate.

**SIR DAVID MAXWELL FYFE:** Yes, my Lord, the prosecution do not ask for any more than the three days. It might conceivably be a little less, but we do not ask for any more than the three days.

**MR. JUSTICE JACKSON:** I should like, your Honour, to call your attention to this. I hope it is not expected that we will mimeograph, and run off on our mimeograph machines, 20 days of speeches or anything of that sort. We simply cannot be put under that kind of a burden. A citizen of the United States is expected to argue his case in the highest court of the land in one hour, and counsel's own clients here have openly scoffed at the amount of time that has been asked.

This is not a sensible amount of time to give to these cases, and I must protest against being expected to mimeograph 20 days of speeches. It really is not possible.

**THE PRESIDENT:** The Tribunal would like to know whether the prosecution intend to let them have copies of their speeches at the time that they are delivered.

**SIR DAVID MAXWELL FYFE:** As far as the closing speech of the Attorney General is concerned, we certainly did expect and do hope to give the Tribunal copies of the speech.

**THE PRESIDENT:** And translations?

**SIR DAVID MAXWELL FYFE:** Yes, that will be done. My Lord, with reference to this, it was Dr. Nelte who said that it would take a long time to translate. I know, as far as translating into English is concerned, we had the problem of several days of speeches the other day, and that was done by our own translators in one day. So I hope that perhaps Dr. Nelte has been a little pessimistic about that side of the problem.

**THE PRESIDENT:** The Tribunal will consider the matter.

Now, the Tribunal will go on with the cross-examination.

**MR. JUSTICE JACKSON:** I think perhaps, your Honour, the photographs in evidence are a little unintelligible if the record of the description of them is not given. I shall read it briefly. It is a description of torture cabinets which were used in the foreign workers' camp in the grounds of No. 4 Armour Shop, and of those of the dirty neglected Russian camp. I quote:

"Photograph 'A' shows an iron cupboard which was specially manufactured by the firm of Krupp to torture Russian civilian workers to an extent that cannot possibly be described by words. Men and women were often locked into a compartment of the cupboard, in which hardly any man could stand up for long periods. The measurements of this compartment are, height 1.52 metres, breadth and depth 40 to 50 centimetres each. Frequently even two people were kicked and pressed into one compartment. The Russian—"

I will not read the rest of that.

"Photograph 'B' shows the same cupboard as it looks when it is locked. Photograph 'C' shows the cupboard open.

In photograph 'D' we see the camp that was selected by the Krupp Directorate to serve as living-quarters for the Russian civilian workers. The individual rooms were 2 to 21 metres wide, 5 metres long, and 2 metres high. In each room up to 16 persons were accommodated in double-tier beds."

I think that covers it.

**THE PRESIDENT:** Mr. Justice Jackson, one moment. I think you ought to read the last three lines of the second paragraph, beginning, "At the top of the cupboard."

**MR. JUSTICE JACKSON:** Oh, yes, I am sorry.

"At the top of the cupboard, there are a few sieve-like air holes through which cold water was poured on the unfortunate victims during the ice-cold winter."

**THE PRESIDENT:** I think you should read the last three lines of the penultimate paragraph in view of what the defendant said about the evidence.

**MR. JUSTICE JACKSON:** "We are enclosing two letters which Camp Commandant Lowenkamp had smuggled out of prison in order to induce the undersigned Hoffer to give evidence favourable to him."

And perhaps I should read the last:

"The undersigned, Dahn,"—one of the signers—"personally saw how three Russian civilian workers were locked into the cupboard, two in one compartment, after they had first been beaten on New Year's night, 1945. Two of the Russians had to stay the whole of New Year's night locked into the cupboard, and cold water was poured on them as well."

I may say to the Tribunal that we have upwards of a hundred different statements and depositions relating to the investigation of this camp. I am not suggesting offering them, because I think they would be cumulative, and I shall be satisfied with one more, Document 313-D, which will become Exhibit USA 901, which is a statement by a doctor.

**THE PRESIDENT:** Mr Justice Jackson, was this camp that you are referring to a concentration camp?

**MR. JUSTICE JACKSON:** Well, it was, as I understand it, a prisoner-of-war and a labour camp. There were labour camps and prisoner-of-war camps at Essen. I had not understood that it was a concentration camp, but I admit the distinction is a little thin at times.

This document reads:

"I, the undersigned, Dr. Apolinary Gotowicki, a doctor in the Polish Army, was taken prisoner by the Germans on 3rd January, 1941, and remained as such until the entry of the Americans. I gave medical attention to the Russian, Polish and French prisoners of war who were forced to work in various places of Krupp's factories. I personally visited the Russian P.O.W. camp in the Raumstrasse in Essen, which contained about 1,800 men. There was a big hall in the camp which could accommodate about 200 men comfortably in which 300 to 400 men were crowded together in such a manner that proper medical treatment was not possible. The floor was cement and the palliasses on which the people slept were full of lice and bugs. Even on cold days the room was never heated, and it seemed to me as a doctor monstrous that human beings, should be forced to live in such conditions. It was impossible to keep the place clean because of the overcrowding of these men who had hardly room to move about normally. Every day at least ten people were brought to me whose bodies were covered with bruises on account of the continual beatings with rubber tubes, steel switches or sticks.

The people were often writhing with agony and it was impossible for me to give them even a little medical aid. In spite of the fact that I protested, made complaints and petitions, it was impossible for me to protect the people or see that they got a day off from work. It was hard for me to have to watch such suffering people being forced to do heavy work. I visited personally, at risk of danger to myself, gentlemen of the Krupp Administration as well as gentlemen from the Krupp Directorate to try to get help. It was strictly forbidden, as the camp was under the direction of the SS and Gestapo, and according to well-known directives, I had to keep silent, otherwise I could have been sent to a concentration camp. I have brought my own bread innumerable times to the camp in order to give it to the prisoners as far as it was possible, although bread was very scarce for me. From the beginning of 1941 conditions did not get better but worse. The food consisted of a watery soup which was dirty and sandy, and often the prisoners of war had to eat cabbage which was bad and stank. I saw people daily who, on account of hunger or ill-treatment, were slowly dying. Dead people often lay for two or three days on the beds until their bodies stank so badly that prisoners took them outside and buried them somewhere. The dishes out of which they ate were also used as toilets because they were too tired or too weak from hunger to get up and go outside. At 3 o'clock, they were wakened. The same dishes were then used to wash in and later for eating out of. This matter was generally known. In spite of this it was impossible for me to get even elementary help or facilities for getting rid of epidemics or for treating cases of illnesses or starvation. There was no proper medical aid for the prisoners. I never received any medical supplies myself. In 1941 I alone had to look after these people, but it is quite understandable that it was impossible for me, as the only doctor, to look after all of these people, and apart from that I had scarcely any medical supplies. I could not think what to do with the large numbers who came to me daily crying and complaining. I myself often collapsed and, in spite of this, I had to take everything upon myself and watch people perish and die. A report was never made as to how the prisoners of war died.

I have seen with my own eyes the prisoners coming back from Krupp's and how they collapsed on the march and had to be wheeled back on barrows or carried by their comrades. It was in such a manner that the people came back to the camp. The work which they had to perform was very heavy and dangerous and many cases happened where people had cut their fingers, hands or legs. These accidents were very serious and the people came to me and asked for medical help. But it was not even possible for me to keep them from work for a day or two, although I had been to the Krupp directorate and asked for permission to do so. At the end of 1941, two people died daily, and in 1942 the deaths increased to three and four. I was under Dr. May and I was often successful in getting him to come to the camp to see the terrible conditions and listen to the complaints, but it was not possible for him to get medical aid from the Medical Department of the Wehrmacht or Krupp's, or to get better conditions, treatment or food.

I was a witness during a conversation with some Russian women who told me personally that they were employed in Krupp's factory and that they were beaten daily in the most bestial manner. The food consisted of watery soup which was dirty and unfit for consumption; and its terrible smell could be noticed from a distance. The clothing of these people was ragged and torn and on their feet they had rags and wooden shoes. Their treatment, as far as I could make out, was the same as that of the prisoners of war.

Beating was the order of the day. The conditions lasted for years, from the very beginning until the day the American troops entered. The people lived under great fear and it was dangerous for them to describe to anyone anywhere the conditions which existed in their camps. The position was such that any discovered doing so, could be murdered with impunity by members of the guards, the SS or Gestapo. It was possible for me as a doctor to talk to these people; they trusted me and knew that I was a Pole, and would never betray them to anyone.

(Signed) Dr. Apolinary Gotowicki."

**BY MR. JUSTICE JACKSON:**

Q. Now, you have explained that some of these conditions were due, in your judgement, to the fact that bombing took place and the billets of the prisoners and workers were destroyed.

A. That is true, but it does not mean that such conditions, if they really existed, could be considered as general.

Q. I'm sorry. Would you please repeat your answer

A. That is true, but I should like to point out that the conditions described in this affidavit cannot be considered as general; apart from that, I do not believe that this description is correct, but I cannot speak about these things since you, will not expect me to be intimately acquainted with what happened in the camps of the Krupp plant.

Q. Well, in the first place, was it considered proper by you to billet forced workers and prisoners of war so close to military targets as these prisoners were?

A. I would rather not tell you here things which every German has at heart. Military targets! The distinction between military and other targets no longer existed, and the camps, therefore, could not be near military targets.

Q. You would not consider the Krupp plants proper targets?

A. The camps were not in the Krupp works, they were near the city of Essen. On principle, we did not construct camps near the works which we expected would be bombed; and we did not want the camps to be destroyed.

Q. Did you notice that one of the photographs in evidence shows the plant—the camp directly against the works?

A. May I see it again, please?

*(The photograph was shown to the defendant.)*

A. Some large factory is recognizable in the background of this photograph, but that does not alter my statement, that in almost all cases we constructed the camps outside the cities. I do not know why this particular instance is different, and I cannot even say whether this is a camp or just a barracks for changing clothes, or anything which had to be near the camp. I still believe that these cupboards were cupboards for clothes, and this is one of the many barracks which were necessary so that the workers could change clothes before and after their work. Any expert in Germany can tell you that these are wardrobes and not some special cupboards, because they are mass-produced articles; this is also confirmed by the fact that there are air vents at the top, for every wardrobe has these ventilation holes at the top and bottom.

Q. As Production Minister, you were vitally interested in reducing the sickness rate among workers, were you not?

A. I was interested in a high output of work, that is obvious; and in addition, in special cases ...

Q. Well, special cases—part of production is in all cases, is it not, dependent upon the health of your labour force, and is it not a fact, as a man engaged in production, that the two greatest problems in manpower and production are the health of the workers and rapid turnover, and that those factors influence production?

A. These two factors troubled us, but not as extensively as your words might suggest. Cases of sickness which, in my opinion, were normal, accounted for a very small percentage of loss in production. However, propaganda pamphlets dropped from aircraft were telling the workers to feign illness, and detailed instructions were given to them on how to do it. And to prevent that, the authorities concerned introduced certain measures which I considered proper.

Q. What were those measures?

A. I cannot tell you in detail, because I myself did not institute these penalties, nor did I have the power to do so; but as far as I know, they were ordered by the Plenipotentiary for Manpower Mobilization in collaboration with the police or State authorities; but the jurisdiction in this connection was with the authorities responsible for legal action.

Q. Now, if you did not know what they were, how can you tell us that you approved of them? We always get to this blank wall that nobody knew what was being done. You knew that they were at least penalties of great severity, did you not?

A. When I say that I approved, I am only expressing my wish not to dodge my responsibility in this respect. But you must understand that a minister of production, particularly in view of the air attacks, had a tremendous task before him, and that I could only take care of matters outside my own field if some particularly important factor forced me to do so. Otherwise, I was glad if I could finish my own work, and, after all, my task was by no means a small one.

I think that if during the German air attacks on England you had asked the British Minister of Munitions whether he shared the worries of the Minister of Labour and whether he was dealing with them, then he would with justification have told you that he had something else to do at that time, that he had to keep up his production and that he expected the Minister of Labour to manage affairs in his sector; and no one would have raised a direct accusation against the British Minister of Munitions on that account.

Q. Well, production was your enterprise, and do you mean to tell me that you did not have any records or reports on the condition of the workers who were engaged in production, which would tell you if there was anything wrong in the sick rate or anything wrong in the general conditions of labour?

A. What I knew is contained in the reports of meetings of the Central Planning Board; there you will get a picture of what I was told. There were many other meetings but I cannot remember in detail all I knew, because there were many things outside my sphere of activity. Naturally, it is a matter of course that anyone closely concerned with the affairs of State will also hear of matters not immediately connected with his own sphere, such as of unsatisfactory conditions existing in other sectors; but one not having to deal with these matters later on does not remember about them in detail. You cannot expect that of me. But if you have any particular matter in mind I shall be glad to give you information on it if I can.

Q. All right; assume that these conditions had been called to your attention and that they existed. With whom would you have taken it up to have them corrected? What officer of the Government?

A. Normally, a minister would send a document to the Government authorities responsible for such conditions. I must claim for myself that when I heard of such deficiencies, I tried to remedy them by establishing direct contact with the authority responsible, in some cases the German Labour Front, where I had a liaison officer, or in other cases my letter was transmitted to Sauckel through my Office of Manpower Deployment. My practice in this respect was that, if I did not receive a reply, I considered the matter settled; for I could not in such a case pursue the matter further and make additional inquiries whether it had been dealt with or not.

Q. With Krupp's, then, you would not have taken it up? You think they had no responsibility for these conditions?

A. During visits to Krupp's discussions certainly took place on the conditions which generally existed for workers after air attacks; this was a matter of great worry for us, particularly with regard to Krupp's. I cannot remember ever being told that foreign workers or prisoners of war employed at the Krupp factories were in a particularly bad condition. Temporarily they all lived under very primitive conditions; German workers lived in cellars during those days, and six or eight people were often quartered in a small cellar room.

Q. In a statement some time ago you said you had a certain responsibility as a minister of the Government for the conditions. I should like you to explain what responsibility you referred to when you say you assume a responsibility as a member of the Government.

A. Do you mean the declaration I made yesterday that I—

Q. Your common responsibility, what do you mean by your common responsibility, along with others?

**A.** Oh, yes. In my opinion, a State functionary has two types of responsibility. One is the responsibility for his own sector and for that, of course, he is fully responsible. But above that, I think that in decisive matters there is and must be, among the leaders, a joint responsibility, for who is to take responsibility for general developments if not the close associates of the head of State?

This joint responsibility, however, can only be applied to fundamental matters, it cannot be applied to details connected with other ministries or other responsible departments, for otherwise the entire discipline in the life of the State would be quite confused, and no one would ever know who is individually responsible in a particular sphere. This individual responsibility in one's own sphere must, at all events, be kept clear and distinct.

**Q.** Well, your point is, I take it, that you as a member of the Government, and a leader during this period of time, acknowledge a responsibility for its broad policies, but not for all the details that occurred in their execution. Is that a fair statement of your position?

**A.** Yes, indeed.

**MR. JUSTICE JACKSON:** I think that concludes the cross-examination.

**THE PRESIDENT:** Do any of the other prosecutors wish to cross-examine?

**BY GENERAL RAGINSKY:**

**Q.** Defendant Speer, when you told your life story to the Tribunal and answered the questions of Justice Jackson, I think you omitted some substantial matters. I would like to ask you a few questions.

**A.** I left out such points as I did not wish to contest, since they are, at any rate, contained here in the documents; I would have a tremendous task if I were to go into all these points in detail.

**Q.** I would like to recall these points, and I would like to ask you to answer them briefly.

Did I understand you correctly that, in addition to your ministerial position, you were also the personal architect of Hitler after the death of Professor Todt? Did you hold this position?

**A.** Yes.

**Q.** Were you General Inspector of Roads?

**A.** Only after Dr. Todt's death.

**Q.** Yes, of course. Were you General Inspector of Waterpower and Power Plants?

**A.** Yes.

**Q.** General Plenipotentiary for Building in the Central Administration of the Four-Year Plan?

**A.** Yes.

**Q.** Director of the Todt Organisation?

**A.** Yes.

**Q.** You were associated with the technological department of the National Socialist Party? You were the leader of the Union of National Socialist Technicians?

A. Yes.

Q. And in addition to these posts, did you have any other leading positions?

A. Oh, I had ten or twelve positions. I cannot give you a list of them all now.

Q. Were you not one of the leaders of the Reich League of Culture?

A. No, no, that is not correct. I cannot tell you for certain, but I think I was a senator or something like that.

Q. Were you a member of the Committee of the Academy of Culture? Were you a member of the Committee of the Academy of Arts?

A. Yes, that also.

Q. I shall not mention the other posts you have held, in order to shorten the cross-examination. Do you remember your statements during the interrogation by Colonel Rosenblith on 14th November, 1945?

A. No, not in detail.

Q. I will remind you of one question, and will you tell me whether or not your answer was put down correctly. It was the question whether you acknowledged that in his book 'Mein Kampf' Hitler stated bluntly his aggressive plans for the countries of the East and West and, in particular, for the Soviet Union. You answered, "Yes, I acknowledge it." Do you remember that?

A. Yes, that is perfectly possible.

Q. And do you confirm that now?

A. No.

Q. You do not confirm that now?

A. I must explain that at the time I was ashamed to say that I had not read the whole of 'Mein Kampf'. I thought that would sound rather absurd.

Q. All right, we shall not waste time. You were ashamed to admit that, or are you ashamed now? Let us go on to another question.

A. Yes, I cheated at that time.

Q. You cheated at that time; maybe you are cheating now?

A. No.

Q. It does not matter. You worked on the staff of Hess, did you not?

A. Yes.

Q. You worked with Ley?

A. Yes, in the Labour Front.

Q. Yes, the German Labour Front. You had a high rank in the Nazi Party, as you stated here today; you said that today in Court, did you not?

A. No, it was not a high rank; it did not in any way correspond to the position which I occupied in the State.

Yesterday, in Court, you said that you were one of Hitler's close friends. You now want to say that so far as the plans and intentions of Hitler were concerned, you only learned about them from the book 'Mein Kampf'?

A. I can give you an explanation of this. I was in close contact with Hitler, and I heard his personal views; these views of his did not lead one to the conclusion that he had any plans of the sort which have been revealed in the documents here, and I was particularly relieved in 1939 when the non-aggression pact with Russia was signed. After all, your diplomats too must have read 'Mein Kampf'; nevertheless, they signed the non-aggression pact. And they were certainly more intelligent than I am—I mean in political matters.

**Q.** I do not think we should now examine who read 'Mein Kampf' and who did not; that is irrelevant.

So you contend that you did not know anything about Hitler's plans?

**A.** Yes.

**Q.** All right, please tell us this. As chief of the Main Office of Technology of the Nazi Party, what were your tasks?

**A.** In the Party?

**Q.** You probably know it better than I, since you were the head of that office.

**A.** I only took over that task or that office in 1942; and in 1942, during the war, this Main Office of Technology of the NSDAP had no task to perform. I took the officials who were in that department into my ministry, and there they worked as State functionaries. Detailed information on this is available in the written testimony of the witness Sauer, and that is contained in my document book.

**Q.** What is contained in the testimony of the witness Sauer?

**A.** The document book also contains a decree which I issued at the end of 1942, and in which I ordered the transfer of these tasks to the State.

**Q.** But you did not answer my question. In order to clarify this, I will read what Sauer said on this point, and you will please state whether it is correct or not.

On the tasks of the Main Office of Technology of the Party, Sauer said:
"The task of the Main Office of Technology of the Party was the unified direction of technical organisations of German engineers in scientific, professional and political fields."

It was a political organisation, was it not?

**A.** No, it was chiefly a technical organisation.

**Q.** A technical organisation which occupied itself with political questions.

In the document book which has been presented and partly quoted by your defence counsel, there are indications of the tasks of the Main Office of Technology. From one document it is obvious that the engineers were to be taught the National Socialist ideology, and that this organisation was also a political one, and not only a technical one.

**A.** Where does it say so? May I have the document?

**Q.** Of course, the document book of the defence. I shall hand it to you, if you want to have it. You will see there the structure of the Kreis leadership.

**A.** The translation said it was from my document book, but it is not from my document book. It is from the organisational handbook of the NSDAP, and—

**Q.** That is the structure of the Kreis leadership of the NSDAP. That is Document 1893-PS, which has been presented by your defence counsel.

A. Yes, but in my document book it says that the Main Office of Technology in the NSDAP did not have a political task. This is an extract from the organisational handbook of the NSDAP, and I would not have included it in my document book if I had not had the precise impression that it demonstrates particularly well that, in contrast to all other agencies, the Main Office of Technology had a non-political task within the Party.

Q. Was the National Socialist Union of German Technicians a political organisation?

A. By no means.

Q. By no means? Tell me, please, did not the leaders of this union have to be members of the Nazi Party?

A. They did not have to be members, as far as I know. I never paid any attention to whether they were members or not.

THE PRESIDENT: Shall we adjourn now?

*(A recess was taken.)*

**BY GENERAL RAGINSKY:**

Q. You were one of the leaders of the Central Planning Board. Was the search for new sources of raw materials part of your programme?

A. I do not understand the meaning of the question?

Q. Was the search for new sources of raw materials part of the programme of the Central Planning Board?

A. No, not actually.

Q. All right. I shall read to you from your document book. Will you listen, please? Otherwise, we shall lose too much time with you. This is the order dated 22nd April, 1942, signed by Goering; it is in your document book in the first volume, Page 14 of the Russian text and Page 17 of the English text. It states:

> "With a view to assuring priority of armaments as ordered by the Fuehrer, and to embrace all the demands which are thereby made on the total economy during the war, and in order to bring about an adjustment between a secure food supply and the raw material and manufacturing facilities in the economy, I order:
>
> In connection with the Four-Year Plan a Central Planning Board shall be organised."

Farther on it mentions who the members of the Central Planning Board were. In the third part the tasks of the Central Planning Board are enumerated. I shall read that into the record:

> "Point C: The distribution of existing raw materials, especially iron and metals, among the places requiring them.
>
> Point B: The decision as to the creation of new plants for production of raw material or enlargement of the plants existing."

This is written in your document book.

A. Well, there is a difference. I was told "sources of raw materials"; I understand "sources of raw materials" to mean ore, for example, or coal beds. What this paragraph says is the "creation of new means of producing raw materials"; that means the building of a factory for steel production, for instance, or an aluminium factory.

I myself said that an expanding supply of raw materials for industry was important, and that I took over this task.

Q. Yes. Of course, it is rather difficult to deny it, since it is written here in the document.

A. No. These are technical expressions, and it may be that since they were retranslated into German, they were rendered inaccurately. The meaning of the paragraph is actually quite clear, and every expert can confirm it. It is the same activity—

Q. I understand the sense. Tell us, when you enumerated the members of the Central Planning Board, was it just accidental that you did not name Funk as a member of that board?

A. No. Actually Funk worked hardly at all on the Planning Board, and therefore I did not list him. He became a member officially only in September, 1943, but even after that time he took part in only one or two meetings, so that his activity was very slight.

Q. I did not ask you about his activity; I am asking you whether Funk was a member of the Central Planning Board.

A. Yes, from September, 1943.

Q. And it was purely through accident that you did not name him? Or did you have any particular purpose in not naming him?

A. I actually named only the three members who were on the Central Planning Board from the very beginning, since its foundation, because I was speaking only of the foundation of the Board. That explains the error. I did not want to occupy the Tribunal's time with something which was generally known.

Q. All right. You have maintained here that you were concerned only with peaceful construction, and that, as far as the appointment to the post of Minister of Armaments was concerned, you accepted it without any particular desire, and you even had your qualms about it. Do you still maintain the same view?

A. May I have the question repeated?

Q. If you please. You stated here several times, in replying to the questions of your defence counsel, that you accepted the post of Minister of Armaments without any special desire for it, and that you had your qualms about it; and you did not particularly care to accept it. Do you still maintain that now?

A. Yes.

Q. I shall remind you of what you said to the representatives of industry in the Rheno-Westphalian district. Do you remember what you said to them? I shall quote one paragraph from your speech. You said:

"In the spring of 1942, without hesitation I accepted the demands propounded by Hitler as a programme which must be fulfilled, which I am fulfilling now, and which will be fulfilled."

Did you say that?

**A.** Yes. But this has nothing to do with your statement. The demands which are meant here are demands for an increase in military armaments. Those are the demands I accepted. But, in addition, it was a matter of course that I immediately accepted the appointment as Armament Minister without any qualms. I have never denied that. I only said that I would rather be an architect than an armament minister, which has probably been misunderstood.

**Q.** And now we shall listen to what you said to the Gauleiter in your speech in Munich:

"I gave up all my peace-time activities, including my actual profession (architecture), to dedicate myself without reservations to the war task.
The Fuehrer expects that of all of us."

Is this the sort of thing which you are saying now?

**A.** Yes, I believe that was the attitude in your country, too.

**Q.** I am not asking you about our country. We are now talking about your country. I am asking you whether you now affirm before the Tribunal what you then said to the Gauleiter.

**A.** Yes. I only wanted to explain this to you, because apparently you do not appreciate why in time of war one should accept the post of Armament Minister. If the need arises, that is a matter of course, and I cannot understand why you do not appreciate that and why you want to reproach me for it.

**Q.** I understand you perfectly.

**A.** Good.

**Q.** When you made your speech before the Gauleiter, you did not, of course, think that you would be held responsible before the International Military Tribunal for the words which you then spoke.

**A.** Excuse me; one moment, please. I want to say something else in answer to your question. That this is my view, and that I think it quite proper, is evident from the fact that you quoted it from my document book, otherwise I would not have included it in my own document book. I hope you consider me sufficiently intelligent to be capable of making up my document book correctly.

**Q.** Quite so, quite so. But these documents are not only in your possession, they are also in the possession of the prosecution. However, we shall pass on to the next question.

In response to the questions of your defence counsel, you testified about the principles and tasks of your ministry. In connection with this, I should like to ask you a few questions. Do you remember the contents of your article entitled "Increase of Production," which was published in Das Reich on 19th April; 1942?

You will be given a copy of this article in a second.

**GENERAL RAGINSKY:** Mr. President, I submit this article as Exhibit USSR 479.

**BY GENERAL RAGINSKY:**

**Q.** I shall remind you briefly of what you wrote about the principles of your ministry.

"One thing, however, will be necessary, and that is energetic action, including the most severe punishment, in cases of offences committed against the interests of the State ... severe prison sentences or death ... The war must be won."

Did you write this?

Now, I shall remind you of another article of yours. You will be given a copy of it.

A. Just a moment. May I ask you to read the whole paragraph? You left out a few sentences in the middle.

Q. Yes, yes, I omitted something, but I shall ask you some questions on that later.

A. But it shows for what offences prison and death sentences were provided. That is surely relevant. I believe you should quote the passage fully, otherwise a wrong impression is given.

Q. You will give your comments or explanations to the questions afterwards. But meanwhile listen to the questions as I put them to you. If you want to give your explanation with regard to this, you are entitled to do so later.

**THE PRESIDENT:** No, no, General Raginsky, the Tribunal would prefer to have the comments now.

**GENERAL RAGINSKY:** Mr. President, if the defendant wishes to give an explanation with regard to this article, I shall let him do so, of course.

**THE WITNESS:** The text which you omitted reads as follows:

"At my suggestion, the Fuehrer ordered that those heads of concerns and employees, and also those officials and officers who attempt to secure material or labour by giving inaccurate information will receive severe prison sentences or the death sentence."

The reasons for this were as follows: When I took over my office, the demands addressed to the central department were increased by the intermediate departments handling the demands. Each of the many intermediate departments added something of its own, so that the demands reaching me were quite enormous and incredible, and made planning quite impossible.

For example, on account of these additions, the demands which I received for copper in one year amounted to more than the whole world's yearly production of copper. And in order to prevent this and obtain accurate indications, I issued an order to deter these officials, officers, heads of concerns, and employees from giving false figures.

In my Gauleiter speech I spoke of this, and I said the result of this decree would surely be that no one would any longer dare to forward false information and demands to higher offices, and that was the purpose of the decree; I said that it would never be necessary to put the decree into effect, since I did not believe that the heads of concerns, employees, officials and officers would, in view of such a severe penalty, have enough boldness to continue supplying such false statements.

In fact, no penalty was ever imposed, but the result of the decree was that demands for materials and workers reaching me decreased considerably.

**BY GENERAL RAGINSKY:**

Q. You maintained that your obligations and duties as a Minister included only production. Did I understand you correctly?

A. Yes, armaments and war production.

Q. And the supply of industry with raw materials, was not that included in your duties?

A. No, that was my task from September, 1943, onwards, when I took over the whole of production. That is true, then I was in charge of the whole of production, from raw materials to the finished products.

Q. In the book Germany at War, which was published in November, 1943—you will be given this volume now—and I submit this document to the Tribunal as Exhibit USSR 480—in this book it says:

"On the basis of the Fuehrer decree of 2nd September, 1943, relative to the concentration of war economy, and of the decree of the Reichsmarschall of the Greater German Reich and the Plenipotentiary of the Four-Year Plan for Central Planning of 4th September, 1943, Reich Minister Speer will now direct the entire war economic production in his capacity as Reich Minister for Armaments and War Production. He alone is competent and responsible for guiding, directing, and controlling the industrial war economy."

Is this correct? I ask you to answer briefly, is it correct or not?

A. This is expressed rather unprofessionally, because the term "industrial war economy" does not quite cover the concept "armament and war production." This was not drawn up by an expert but otherwise it agrees with what I have testified. I said that war production embraced the whole of production.

Q. Yes, but after September, 1943, you were responsible not only for war industry but also for the whole war economy as well, and those are two different things.

A. No, that is the mistake. It says here "industrial war economy," which means something like production, war economy or production in trade and industry, with that qualification; and when it says earlier "the entire economic production," the person who wrote this also meant production. But the concept—

Q. You mentioned here already that having accepted the post of Minister in 1942, you inherited a great and heavy task. Tell us briefly, please, what was the situation with regard to essential raw materials and, in particular, with regard to metals used in the war industry?

**THE PRESIDENT:** Well, General Raginsky, is it necessary for us to go into details? Is it not obvious that a man who was controlling many millions of workers had a large task? What is this directed to?

**GENERAL RAGINSKY:** Mr. President, the question is preparatory, it leads to another question and inasmuch as it is connected—

**THE PRESIDENT:** Yes, but what is the ultimate object of the cross-examination? You say it is leading to something else. What is it leading to?

**GENERAL RAGINSKY:** The object is to prove that the defendant Speer participated in the economic plundering and looting of occupied territories.

**THE PRESIDENT:** Yes, then ask him directly about that.

**GENERAL RAGINSKY:** I am just coming to that now.

**BY GENERAL RAGINSKY:**

Do you acknowledge the fact that you participated in economic plundering of occupied territories?

**A.** I participated in the economic exploitation of the occupied countries, yes; but I do not believe the term "plundering" is very clearly defined. I do not know what is meant by "plundering of an occupied territory."

**Q.** To make up the deficit of essential raw materials, did you not export metals for the war industry from Belgium, France and other occupied territories?

**A.** Of course I did not export them myself, but certainly I participated in some way. I was not responsible for it, but certainly I urged strongly that we should obtain as much metal from there as possible.

**Q.** I am satisfied with your answer and the Tribunal will draw its conclusions.

Do you remember Hitler's order about concentration of war economy, published on 2nd September? You will be given a copy of this order at once. This document is being submitted as Exhibit USSR 482. I do not intend to read all of this as it will take too much time, but I would like to read into the record a few paragraphs of this order, which begins:

> "Taking into consideration the stricter mobilization and uniform commitment of all economic forces required by the exigencies of war, I order the following":

Paragraph 2:

> "The powers of the Reich Minister of Economics in the sphere of raw materials and production in industry and trade are given to the Reich Minister for Armament and Munitions. The Reich Minister for Armament and Munitions, in view of the extended scope of his tasks, will be known as Reich Minister for Armament and War Production."

Did you see this decree?

**A.** Yes, I know it.

**Q.** Will you, in connection with this order, tell us briefly and concisely how the functions between you and Funk were divided?

**A.** Well, that is shown in the text. I was in charge of all production, from raw materials to the final product, and Funk was in charge of all general economic questions, primarily the questions of financial transactions, securities, commerce, foreign trade, and so forth. This, however, is not exhaustive, but broadly describes the division.

**Q.** That answer satisfies me. In connection with this order, did you receive plenipotentiary powers for the regulation of exchanging of goods and goods traffic?

**A.** I do not quite understand what you mean.

**Q.** All right. So as not to lose any time, you will be given a document signed by you and Funk, and dated 6th September, 1943. This document I present to the Tribunal as Exhibit USSR 483. I shall read the first sentence of the first paragraph:

"In so far as existing laws prescribe the authority of the Reich Minister of Economics in the regulation of goods traffic, this authority for the period of the war will be exercised by the Minister for Armament and War Production."

In this way your role in the war effort of Germany, your role as head of the German war economy during the period of the war, was much wider in scope than that which you have described here to the Tribunal, is not that so?

A. No, I did not try to picture the situation differently, and I said that in time of war the Armament Minister holds the most important position of all in the Reich; and that everyone has to work for him. I do not believe that I could have given a more comprehensive description of my task. This matter of the goods traffic is of quite subordinate significance. I cannot even say what is meant here by "goods traffic." It is a technical term which I do not quite understand.

Q. Yes, but this document is signed by you and now you do not know exactly what is meant by it. You signed it together with Funk.

A. Of course.

Q. Tell us, how was contact between your Ministry and the German Labour Front maintained, and was there co-operation between the two organisations?

A. There was a liaison man between the German Labour Front and my office, just as between all other important offices in the Reich.

Q. Will you not name that officer?

A. It was my witness Hupfauer who later was chief of the central office under me.

Q. You testified that a number of concerns, engaged in producing textiles and processing of aluminium and lumber, etc., should not be included in the list of war economy concerns. Did I understand you correctly? Did you maintain that?

A. No, that is a mistake. That must have been wrongly translated.

Q. What is the correct interpretation?

A. I think there are two mistakes here in the translation. In the first place, I did not speak of war economy in my testimony, but I used the term "armament." I said that this term "armament" included textile concerns and wood and leather processing concerns. But armament and war economy are two entirely different terms.

Q. And the textile industry is wholly excluded from the term "armament"?

A. I said that various textile concerns were incorporated in armament industry, although they did not produce armaments in the strict sense of the word.

Q. Did not the textile industry manufacture parachute equipment for the Air Force?

A. Yes, but if you consult the Geneva Prisoner-of-War Agreement you will see that it is not forbidden to manufacture that ... for prisoners of war to manufacture that. I have the text here, I can read it to you.

Q. And do you want us seriously to accept that powder can be manufactured without cellulose, and are you for that reason narrowing down the conceptions of war industry and war production?

A. No, you have misunderstood me completely. I wanted to make the concept "armament industry" as broad as possible in order to prove that this modern conception of armament industry is something entirely different from the industries producing armaments in the sense of the Geneva Convention.

Q, All right. You spoke of your objection to using foreign workers, and your reasons for this objection were indicated by Schmelter in his testimony. He was in charge of labour in your Ministry. This testimony was presented by your defence counsel; I shall read only one paragraph and will you please confirm whether it is correct or not:

> "In so far as he—Speer—repeatedly mentioned to us that utilisation of foreign workers would create great difficulties for the Reich with regard to the food supply for these workers ..."

Were these the reasons for your objection?

A. The translation must be incorrect here. I know exactly how the text reads and what the sense of this statement is. The sense is entirely correct. The question was this: If we brought new workers to Germany we had first of all to make available to them the basic calories necessary to sustain adequately a human being. But the German labourers still working in Germany had to receive these basic calories in any case. Therefore, food was saved if I employed German workers in Germany, and the additional calories for persons doing heavy work and working long hours could again have been increased. That was the sense of Schmelter's statement.

Q. Defendant Speer, you digressed from a direct answer to my question—

A. I would gladly—

Q. You are now going into details which are of no interest to me. I asked you whether this particular passage which I read from the testimony of Schmelter was correct or not.

A. No, it was falsely translated. I should like to have the original in German.

Q. The original is in your document book and you can read it. I will pass to the next question.

A. Yes, but it is necessary to show it to me now. In cross-examination by the Soviet prosecutor I do not have to take my document book to the stand with me.

**THE PRESIDENT:** You must give him the document if you have got the document.

**GENERAL RAGINSKY:** Mr. President, this document is contained in the document book presented by the defence counsel. The Tribunal has the original, I only have the Russian translation. Schmelter's affidavit was submitted to the Tribunal yesterday.

**THE PRESIDENT:** Have you got it, Dr. Flaechsner?

**DR. FLAECHSNER:** Yes.

*(The document is handed to the witness.)*

**THE PRESIDENT:** Thank you.

**THE WITNESS:** On what page, approximately?

**GENERAL RAGINSKY:** It is Page 129 in the Russian translation, answer to Question No. 13, the last paragraph.

**THE WITNESS:** Yes. It says in the German text:

"He"—that is, Speer—"referred repeatedly to the fact that the employment of foreign workers would cause greater difficulties in production and would depend on whether the Reich would supply additional food."

I explained that. I explained the reasons for that; I think, if you are not convinced, that this explanation of mine is also mentioned later in the affidavit.

**BY GENERAL RAGINSKY:**

Your deputy, Schieber, in reply to the question whether Speer knew that the workers which he requested from Sauckel were brought from occupied territories, answered:

"Well, that was the great debatable question. We always said that Sauckel would only create partisans if he brought workers to Germany against their will."

In connection with this, I am saying that you not only knew that the people who were working in your industries were enslaved workers, but that you also knew of the methods which Sauckel used. Do you confirm that?

A. I knew that some of the workers were brought to Germany against their will. I have already said so. I also said that I considered this compulsory recruitment wrong and disastrous for production in the occupied territories. This is a repetition of my testimony.

Q. It is of no use to repeat your testimony. Tell us, did you not insist that Sauckel should supply you with forcibly recruited workers beyond the demands which you had already made? I will remind you of your letter to Sauckel, this will expedite the proceedings. On 6th January, 1944, you wrote to Sauckel:

"Dear Party-Comrade Sauckel; I ask you, in accordance with your promise to the Fuehrer, to assign these workers so that the orders issued to me by the Fuehrer, may be carried out on time. In addition there is an immediate need of 70,000 workers for the Todt Organisation to meet the time limit set on the Atlantic Wall by the Fuehrer in Order No. 51; notification of the need for this labour was given more than six months ago, but it has not yet been complied with."

Did you write this letter? Do you confirm it?

A. Yes. I even admit that I included this letter in my document book, and for the following reasons: The conference, at which Hitler ordered that

*Speer presenting the Knight's Cross with Swords to the director of this munitions factory for quickly resuming output after being bombed by the Allies. May 1944.*
Bundesarchiv, Bild 146-1981-052-06A / CC-BY-SA

one million workers were to be brought from France to Germany, took place on the 4th of January, 1944. On the same day I told General Studt, my representative in France, that the requirements for reserved industries in France were to be given priority over the requirements for Germany. Two days later I told Sauckel, in the letter which you now have in your hand, that my need in France amounted to 800,000 workers for French factories and that requirements for workers on the Atlantic Wall had not yet been fully met, that they should therefore be provided first, before the one million workers were sent to Germany. I said yesterday that through these two letters the programme which had been ordered by Hitler was rendered abortive, and that it was the purpose to inform the military commander, who also received this letter, that the workers were to be used first in France; that information was very valuable to the military commander.

**Q.** Defendant Speer, did you know that, in the factories of which you were in charge, some of the forced labourers were convicts whose prison terms had already expired? Did you know that?

**A.** During my period of office I did not know it; I learned of it here from a document.

**Q.** You claim that you did not know it?

**A.** I know what you mean; it is mentioned in the Schieber letter of 4th May, 1944, which is in my document book, but I could not possibly remember all these details.

**Q.** You cannot remember, but Schieber, on 4th May, 1944, in a special letter addressed to you personally, wrote to you about it and you could not possibly have not known it. The fact that this letter is included in your document book does not change the situation.

**A.** On the receipt of this letter I then wrote to Himmler with regard to the workers who had served their prison sentences. I can submit this letter at any time, I left it out to avoid making the document book too long. This letter shows that I asked Himmler to let these workers, who had served their sentences, remain free. Himmler's point of view was that these workers should remain in custody.

**Q.** Do you remember the letter from the OKW of 8th July, 1943, on the subject of manpower for mining? Do you remember that letter and its contents?

**A.** No.

**Q.** I shall remind you.

**GENERAL RAGINSKY:** This document was submitted to the Tribunal as Exhibit USA 455 and has been quoted here several times. I think, therefore, that it is not necessary to read all of it into the record, but I will read just a few basic points.

**BY GENERAL RAGINSKY:**

**Q.** The Fuehrer's order to assign 300,000 Russian prisoners of war to coal mining is mentioned in this letter. Do you remember this order?

**A.** I should like to see it.

**Q.** You will be given a chance to see it. In paragraph a of this document it is mentioned that all prisoners of war taken in the East after 5th July, 1943, are to be brought to the camps of the OKW and turned over to the Plenipotentiary for Labour Mobilization for employment in the coal mining industry.

In paragraph 4 of this document it states:

"All male prisoners, from 16 to 55 years of age, captured in guerrilla fighting in the operational army area of the Eastern commissariats, the Government General and the Balkans, will in the future be considered prisoners of war. The same applies to males in the newly conquered regions of the East. They are to be sent to prisoner-of-war camps, and are to be brought from there for labour commitment in the Reich."

This letter was also sent to you and therefore you knew what kind of methods were used to obtain workers for your coal industry. Do you admit that?

**A.** No, I do not admit it.

**Q.** All right.

**A.** I do not know whether you mean that the prisoners who were taken in the fighting against partisans in the operational area were to be sent to the mines. I assumed at the time that they were taken prisoner in battle, and a partisan captured in battle is, of course, a prisoner of war. Here the assertion was made that in particular the prisoners taken in the partisan areas were not treated as prisoners of war. But this document seems to me to be evidence to the contrary. It shows that prisoners taken in the partisan areas were treated as prisoners of war.

**Q.** I am definitely not interested in your comments on this document.

I asked you whether you knew in what particular way, and through what particular methods, you were receiving workers for your coal industry, and you answered that you did not admit knowledge of it; I think that covers the question with regard to the document. We will pass on to the next document.

On 4th January, 1944 you participated in a meeting which took place in Hitler's headquarters and at which the question of utilisation of manpower for 1944 was. discussed. You stated that you would have to have an additional 1,300,000 workers. During this meeting it was decided that Sauckel would furnish not less than 4,000,000 workers from occupied territories in 1944, and that Himmler would help him to supply this number. The minutes of the meeting, signed by Lammers, stated that the decision of all participants in the meeting was unanimous. Do you acknowledge that, as a participant in this meeting and as a Reich Minister, you are among those responsible for the forced deportation to Germany of a few million workers?

**A.** But this programme was not carried out.

**Q.** Defendant Speer, if you do not answer my questions, we shall lose too much time.

**THE PRESIDENT:** But, General Raginsky, from the outset of this defendant's evidence, if I understand it, he has admitted that he knows that prisoners of war and other workers were brought to Germany forcibly, against their will. He has never denied it.

**GENERAL RAGINSKY:** Yes, Mr. President, he admitted it. But the question now is whether he admits that he himself is responsible for the decision taken at this meeting which he attended on 4th January. He did not answer that and I am asking him again.

**BY GENERAL RAGINSKY:**

**Q.** I shall repeat my question. I am not asking you whether Sauckel really carried through this programme. I am asking you whether on 4th January you participated in a decision taken at Hitler's headquarters that Sauckel, with the assistance of Himmler, should forcibly deport 4,000,000 people from occupied territories. You participated in that decision, did you not? It is obvious from the minutes which state that the decision was unanimous. Now, do you accept responsibility for this decision?

**A.** As far as my responsibility is concerned I assume the Tribunal will decide the extent of it. I cannot establish it myself.

**Q.** Now, I shall read to you an excerpt from a document presented to the Tribunal as Exhibit USA 184. This document mentions a decision of Sauckel to the effect that mobilization and drafting of two age groups—1926 and 1927—will be carried through in all newly occupied Eastern territories. This document also states that "the Reich Minister of Armament and Munitions approved this order," and the document ends with the following sentence:

"Mobilization and selection must be speeded up and carried through with the greatest energy and all appropriate measures must be applied."
Do you remember this order?

**A.** I have read this document here; it is correct.

Q. Now we shall pass on to the next question. You stated here that you were highly critical of Hitler's entourage. Will you please name the persons whom you criticized?

A. No, I will not name them.

Q. You will not name these persons because you did not criticise anybody, am I to understand you in that way?

A. I did criticise them, but I do not consider it right to name them here.

Q. Well, I will not insist on an answer to this question.

You had some differences with Hitler. Tell us, did they begin after you had convinced yourself that Germany had lost the war?

A. I made clear statements on this point yesterday.

Q. You spoke here quite extensively about your opposition to the destruction of industries in the Western areas of the Reich before the withdrawal of the German armed forces. But did you not do that only because you counted upon the reoccupation of these regions in the near future, and because you wanted to save these industries for your own use?

A. No, that was not the reason. I explained in detail yesterday that this reason served as my pretext to prevent the destruction. If, for instance, you look at my memorandum dealing with the motor fuel situation, it is obvious that I did not believe a reoccupation was possible, and I do not think that any military leader in 1944 considered a re-occupation of France, Belgium or Holland possible. That also applies to the Eastern territories, of course.

Q. I think it would be better if we referred to the document. That is the right way of doing it and it would save time. It is a draft of a telegram which you prepared for Gauleiter Buerkel, Wagner and others. I shall read from Page 56 of your document book.

"The Fuehrer has stated that he can in a short time accomplish the reoccupation of the territories which are at present lost to us, since in continuing the war the Western areas are of great importance for armament and war-production."

What you stated in your testimony is quite different from what you wrote to the Gauleiter.

A. No, my counsel quoted and explained all this yesterday. I should like to see the document again. I do not know whether it is necessary to repeat this whole explanation, it was given yesterday and lasted about ten minutes. Either my explanation of yesterday is believed or not.

Q. I do not want you to repeat what you said yesterday; if you do not want to answer me I prefer to pass on to the next question.

**THE PRESIDENT:** General Raginsky, if you asked him a question which was asked yesterday, he must give the same answer if he wants to give a consistent answer.

**GENERAL RAGINSKY:** Mr. President, I am asking him this question again because in my view he answered it very wrongly yesterday. But to repeat yesterday's answer would be an absolute waste of time. If he does nor want to answer truthfully, then I shall pass on to the next question.

**THE PRESIDENT:** The witness says: "I did answer the question truthfully yesterday, but if you want me to repeat it again, I will do it but it will take ten minutes to do it." That is what he said and it is a perfectly proper answer.

**GENERAL RAGINSKY:** I prefer to pass on to the next question.

**BY GENERAL RAGINSKY:**

Q. Tell us why you sent this telegram about the destruction of industries to the Gauleiter.

A. It was not sent only to the Gauleiter, it was sent to my representatives as well as to the Gauleiter. The Gauleiter had to be informed, because they could, on their own initiative, have ordered destruction to be carried out, and, since they were not subordinate to me but to Bormann, I had to send this teletype message which I had drafted to Bormann with the request to forward it to the Gauleiter.

Q. You stated that the supporters of Hitler's "scorched earth" policy were Ley, Goebbels and Bormann. Now, what about those who are alive today, those who are now sitting in the dock. Did not any of them support Hitler in this policy?

A. As far as I recall, none of those now in the dock were in favour of the "scorched earth" policy. On the contrary, Funk, for example, was one of those who opposed it very strongly.

Q. This policy was advocated only by people who are now dead?

A. Yes, and probably they killed themselves because they advocated this policy and did other such things.

Q. Your defence counsel has submitted to the Tribunal several letters addressed to Hitler, dated March, 1945. Tell us, did Hitler, after receiving these letters, lose confidence in you?

A. I said yesterday that violent disputes followed these letters, and that Hitler wanted me to go on leave, on permanent leave, that is; in effect he wanted to dismiss me. But I did not want to go.

I have heard this before. But nevertheless, Hitler appointed you, Speer, on 3rd March, 1945, to be in charge of the total destruction of all industries.

A. Yes, that is, I was competent for the destruction or non-destruction of industry in Germany until 19th March, 1945. Then a Hitler decree, which has also been submitted, took away from me this power to carry out destruction, but Hitler's decree of 30th March, 1945, which I drew up, returned this power to me. The main thing, however, is that I have also submitted the orders which I issued on the strength of this power; they show clearly that I prohibited the carrying out of destruction, and thereby my purpose was achieved. Not Hitler's decree, but my executive order was decisive. That order is also among the documents.

Q. In spite of the fact that Hitler received such letters from you, he did not regard you as a man opposing him?

A. Hitler said, in the talk which I had with him at that time, that both for domestic and for foreign political reasons he could not dispense with my services. That was his explanation. I believe that already then his confidence in me was shaken, since in his testament he named another as my successor.

Q. And the last question. In April, 1945, you wrote, in the Hamburg radio studio, a speech which you intended to deliver if Berlin fell. In this speech, which was not delivered, you advocated the banning of a Werewolf organisation. Tell us, who was in charge of the Werewolves.

A. Reichsleiter Bormann was in charge of the Werewolves.

Q. And besides Bormann, who?

A. No, just Bormann. As far as I know—I am not quite certain—the Werewolf organisation was subordinate to Bormann.

Q. That is understood. If Bormann were still alive, then you would have said that Himmler was the leader of this organisation. One could hardly expect another answer.

**GENERAL RAGINSKY:** I have no more questions of the defendant.

**THE PRESIDENT:** Dr. Servatius, did you want to ask something which arises out of the cross-examination?

**DR. SERVATIUS:** I have only a few questions on the cross-examination.

**BY DR. SERVATIUS:**

Q. Witness, you stated that after air raids, deficiencies arising in the concerns were reported by you to the DAF or to Sauckel. That is correct, is it not?

A. No, not quite in this form. I was asked whether I received occasional reports on such conditions. I said yes, I passed them on to Sauckel or to the DAF because they were the competent authorities.

Q. What did these reports which were sent to Sauckel contain?

A. As far as I remember, I said in the examination that I did not exactly recall receiving such reports. In any case, the question was only a theoretical one: what would I have done if I had received such reports. I thought that reports had certainly reached me, but I can no longer recall their specific contents.

Q. What was Sauckel to do?

A. Against the air raids Sauckel could not do anything either.

Q. If you sent the reports to him, it meant that he was to provide help?

A. Yes, or that he, as the competent authority, would have precise information on conditions in his field of work, even if he could not help.

Q. His field was the recruiting of manpower.

A. Yes, also labour conditions.

Q. Labour conditions could be improved only through material deliveries, through food deliveries, and so forth.

A. Of course, but in the last analysis the Plenipotentiary for Labour Mobilization was responsible for working conditions. That is obvious from the decree which Goering signed. Naturally, it was also the concern of other authorities to create good working conditions; that is quite clear.

Q. But, after all, it was not a question of issuing a decree, but of giving practical help.

A. Practical help after air raids was not given by the central agency, that was impossible since transport and telephone connections were generally dislocated; but it was given by the local authorities.

Q. In other words, Sauckel could not do anything?

A. No, not personally, but his local offices under him participated in rendering aid.

Q. But he had to turn to you for any material, since everything was confiscated for armament?

A. As far as building material was concerned, he could get it only from me, and he did in fact receive large amounts of it. I must add that Sauckel did not receive the material himself, but, as far as I recall, generally the German Labour Front received it, since the DAF actually took care of the camps.

Q. Which were the responsible agencies? Were you not the agency which cared for the plants?

A. Not in the sense which you mean. You want me to answer that I was responsible for the working conditions.

THE PRESIDENT: Dr. Servatius, the Tribunal thinks that we have been over all this already with the witness.

DR. SERVATIUS: Mr. President, I think this question has not yet been dealt with. Yesterday internal administration was discussed. A second series of agencies existed for taking care of the factories, namely through the Armament Commission and the Armament Inspection Office, and there was a third possibility open to the witness Speer for making contact with the factories, the Labour Mobilization Engineers. In this connection I wanted to ask him another question.

THE WITNESS: I shall be glad to answer it.

BY DR. SERVATIUS:

Q. Did not the Labour Mobilization Engineers constitute your only real possibility of improving conditions in the concerns and did you have direct supervision?

A. I must define for you the task of the Labour Mobilization Engineers: it was an engineering task, that is shown in their title.

Q. It was limited to this engineering task?

A. Yes.

DR. SERVATIUS: Then, I have no more questions.

DR. FLAECHSNER (**counsel for the defendant Speer**): Mr. President, I have only two questions arising out of the cross-examination.

RE-DIRECT EXAMINATION BY DR. FLAECHSNER:

Q. One of the questions is this: Herr Speer, I refer once more to the answer which you gave to Justice Jackson at the end of the cross-examination, and to clarify that answer I would like to ask you this: In assuming a common responsibility, did you want to acknowledge measurable guilt or co-responsibility under the penal law, or did you want to record an historical responsibility before your own people?

A. That question is very difficult to answer; it is actually one which the Tribunal will decide in its verdict. I only wanted to say that even in an authoritarian system the leaders must accept a common, united responsibility, and that it is impossible after the catastrophe to avoid this responsibility. If the war had been won, the leaders would presumably have laid claim to full responsibility. But to what extent that is punishable or immoral, that I cannot decide and it is not for me to decide.

Q. Thank you. Secondly the American prosecution showed you a number of documents which, for the most part, I believe even entirely, were relative to the conditions of the Krupp labour camps. You said that you yourself had no knowledge of these conditions. Did I understand you correctly?

A. I did not know the details necessary to be able to deal adequately with these documents individually.

DR. FLAECHSNER: I have no more questions, Mr. President. However, I must reserve the right, in connection with these affidavits introduced as evidence against my client—the position is actually not quite clear to me—to decide whether it is necessary to cross-examine the persons who made the affidavits. I regret that, but I may possibly have to do it. I had no previous knowledge that these would be introduced here.

Then, Mr. President, I need just five minutes to finish my documentary evidence.

THE PRESIDENT: Yes. Dr. Flaechsner, with reference to these affidavits, if you want to cross-examine any witness you must apply in writing to do so, and you must do so promptly. Because there are only two—I think I am correct in saying that there are only two other of the defendants to be examined, and unless the application comes in soon, it will not be possible to find the witnesses or to bring them here in time.

Now, you say you will finish in five minutes?

DR. FLAECHSNER: Yes.

THE PRESIDENT: I think you may as well finish now, then. However, Dr. Flaechsner, first the Tribunal has one or two questions to put to the defendant.

BY THE TRIBUNAL (Mr. Biddle):

Q. Defendant, you spoke of not using the Western prisoners in war industry and in the making of munitions, do you remember?

A. Yes.

Q. Were there regulations to that effect?

A. Yes.

Q. There were regulations to that effect?

A. Yes, as far as I know, but my memory may be faulty on this point. I only recall talks with Keitel about employment in individual cases, and these Keitel turned down. Otherwise I had no knowledge.

Q. You never saw any regulation which made that distinction, did you?

A. No.

Q. And with respect to civilians from non-occupied countries, they were used in war industries, I suppose, were they not?

A. Foreign workers were employed without consideration for any agreement.

Q. That is just what I want to know.

Now, you said the concentration camps had a bad reputation, remember? I think those were your words, were they not, "a bad reputation"? Is that right?

A. Yes.

Q. What did you mean by "bad reputation"? What sort of reputation, for what?

A. That is hard to define. It was known in Germany that a stay in a concentration camp was an unpleasant experience. I knew that, but I did not know any details.

Q. Well, even if you did not know any details, is not "unpleasant" putting it a little mildly? Wasn't the reputation that violence and physical punishment were used in the camps? Was not that the reputation that you meant? Is not it fair to say that, really?

A. No, that is going a little too far, on the basis of what we knew. I assumed that there was ill-treatment in individual cases, but I did not assume that it was the rule. I did not know that.

Q. Did you not know that violence or physical force was used to enforce the regulations if the internees did not obey them?

A. No, I was not aware of that. I must explain that, during the time I was a Minister, strange as it may sound, I became less disturbed about the fate of concentration camp inmates than I had been before I became a Minister, because while I was in office I heard only good and reassuring reports about the concentration camps from official sources. It was said that the food was being improved, and so on and so forth.

Q. Only one other question. I was interested in what you said at the end about all of the leaders being responsible for certain general principles, and certain fateful decisions. Can you particularize? What did you mean? What principles? Did you mean going on with the war, for instance?

A. I think that, for example, the beginning of the war or the continuing of the war were basic decisions which ...

Q. You deem the beginning of the war and the continuing of the war were basic decisions for which all the leaders were responsible?

A. Yes.

MR. BIDDLE: Thank you.

THE PRESIDENT: The defendant can return to the dock.

THE PRESIDENT: You may as well finish tonight, Dr. Flaechsner.

DR. FLAECHSNER: Yes, gladly.

I should like, supplementing yesterday's evidence, to submit a letter from Speer to Sauckel, of 28th January, 1944, which was quoted here yesterday; it will be Exhibit 31.

Then, another letter from Speer to Sauckel of 11th March, 1944; that will be Exhibit 32.

Then, the executive order for implementing the decree for destruction mentioned by the defendant yesterday, which the Tribunal will find on Page 81 of the English Document Book; I submit it as Exhibit 33.

Then, as Exhibit 34, I should like to submit a letter from Hitler to Speer, dated 21st April, 1944.

**THE PRESIDENT:** Will you give us the date of Exhibit 33? You said Page 81. Did you mean Page 81 of the original which is 85 in the English?

**DR. FLAECHSNER:** No, in the English text, Mr. President.

**THE PRESIDENT:** What is the date of the document?

**DR. FLAECHSNER:** It is an execution order for the Fuehrer decree of 19th March, 1945,

**THE PRESIDENT:** That does not seem to be right, because Page 81 of our copy is the end of—

**MR. BIDDLE:** It is on Page 80.

**THE PRESIDENT:** Well, the decree of 22nd March, 1945? Is that the thing you mean?

**DR. FLAECHSNER:** Yes.

**THE PRESIDENT:** Then it is on Page 80.

**DR. FLAECHSNER:** It is the execution order for the Fuehrer decree of the 19th of March ....

**THE PRESIDENT:** Very well.

**DR. FLAECHSNER:** The next document, Mr. President, is on Page 55 of the English text and Page 52 of the original, the same as the French text. It is the letter from Hitler to Speer, already mentioned, dealing with the instructions given to Dorsch for the construction of fighter planes. That is Exhibit 34.

I have to submit Exhibit 35 later.

As Exhibit 36 I submit the interrogatory of Kehrl. It is signed by the witness, Hans Kehrl, and the signature is certified by an officer of the internment camp; the signature of a representative of the prosecution and my own signature are also on it.

**THE PRESIDENT:** What page is that—36?

**DR. FLAECHSNER:** Exhibit 37 is the—

**THE PRESIDENT:** No. 36. We want the page of it.

**DR. FLAECHSNER:** 36 is on Page 105 in the original.

On Page 113 of the document book, Mr. President, is an excerpt from the interrogation of the witness Schieber, which I submit as Exhibit 37. It is submitted in German and English. The record is certified by a member of the prosecution and by me.

In the second book, on Page 127, the Tribunal will find the interrogation of the witness Schmelter, which I submit as Exhibit 38. It is certified in the same way. On Page 136 of Document Book 2 I submit the testimony of the witness Hupfauer, who was also mentioned here today. That will be Exhibit 39.

On Page 142 of Document Book 2 the Tribunal will find the interrogation of the witness Sauer. I submit this as Exhibit 40, again in English and German. The English record is certified by a member of the prosecution and by me.

On Page 148 of my second document book the Tribunal will find the record of the examination of Frank, carried out in Ludwigsburg by the prosecution and by me. The record is certified by the prosecution and by me.

**THE PRESIDENT:** That was 41, was it not?

**DR. FLAECHSNER:** That was 41, Mr. President.

On Page 153 of the document book is the record of the examination of Roland, which will be Exhibit 42. This also is in English and in German, and is certified in the usual way.

On Page 165 of the document book is the record of the examination of the witness Kempf, carried out on 3rd May at Kransberg by the prosecution and by me. It is certified in the usual way, and will be Exhibit 43.

**THE PRESIDENT:** How many more have you got?

**DR. FLAECHSNER:** There are two more.

On Page 176 of the document book is the interrogatory of Guderian, who was questioned at Hersbruck. The record is in English and German, and the English is certified by me and the prosecution. That is Exhibit 44.

On Page 181 of the document book—this will be Exhibit 45—the Tribunal will find the testimony of the witness Stahl, also in English and German, the English being certified by the prosecution and by me.

Finally, on Page 186 of the document book there is the interrogatory of Karl Brandt, which is certified by the camp authorities. It is in English and German, and will be Exhibit 46.

**THE PRESIDENT:** Is that all?

**DR. FLAECHSNER:** That is all.

Mr. President, yesterday the defendant referred to excerpts of the Fuehrer conference of 3rd to 5th January. This document has not yet been translated, and with your permission, I shall submit it later. The prosecution has already seen it and has no objection.

Those are the documents I wanted to submit. I believe that the Tribunal does not wish to hear comments on the documents in the document book, especially as the documents have already been presented by the Soviet prosecution in great detail. That concludes my case for the defendant Speer.

**THE PRESIDENT:** The Tribunal will adjourn.

*(The Tribunal adjourned until 22nd June, 1946, at 1000 hours.)*

# Concluding Speech from the Defense

## TUESDAY, 23RD JULY, 1946

**THE PRESIDENT:** I call on Dr. Flaechsner, counsel for the defendant Speer.

**DR. FLAECHSNER (for the defendant Speer):** Mr. President, may it please the Tribunal:

The prosecution has charged the defendant Speer under all four Counts of the Indictment which essentially cover the stipulations of Article 6 (a) to (c).

The French prosecution, which substantiated more definitely the individual charges against the defendant Speer, refrains from charging the defendant Speer with the violation of Article 6 (a) of the Charter and demands only the application of Article 6 (b) and (c) against Speer. However, since the legal concept of conspiracy has frequently been dealt with during the oral proceedings by citing the person of the defendant Speer as an example, and since it was asserted that the defendant Speer also had made himself guilty within the meaning of Article 6 (a) of the Charter, details must be given by way of precaution.

The defendant has, in addition, been charged with the planning, preparation, initiation or waging of a war of aggression or a war violating international treaties, although, at the time when the defendant assumed the office of Minister of Armaments, which was only expanded to a Ministry for Armament and Munitions one and a half years later, the German Reich was already at war with all the countries to which it capitulated in May, 1945. Thus, at the time the defendant took charge of government affairs, all the events mentioned under Article 6 (a) had without exception taken place, and the defendant Speer's activity did not alter the existing situation to the slightest extent.

The defendant had done nothing at all to bring about this situation. His previous activity was that of an architect, who occupied himself exclusively with peace-time construction and did not contribute by his activity either to the preparation or the waging of a war violating international treaties. I refer to my document book, Page 29, Document 1435-PS.

If the circumstances which Article 6 (a) of the Charter materially and legally characterise as criminal acts applied to International Law, and if the individual criminality of persons who bring about these conditions were generally recognized in International Law, the defendant Speer in my opinion could still not be held responsible for these conditions, for not the slightest evidence has been produced during the trial thus far that Speer contributed in the least towards bringing about these conditions. In this connection we must consider that criminality of attitude requires that the person in question must have contributed in some way to bringing about the circumstances which have been declared punishable, i.e., he must have functioned as a cause of the result which has been declared punishable. If, however, as in the case under consideration, the defendant Speer entered the Government without having contributed anything at all to the so-called crimes against peace, he cannot be charged with criminal responsibility for this, even if such responsibility were applicable to other members of the Government.

The prosecution has asserted that by joining the Government the defendant had accepted and approved the preceding crimes against peace. This is a concept taken from the field of civil law and it cannot be applied to criminal law. Criminal law applies only to circumstances consisting of actions which serve to bring about the circumstances declared punishable. Nor is this altered by the introduction of the legal concept of conspiracy. In this connection reference may be made to Dr. Stahmer's detailed statement on conspiracy. The legal views set forth in that statement are also made the subject of my own statement. I refer to it, and to Professor Jahrreiss's statements, in order to avoid repetition. It can, therefore, be confirmed that the defendant Speer cannot be charged with a so-called crime against peace.

The personal interrogation of the defendant and the cross- examination regarding his activity in the Party have shown that Speer, by virtue of his position as an architect, exercised only architectural and artistic functions even in the Party organisation. Speer was the commissioner for building in the Hess staff; it was a purely technical assignment and had nothing at all to do with any form of preparation for war. The Party, which strove to seize and influence all the vital functions of the people, had created the position of Commissioner for Building to ensure uniformity in Party buildings. In their building projects, the Gauleiter and the other Party offices could consult this office, but they availed themselves of the opportunity only to a very limited extent.

**THE PRESIDENT:** Dr. Flaechsner, the Tribunal thinks it might be appropriate at some time convenient to you if you were to deal with the question of the meaning of the words "waging of a war of aggression" in Article 6 (a). I do not want to interrupt you to do it at this moment in your speech but at some time convenient to you the Tribunal would like you to give your interpretation of the words in Article 6 (a), "waging of a war of aggression."

**DR. FLAECHSNER:** Yes, Mr: President. Perhaps I might return to this point later, Mr. President, when I have concluded this topic.

Naturally it was from purely artistic reasons that the Party took over responsibility for building. It strove to give its buildings a uniformly representative character. Considering the peculiar nature of the architectural demands, it was natural that each architect should follow his own line in solving the problems put to him. The activity of the defendant as Commissioner for Construction was therefore relatively restricted and of minor importance, since he did not even have an office of his own at his disposal. It would be erroneous to try to deduce therefrom any participation by the defendant in any crimes against the peace. The same is true of the defendant's other functions prior to and during the war, up to his assumption of office as minister.

Although the defendant was given the task of replanning the towns of Berlin and Nuremberg, this activity had nothing at all to do with crimes against the peace; on the contrary, his activities must rather be regarded as hampering war preparations; as his task required large quantities of raw materials and equipment, which might otherwise have been used directly or indirectly for rearmament. The construction projects assigned to Speer were, moreover, calculated and planned far ahead. They could only give Speer the impression that Hitler was counting on having a long period of peace. The defendant cannot, therefore; be said, prior to his assumption of office as Reich Minister, to have contributed directly or indirectly to the emergence of the events characterised by Article 6 (a) of the Charter as crimes against peace. The fact, too, that the defendant was a member of the Reichstag after 1941 cannot be quoted in support by the prosecution, because, as the prosecution itself pointed out, the Reichstag sank into complete insignificance under the totalitarian regime and became merely an institution Which accepted and acclaimed the Fuehrer's decisions.

Responsibility for war guilt is out of the question here too; for no activity on the part of the Reichstag in connection with extending the war to the Soviet Union and the United States can be recognized.

The French prosecution, therefore, rightly refrained from charging the defendant with the violation of Article 6 (a) of the Charter.

The prosecution further charges the defendant Speer with having participated in war crimes committed during his term of office by forcibly transferring workers from the occupied countries to Germany, where they were employed for the purpose of waging war or of producing war materials. The following should be said in this connection:

The prosecution charges the defendant with violations of Article 52 of the Hague Convention on Land Warfare, which states that services may only be demanded of nationals of the occupied country to cover the requirements of the occupying forces, that they must be in proportion to the resources of the country and that they must not oblige the persons concerned to take part in military actions against their native land. In Article 2, the Hague Convention on Land Warfare lays down that all countries participating in the war in question must be signatories (General participation clause— Allbeteiligungsklausel). As the Soviet Union was not a signatory of the Convention on Land Warfare, the latter could apply to conditions created by the war against the Soviet Union only if the legal principles laid down in the Convention were considered as universally valid International Law. We must start, therefore, from the principle that those areas belonging to signatories of the Hague Convention on Land Warfare must be judged on a different legal basis from areas belonging to non-signatories of the Treaty. In examining the question, we must first decide whether the deportation of labourers from territories occupied in war time by an enemy power can be justified on the basis of Article 52 of the Hague Convention. Article 52 constitutes a limitation of Article 46 of the Hague Convention on Land Warfare, which lays down the principle that the population of occupied territories and their property are, on principle, to be subjected to as little damage as the necessities of war will allow: Starting from this principle, we must examine whether it involves the absolute prohibition of deportation for the purpose of securing labour for the essential war economy of a belligerent country. It must be remembered in this connection that the situation is altered if the deportation carried out by the occupying belligerent State is in accordance with agreements made with the government of the country occupied. The prosecution has taken the view that such agreements are legally invalid because they were made under the pressure of the occupying power, and because the government existing in France during the time of the occupation could not be considered as representing the French nation.

The first point does not support the prosecution's contention. The contents of treaties concluded under International Law will always be influenced by the respective power of the contracting parties. In every peace treaty concluded between a victor and a vanquished State, this difference of power will be reflected in the contents. This is not, however, contrary to the nature of treaty-making.

The second point, by virtue of which the prosecution rejects the plea of an agreement between the German Government and the French Government then in power relating to the assignment of labour, is equally ineffectual. The so-called Vichy Government then in power was the only government existing in French territory; it was the lawful successor of the government in office before the occupation, and as regards International Law, it is to be particularly noted that States which were of that time involved in the war maintained diplomatic relations with it.

It cannot, moreover, be assumed that the willingness shown by the French Government in this agreement to co-operate with the German Reich, which was then gaining military victories, ran counter to the real feeling of the French people. Reference can be made in this connection to Document 124-R, Page 34 of my document book. Particular attention must be paid to the economic situation of occupied France at the time. After France's capitulation, the total blockade was extended to cover the whole of French territory in Europe, with the result that raw materials not produced in France were no longer obtainable and production was considerably reduced. Important sections of French production were in this way put out of action and many workers deprived of the means of earning a living.

The French Government did not pledge itself unconditionally to send workers to Germany, but made this dependent on reciprocal concessions such as the release of prisoners of war, etc. Whether, and in what measure, the hopes placed in the treaty by the French Government were actually fulfilled, is irrelevant in determining whether the treaties in question were authentic treaties or not. From the legal point of view there is no doubt that these agreements have the character of treaties. From this point of view, there is no justification for the accusation made by the prosecution that workers were taken from occupied French territory against their will and therefore illegally. No judgement of the legality of the measures relating to the workers from Belgium and Holland can be based on agreements such as those concluded between the German and French government departments, since in those countries the government had left the country and consequently no political authority existed. The General Secretaries remaining there could not be considered as representatives of the government and the decrees regulating the dispatch of workers to Germany were enacted by order of the Reich Commissioners or the German military Commander-in-Chief.

Dr. Steinbauer in his exposition on the defendant Seyss- Inquart's activities in Holland has already explained in detail that particular rules must apply to those countries and to the dispatch, of labourers from them. In order to avoid repetition, I refer you to his remarks.

As regards the eastern countries, we must start with the fact that the Soviet Union did not sign the Hague Convention on Land Warfare. It remains, however, to be examined whether the principle laid down in Article 46 of the Hague Convention on Land Warfare, with reference to the treatment of civilians in war and, in the case of occupation of a belligerent country, by the enemy, must not be considered as a universally valid International Law and therefore applicable even if the belligerent country concerned is not specifically a party to the Hague Convention of Land Warfare. An examination of this question would show the deportation of workers from occupied territories to be illegal unless some special factor emerges to remove its illegality.

A state of emergency in the sense of International Law can be considered as such a factor. It is true that it is a matter of International Law whether and in what measure such an emergency can legalise a practice which is in itself illegal, but such a state of emergency must be admitted in cases when a State is fighting for its bare existence. It may be considered that after the Allies had declared the unconditional surrender of Germany to be their goal, such a state of emergency existed for the German State, since there remained no doubt that the enemy intended to destroy the existing German State to its very foundations.

This state of emergency may, however, be considered as existing at an earlier period, when it became clear that the war had ceased to be a settlement of differences between two States, in the sense of the Hague Convention on Land Warfare, and had become a war aimed not only against the fighting forces of the belligerent nations, but also, and primarily, at their economic forces and thus at their so-called war potential. The Hague Convention on Land Warfare is based upon a conception of war which was already out of date in the First World War and much more so in the second. If in the

First World War the belligerents sought to attack each other's economy by blockade and counter-blockade, this is all the more true of the Second World War, in which, in addition to the more indirect effects of the blockade, they introduced the element of direct attack on the enemy by destroying his productive installations by means of air attacks. In contrast to the conception of war on which the Hague Convention on Land Warfare is based, a complete change has come about. In view of the fact that a country can only resist an adversary who is well equipped from the technical point of view if it has at its disposal an unimpaired capacity for production, the main objective in the war was the destruction of the enemy's capacity for production. This was the aim of the British blockade not only of Germany but of every country in the German sphere of influence.

Dr. Kranzbuehler has already discussed the questions connected with this subject. I refer to the relevant parts of his statement.

From this point of view, too, the war in the air was waged primarily not only to attack German national territory but also to destroy production capacity and potentialities in the occupied territories. Continuous air raids were directed against economic targets in France, Belgium, Holland, Czechoslovakia, Poland and Austria, and had as their further aim the interruption and disruption of the whole system of communications, not only on the front and immediately behind it, but; also hundreds of kilometres away from it, in order to paralyse vital functions of the adversary. The Allied air offensive against Japan is a particularly clear indication of this. This war went beyond the bounds of the Hague Convention on Land. Warfare. It ceased to make any further distinction between the adversary's territory proper and the occupied territories, which were likewise included in the enemy blockade. In this war, which sought not only to destroy the adversary, as a nation but also to ruin its economic system and its power of production, we may speak of that as a real national emergency.

When the defendant Speer was appointed Minister, the economic war just described was in full swing on both sides; in fact the task assigned to Speer's department was that of solving the production problems caused by it. Speer therefore found himself in the midst of this economic war; and we now have to decide whether and to what extent the measures taken on the German side were capable of alleviating the state of emergency.

**THE PRESIDENT:** Dr. Flaechsner, I would like to ask you this question. Is there any communication between States, either at the League of Nations or elsewhere, since the war of 1914-18, which suggests that the Hague Rules on Land Warfare were no longer applicable? Perhaps you would consider that question and answer it at your convenience?

**DR. FLAECHSNER:** Mr. President. I can answer this question immediately, in the negative. In the period between the two wars these problems were dealt with only very superficially and, as far as I am acquainted with the facts, the questions considered lay in the sphere of naval warfare and also land warfare in connection with the treatment of prisoners of war. The Hague

*Speer and Generaloberst Eduard Dietl, commander of the 20th Mountain Army on the northern Eastern Front, February 1944.*
Bundesarchiv, Bild 183-J16636 / CC-BY-SA

Convention on Land Warfare itself contained no additions or amendments whatsoever, apart from separate agreements concerning particular methods of conducting warfare. I might add that in the meantime various methods of warfare have been banned by treaties. But as far as principles are concerned, and that is the basis of my argument, the principles laid down in the Hague Convention have undergone no changes through treaties in the meantime.

**THE PRESIDENT:** Yes, then I understand you to say there has been no communication between States, since the 1914-18 war, which suggests that the Hague Rules on Land Warfare are no longer applicable?

**DR. FLAECHSNER:** Yes, that is correct.

We must also decide whether and to what extent the measures taken on the German side were effective in remedying the state of emergency.

In the course of the trial, the prosecution has claimed on several occasions that the imported labour was to be used to release workers for service at the front. This is certainly one reason why recourse was had to foreign workers, but it is by no means the only decisive reason, not even the most decisive reason. It is a fact that the total blockade of the German Reich carried out by the adversary compelled the Reich to an increasing extent to build plants for the production of substitute raw materials in order to carry on the war in the technical form which it had now assumed. It is also a fact that the disturbances caused in economic life by air warfare made it essential to employ an increased number of workers. Merely as an example, let me say how much additional labour was necessary for the repair of air raid damage. This situation involved a state of emergency in so far as the waging of a war of self-preservation would no longer have been possible without the erection of such additional production plants.

Should it be contended that it is impossible to speak of an emergency overriding the illegality of the proceedings in terms of International Law, since the war was begun as a war of aggression and was therefore illegal from the outset, it may at least be said in favour of the defendant Speer that he believed in the existence of such a state of emergency and had reason to do so.

The examination of evidence has revealed that the underlying causes which led to the war, so far as they have been exposed here by the prosecution, were not known to most of the defendants, and least of all to the defendant Speer.

In so far as the deportation of foreign workers to the Reich constitutes an objectively illegal measure according to International Law, it remains to be examined what share of it can be charged to the defendant Speer. At his interrogation prior to the beginning of the trial, on 18th October, 1945, the defendant Speer admitted knowing that, at least as far back as September, 1942, foreign workers had ceased to come voluntarily to the Reich. He said he had countenanced that because there was no possibility of meeting the labour requirements otherwise. It must be concluded from this declaration that the defendant was convinced of the necessity for this emergency measure. Subjectively, therefore, he must be credited with believing in the existence of such a state of emergency overriding illegality. But in the firs place we must examine to what extent the defendant Speer actually contributed to the dispatch of deportees to Germany. Here we must start from the principle that the defendant Speer had a purely technical assignment which he described adequately in his evidence, to which reference can be made. In order to carry out this assignment, he stated his labour requirements. The way in which these requirements were met has been described in detail by the witnesses Schieber and Schmelter. Requirements were submitted in terms of totals needed and it was incumbent upon the defendant Sauckel to satisfy them. These requirements referred to the total number of workers as a whole, and it was the defendant Sauckel's task to meet these requirements as far as possible and in accordance with his judgement. He had power to exhaust the entire resources of the home labour potential as well as to recruit foreign labour. The witnesses Schieber, Kehrl and Schmelter stated in the course of their interrogations that the defendant Speer tried to procure German worker) in the first place for assignments given to him by the Government. The testimony of the witness Sauer shows that the obtaining of the labour requirements necessary to enable him to accomplish his assignment of increasing armament production was of considerable—though not decisive—importance (Document Book II, Page 146).

According to this testimony, the number of workers in the armament finishing industry rose from 4,000,000 to 4,900,000 during the defendant's activity as Armament Minister, while the manufacture of armament parts increased five and a half times up to seven times in many departments. It must therefore be borne in mind that the increase in armament production which the defendant Speer was required to produce was achieved in the first place not so much through an increase in the number of workers employed as by means of technical and organisational measures. It follows from this again that, for the defendant, the procurement of labour was admitted to be an important, though not decisive, element in the fulfilment of the task assigned to him. The defendant made the credible statement that he had applied to Sauckel for workers, but had stressed the fact that he wanted German workers first of all. In the defendant's opinion, an increased number of workers could have been found in the economic sector under his control without having recourse to foreign labour to the extent which was done. The measures taken by the defendant to prevent the transfer of workers from the West into the Reich have been adequately described in the evidence. In taking those measures, i.e., in transferring the production of consumer goods and the manufacture of high priority armament products such as, for instance, forged parts, railway equipment, etc., to the western countries and in establishing blocked industries there, Speer was actuated by the knowledge that the conscription of workers from France as well as from Belgium and Holland would be checked. The result of his talks with the French Minister Bichelonne, as the defendant explained during his interrogation, was for all practical purposes the end of the deportation of workers to Germany. The results have been accurately described by the General Plenipotentiary for Labour Mobilization at the session of the Central Planning Board held on 1st March, 1944 (see Page 32 of my document book). In spite of all the opposition made to this policy (see Sauckel's letter to Hitler dated 17th March, 1944, Document 3819-PS) Speer persevered in his purpose. The decision adopted at Hitler's conference on 4th January, 1944, a report of which was submitted by the prosecution under Document 556-PS, also reveals that the blocked industries, the abolition of which was urged by Sauckel, were to remain out of bounds to Sauckel's labour conscription. Speer wanted to employ the French workers in France in all effort to transfer the production of consumer goods and products which did not represent armament production to the occupied western territories. He wished to utilise for armament production the German workers released in consequence of the closing down of German plants (see Document 124-R, pp. 33/34 of Speer Document Book). In this manner Speer was able to increase production, because German workers, on account of the elimination of language difficulties, could more easily be retrained and because there were no difficulties regarding food. (Compare Kehrl, Page 110, Speer Document Book.)

The result of this policy was that workers from the western areas were mainly used in the production of civilian goods—not in armament production.

On the question of employment of foreign labour in the blocked industries it must also be said: The statute is based on two factual circumstances: deportation for forced labour and forced labour itself.

Compulsory labour in France was ordered by a decree from the French Government. According to International Law there could be no objection to this, unless the view was taken that the French Government was not entitled to take such measures and to issue such decrees. As the defendant Speer stated, the French economic leadership obtained its independence through the agreement with Bichelonne, naturally with the restrictions imposed by the agreement.

As established by Berck (see Document Book I, Page 38, Document 1289-PS), co-worker of the defendant Sauckel, 20 per cent went from the blocked industries of France to French economy, whereas more than 40 per cent went from the consumer goods industry into French hands. It follows that the French armament industry did not manufacture weapons and actual implements of war, for the German authorities would scarcely have left these to the French agencies. In the session of 20th June, 1946, the Tribunal summarised its misgivings as to the manner in which we presented our evidence by stating that questions of suitability were irrelevant; on the other hand the defence may be said to represent the viewpoint that this speech was only intended to clarify the question of legality If the French Government was justified in decreeing compulsory labour service and if plants, employing French workers on the basis of this decree or on the basis of voluntary labour contracts, were provided with German orders, no legal objection could be raised. The establishment of blocked industries which prevented the withdrawal of workers and their transfer to Germany, and the removal of branches of production to France, Belgium and Holland, obtained the objective, i.e., satisfaction of the requirements of the German economy, in a manner which was legally unobjectionable. Even though the defendant Speer did not completely check the transfer of workers, he nevertheless did succeed in decreasing their commitment appreciably. Instead of the policy pursued by other Reich offices of removing foreign workers to the Reich, the defendant aimed at employing the labour needed for his purpose in the workers' homeland (Speer Exhibit 9, Page 24, and Speer Exhibit 11, Page 27, of the Speer Document Book). To this extent he counteracted the tendency to deport workers from their native country.

In order to prove the assertion that Speer played a decisive part in intensifying deportation of workers for forced labour, the prosecution refers to Document 556-PS, which is a file memo by Sauckel of a telephone conversation he had with Speer on 5th January, 1941. In contrast to this as Speer Exhibit 35, the copy of the minutes of the Fuehrer conference of 3rd and 5th January, 1941, which was the subject of the telephone conversation, has been submitted. Even if sharp remarks by Hitler are reproduced here also, the exhibit nevertheless does not reveal the tendency which was noted by Sauckel in his file memo.

The defendant Speer was already at that time on bad terms with Sauckel. The order issued to Speer in the minutes of the Fuehrer conference, with reference to the control of the French armament industry, gave him a pretext for the establishment of blocked industries. For all practical purposes the termination of labour commitments from France was thereby achieved, just the opposite, therefore, of what the prosecution would like to prove. Reference must be made in this connection to Document 22-RF. There it is asserted that owing to the Speer-Bichelonne agreement, labour, commitments to Germany from October, 1943, onwards were one-tenth less (compare Page 41 of my document book).

In weighing the question as to what extent this exonerates the defendant, it is of no importance whether he acted in such a way for reasons of expediency or because he considered the other procedure as illegal. The only thing that matters in this case is the result, which actually put a practical stop to the transfer of workers to Germany, as is evident from the document quoted, 22-RF.

It is finally clear from the Fuehrer minutes of 19th to 22nd June, 1944 (Speer Exhibit 12, Page 19 of the Speer Document Book), and from the testimony of Seyss-Inquart (11th June, 1946) that in spite of the loss of industry in the western territories and the intention of other departments to bring the unemployed workers to Germany, Speer succeeded in maintaining his blocked industries, and thus the plan to commit more foreign workers to Germany finally collapsed. In the case of the defendant Speer we cannot say that it was his duty to examine how far Sauckel's measures were admissible from the point of view of International Law, and this for the following reasons:

When he took over his post in the year 1942, the transfer of foreign workers to Reich territory had already been in operation for some time. Speer relied on the assumption that the legal foundations for these measures had been examined before their introduction. It was not his duty, in the eyes of the law, to examine them independently; he could be sure that the offices which handled the mobilization of labour commitment had examined the legal basis of their activity. During his years of office, the General Plenipotentiary for the Employment of Labour had repeatedly confirmed the fact that the transfer of workers to the Reich was carried out strictly within legal limits. He could depend on it that the authorities who were entrusted by the State with the tasks of labour procurement would on their side examine the measures they took in order to carry out these tasks, from the point of view of their legal admissibility. The activity of the defendant within the framework of the Government could, if transferred to the sector of civil law, be compared with that of the technical works manager of a factory, and in this case Sauckel's position would correspond to that of a director of the personnel office. In such a case the technical works manager's duty is not to examine if and to what extent the employment contracts concluded with the individual workers conform to legal regulations. He has only to see that the manpower he is given to carry out his tasks is employed in the right place and in the right manner. This cannot be countered with the argument that the defendant Sauckel merely considered himself as the deputy of the defendant Speer. This would not present a fair picture of the way in which the different tasks had been distributed between the two co-defendants by the heads of the State. The fact cannot be overlooked that of all the sectors of economy which sent in their requests to the defendant Sauckel, those presented by the defendant Speer were the most important for the conduct of the war and therefore had priority over the others. This does not mean, however, that it was Sauckel's duty to satisfy all the demands of the department represented by Speer before all the others. He did not do so, as can be seen from the evidence, in particular from the testimonies of the witnesses Schieber (Document Book II, Page 114) and Kehrl (Document Book I, Page 106), and could not even do so, as the demands of the other branches of economy, which were all known as consuming agents, "Bedarfstrager," were very often equally urgent, and the labour potential at hand was not sufficient to fulfil all the demands to the same extent. Had Sauckel not been more than a "deputy of Speer," a mere tool who had only to carry out the instructions of Speer, the profound differences between the two could never have come into existence.

It has been emphasized by the prosecution that the appointment of the defendant Sauckel as Plenipotentiary for the Employment of Labour was only made possible through the intervention of the defendant Speer, and that this gave reason to believe that Sauckel had been more or less a tool of the defendant Speer or depended on him to a large extent. This assumption does not correspond with the actual facts.

When he took over his office as Armament Minister, the defendant Speer soon discovered that the supplying of workers to plants had been carried out until then by the Ministry of Labour, which could not cope with the demands made on it. Within the field of work of the Ministry of Labour, this activity represented only a small fraction of its overall functions.

The defendant Speer declared, in the course of his interrogation, that the Ministry of Labour could not overcome sufficiently the obstructive tactics of the different Gauleiter in their districts, because it was the ambition of every Gauleiter to do everything within his power to prevent the transfer of workers from his Gau to another. The department of the Ministry of Labour, which was organised on purely bureaucratic lines, did not seem to the defendant Speer to be equal to its task, and the suggestion was made to the State leadership that a Gauleiter should be entrusted with this charge. When Speer's suggestion was followed up by the request that a Gauleiter charged with the procurement of labour should be put under him, it was not granted by the State leadership because of other existing competencies. The person proposed by Speer was also turned down, and the defendant Sauckel was appointed instead. So that in Speer's endeavours to create a Plenipotentiary for the Employment of Labour the reasons involved were merely of an organisational nature, with the purpose of overcoming the above-mentioned opposition, which was directed against the activity of the Labour Procurement Office in the Ministry of Labour. But to draw from these facts the conclusion that the defendant Speer was responsible for all the measures ordered by the defendant Sauckel would be erroneous.

The fact that the defendant, as a member of the Central Planning Board, participated in sessions at which the problem of the procurement of labour was discussed, cannot be used to support the claim of the prosecution. The prosecution attempts to prove from the sessions of the Central Planning Board that the defendant Speer played a leading part in the procurement of labour from foreign countries. In reply to this the following must be stated: The prosecution has only submitted the text of the minutes of a session, but not the decisions which were made on the basis of this session. And yet it is exactly these that are decisive. Since all the defendant Speer's reports, including also the notes on the decisions of the Central Planning Board, were placed by him at the disposal of the Allied authorities, it would have been easy for the prosecution to have presented such decisions, which would have shown the decisive co-operation of the defendant in the procurement of labour. But such conclusions do not exist and, therefore, the fact that at the conferences of the Central Planning Board questions of labour mobilisations were mentioned should not lead to the conclusion that the Central Planning Board had taken this point over in its sphere of activity.

The decree regarding the establishment of the Central Planning Board is given under No. 42 in Exhibit Speer 7. The scope of the Central Planning Board in labour questions is clearly outlined, and it is stated that the procurement and distribution of labour need not be included in the sphere of competence of the Central Planning Board, as the new office of the Plenipotentiary for the Employment of Labour has been specially created for it. It is clear also from the testimony that when the co-defendant Sauckel discussed questions concerning the policy of labour commitment before the Central Planning Board, he underlined sharply his independence of the Central Planning Board, and stressed the fact that when he made his decisions he was responsible only to the Fuehrer in the last instance, and was independent of the Central Planning Board. For this I refer to the testimonies of the witness Kehrl and the witness Schieber (Speer Exhibits 36 and 37). This does not mean that no attempts were made in the Central Planning Board to exert an influence in the sphere of the General Plenipotentiary for the Employment of Labour. These attempts, however, did not have any results.

In principle we must take the stand that the responsibility of the defendant Speer for the transportation of labour from the occupied territories to the Reich cannot be deduced from his activity within the Central Planning Board.

If the prosecution charges the defendant with the fact that he knew that a great portion of the workers made available to him by Sauckel had been brought to Germany against their will and that he used these workers in the industry which was under his control, this conclusion is open to legal criticism. If and in so far as the removal of workers to the Reich was a violation of International Law, this crime would be limited at the most to the removal of workers to the Reich. The fact that the persons removed into Reich territory were assigned to work is, legally speaking, a new fact to which the prosecution applies the concept of "slave labour."

In this connection the following should be considered: By reason of the Reich Service Law and the decree which enforced it there existed for every German an obligation to contribute his services to the war effort. Through the Labour Office as the highest authority, the leaders of the State could assign the labour of every State national to any purpose they considered appropriate, and they did so.

Foreign workers who were removed to Germany likewise became subject to this regulation. We on our part do not deny that the Hague Convention on Land Warfare itself contains no provision which would support the extension of compulsory labour service from German nationals to the inhabitants of the occupied territories. Since the Hague Convention on Land Warfare reflects the influence of a different concept of warfare, it is impossible that it should have taken into consideration conditions produced by economic warfare. Yes, it is not possible to answer in the affirmative the question of whether the Hague Convention on Land Warfare finally and definitely regulates all the powers of an occupation authority. Such an answer is contradicted by the practice of all the nations which participated in this war. But here too we can resort to the above-mentioned concept of "national emergency" to obtain a correct evaluation and appreciation of the case. It should be admitted that the prosecution is right in that this extension of liability to compulsory labour can be justified from that point of view only.

If we accept the prosecution's contention that there is no legal justification for the extension of liability to compulsory labour to foreign nationals of occupied territories, we are still obliged to check the extent to which the defendant Speer has made himself guilty of the employment of labour subject to such compulsion. In this connection we may refer to what was said earlier about deportation. That the defendant Speer, although he was not responsible for this, still attempted to mitigate the living conditions of these workers, and that he also took steps to correct bad conditions—in so far as these came to his attention—is shown by Exhibits 3, 4 and 5 of the Speer Document Book (Pages 7, 8, 9 of the Speer Document Book). Reference must also be made to the testimony of the defendant himself, in direct examination as well as in cross- examination, where he described his activity in that field.

Justice Jackson, the American Chief Prosecutor, when placing before the defendant Speer during his cross-examination a series of documents intended to demonstrate the bad treatment of foreign workers by the firm of Krupp in Essen, himself stated that he did not intend to hold the defendant Speer responsible for such individual incidents.

The documents involved were Dr. Jager's affidavit—Document 288-D—discussed by Dr. Servatius; and a letter of the Locomotive Manufacturing Department of the firm of Krupp, dated February, 1942, shortly after the defendant Speer's appointment as Reich Minister. The conditions described therein had caused Speer to intervene with Hitler in March, 1942 (Speer Exhibit 3, Page 7 of the Speer Document Book). A further document submitted—321-D—describes the conditions under which Russian workers came to Essen in 1941, that is, before the defendant Speer took office. Document 258-D, Exhibit USA 896, which was submitted during cross-examination, as stated by Justice Jackson, was not produced in order to incriminate the defendant, and may therefore be passed over.

Further documents submitted all deal with incidents in the Krupp Works. As far as he was able to do so, the defendant explained all of them. These documents show that abuses of a general nature, for which the firm of Krupp might be held responsible, were caused by air bombardments and the resulting demolition of living quarters. But even if the incidents cited had actually occurred on the premises of that firm—which the defence is not in a position to verify—these incidents would not supply adequate ground for the assumption that the conditions under which foreign labourers worked in armament industries were the same everywhere. No conclusions may be drawn as to a whole system simply by selecting and investigating one firm. Only evidence showing the general prevalence of such conditions would be relevant.

It is true that this activity of the defendant Speer would not affect the criminal evaluation of his actions in principle, but it would be of decisive import in establishing the degree to which he participated.

When the defendant took office, the practice of employing foreign workers and prisoners of war was already in existence. Thus he cannot be considered as the originator of this policy, which fact must also be taken into consideration when passing judgement; for it appeared impossible to depart from the established practice. The employment of foreign workers in German economy was nothing unusual. Many foreign labourers were employed in agriculture, mining and surface and underground construction in peace time as well.

During the war many foreign labourers from both East and West had already been brought to Germany before the defendant Speer took office, and only part of these belonged to the sector under Speer's control.

In order to define the spheres of responsibility of the two defendants Sauckel and Speer, it will be shown below how the assignment and distribution of workers were handled in the establishments last controlled by the defendant Speer. Acting as organs of the Speer Ministry, commissions and pools assigned certain production tasks to individual establishments as part of the armament programme. The factory then calculated the number of workers needed. This was reported simultaneously to the Armament Command and to the Labour Office, where the labour requirements of all employers in need of workers were recorded. The Armament Commands examined all requests received from plants under their jurisdiction and passed them on to the Armament Production Office. Labour requirements reported to the Labour Offices were forwarded by these in turn to the Gau Labour Offices. Armament Inspection Offices collected the requests and forwarded them to the Speer Ministry, Labour Mobilization Division. The Gau Labour Offices directed applications which they received to the General Commissioner for the Mobilization of Labour. It must be noted in this connection that in 1942 the Speer Ministry controlled only construction work and ground forces armament. Navy and air armament made their requests for labour independently. In the spring of 1943, Navy armament was assigned to the Speer Ministry, and from that time on, labour requisitions for this purpose were handled through the Labour Mobilization Division. In the autumn of 1943 the rest of production was added, while aircraft armament continued to handle its requisitions independently through the General Plenipotentiary for the Mobilization of Labour until August, 1944.

An account of these details is indispensable to disprove the prosecution's assumption that Speer was the main beneficiary of Sauckel's mobilization of labour. The fact that alongside of the Speer Ministry there existed essential consuming agencies of equal importance, as, for instance, the Wehrmacht Administration, the Transport System and so forth, need be mentioned only incidentally, but has also been, confirmed by the testimony of witnesses. The General Plenipotentiary for the Mobilization of Labour distributed the labour at his disposal among the various consuming agencies and assigned the required labour to the Gau Labour Office; who in turn referred them to the local labour offices where workers were assigned to individual establishments on the strength of applications previously examined by the Armament Offices. An exception to this cumbersome procedure was made .by the introduction of the so-called "red-slip process" which was used in the case of exceptionally urgent production assignments (I refer to Page 120 of my document book). A certain number of red slips were issued monthly by the General Plenipotentiary for the Mobilization of Labour and placed at the disposal of the Armaments Ministry for distribution by the latter to the plants under its supervision through the industry's administrative agencies.

The plant itself then presented these red slips to the Labour Office, which had to satisfy these "red-slip" requests for workers regardless of the requirements of other consuming agencies. Not until this had been done could allocations be made to other establishments. General requests for labour were involved in all instances. The allocations were exclusively in the hands of labour authorities directed by the defendant Sauckel, so that neither the individual factory nor the offices of the defendant Speer nor the defendant Speer himself had any influence on the distribution. The question of whether local, foreign or prisoner-of-war labour should be used to satisfy requisitions was left for the Labour Authorities to decide (Document Book, Pages 8 and 9).

In concluding the presentation of evidence, the prosecution submitted the decree of 1st December, 1942 (Document 4006- PS), issued jointly by Speer and Sauckel. The prosecution contends that this document and the decree of 22nd June, 1944, submitted at the same time, furnish a basis for appraisal of the power ratio between Speer and Sauckel. Some comment on this is therefore appropriate.

The decree of 1st December, 1942, leaves no doubt that the General Plenipotentiary for the Mobilization of Labour was authorized to examine requests for labour submitted to him which came from the armaments industry. Thus, when a factory asked for additional labourers in order to carry out the production job assigned to it, the General Plenipotentiary for the Mobilization of Labour reserved to himself the right to examine the requests submitted with a view to determining whether they were necessary. The intention was to make each factory practise the greatest possible economy in the use of labour within its own precincts. Another purpose of these commissions was to determine the extent to which an establishment might be able to release its own labour for work in other plants, without prejudice to the task assigned to it. It was the task of the Armaments Ministry and of the agencies subordinate to it to determine the sequence of priority of requests for labour received by establishments under its jurisdiction. They also had to determine which of the plants was in a position to release workers for other plants manufacturing similar products for similar Wehrmacht requirements. To give an example: The supply programme of a plant manufacturing component parts for vehicles was modified: then it was left to the Armaments Commands to decide that the labour power thus set free should be assigned to another factory in the same line of production. In general, the allotment of labour remained in the hands of the General Plenipotentiary for the Mobilization of Labour. The agencies of Speer's Ministry were merely concerned with directing the labour already available in this economic branch which had been procured and assigned to these establishments by the General Plenipotentiary for the Mobilization of Labour. The procurement of other labour remained in the hands of the General Plenipotentiary for the Mobilization of Labour; and the General Plenipotentiary for the Mobilization of Labour participated authoritatively in the examination of the question as to what extent plants could release labour in order to make it available to others. (The so-called combing- out action.) The authority of the General Plenipotentiary for the Employment of Labour was therefore not limited to any extent through this mutual agreement between him and the Reich Minister for Armament and War Production. His task, now as before, was merely to procure labour for the plants; he was even given a considerable amount of authority in labour questions, to look over the armament plants under the control of the defendant Speer, and to examine if and to what extent these plants could release workers for other plants. The decree of 22nd June, 1944, ordained that labour which was already available was to be used in accordance with the directives of the Central authorities or according to the orders of the Chairman of the Armament Commission. It must also be noted in this respect that it was not a matter of using new labour which was unskilled in armament work and which was still procured through the General Plenipotentiary for the Employment of Labour, but solely of so-called transfer actions from one armament plant to another. Therefore the Sauckel agencies, in accordance with this decree, could no longer check the demands for labour made by the plants which were controlled by the Speer Ministry, if the Chairman of the Armament Commission had recognized these demands. This decree did not bring any change in the basic distribution of authority, according to which the General Plenipotentiary for the Employment of Labour had to procure the required workers and to handle the whole allocation of labour. If the agencies of the General Plenipotentiary allocated labour in response to demands which had been checked, then it was left to their judgement as to what type of labour, whether native or foreign, etc., was to be furnished: The authority of the agencies of the Minister for Armament in questions of the commitment of labour was limited to a large extent to the execution of so-called transfer actions, i.e., the assignment of labour from one armament plant to another. It would be wrong to try to conclude from these decrees that there was a considerable limitation of the authority of the General Plenipotentiary for the Employment of Labour and a fundamental expansion of authority on the side of Speer. It would be just as wrong to conclude from this that the influence of the Armament Ministry had been increased over other authorities of the General Plenipotentiary for the Employment of Labour.

In order apparently to characterise the relationship between Speer and Sauckel, the prosecution has finally submitted a file note by General Thomas, the Director of the War Economy and Armament Division in the OKW, regarding a discussion which took place on 24th March, 1942, between the defendant Speer on the one hand, and himself aid the directors of the Armament Offices of the three branches of the Wehrmacht on the other hand, in which Thomas states that the Fuehrer considered Speer as his main authority and his agent for all economic spheres. This note can only be understood in connection with the report of the account given by General Thomas of his activity as Director of the War Economy and Armament Office, and which has been presented to the. Tribunal in excerpt form in Document 2353-PS. Prior to Speer's appointment as Minister for Armament, Thomas had to try to bring about an expansion of the position of General Plenipotentiary for Economy, as it has been provided in the Reich Defence Law, so that it should become an office which would control the whole war economy. When the armament economy was confronted with heavy demands in connection with the first winter campaign in Russia and the losses which had been sustained there, and Hitler, after the death of Dr. Todt, appointed Speer to be his successor in the Ministry for Armaments and Munitions, Thomas thought he would find in Speer a personality who would receive the authority which he had striven to obtain for the General Plenipotentiary for Economy. This, however, did not occur. As has been shown from the evidence, Speer was only entrusted with the equipment of the Army and construction tasks. The control of the new office of the General Plenipotentiary for the Employment of Labour by his Ministry, for which the defendant Speer was striving, was not sanctioned by Hitler. Speer's rights as Minister for Armament are stated in the decree. The expectations which General Thomas held as regards the Appointment of Speer were therefore not fulfilled in any way. Speer only received increased authority when, in the year 1943, he took over industrial production from the Ministry of Economics. But even then he was still far from having the complete field of tasks which General Thomas had expected he would obtain. Relying on his expectations, General Thomas thought that he had found in the person of Speer the man appointed by Hitler who would be decisive for all economic questions. In the file note of General Thomas, which confines itself merely to generalities, it is a matter of an expression of opinion which was not justified by the actual state of affairs. It offers no grounds on which to answer the question as to how we must distribute responsibility for the policy of the labour commitment to which the prosecution objects.

In summarising it must be stated to this count of the Indictment:

Speer is not responsible for the means employed for the procurement of foreign workers, nor for their removal to Germany. He is at the most responsible for the utilisation of part of this manpower in Germany.

As a further count of the Indictment it has been stated that the defendant employed prisoners of war in the economic sector which was under his direction, and that he thereby violated Article 32 of the Geneva Convention of July, 1929, regarding the treatment of prisoners of war. The defendant never denied that he employed prisoners of war in plants under his control. This, however, cannot be regarded simply as a violation of Articles 31 and 32 of the previously mentioned agreement. The expression "armament economy" and/or "armament plant" has not the same meaning as "plant" and/or "economy", the task of which is the manufacture of arms and of direct war requirements.

The term "armament plant" can only be understood from its development. When, at the beginning of rearmament, there began to be a limitation of raw materials, plants which were working for rearmament were given preference in obtaining raw materials. These plants were controlled by the armament inspectors of the Wehrmacht, and were called "armament plants". In addition to all other plants, those used for manufacturing iron, steel and metals, as well as those plants which manufactured machine-boilers and vehicles and appliance, also those used for the entire manufacture of raw steel, the first stage of processing to the finished product (foundries, rolling works, forges), as well as the whole remaining subsidiary supply industry, came under the term "armament plants", for example, electro-technical plants, plants which produced optical instruments, plants which manufactured ball-bearings, cog-wheels, etc. This is shown by the testimony of the witness Schieber. (Question 9, Document Book, Page 114.)

Only 30-35 per cent roughly of the whole iron production was used for the production of armaments to the extent previously described, and 60 per cent for the maintenance of production for other consumers (Reich Railways, the construction of merchant vessels, agricultural machines, export goods, appliances for the chemical industry, etc.). We refer to the testimony of the witness Kehrl, which has been submitted under Exhibit Speer 36, and particularly to his answer to question 5.

Since the iron quota assigned to the armament industry also includes the production of raw steel and the different stages of manufacture, it can be safely presumed that of all the plants which were combined in the armament inspections, only approximately 20-30 per cent manufactured armament products in the sense implied in the Geneva Convention. These details had to be examined in order to gain an idea as to what extent Article 31 of the Geneva Convention could be violated by the employment of prisoners of war.

The prosecution has presented an affidavit of the American economic statistician Deuss under Document 2520-PS, in order to prove thereby how many prisoners of war and foreign workers were employed in the armament industry. This compilation, which is principally supported by figures taken from the documents in the possession of the defendant Speer, does not, however, state in which branches of the armament industry the individual prisoners of war worked. A big enterprise, which, because it falls under one of the above- listed categories, and as a result thereof was considered an armament plant in its entirety, needed only to manufacture a fraction of, or perhaps even no weapons or equipment at all, which stand in direct relationship to war activities. If prisoners of war are employed in it, then their occupation does not represent a violation of Article 31 of the Geneva Prisoner-of-War Convention. Such a plant, however, appears in its entirety in Deuss's affidavit. The affidavit thereby loses its value as evidence as to what extent Article 31 of the Geneva Convention was violated. Thus we have no proof of whether and to what extent Article 31 was violated by the employment of prisoners of war in the armament industry.

The French prosecution has taken the point of view that the employment of French civilian workers, who had been released from confinement as prisoners of war and who were employed in the armament industry, was also to be considered a violation of Article 31. This is not applicable. From the time of their release the former prisoners of war were free people who were unlimited in their freedom of movement, and who were restricted only by the obligations embodied in their labour contracts. In addition to this, no French prisoner of war could be forced to agree to his release under the obligation of putting himself as a worker at the disposal of German industry. It was his own free decision if he preferred circumstances, the advantages apparently appeared far greater than the protection which they enjoyed as prisoners of war. If they did so, then their occupation, even in work which in itself is prohibited for prisoners of war in accordance with Article 31, cannot be considered a violation of this article.

The employment of prisoners of war in the industry of the country which is holding them prisoner is not prohibited by the Geneva Prisoner-of-War Convention. Only that work is prohibited which is directly connected with military operations, for example, the use of prisoners of war for fortification works for a combat unit. The defendant Speer cannot be accused of anything of that kind. It is also prohibited for them to manufacture and transport weapons of all kinds, as well as to transport war material for combat units. In the armament economy under the control of the defendant Speer, the only thing which could be considered as a violation of the aforementioned rule is the manufacture of weapons and munitions of all kinds. Such a violation, however, has so far not been proved by the prosecution at all.

It must furthermore be examined how the assignment of prisoners of war to plants took place. According to the testimony of the defendant Sauckel, this was done by the War Economy Officers with the Military District Commanders, who submitted the number of prisoners of war available for work to the Gau Employment Office, and the transfer of the prisoners of war to the plants then took place in the same manner as with ordinary labour.

The only difference was that the camp officers—the prisoners of war were billeted in so-called enlisted men's camp (Stammlager)—were responsible for seeing that the directives issued by the OKW for the employment and treatment of prisoners of war were complied with. It was the responsibility of these camp officers to prevent, in the employment of prisoners of war, violations of Article 31 of the Prisoner-of-War Convention. The Commitment Officers (Einsatzoffiziere) appointed by the camp commanders had constantly to control and examine the working conditions and the nature of the occupation of prisoners of war in armament plants, and they had to watch and see that no prohibited work was imposed on the prisoners of war. The defendant Keitel has given an exact description of the manner in which the control of prisoners of war in the home area was carried out. Documents have also been submitted which give information about the treatment of prisoners of war.

The prisoners of war who were confined in assembly camps were constantly 3 being examined by Camp Commitment Officers to see that their employment was in accordance with Articles 31 and 32 of the Geneva Prisoner-of-War Convention. As far as French prisoners of war were concerned, a special

*The arrest of the Flensburg Government. Karl Doenitz is in the centre in the dark coat, followed by Albert Speer (bareheaded), accompanied by Alfred Jodl.*
Bundesarchiv, Bild 146-1985-079-31 / CC-BY-SA

authority existed for them in the person of Ambassador Scapini, who had to forward to the OKW any complaints which were made against the use of prisoners of war for labour in a way which violated International Law.

Complaints of this kind by Ambassador Scapini were immediately investigated, and if they were found to be justified, improvements were made. It is, of course, possible that mistakes sometimes occurred in view of the vast organisation necessitated by the large number of French prisoners of war. Measures for the correction of mistakes of this kind, are, after all, provided by the Geneva Prisoner-of-War Convention itself in its regulations. These regulations were also effective in the last war. The representatives of the protecting powers intervened against bad conditions which had been brought to their attention through complaints, and they also demanded and achieved their abolition. If such mistakes were recognized and reported, they were then immediately remedied. It would be wrong to try to conclude from individual occurrences that there was a pre-meditated system. The protection which prisoners of war found in the Labour Commitment Offices even laid defendant Speer open to criticism by individual plant directors as being too extensive.

In this respect, as far as the defendant Speer's position in law is concerned, we must first examine whether the employment of prisoners of war in the armament industry is to be fundamentally regarded as a violation of the rules of International Law. After the previous statements as to the character of the plants which were combined in the armament industry, this must be answered in the negative. Only in so far as prisoners of war were actually employed in the production of arms and in the production of urgent war materials could there be any suggestion of a violation of Article 31. That this regulation may have been violated in individual cases we will not deny. If, for example, as the photographs submitted by the American prosecution show, prisoners of war were used near the front lines to unload munition trains, then this undoubtedly represents a violation of the regulations of Article 31. The defendant Speer, however, cannot be accused of such incidents, as they do not fall under his competence. To conclude from this fact of the employment of some prisoners of war in the armament industry that a violation on a large scale of the regulations of the Geneva Prisoner-of-War Convention did take place, is not justified.

**THE PRESIDENT:** The Tribunal will adjourn.

*(A recess was taken until 1400 hours.)*

**M. LANOIRE:** Mr. President, I would request the permission of the Tribunal, to make a very short statement in the name of the French prosecution. Even though it is not the custom that the prosecution should intervene in the course of the discussion, the counsel for Speer gave a few opinions which it seems to me I must underline, and also request the Tribunal to put them aside.

**THE PRESIDENT:** The Tribunal does not think it is appropriate that the speeches of the defendants' counsel should be interrupted by counsel for the prosecution. Counsel for the prosecution are going to speak afterwards, and they will then have a full opportunity of answering the speeches that have been made on behalf of the defendants.

**M. LANOIRE:** Certainly, Mr. President.

**THE PRESIDENT:** Dr. Flaechsner, if you will wait one moment, I have an announcement to make. The Tribunal refers to its Order of 23rd February, 1946, paragraph 8 of that Order, which is on the subject of the statements which the defendants may make, under Article 24 of the Charter.

In view of the full statements already made by the defendants and their counsel, the Tribunal assumes that if it is the defendants' desire to make any further statements, it will be only to deal with matters previously omitted. The defendants will not be permitted to make further speeches or to repeat what has already been said by themselves or their counsel, but will be limited to short statements of a few minutes each to cover matters not already covered by their testimony or the arguments of counsel.

That is all.

**DR. FLAECHSNER (for the defendant Speer):** Mr. President, your Honours, I now continue my speech. A further charge of the prosecution refers to the violation of Article 32 of the Geneva Prisoner-of-War Agreement, according to which prisoners of war were employed in unhealthy work, in so far as prisoners of war had been employed in mines. For this reference is made to the minutes of a Central Planning meeting where the employment of Russian prisoners of war in mines is discussed. The employment of Russian prisoners of war in mines is not to be considered as forbidden in itself, and it has been practised in all industrial nations. The employment of Russian prisoners of war in mines is, therefore, not to be objected to, in so far as the prisoners concerned were in a physical condition that enabled them to do heavy mining work. It has not been established and proved by the prosecution that these prisoners of war were not physically fit for the work given them. From the fact that the employment of prisoners of war in mines was discussed and approved, it cannot be concluded that Article 32 of the Prisoner-of-War Agreement was violated. The treatment of prisoners of war has to be examined legally from various points of view. The German Government has taken the point of view that Soviet prisoners of war should be treated on a different legal basis from the subjects of the Western States, who were all parties to the treaty of the Geneva Prisoner-of-War Convention of 1929, whereas the Soviet Union did not sign this agreement.

The Soviet Prosecution has presented Document EC-338, Exhibit USSR 356, an investigation according to International Law of the Foreign Counter-Intelligence Office (Amt Ausland/Abwehr) in the High Command of the Wehrmacht, concerning the legality of the regulations issued on the treatment of Soviet prisoners of war, and levelled sharp criticism at the latter. The essential point is that in this report the view is expressed that, as a matter of fundamental principle, Soviet prisoners of war cannot be treated according to the rules of the Geneva Prisoner-of-War Agreement because the Soviet Union did not participate in this. Moreover, this report refers to the decree of the Soviet Union of 1st July, 1941, concerning the treatment of prisoners of war, regarding which the opinion of the Military Intelligence of the Wehrmacht confirms that on essential points it agrees with the rules of the Geneva Prisoner-of-War Agreement. It is, however, characteristic that in this decree it is ordered that non-commissioned officers and enlisted men taken as prisoners of war may be put to work for industry and agriculture inside the camp or outside, and that the only restriction is that the use of prisoner-of-war labour is forbidden:

(a) in the combat area,
(b) for personal needs of the administration as well as the needs of other prisoners of war. (So-called "orderly service"; see Page 12-13 of the document book.)

An order restricting the use of prisoner-of-war labour according to Articles 31 and 32 of the Geneva Prisoner-of- War Agreement is not to be understood from the above- mentioned command. It now remains to investigate whether the stipulations of Articles 31 and 32 of the Geneva Prisoner-of- War Agreement are based on general rules of International Law which should be observed even if there were no special ruling by treaty, such as the Geneva Prisoner-of-War Agreement represents. This cannot generally be affirmed. The above-mentioned treaty regulations cannot be regarded as the prescription by treaty of generally valid legal concepts if so important a member of the family of International Law as the Soviet Union does not accept a ruling of this sort.

Proceeding from this idea, the employment of Soviet prisoners of war in work forbidden by Article 31 of the PW Agreement is not to be objected to. The Italian military personnel interned in Germany after Italy's fall do not come under the regulations of the Geneva Prisoner-of-War Agreement since no state of war existed between Germany and Italy. Moreover, these military internees did not come under the restrictions of Article 31 in their employment as manpower. It must, however, be pointed out that these military internees are comprised in the enumeration by Mr. Deuss of prisoners of war occupied in the armament industry.

In conclusion, the following is to be said on this point:

The procurement of prisoners of war for the factories was effected exclusively through the offices of the General Plenipotentiary for Labour Commitment. The control of the proper allocation in accordance with the Prisoner-of-War Agreement depended on the Labour Commitment Officer of the Stalag, who in return was himself finally responsible to the General for Prisoner-of-War Matters at the Army High Command. It was not possible for the defendant Speer to have any influence on the distribution of prisoners of war and their occupation. The prosecution has not been in a position to produce any evidence from which the participation of the defendant Speer in unlawful employment of prisoners of war might be deduced. This assertion of the prosecution has remained unproved.

The prosecution has now further brought against the defendant the charge that the Todt Organisation, at the head of which Speer was placed in February, 1942, after Dr. Todt's death, used native workers to build fortifications in the French coastal areas. As far as the Todt Organisation is concerned, it was a purely civilian institution of the General Construction Inspector for road maintenance. It worked on a private economic basis, that is, it allocated the construction work that it intended to carry out to private firms, also to foreign firms, which were established in the respective countries, and it merely supervised the execution of the constructions. The private firms could undertake the procurement of the necessary materials and labour themselves. For the very reason that native construction enterprises were used, it was possible to eliminate the difficulties which otherwise would have obstructed the execution of the work. The workyards of the Todt Organisation enjoyed a certain favour with the natives because the workmen had the assurance that they could not be compelled to go to Germany to work in industry there because these tasks of construction of the Organisation Todt were considered as urgently important. The workers went voluntarily to the firms which were working for the Todt Organisation to obtain this security. The example quoted by the defendant Speer during cross-examination, of 50,000 Todt Organisation workers who were once taken from France to Germany to repair damages caused to two West German valley dams by air attacks, made such a bad impression on the workers employed in other Todd Organisation construction sites that there was nothing else left to be done but to send these 50,000 workers back to France. In the meantime, many workmen of the Todt Organisation construction sites in France disappeared, because they feared they would be taken to Germany sooner or later against their will, while up to then they had regarded employment in enterprises which worked for the Todt Organisation as insurance against an eventual transfer to Germany. Only the return of the above-mentioned 50,000 workers to France, which was brought about by the defendant Speer when these unfavourable consequences developed, restored the hitherto existing state of confidence.

Here, too, the fact should be emphasized that as a result of the event described the Todt Organisation workers were free to go where they wished, in France in any case, and that no coercion was used against them. The consequences of this were that when the protected plants (Sperrbetriebe) were established in France, all enterprises working for the Todt Organisation were declared protected plants and therewith removed from the possibility of being employed on other work. This instance shows that the view of the prosecution that the workers of the Todt Organisation were forced into the Todt Organisation plants against their will is wrong.

As it is established that the French Government agreed to the use of French workers in construction sites under administration of the Todt Organisation, as well as in any other armament industries in Germany and the occupied territories, every illegality is excluded. It should not be left unmentioned here that after the conclusion of the Armistice Agreement with France the latter had no more part in military hostilities. The Armistice Treaty certainly did not mean an agreement for a truce but, de facto, a final stopping of hostilities, and was to serve as a preparation for the conclusion of peace; it was a peace situation but did not yet mean the definite return to peace-time conditions regulated by treaty. A resumption of hostilities was, however, according to both partners to the Armistice, completely out of the question. The Armistice was exclusively to regulate the situation until the definite conclusion of peace. Prescriptions of the Hague Convention, as well as of the Prisoner-of-War Agreement, concerning the restriction that performance of services cannot be allowed to violate the loyalty towards one's own country which is still fighting, do not apply because the country was no longer at war. After a general armistice, the production of arms and munitions can no longer be directed against the party which has retired from hostilities, but only against other partners still in the field. The aforementioned principle of respecting the loyalty to one's own country can no longer be applied in such cases.

It must, moreover, be pointed out that the Todt Organisation was in no way a para-military organisation as has been falsely asserted. Apparently this false assumption has been strengthened by the fact that the German members of the administration of the Todt Organisation abroad wore a uniform. These people were considered as Wehrmacht followers, but on the other hand the labour engaged by the firms and the construction workers of the firms as well as the technical personnel were in no such relation. The charge cannot be made, therefore, that these native workers were indirectly incorporated into a Wehrmacht organisation.

A further charge against the defendant Speer consists in the fact that prisoners from concentration camps were employed in the economic sector controlled by him. The defendant has admitted this. A penal responsibility because of this fact does not, however, stand the test of legal examination. The employment of convicts for work of an economic nature has always been a practice in Germany. It could be carried out in various ways, partly by employment within the convict prison itself, partly outside. Owing to the lack of labour due to the aggravation of the economic war, it was necessary to draw upon the labour available in the concentration camps.

The prosecution has submitted documents from which can be seen how much trouble was taken by the offices subordinate to the Reich Minister Himmler to use the reserves of labour contained in the concentration camps for the construction of their own SS plants, and the defendant Speer has supplied information during his hearing before the Tribunal on 20th—21st June regarding the efforts of Himmler towards building up a separate armament industry of his own, and subordinate to him only, which would have had the result that any control over the production of arms in these intended SS plants would have become impossible, so that the SS could have provided themselves with weapons without the Army or any other offices being able to control them.

The defendant Speer successfully fought against this. It was agreed that Himmler would release a part of the inmates of the concentration camps to be employed in the armament industry. Hereby the inmates of the concentration camps gained an improvement of their situation, since in the first place they obtained the higher food rations provided for workmen or for those doing long shifts or heavy work, as has been attested by witness Riecke; moreover, they left the large concentration camps and were no more under SS control during working-hours, but were subject to the control of foremen and skilled workmen appointed by the plants themselves.

It is true that to avoid transportation and marching difficulties special camps were erected near the plants or working-places where they were employed, and these were not accessible to the control of the plant managers nor to the control of the offices of the defendant Speer, but stood exclusively under the control of the offices in charge of the administration of the concentration camps. For the conditions prevailing in such camps neither the plant manager nor the offices of the defendant Speer can be held responsible if abuses occurred there. In general, as attested by the letter of the department chief Schieber of 7th May, 1944, to the defendant Speer (Document Book II, Page 88), the inmates preferred work in such plants to work under the administration of the concentration camp itself. And Schieber quite clearly states in his letter that for these reasons more scope should be given to the employment of concentration camp inmates in order to improve their lot. But he further states that the number of concentration camp inmates employed in the armament industry amounted to 36,000 and that this figure was decreasing. Against this, the defendant's assertion at his interrogation that the total number of concentration camp workers employed in the armament industry amounted to one per cent of the total number of workmen employed in the whole armament industry is calculated too high. Of 49 million workmen engaged in the final processing of armaments, the figure of 36,000 represents only seven per thousand. The number of concentration camp inmates employed in the armament industry represents a very small part of the total labour employed in the final processing of armaments, that is of the total labour employed in the plants manufacturing finished products.

These figures show how misleading the assumption of the prosecution is, that the employment of such prisoners in the armament industry had resulted in an increased demand for such labour and that this increased demand was satisfied by the sending into concentration camps of persons who under normal conditions would never have been sent there. The opinion that the fact of the employment of prisoners from concentration camps in the armament industry led to an increase in the number of concentration camp inmates is disproved by the letter of Schieber already mentioned (Exhibit No. 6, Page 88), and by his testimony, also submitted as Exhibit No. 37, Document Book No. 51. According to this the employment of concentration camp inmates in the armament industry occurred for the first time in the autumn of 1943, and the number of prisoners employed there reached its peak with the maximum figure of 36,000 in March, 1944, and from that time on not only did not increase, but, on the contrary, decreased.

Therefore the conclusions of the prosecution in no way bear examination. Not even proof has been brought forward that Speer had attempted to have people sent to concentration camps.

At his interrogation, the defendant admitted that everywhere in Germany people were afraid of being sent to a concentration camp. The population's dread of concentration camps was quite justified, for it depended only on the judgement of the police authorities, led by Himmler, whether a person was sent to a concentration camp or not; further, because there was no legal authority which might have made it possible to check the charges resulting in a transfer to a concentration camp, and finally, and this is the main reason, because it was left entirely to the discretion of the concentration camp authorities to decide for how long one was to be held in a concentration camp.

The prosecution has further asserted that Speer went on having concentration camp inmates work in the armament industry after he had obtained knowledge of conditions prevailing in the Mauthausen camp from a visit he made there. That this was not the case is proved by the evidence of the defendant on this point. As it was only a hurried visit, the purpose of which was merely to instruct the camp administration to desist from tasks undertaken in defiance of the prohibition, and which served purely peace-time purposes, and instead of this to place labour at the disposal of the armament industry, the defendant Speer could only obtain a superficial impression of the living conditions in the camp. Up to this point, his evidence may be referred to.

Moreover, through witnesses for the prosecution, detailed reference has been made to the fact that during such visits to concentration camps by personalities of high standing, the camps were shown from the best side only, and that any signs of atrocities, etc., were carefully removed so that the visitor should not get a bad impression of the camp—see the statement of the witness Blaha on 1st January, 1946.

In connection with this question, we will deal with the further charge of the prosecution, which asserts that Speer had approved of the use of Hungarian Jews as labour for the construction of the bomb-proof aircraft factories ordered by Hitler. On this point, reference must be made to the evidence of the witness Milch and that of the witness Frank. Milch stated that Speer, who was ill at the time, strongly opposed these constructions, but that Hitler, who demanded the undertaking of the work, gave the commission directly to Dorsch, the leader of the Todt Organisation, to carry them out. So that the controversy between Hitler and Speer should not become known to outsiders, Dorsch officially remained subordinate to Speer, but in this matter he had to deal directly with Hitler alone, and was immediately subordinate to him. In his evidence Milch further stated that the proposed constructions were never carried out. I have submitted Hitler's order to Speer of gist April, 1944, as Exhibit 34, Page 52, in my document book. This order clearly shows that Hitler designated Dorsch as being directly responsible to him, since the appointment of Speer, who was given the duty of adjusting these building tasks to the building plans under him, was of a purely formal nature. The evidence given by Field-Marshal Milch is thus confirmed by this letter.

To support the opinion of the prosecution that the defendant Speer had contributed to sending people to concentration camps, a statement is quoted which was made by Speer at a sitting of the Central Planning Board of 30th October, 1942, on the question of shirkers. In this connection, one must look at the evidence of the defendant Speer in the witness box, in which he declared that upon this statement no steps to stop this evil were taken with the General Plenipotentiary for Labour Commitment either by the Central Planning Board or by himself. Actually, nothing was done about it at that time. It was only in November, 1943, that Sauckel issued a decree against shirkers. The term "shirker" is applied to those workers who, in order to evade the fulfilment of their working obligations, simulate illness or stay away from work under the pretext of reasons that do not stand the test of examination, or even without any reason at all.

It may incidentally be mentioned here that economic warfare did not neglect even this question. Efforts were made in every imaginable way to undermine the willingness to work of the working people. By dropping leaflets and through other channels of information, advice was given to the workers as to how they could report sick; what means they were to use in order to succeed in feigning illness at medical examinations; they were invited to work slowly, etc. At first this propaganda succeeded only in isolated cases. As, however, such isolated cases very easily have an unfavourable influence on the working discipline of the personnel as a whole, the defendant Speer discussed the possibility of police intervention. Speer did not, however, take any initiative of any kind which would have led to practical action on the part of the police. It was not until a year later that a decree was issued by the General Plenipotentiary for Labour Commitment, first making it an obligation for the employer to use disciplinary penalties. In particularly grave cases, the trustees for production could ask for punishment by a court. Based on this decree sentences could be pronounced providing for transfer to a workers' training camp for a term of 56 days. Only in exceptionally grave cases of infractions of the labour laws did the decree of the General Plenipotentiary for Labour Commitment provide for transfer to a concentration camp.

It must be mentioned here that this decree was applicable both to native and foreign workers in the same way, for in no case were native workers to be treated differently. In the cross-examination of defendant Sauckel, the French prosecution produced the document relative to a meeting of Sauckel's labour authorities at the Wartburg. At this meeting Dr. Sturm, the specialist on questions of labour law with the General Plenipotentiary for Labour Commitment, gave a lecture on the punishment of workmen, and it was thereby established that only an infinitesimal percentage of workers had to be sentenced to penal punishment.

But from this it is again evident that the prosecution has brought forward no proof for the assertion that, as a consequence of Sauckel's decree concerning shirkers, the concentration camps were filled; so that conclusive proof is lacking that Sauckel, or respectively, the defendant Speer, contributed by any measures they took to the filling of concentration camps.

In his statement before the Central Planning Board of 22nd May, 1944 (P. 49 in my document book), Speer pointed out that the escaped prisoners of war who were apprehended by the police had to be brought straight back to their work. From this remark we see the basic attitude of the defendant Speer, who did not want to see the escaped prisoners of war thrown into concentration camps but demanded that they be immediately incorporated into industry. So far the prosecution has not been able to bring forward any reliable proof for the assertion that Speer had the concentration camps filled in order to obtain labour from them.

Mr. President, perhaps now I may go into the question which you asked me at the beginning of my plea as to how I interpret paragraph 6A of the Charter in regard to the defendant Speer, especially in regard to the terminology: "The waging of a war of aggression." I should like to say the following: The Charter, under 6A, cites, among other punishable actions, the execution of a war of aggression. As for the definition of a war of aggression, I need say nothing here Professor Jahrreiss has already done that in detail. Here it is only the interpretation of the term "the execution of a war of aggression" that is in question. My point of view is that a war of aggression can be waged only by the person who has supreme command. All others are only led, even if their participation may mean a considerable contribution to the war.

In the case of the defendant Speer, therefore, the waging of a war of aggression cannot be applied. I should like to point out the following as well: In a session on about 28th February or 1st March, one of the judges told justice Jackson that the prosecution had represented the point of view that the charge of a war of aggression was concluded with its outbreak. I can only share this opinion.

During the hearing of evidence I had ample opportunity to state the activities of the defendant Speer during the last phases of the war from June, 1944. I can, therefore, confine myself now to proving in regard to this detailed chronological description that the entire testimony of Speer is covered almost completely by testimonies of other witnesses and by documents. The written statements of witnesses, which I refrained from reading before the Tribunal, run entirely along the same lines, although the witnesses came from different camps and expressed themselves in a completely unbiased manner.

Beginning with June, 1944, the defendant Speer readily reported to Hitler on the situation of his armament production, and he emphatically pointed out at the same time that the war would be lost if such decline of production were allowed to continue. This is proved by the memoranda of Speer to Hitler submitted as Speer Exhibits Nos. 14, 15, 20, 21; 22, 23, and 24. As stated by the witness General Guderian, Chief of the General Staff of the Army (compare Question 6, Page 179 of my document book), Hitler, as from the end of January, 1945, defined any such information as high treason and subjected it to corresponding punishment. Nevertheless, as it appears also from the statement of General Guderian, Chief of the Army General Staff, Speer stated clearly time and again to Hitler as well as to Guderian his opinion about the prospects of the war.

Hitler had especially forbidden that third persons should be informed about the true situation of the war. Notwithstanding this, after the severest orders for destruction had been issued by Hitler, Speer informed the Gauleiter and the Commanders-in-Chief of various army groups that the war was lost and thus achieved that Hitler's policy of destruction was at least partly prevented. This is evident from the testimonies of witnesses Hupfauer, Kempf and von Poser.

Hitler declared to Speer on 29th March, 1945, that the latter would have to take the consequences customary in such cases, if he continued to declare that the war was lost. This conversation is contained in the testimony of the witness Kempf. In spite of this, Speer two days later travelled to Seyss-Inquart (on 1st April, 1945) in order to explain to him, too, that the war was lost. The witness Seyss-Inquart and the witness Schwebel in the interrogations of 11th June, 1946, and 14th June, 1946, stated here unanimously that this conversation with Speer of 1st April, 1945, occasioned the conferences of Seyss-Inquart with the Chief of the General Staff of General Eisenhower, General Smith. This led finally to the handing over of Holland to the Allies.

On 24th April, 1945, Speer flew once again to Berlin, which was already besieged, in order to persuade Hitler that the senseless fight should be given up, as is evident from the testimony of the witness Poser. In his last will Hitler dismissed Speer on 29th April, 1945 (Document 3569-PS, Page 87 of the Document Book Speer).

The American Chief Prosecutor, Chief Justice Jackson, has, therefore, been obliged to admit to the defendant Speer during his cross-examination that he, Speer, was evidently the only man who told Hitler the whole truth.

The representatives of the prosecution have produced no evidence that destructions of industries took place in Poland, the Balkans, Czechoslovakia, France, Belgium, Holland during the German retreat. This is in the first place a merit of the defendant Speer who prevented the destruction of the industries of these countries as ordered by Hitler, partly through a purposely false interpretation of existing orders. That Speer was convinced as early as the summer of 1944 that this destruction should be prevented in the general European interest is evident from the testimony of the witness von Poser. It would have been easy, by relevant execution of the orders, to cripple completely the highly-developed industries of Central Europe and of the occupied Western European countries for 2-3 years and with them the entire industrial production and civilised life of these peoples, in fact, to make rebuilding by their own labour quite impossible for years to come.

The witness Seyss-Inquart has stated in his interrogation on 11th June of this year, that the prepared destruction of only 14 plants in Holland would have absolutely destroyed the basis of existence of this country. The destruction of all power plants in these countries would have produced a similar effect as the destruction in 1941 by the Soviets of the 2-3 power plants in the Donetz territory. In spite of all efforts, it was not until the summer of 1943 that some scanty production could start again there. Similar but still more far-reaching consequences had to be expected from the carrying out of Hitler's orders on the European continent.

After the success of the invasion of these occupied territories Speer gave the authorisation to undertake no destructions, as is confirmed by the witnesses von Poser, Kempf, Schieber, Kehrl, Rohland, Seyss-Inquart, Hirschfeld, and by Speer Document 16, question 12, Page 112; Schieber for Upper Italy, question 25, Page 1 19; Rohland for Luxembourg and Lorraine, question 5, Page 1571; Kempf for the Balkans, Czechoslovakia, Polish Upper Silesia, France, Belgium, Holland, Luxembourg; Seyss-Inquart for Holland, Page 11,210 of the German transcript; Hirschfeld for France, Belgium, Czechoslovakia, Upper Italy, Hungary, the Balkans, Poland.

Immediately after the appointment of the co-defendant Doenitz as successor to Hitler, he submitted to him orders prohibiting- any destruction in the still occupied territories of Norway, Czechoslovakia and Holland, as well as Werwolf activities, as is shown in the testimony of the witnesses von Poser and Kempf.

Although Speer had no direct authority for carrying out the destruction of industries in the occupied territories, he had to accomplish this task at his own responsibility and through his agencies within the borders of the so-called Greater German Reich. He had to keep especially busy in this connection in order to obstruct the total destruction of all real values which was obstinately demanded by Hitler. Information on this will to destroy on the part of Hitler and many of his Gauleiter is furnished in the testimonies of witnesses Guderian, Rohland, Hupfauer, von Poser, Stahl and Kempf.

The most important document in this regard is the letter of Speer to Hitler of 29th March, 1945, submitted as Speer Exhibit 26, in which Speer repeats again Hitler's remarks during the conversation on 18th March, 1945. This document shows clearly that Hitler had made up his mind to destroy completely the foundations of the life of the German people. This document should be especially rich in information about Hitler's time for any future historian. In connection therewith follows the evidence of General Guderian who certifies that in February, 1945, Hitler

(1) confused his inevitable fate with that of the German people,
(2) wished to continue this senseless fight by all means and thereby
(3) ordered the reckless destruction of all things of real value.

That is Guderian on Page 177 and Page 179 of my document book.

Also the demolition and evacuation orders of Hitler and Bormann, which were issued the day after the conference with Speer and are of impressive clearness, have been submitted to the Tribunal as documents under Speer Exhibit Nos. 25-28.

Already since the middle of March, 1944, Speer, considering this war inevitably lost, was determined to undertake everything in order to maintain the most urgent vital necessities for the German people, as has been confirmed by the witness Rohland. Notwithstanding the growing danger to himself, he repeated this determination with increasing urgency to his collaborators, as the witnesses Kempf, von Poser and Stahl can certify for the months of July and August, 1944, and the witnesses Stahl, Kempf, von Poser, Rohland and Hupfauer for the critical period from February, 1945, onwards.

Numerous orders of Speer dealing with the preservation of industrial plants, issued between September, 1944, and the end of March, 1945, have been submitted to the Tribunal. They were at first partly issued without Hitler's authorisation, but by clever use of Hitler's hope that these territories could be re-conquered were in part subsequently approved by him.

The testimonies of the witnesses Rohland, Kempf and von Poser, as well as Speer's numerous memoranda regarding the war situation, prove that, without sharing it, he profited by Hitler's illusion in order to prevent these demolitions.

Since the beginning of February, 1945, Hitler no longer lent his ear to any such argumentation. On the contrary, the introduction to his demolition orders of 19th March, 1945, shows that he considered it necessary to oppose actively such argumentation. In counter-orders such as those of 30th March, 1945 (Speer Exhibit No. 29, Page 81 of the document book), to all industrial plants, as well as those of 4th April, 1945, for all sluices and dams, Speer gave instructions—contradictory to the intentions of the orders issued by Hitler—

not to undertake any industrial demolitions. This likewise is corroborated by the witnesses Kempf, von Poser and Rohland.

During the month of March the executive power for the demolition of industrial plants and of other objects of value was transferred from Speer to the Gauleiter.

During this period Speer acted in open insubordination, and on trips to the danger zones he arranged for the sabotage of these orders. Thus, for instance, by clever planning he withdrew the stocks of explosives from the grasp of the Gauleiter, as stated by the witnesses von Poser, Kempf and Rohland, and gave orders that the so-called industrial explosives, which were used for demolition, should no longer be produced, as is proved by the statement of the witness Kehrl, the Chief of the Office for Raw Products of Speer's Ministry.

It seems important that Speer had urgently drawn Hitler's attention to the consequences which the demolitions would have for the German people, as is shown in Speer's submitted memorandum dated 15th March, 1945 (Speer Exhibit No. 23). In this Speer, for example, has established that by the planned demolition of industrial plants and bridges, in the Ruhr for instance, the reconstruction of Germany by her own forces after this war would be made impossible. Thus it is without doubt mainly to Speer's credit that the industrial reconstruction of Western and Central Europe can progress already today, and that in France, Belgium and Holland, according to their latest reports, production has already reached the level of the peace-time production of 1938.

Speer was the Minister responsible for the means of production, i.e., the factories and their installations. Thus he sat in the transmission centre through which Hitler's intentions for the carrying out of these demolitions must necessarily pass. We have noticed in this trial how in an authoritative system such centres are in the position to carry out on a big scale the orders of the head of the State. It was a fortunate coincidence that, at this decisive period, a clear-thinking man like Speer directed this office from which the industrial demolition must be directed.

But with increasing intensification Speer took measures beyond his sphere of action, in order to ease the transition for the German people and at the same time to shorten the war. Thus Speer tried to prevent the destruction of bridges. Every German knows that up to the last days of the war and to the farthest corner of the German Reich bridges were destroyed in a senseless way.

Nevertheless his efforts had no doubt a partial success. The numerous conferences which Speer held in this connection with military commanders are testified to by the witnesses Kempf and Lieutenant-Colonel von Poser. This witness was Speer's liaison officer with the Army, and accompanied him on all trips to the front.

These conferences were partially successful. Finally by the middle of March, 1945 the Chief of the General Staff of the Army, General Guderian, and Speer,

*Speer photographed in his cell during the Nuremberg trials.*

according to the latter's proposal, tried to obtain Hitler's agreement to alter his demolition orders regarding bridges, but they did not succeed. This is confirmed by the witness General Guderian.

Knowing that the consequences of those bridge demolitions were unpredictable, Speer finally, on 6th April, 1945, issued six orders in the name of General Winter of the Supreme Command of the Wehrmacht which were directives for the sparing of the bridges of essential railway lines in the Reich and in the entire Ruhr territory. These unauthorised orders were confirmed by the statements of the witnesses von Poser and Kempf.

At the end of January, 1945, he noticed that from a long- range point of view the guarantee of sufficient food supplies for the German people and the spring tilling of fields for the harvest of 1945 in particular were endangered. Speer, therefore, allowed the requests for armament and production, which were in his jurisdiction, to be superseded and gave priority to the supply of food.

That this did not apply only to the actual food situation but was effected mainly in order to relieve the transition period after the occupation by the Allied troops is proved by the statements of the witnesses Hupfauer, Kempf, Rohland, von Poser, Riecke, Secretary of State in the Ministry of Food, Milch, Kehrl and Seyss-Inquart.

When Speer believed that he had new reasons for apprehension that Hitler, induced by his close collaborators in Party circles, would use poison gas in the autumn of 1944 and in the spring of 1945, he opposed this determinedly, as was proved in his cross-examination by the U.S. Prosecutor, Mr. Justice Jackson, and by the testimony of the witness Brandt. Speer's statement that due to this apprehension he had closed down the German poison gas production as early as November, 1944, was confirmed by the witness Schieber. Speer at the same time established that the military authorities unanimously opposed such a plan.

Finally, since the end of February, 1945, the defendant Speer had tried by means of conspiracies to have the war brought to an earlier end.

The statements of the witnesses Stahl and von Poser show that Speer had planned other violent measures. Chief Justice Jackson has established, too, in the course of Speer's cross-examination, that the prosecution knew of further plans which were to be executed under Speer's leadership.

Apart from all these activities, Speer's political attitude is illuminated by two facts:

1. In Speer's memorandum addressed to Hitler, submitted as Exhibit 1, the defendant establishes that Bormann and Goebbels called him alien and hostile to the Party, and that a continued collaboration would be impossible, should he and his assistants be judged by party-political standards.
2. In their Government list of 20th July, 1944, the anti- Hitler conspirators nominated Speer as Armament Minister and as the only Minister of the Hitlerite system, as stated by the witnesses Ohlendorf, Kempf and Stahl.

Would these circles have proposed Speer as Minister, both in Germany and abroad, if he had not been considered an honest and unpolitical expert for a long time? Is not the very fact that he, as one of the closest collaborators of Hitler, was chosen for this post a further proof of the high esteem in which he was held by the opposition?

My Lords, let me say a few more fundamental words about the Speer case itself. When the defendant took over the office of Minister at the age of 36, his country was in a life-and- death struggle. He could not evade the task with which he had been charged. He devoted his entire energy to the solution of the task, which seemed almost insoluble. The success he obtained there did not cloud his view of the actual condition of things. He realised only too late that

Hitler was not thinking of his people, but only of himself. In his book 'Mein Kampf', Hitler wrote that the government of a people always had to remain conscious of the fact that it should not plunge the people into disaster. Its duty was rather to resign at the right time, so that the people could continue to live. Naturally, such principles were valid only for governments in which Hitler had no part. As far as he himself was concerned, however, he was of the point of view that if the German people should lose this war, they would have proved themselves the weaker nation, and would no longer have any right to live. In contrast to this brutal egoism, Speer had preserved the feeling that he was the servant of his people and his nation. Without consideration for his person and without consideration for his safety, Speer acted as he considered it his duty to act towards his people.

Speer had to betray Hitler in order to remain loyal to his people. Nobody will be able to disregard the tragedy which lies in this fate.

# Concluding Speeches from the Prosecution

## FRIDAY, 26 JULY 1946

**THE PRESIDENT:** I call on the Chief Prosecutor of the United States of America.

**JUSTICE JACKSON:** Mr. President and members of the Tribunal:

An advocate can be confronted with few more formidable tasks than to select his closing arguments where there is great disparity between his appropriate time and his available material. In eight months—a short time as State trials go—we have introduced evidence which embraces as vast and varied a panorama of events as has ever been compressed within the framework of a litigation. It is impossible in summation to do more than outline with bold strokes the vitals of this trial's sad and melancholy record, which will live as the historical text of the twentieth century's shame and depravity.

In opening this case I ventured to predict that there would be no serious denial that the crimes charged were committed, and that the issue would concern the responsibility of particular defendants. The defendants have fulfilled that prophecy. Generally, they do not deny that these things happened, but it is contended that they "just happened", and that they were not the result of a common plan or conspiracy.

One of the chief reasons the defendants say why there was no conspiracy is the argument that conspiracy was impossible with a dictator. The argument runs that they all had to obey Hitler's orders, which had the force of law m the German State, and hence obedience could not be made the basis of a criminal charge. In this way it is explained that while there have been wholesale killings, there have been no murderers.

This argument is an effort to evade Article 8 of the Charter, which provides that the order of the Government or of a superior shall not free a defendant from responsibility but can only be considered in mitigation. This provision of the Charter corresponds with the justice and with the realities of the situation, as indicated in defendant Speer's description of what he considered to be the common responsibility of the leaders of the German nation; he said that ... with reference to decisive matters, there was a joint responsibility. There must be a joint responsibility among the leaders, because who else could take the responsibility for the development of events, if not the close associates who work with and around the head of the State?

And again he told the Tribunal that ... it was impossible after the catastrophe to evade this joint responsibility, and that if the war had been won, the leaders would also have laid claim to joint responsibility.

Like much of defence counsel's abstract arguments, the contention that the absolute power of Hitler precluded a conspiracy crumbles in the face of the facts of record. The Fuehrerprinzip of absolutism was itself a part of the common plan, as Goering has pointed out. The defendants may have become the slaves of a dictator, but he was their dictator. To make him such was, as Goering has testified, the object of the Nazi movement from the beginning. Every Nazi took this oath:

> "I pledge eternal allegiance to Adolf Hitler. I pledge unconditional obedience to him and the Fuehrers appointed by him."

Moreover, they forced everybody else in their power to take it. This oath was illegal under German law, which made it criminal to become a member of an organisation in which obedience to "unknown superiors or unconditional obedience to known superiors is pledged". These men destroyed free government in Germany and now plead to be excused from responsibility because they became slaves. They are in the position of the boy of fiction who murdered his father and mother and then pleaded for leniency because he was an orphan.

What these men have overlooked is that Adolf Hitler's acts are their acts. It was these men among millions of others, and it was these men leading millions of others, who built up Adolf Hitler and vested in his psychopathic personality not only innumerable lesser decisions but the supreme issue of war or peace. They intoxicated him with power and adulation. They fed his hates and aroused his fears. They put a loaded gun in his eager hands. It was left to Hitler to pull the trigger, and when he did they all at that time approved. His guilt stands admitted, by some defendants reluctantly, by some vindictively. But his guilt is the guilt of the whole dock, and of every man in it.

The last stand of each defendant is that even if there was a conspiracy, he was not in it. It is therefore important in examining their attempts at avoidance of responsibility to know, first of all, just what it is that a conspiracy charge comprehends and punishes.

In conspiracy we do not punish one man for another man's crime. We seek to punish each for his own crime of joining a common criminal plan in which others also participated. The measure of the criminality of the plan and therefore of the guilt of each participant is, of course, the sum total of crimes committed by all in executing the plan. But the gist of the offence is participation in the formulation or execution of the plan. These are rules which every society has found necessary in order to reach men, like these defendants, who never get blood on their own hands but who lay plans that result in the shedding of blood. All over Germany today, in every zone of occupation, little men who carried out these criminal policies under orders are being convicted and punished. It would present a vast and unforgivable caricature of justice if the men who planned these policies and directed these little men should escape all penalty.

These men in this dock, on the face of this record, were not strangers to this programme of crime, nor was their connection with it remote or obscure. We find them in the very heart of it. The positions they held show that we have chosen defendants of self-evident responsibility. They are the very highest surviving authorities in their respective fields and in the Nazi State. No one lives who, at least until the very last moments of the war, outranked Goering in position, power, and influence. No soldier stood above Keitel and Jodl, and no sailor above Raeder and Doenitz. Who can be responsible for the double-faced diplomacy if not the Foreign Ministers, von Neurath and Ribbentrop, and the diplomatic handyman, von Papen? Who should be answerable for the oppressive administration of occupied countries if Gauleiter, Protectors, Governors and Commissars such as Frank, Seyss-Inquart, Frick, von Schirach, von Neurath, and Rosenberg are not? Where shall we look for those who mobilised the economy for total war if we overlook Schacht and Speer and Funk? Who was the master of the great slaving enterprise if it was not Sauckel? Where shall we find the hand that ran the concentration camps if it was not the hand of Kaltenbrunner? Who whipped up the hates and fears of the public, and manipulated the Party organisations to incite these crimes, if not Hess, von Schirach, Fritzsche, Bormann and the unspeakable Julius Streicher? The list of defendants is made up of men who played indispensable and reciprocal parts in this tragedy. The photographs and the films show them again and again together on important occasions. The documents show them agreed on policies and on methods, and all working aggressively for the expansion of Germany by force of arms.

Each of these men made a real contribution to the Nazi plan. Each man had a key part. Deprive the Nazi regime of the functions performed by a Schacht, a Sauckel, a von Papen, or a Goering, and you have a different regime. Look down the rows of fallen men and picture them as the photographic and documentary evidence shows them to have been in their days of power. Is there one who did not substantially advance the conspiracy along its bloody path towards its bloody goal? Can we assume that the great effort of these men's lives was directed towards ends they never suspected?

To escape the implications of their positions and the inference of guilt from their activities, the defendants are almost unanimous in one defence. The refrain is heard time and again: these men were without authority, without knowledge, without influence, without importance.

In the testimony of each defendant, at some point there was reached the familiar blank wall: nobody knew anything about what was going on. Time after time we have heard the chorus from the dock:

"I only heard about these things here for the first time."

These men saw no evil, spoke none, and none was uttered in their presence. This claim might sound very plausible if made by one defendant. But when we put all their stories together, the impression which emerges of the Third Reich, which was to last a thousand years, is ludicrous. If we combine only the stories of the front bench, this is the ridiculous composite picture of Hitler's Government that emerges. It was composed of:

- A No. 2 man who knew nothing of the excesses of the Gestapo which he created, and never suspected the Jewish extermination programme although he was the signer of over a score of decrees which instituted the persecution of that race;
- A No. 3 man who was merely an innocent middleman transmitting Hitler's orders without even reading them, like a postman or delivery boy;
- A Foreign Minister who knew little of foreign affairs and nothing of foreign policy;
- A Field-Marshal who issued orders to the armed forces but had no idea of the results they would have in practice;
- A Security Chief who was of the impression that the policing functions of his Gestapo and SD were somewhat on the lines of directing traffic;
- A Party philosopher who was interested in historical research, and had no idea of the violence which his philosophy was inciting in the twentieth century;
- A Governor-General of Poland who reigned but did not rule;
- A Gauleiter of Franconia whose occupation was to pour forth filthy writings about the Jews, but who had no idea that anybody would read them;
- A Minister of the Interior who knew not even what went on in the interior of his own office, much less the interior of his own department, and nothing at all about the interior of Germany;
- A Reichsbank President who was totally ignorant of what went in and out of the vaults of his bank;
- A Plenipotentiary for the War Economy who secretly marshalled the entire economy for armament, but had no idea it had anything to do with war.

This may seem like a fantastic exaggeration, but this is what you would actually be obliged to conclude if you were to acquit these defendants.

They do protest too much. They deny knowing what was common knowledge. They deny knowing plans and programmes that were as public as 'Mein Kampf' and the Party programme. They deny even knowing the contents of documents which they received and acted upon.

These defendants, unable to deny that they were the men in the very highest ranks of power, and unable to deny that the crimes I have outlined actually happened, know that their own denials are incredible unless they can suggest someone who is guilty.

The defendants have been unanimous, when pressed, in shifting the blame on other men, sometimes on one and sometimes on another. But the names they have repeatedly picked are Hitler, Himmler, Heydrich, Goebbels and Bormann. All of these are dead or missing. No matter how hard we have pressed the defendants on the stand, they have never pointed the finger at a living man as guilty. It is a temptation to ponder the wondrous workings of a fate which has left only the guilty dead and only the innocent alive. It is almost too remarkable.

The chief villain on whom blame is placed—some of the defendants vie with each other in producing appropriate epithets—is Hitler. He is the man at whom nearly every defendant has pointed an accusing finger.

I shall not dissent from this consensus, nor do I deny that all these dead and missing men shared the guilt. In crimes so reprehensible that degrees of guilt have lost their significance they may have played the most evil parts. But their guilt cannot exculpate the defendants. Hitler did not carry all responsibility to the grave with him. All the guilt is not wrapped in Himmler's shroud. It was these dead men whom these living chose to be their partners in this great conspiratorial brotherhood, and the crimes that they did together they must pay for one by one.

It may well be said that Hitler's final crime was against the land he had ruled. He was a mad "messiah" who started the war without cause and prolonged it without reason. If he could not rule he cared not what happened to Germany. As Fritzsche has told us from the stand, Hitler tried to use the defeat of Germany for the self-destruction of the German people. He continued the fight when he knew it could not be won, and continuance meant only ruin. Speer, in this courtroom, has described it as follows:

"... The sacrifices which were made on both sides after January, 1945, were senseless. The dead of this period will be the accusers of the man responsible for the continuation of that fight, Adolf Hitler, and the ruined cities which in this last phase lost tremendous cultural values and in which a colossal number of dwellings were destroyed .... The German people remained faithful to Adolf Hitler until the end. He betrayed them knowingly. He finally tried to throw them into the abyss ...."

Hitler ordered everyone else to fight to the last and then retreated into death by his own hand. But he left life as he lived it, a deceiver; he left the official report that he had died in battle. This was the man whom these defendants exalted to a Fuehrer. It was they who conspired to get him absolute authority over all of Germany. And in the end he and the system they had created for him brought the ruin of them all. As stated by Speer in cross-examination:

"... the tremendous danger of the totalitarian system, however, only became really clear at the moment when we were approaching the end. It was then that one could see what the principle really meant, namely, that every order should be carried out without criticism. Everything that has become known during this trial, especially with regard to orders which were carried out without any consideration, has proved how evil it was in the end.... Quite apart from the personality of Hitler, on the collapse of the totalitarian system in Germany it became clear what tremendous dangers there are in a system of that kind. The combination of Hitler and this system has brought about these tremendous catastrophes in the world."

We have presented to this Tribunal an affirmative case based on incriminating documents which are sufficient, if unexplained, to require a finding of guilt on Count One against each defendant. In the final analysis, the only question is whether the defendants' own testimony is to be credited as against the documents and other evidence of their guilt. What, then, is their testimony worth?

The fact is that the Nazi habit of economising in the use of truth pulls the foundations out from under their own defences. Lying has always been a highly approved Nazi technique. Hitler, in 'Mein Kampf', advocated mendacity as a policy. Von Ribbentrop admits the use of the "diplomatic lie". Keitel advised that the facts of rearmament be kept secret so that they could be denied at Geneva. Raeder deceived about rebuilding the German Navy in violation of Versailles. Goering urged Ribbentrop to tell a "legal lie" to the British Foreign Office about the Anschluss, and in so doing only marshalled him the way he was going. Goering gave his word of honour to the Czechs and proceeded to break it. Even Speer proposed to deceive the French into revealing the specially trained among their prisoners.

Nor is the lie direct the only means of falsehood. They all speak with a Nazi double meaning with which to deceive the unwary. In the Nazi dictionary of sardonic euphemisms "Final solution" of the Jewish problem was a phrase which meant extermination; "Special treatment" of prisoners of war meant killing; "Protective custody" meant concentration camp; "Duty labour" meant slave labour; and an order to "take a firm attitude" or "take positive measures" meant to act with unrestrained savagery. Before we accept their word at what seems to be its face value, we must always look for hidden meanings. Goering assured us, on his oath, that the Reich Defence Council never met "as such". When we produced the stenographic minutes of a meeting at which he presided and did most of the talking, he reminded us of the "as such" and explained this was not a meeting of the Council "as such" because other persons were present. Goering denies "threatening" Czechoslovakia. He only told President Hacha that he would "hate to bomb the beautiful city of Prague".

Besides outright false statements and those with double meanings, there are also other circumventions of truth in the nature of fantastic explanations and absurd professions. Streicher has solemnly maintained that his only thought with respect to the Jews was to resettle them on the island of Madagascar. His reason for destroying synagogues, he blandly said, was only because they were architecturally offensive. Rosenberg was stated by his counsel to have always had in mind a "chivalrous solution" to the Jewish problem. When it was necessary to remove Schuschnigg after the Anschluss, Ribbentrop would have had us believe that the Austrian Chancellor was resting at a "villa". It was left to cross-examination to reveal that the "villa" was Buchenwald concentration camp. The record is full of other examples of dissimulations and evasions. Even Schacht showed that he, too, had adopted the Nazi attitude that truth is any story which succeeds. Confronted on cross-examination with a long record of broken vows and false words, he declared in justification—and I quote from the record:

"I think you can score many more successes when you want to lead someone if you don't tell them the truth than if you tell them the truth."
This was the philosophy of the National Socialists. When for years they have deceived the world, and masked falsehood with plausibilities, can anyone be surprised that they continue that habit of a lifetime in this dock? Credibility is one of the main issues of this trial. Only those who have failed to learn the bitter lessons of the last decade can doubt that men who have always played on the unsuspecting credulity of generous opponents would not hesitate to do the same now.

It is against such a background that these defendants now ask this Tribunal to say that they are not guilty of planning, executing, or conspiring to commit this long list of crimes and wrongs. They stand before the record of this trial as bloodstained Gloucester stood by the body of his slain King. He begged of the widow, as they beg of you: "Say I slew them not." And the Queen replied, "Then say they were not slain. But dead they are ...." If you were to say of these men that they are not guilty, it would be as true to say that there has been no war, there are no slain, there has been no crime.

**THE PRESIDENT:** I call on the Chief Prosecutor of the United Kingdom of Great Britain and Northern Ireland.

**SIR HARTLEY SHAWCROSS:** May it please the Tribunal; like my distinguished colleague whose succinct, able and eloquent speech I cannot hope to emulate, I desire on behalf of the British Prosecutors at this trial to lay before the Tribunal some comment on those salient and outstanding features of the evidence which, in our submission, make clear the guilt of these defendants. Although throughout these proceedings the representatives of the prosecuting powers have worked in the closest co-operation and agreement and although there are certain matters which I shall be laying before the Tribunal on behalf of all of us, we all thought it right at this final stage, even at the cost of some inevitable repetition and overlapping, that we should prepare our final submissions quite independently, so that the Tribunal and our own countries might know exactly the grounds on which we seek the condemnation of these men; and if it turns out that several of us point to the same evidence or reach similar conclusions, as no doubt it will, that very coincidence reached independently may perhaps add force to our submissions that each of these defendants is legally guilty.

Let them now, accused murderers as they are, attempt to belittle the power and influence they exercised how they will, we have only to recall their ranting as they strutted across the stage of Europe dressed in their brief authority, to see the part they played. They did not then tell the German people or the world that they were merely the ignorant, powerless puppets of their Fuehrer. The defendant Speer has said:

"Even in a totalitarian system there must be total responsibility ... it is impossible after the catastrophe to evade this total responsibility. If the war had been won, the leaders would also have assumed total responsibility."

Had the war been won is it to be supposed that these men would have retired to the obscurity and comparative innocence of private citizenship? That opportunity was not denied to them before the war, had they wished to dissociate themselves from what was taking place. They chose a different path. From small beginnings, at a time when resistance instead of participation could have destroyed this thing, they fostered the Hitler legend, they helped to build up the Nazi power and ideology and to direct its activities until, like some foul octopus, it spread its slime over Europe and extended its tentacles throughout the world. Were these men ignorant of the ends sought to be achieved during that period of the rise to power?

One comes to the defendants Speer and Fritzsche, who have appeared in this trial as experts. Speer has admitted that his responsibility for conscription of labour helped to bring up the total number of workers under him to 14,000,000. He stated that when he took over office in February, 1942, all the perpetrations or violations of International Law of which he could be accused had already been realised. Nevertheless he went on to say:

"The workers were brought into Germany against their will. I had no objection to their being brought to Germany against their will. On the contrary, during the first period until autumn of 1942 I certainly used my energy that as many workers as possible should be brought to Germany in this manner."

Further, workers were placed at his disposal by Sauckel and he was responsible for their allocation priorities.

He acknowledged the receipt of 1,000,000 Soviet labourers in August, 1942. On 4th January, 1944, he demanded 1,300,000 workers for the coming year. Speer produced no defence of this conscription of labour but he did assert that from 1943 he had supported the retention of French workers in France, which is a mere matter of mitigation. The moderation of Speer's manner ought not to hide the fact that this policy, which he cheerfully adopted and applied, was one that meant the most appalling misery and suffering for millions of Soviet and other families.

It displays once again the complete disregard of the fate of other people which s runs like a sordid thread through the evidence in this trial, and no moral awakening regarding the interest of the German people (I repeat "the German people") at the end of the war can offset the participation in this horrible action.

With regard to the treatment of foreign workers Speer's general point was that the evidence for the prosecution is simply that of individual bad instances and should not be taken as the general condition. If it were the general condition he would accept responsibility. The prosecution submit that their evidence, viewed as a whole, is conclusive evidence of general bad conditions.

Some it may be are more guilty than others; some played a more direct and active part than others in these frightful crimes. But when those crimes are such as you have to deal with here—slavery, mass murder and world war, when the consequences of the crimes are the deaths of over 20,000,000 of our fellow-men, the devastation of a continent, the spread of untold tragedy and suffering throughout the world, what mitigation is it that some took less part than others, that some were principals and others mere accessories? What matters it if some forfeited their lives only a thousand times whilst others deserved a million deaths?

In one way the fate of these men means little: their personal power for evil lies for ever broken; they have convicted and discredited each other and finally destroyed the legend they created round the figure of their leader. But on their fate great issues must still depend, for the ways of truth and righteousness between the nations of the world, the hope of future international co-operation in the administration of law and justice are in your hands. This trial must form a milestone in the history of civilisation, not only bringing retribution to these guilty men, not only marking that right shall in the end triumph over evil, but also that the ordinary people of the world (and I make no distinction now between friend and foe) are now determined that the individual must transcend the State. The State and the law are made for man, that through them he may achieve a fuller life, a higher purpose and a greater dignity. States may be great and powerful. Ultimately the rights of men, made as all men are made in the image of God, are fundamental. When the State, either because as here its leaders have lusted for power and place, or under some specious pretext that the end may justify the means, affronts these things, they may for a time become obscured and submerged. But they are immanent and ultimately they will assert themselves more strongly, still, their immanence more manifest. And so, after this ordeal to which mankind has been submitted, mankind itself—struggling now to re-establish in all the countries of the world the common, simple things— liberty, love, understanding—comes to this Court and cries: "These are our laws—let them prevail."

## TUESDAY, 30 JULY 1946

**GENERAL RUDENKO:** Gentlemen of the Tribunal!

I have already indicated in my opening statement that the action of deporting civilians—men, women and children—for forced labour into Germany was one of the most important in the chain of foul crimes committed by the German Fascist invaders.

Long before the Nazi came to power the architect Albert Speer was a personal friend of the architect's draughtsman, Hitler, and remained so till the end. Not only common professional interests but political interests also brought them together. Speer began his career in 1932 with the reconstruction of the "Brown House"—the headquarters of NSDAP in Berlin, and in ten years' time he was at the head of all the military construction and war production in Fascist Germany. Starting with the construction of the building of the Reich's

"Parteitag," Speer ended by setting up the "Atlantic Wall."

Speer held an important post in the Government and military machinery of Hitler's Germany and played a direct and active part in planning and realizing the criminal conspiracy.

What is Speer's line of defence at the trial? Speer presents his case in the following way: he was pressed upon by Hitler to take on the post of Minister; he was an intimate friend of Hitler's, but he knew nothing about his plans; he had been a member of the Nazi Party for fourteen years, but he was far from politics and had never even read 'Mein Kampf'. It is true that upon being given the lie Speer confessed that he had lied during his preliminary interrogation at the inquest.

Speer lied when he denied that he had never belonged to the SA, and then to the SS. The Tribunal possesses the original file of the SS man Albert Speer, who belonged to the personal staff of the SS Reichsfuehrer Himmler.

Speer held also a rather high rank in the Nazi Party. In the Party Chancellery, he was delegate for all technical questions, he headed the chief technical administration of the Party, he directed the union of German National Socialist technicians, he was plenipotentiary for the staff of Hess and a leader of one of the major German Labour Front organisations.

After all this can Speer's declaration that he was a specialist indifferent to politics be taken into consideration? In reality, as a close collaborator of Hitler, Hess, Ley and Goering, he directed the German technique not only as Reichsminister, but also as a Nazi political leader.

Upon succeeding to Todt, Speer, as he himself said in his speech before the Gauleiter, devoted himself completely to the solution of war problems. By means of the pitiless exploitations of the population in the occupied territories and of the prisoners of war of the allied countries, at the expense of the health and lives of hundreds of thousands of people, Speer increased the production of armament and ammunition for the German army. By plundering the raw materials and other resources of the occupied territories, Speer increased the war potential of Hitler's Germany. His powers grew with every month of the war. By Hitler's decree of 2nd September 1943, Speer became plenipotentiary and responsible for the supply of raw materials, for the direction and production of war industry. He was even commissioned to regulate the turnover of commodities and, by Hitler's decree of 24th August, 1944, Speer was, in effect, made dictator of all German authorities in Germany as well as in the occupied territories whose activity was in any way connected with the strengthening of German military power.

And when the Fascist flyers bombed peaceful towns and villages, killing women, old men and children, when the German artillery bombarded Leningrad, when the Hitlerite pirates sank hospital ships, when the "V" bombs destroyed towns in England, all this came as a result of Speer's activity. Under his leadership, the production of gas and of other means of chemical warfare had been widely increased. The defendant himself, when interrogated by Mr. Justice Jackson at the trial, confessed that three factories had been turning out products for chemical warfare and that they were working at full speed till November, 1944.

Speer not only knew of methods used by Sauckel for deporting the population from the occupied territories for slave labour, but he himself took part, together with Sauckel, in conferences with Hitler and in the administration of "Central Planning" where decisions were taken to deport millions of people to Germany from the occupied territories.

Speer kept up a close contact with Himmler; he received from Himmler prisoners for work in war factories; branches of concentration camps were organised in many factories subordinated to Speer; in recognition of Himmler's services Speer supplied the SS with experienced specialists and with supplementary war equipment.

Speer has said a lot here about his having sharply criticized the Hitler environment, that he allegedly had very serious dissensions with Hitler and that, in his letters to Hitler, he had written about the uselessness of continuing the war. When the representative of the Soviet prosecution asked Speer which of the persons close to Hitler he had criticized and in what connection, the defendant answered: "I shall not tell you."

It is quite evident that Speer not only did not want to, but could not tell, for the simple reason that he had never criticized anyone who was close to Hitler; moreover, he could not criticize as he was a convinced Nazi himself, and belonged to this close environment. As to the so-called "serious dissensions", they began—as Speer admitted—when it became clear to him that Germany had lost the war. Speer's letters to Hitler are dated March, 1945. At that time Speer could, without great risk, depict Germany's hopeless condition. It was apparent to everyone and was no longer a subject of discussion. And it was not by accident that after these letters Speer still remained Hitler's favourite. It was precisely Speer whom Hitler appointed on 30th March, 1945, to direct measures for the total destruction of the industrial enterprises, by obliging all Party, State and military offices to render him extensive help.

That is the true picture of the defendant Speer and the real part played by him in the crimes committed by the Hitler clique.

# The Final Statement by the Defendant

## SATURDAY, 31ST AUGUST, 1946

THE PRESIDENT: I call on the Defendant Albert Speer.

ALBERT SPEER (Defendant): Mr. President, may it please the Tribunal: Hitler and the collapse of his system have brought a time of tremendous suffering upon the German people. The useless continuation of this war and the unnecessary destruction make the work of reconstruction more difficult. Privation and misery have come to the German people. After this Trial, the German people will despise and condemn Hitler as the proven author of its misfortune. But the world will learn from these happenings not only to hate dictatorship as a form of government, but to fear it.

Hitler's dictatorship differed in one fundamental point from all its predecessors in history. His was the first dictatorship in the present period of modern technical development, a dictatorship which made complete use of all technical means in a perfect manner for the domination of its own nation.

Through technical devices such as radio and loudspeaker 80 million people were deprived of independent thought. It was thereby possible to subject them to the will of one man. The telephone, teletype, and radio made it possible, for instance, for orders from the highest sources to be transmitted directly to the lowest-ranking units, where, because of the high authority, they were carried out without criticism. Another result was that numerous offices and headquarters were directly attached to the supreme leadership, from which they received their sinister orders directly. Also, one of the results was a far-reaching supervision of the citizen of the state and the maintenance of a high degree of secrecy for criminal events.

Perhaps to the outsider this machinery of the state may appear like the lines of a telephone exchange—apparently without system. But like the latter, it could be served and dominated by one single will.

Earlier dictators during their work of leadership needed highly qualified assistants, even at the lowest level, men who could think and act independently. The totalitarian system in the period of modern technical development can dispense with them; the means of communication alone make it possible to mechanize the subordinate leadership. As a result of this there arises a new type: the uncritical recipient of orders.

We had only reached the beginning of the development. The nightmare of many a man that one day nations could be dominated by technical means was all but realized in Hitler's totalitarian system.

Today the danger of being terrorized by technocracy threatens every country in the world. In modern dictatorship this appears to me inevitable. Therefore, the more technical the world becomes, the more necessary is the

*The defendants at the Nuremberg Trials.
Albert Speer is on the back row, fifth from the right.*
Bundesarchiv, Bild 183-V01057-3 / CC-BY-SA

promotion of individual freedom and the individual's awareness of himself as a counterbalance.

Hitler not only took advantage of technical developments to dominate his own people-he almost succeeded, by means of his technical lead, in subjugating the whole of Europe. It was merely due to a few fundamental shortcomings of organisation such as are typical in a dictatorship because of the absence of criticism, that he did not have twice as many tanks, aircraft, and submarines before 1942.

But, if a modern industrial state utilises its intelligence, its science, its technical developments, and its production for a number of years in order to gain a lead in the sphere of armament, then even with a sparing use of its manpower it can, because of its technical superiority, completely overtake and conquer the world, if other nations should employ their technical abilities during that same period on behalf of the cultural progress of humanity.

The more technical the world becomes, the greater this danger will be, and the more serious will be an established lead in the technical means of warfare.

This war ended with remote-controlled rockets, aircraft traveling at the speed of sound, new types of submarines, torpedoes which find their own target, with atom bombs, and with, the prospect of a horrible kind of chemical warfare.

Of necessity the next war will be overshadowed by these new destructive inventions of the human mind.

In 5 or 10 years the technique of warfare will make it possible to fire rockets from continent to continent with uncanny precision. By atomic power it can destroy one million people in the center of New York in a matter of seconds with a rocket operated, perhaps, by only 10 men, invisible, without previous warning, faster than sound, by day and by night. Science is able to spread pestilence among human beings and animals and to destroy crops by insect warfare. Chemistry has developed terrible weapons with which it can inflict unspeakable suffering upon helpless human beings.

Will there ever again be a nation which will use the technical discoveries of this war for the preparation of a new war, while the rest of the world is employing the technical progress of this war for the benefit of humanity, thus attempting to create a slight compensation for its horrors? As a former minister of a highly developed armament system, it is my last duty to say the following:

A new large-scale war will end with the destruction of human culture and civilization. Nothing can prevent unconfined engineering and science from completing the work of destroying human beings, which it has begun in so dreadful a way in this war.

Therefore this Trial must contribute towards, preventing such degenerate wars in the future, and towards establishing rules whereby human beings can live together.

Of what importance is my own fate, after everything that has happened, in comparison with this high goal?

During the past centuries the German people have contributed much towards the creation of human civilization. Often they have made these contributions in times when they were just as powerless and helpless as they are today. Worth-while human beings will not let themselves be driven to despair. They will create new and lasting values, and under the tremendous pressure brought to bear upon everyone today these new works will be of particular greatness.

But if the German people create new cultural values in the unavoidable times of their poverty and weakness, and at the same time in the period of their reconstruction, then they will have in that way made the most valuable contribution to world events which they could make in their position.

It is not the battles of war alone which shape the history of humanity, but also, in a higher sense, the cultural achievements which one day will become the common property of all humanity. A nation which believes in its future will never perish. May God protect Germany and the culture of the West.

# The Judgment

## 1ST OCTOBER, 1946

MR. BIDDLE: Speer is indicted under all four Counts. Speer joined the Nazi Party in 1932. In 1934 he was made Hitler's architect and became a close personal confidant. Shortly thereafter he was made a department head in the German Labor Front and the official in charge of capital construction on the staff of the deputy to the Fuehrer, positions which he held through 1941. On 5th February, 1942, after the death of Fritz Todt, Speer was appointed Chief of the Organisation Todt and Reich Minister for Armaments and Munitions (after 2nd September, 1943, for Armaments and War Production). The positions were supplemented by his appointments in March and April, 1942, as General Plenipotentiary for Armaments and as a member of the Central Planning Board, both within the Four Year Plan. Speer was a member of the Reichstag from 1941 until the end of the war.

### CRIMES AGAINST PEACE
The Tribunal is of opinion that Speer's activities do not amount to initiating, planning, or preparing wars of aggression, or of conspiring to that end. He became the head of the armament industry well after all of the wars had been commenced and were under way. His activities in charge of German armament production were in aid of the war effort in the same way that other productive enterprises aid in the waging of war; but the Tribunal is not prepared to find that such activities involve engaging in the common plan to wage aggressive war as charged under Count One or waging aggressive war as charged under Count II.

### WAR CRIMES AND CRIMES AGAINST HUMANITY
The evidence introduced against Speer under Counts Three and Four relates entirely to his participation in the slave labor program. Speer himself had no direct administrative responsibility for this program. Although he had advocated the appointment of a General Plenipotentiary for the Utilization of Labor because he wanted one central authority with whom he could deal on labor matters, he did not obtain administrative control over Sauckel. Sauckel was appointed directly by Hitler, under the decree of 21st March, 1942, which provided that he should be directly responsible to Goering, as Plenipotentiary of the Four Year Plan.

As Reich Minister for Armaments and Munitions and General Plenipotentiary for Armaments under the Four Year Plan, Speer had extensive authority over production. His original authority was over construction and production of arms for the OKW. This was progressively expanded to include naval armaments, civilian production and finally, on 1st August, 1944, air armament. As the dominant member of the Central Planning Board, which had supreme authority for the scheduling of German production and the allocation and development of raw materials, Speer took the position that the Board had authority to instruct Sauckel to provide laborers for industries under its control and succeeded in sustaining this position over the objection of Sauckel. The practice was developed under which Speer transmitted to Sauckel an estimate of the total number of workers needed. Sauckel obtained the labor and allocated it to the various industries in accordance with instructions supplied by Speer.

Speer knew when he made his demands on Sauckel that they would be supplied by foreign laborers serving under compulsion. He participated in conferences involving the extension of the slave labor program for the purpose of satisfying his demands. He was present at a conference held during 10th August and 12th August, 1942, with Hitler and Sauckel, at which it was agreed that Sauckel should bring laborers by force from occupied territories where this was necessary to satisfy the labor needs of the industries under Speer's control. Speer also attended a conference in Hitler's headquarters on 4th January, 1944, at which the decision was made that Sauckel should obtain "at least 4 million new workers from occupied territories" in order to satisfy the demands for labor made by Speer, although Sauckel indicated that he could do this only with help from Himmler.

Sauckel continually informed Speer and his representatives that foreign laborers were being obtained by force. At a meeting of 1st March, 1944 Speer's deputy questioned Sauckel very closely about his failure to live up to the obligation to supply 4 million workers from occupied territories. In some cases Speer demanded laborers from specific foreign countries. Thus, at the conference of 8/10-12/1942 Sauckel was instructed to supply Speer with "a further million Russian laborers for the German armament industry up to and including October, 1942". At a meeting of the Central Planning Board on 22nd April, 1943, Speer discussed plans to obtain Russian laborers for use in the coal mines, and flatly vetoed the suggestion that this labor deficit should be made up by German labor.

Speer has argued that he advocated the reorganisation of the labor program to place a greater emphasis on utilisation of German labor in war production in Germany and on the use of labor in occupied countries in local production of consumer goods formerly produced in Germany. Speer took steps in this direction by establishing the so-called "blocked industries" in the occupied territories which were used to produce goods to be shipped to Germany. Employees of these industries were immune from deportation to Germany as slave laborers and any worker who had been ordered to go to Germany could avoid deportation if he went to work for a blocked industry. This system, although somewhat less inhumane than deportation to Germany, was still illegal. The system of blocked industries played only a small part in the over-all slave labor program, although Speer urged its cooperation with the slave

*Spandau Prison in 1951, where Speer spent his 20 year sentence.*

labor program, knowing the way in which it was actually being administered. In an official sense, he was its principal beneficiary and he constantly urged its extension.

Speer was also directly involved in the utilisation of forced labor, as Chief of the Organisation Todt. The Organisation Todt functioned principally in the occupied areas on such projects as the Atlantic Wall and the construction of military highways, and Speer has admitted that he relied on compulsory service to keep it adequately staffed. He also used concentration camp labor in the industries under his control. He originally arranged to tap this source of labor for use in small out-of-the-way factories; and later, fearful of Himmler's jurisdictional ambitions, attempted to use as few concentration camp workers as possible.

Speer was also involved in the use of prisoners of war in armament industries but contends that he utilised Soviet prisoners of war only in industries covered by the Geneva Convention.

Speer's position was such that he was not directly concerned with the cruelty in the administration of the slave labor program, although he was aware of its existence. For example, at meetings of the Central Planning Board he was informed that his demands for labor were so large as to necessitate violent methods in recruiting. At a meeting of the Central Planning Board on 10/30/1942, Speer voiced his opinion that many slave laborers who claimed to be sick were malingerers and stated: "There is nothing to be said against SS and police taking drastic steps and putting those known as slackers into concentration camps." Speer, however, insisted that the slave laborers be given adequate food and working conditions so that they could work efficiently.

In mitigation it must be recognized that Speer's establishment of blocked industries did keep many laborers in their homes and that in the closing stages of the war he was one of the few men who had the courage to tell Hitler that the war was lost and to take steps to prevent the senseless destruction of production facilities, both in occupied territories and in Germany. He carried out his opposition to Hitler's scorched earth program in some of the Western countries and in Germany by deliberately sabotaging it at considerable personal risk.

**CONCLUSION:**
The Tribunal finds that Speer is not guilty on Counts One and Two, but is guilty under Counts Three and Four.

## THE SENTENCE

**THE PRESIDENT:** Before pronouncing sentence on any of the defendants, and while all the defendants are present, the Tribunal takes the occasion to advise them that any applications for clemency of the Control Council must be lodged with the General Secretary of this Tribunal within four days from today.

The Tribunal will now adjourn and will sit again at ten minutes to three.

*(A recess was taken until 2.50 p.m.)*

**THE PRESIDENT:** In accordance with Article 27 of the Charter, the International Military Tribunal will now pronounce the sentences on the defendants convicted on this indictment.

Defendant Albert Speer, on the counts of the Indictment on which you have been convicted, the International Military Tribunal sentences you to twenty years imprisonment.

www.ingramcontent.com/pod-product-compliance
Lightning Source LLC
Chambersburg PA
CBHW020326240426
43665CB00044B/670